# VILLA PARK
# 100 YEARS

Simon Inglis

SPORTS PROJECTS LTD

Villa Park • 100 Years

•

•

Published by Sports Projects Ltd
188 Lightwoods Hill, Smethwick, Warley, West Midlands, B67 5EH

•

ISBN 0 946866 43 0

•

Design, Layout and Scans by Sports Projects Ltd

•

Printed in England by Polar Print Group Ltd

# Contents

# THANK YOU

❖ This book has been a labour of love, not only for me but for the very many fans, former players and people of Birmingham whom I have pestered over the past twelve months. I have also been a bit of a nuisance to many of the folk at Villa Park, and so must thank Doug Ellis and all his staff for giving me the chance to write this official history and for putting up with me in the process.

In addition to those named in the text, particular thanks go to the staff at BIRMINGHAM CENTRAL LIBRARY's local history collection, and especially to Peter Drake; to Andy Cowie (COLORSPORT); the staff at the BIRMINGHAM POST & MAIL library and those at the BRITISH MUSEUM NEWSPAPER LIBRARY in Colindale.

I must also pay tribute to the painstaking research carried out by my friend and fellow football ground nut, Colin Peel, and to all the previous Aston Villa historians who have made my task so much easier. These include Derrick Spinks, Peter Morris (author of the excellent centenary history), and both David Goodyear and Tony Matthews.

Other invaluable sources were Oliver Fairclough's seminal history of Aston Hall; the memories of local author Victor J. Price; Peter Lovesey's history of the AAA, and, it surely goes without saying, the inestimable VILLA NEWS AND RECORD, which I have no hesitation in describing as one of the finest historical sources available to any football club historian. Football writers in the Midlands are also lucky to be able to call upon the collected works of such newspapers as the SPORTS ARGUS (happy 100th birthday to them!), the BIRMINGHAM EVENING MAIL and all its illustrious predecessors.

A number of Villa afficionadoes have been generous with their time, knowledge and collections. Many are mentioned in the text, but I would especially like to thank Ted Small (Stadium Manager), Jon Farrelly, Carl Chinn (another Moseley C of E old boy), and above all the two great doyens of Villa Park, Jack Watts and Terry Weir. Sadly, one of the many older fans whom I interviewed for the book, Alf Pursall, died before the book was completed. So too did Villa's design consultant, Keith Smith, who I feel sure would have wished to help, as he always did with my other books.

Among dozens of other helpers I thank Robert Brooke (WARWICKSHIRE CCC historian), Reg Gower (HANDSWORTH HISTORICAL SOCIETY), Oliver Holland, Dave Ismay and Tamara Williams (in Aston Villa's Special Projects Department), Christian Jahnsen (our friend on the Internet), David Lander, Marie McDonald (SHAKESPEARE BIRTHPLACE TRUST), Brian Mellowship, Ted Pearson (GUNNEBO MAYOR TURNSTILES), Neil Rioch (ASTON VILLA FORMER PLAYERS' ASSOCIATION), Roger St Pierre (cycling history), Ray Spiller (ASSOCIATION OF FOOTBALL STATISTICIANS), Reg Thacker (Aston Villa's archivist) and Keith Whild.

Finally, four individuals deserve special thanks. My parents, Wendy and Harold, not only indulged my youthful obsession with Villa, but found themselves wrapped up in it during the writing of this book. Dad, in particular, spent many hours in libraries and on the road aiding my researches, and never once lost his temper, despite my frequent, last minute demands. Thanks Dad.

My wife, Jackie Spreckley, typed up hours of transcripts and provided all the love and support a deadline-haunted author could possible have wished for, despite her sorrow at Macca's departure. I could not have written this without her.

And last but by no means least, I cannot find words enough to thank Bernard Gallagher of SPORTS PROJECTS. Villa are truly lucky to have such an excellent publisher of their match programme, their club magazine, CLARET & BLUE, and several other publications besides. In truth, this book should really bear his name on the title page too, for it is his design, and throughout its production he has been a constant source of advice, reassurance and support. Above all, he has been a real friend.

PHOTOGRAPHS AND ILLUSTRATIONS KINDLY SUPPLIED BY:

Aston Villa Football Club
Local Studies Dept, Birmingham Central Library
Records Office, Shakespeare Birthplace Trust
The Birmingham Post & Mail
Bernard Gallagher, Sports Projects Ltd
Colorsport Ltd
Albert Wilkes & Son
John Whybrow Ltd
Syndication International
Hulton Deutsch Collection Ltd
RCHME
Chorley Handford
Premier Image Products
Peter Robinson, Football Archive
John Cox
Terry Weir
Simon Inglis
Bill Goulden
Mike Smith
Roy Fifield
Reg Gower
Ted Small
Peter Hing & Jones
Barrie Bailey
George Brannigan

Every reasonable effort has been made to trace the ownership of copyright material and to make due acknowledgement.

# A GREAT MIDLANDS SPORTS GROUND

❖ *If the history of the big plot of land on which the Villa teams play and all its many 'accessories' are included ever comes to be written, it will form quite a romantic tale, full of sporting and financial adventure.*

So wrote the editor of the VILLA NEWS AND RECORD, A. E. Machin, in December 1924. And so it has proved. For now that the history of this big plot of land has been written, it has turned out to be more full of adventure than even I had dared to imagine when I first took on the task in 1996.

In the course of nearly 20 years of studying and writing about the history and development of football grounds, I have always known that Villa Park is special. Even so, I had no idea that this affection had formed so early in my life, until just a week or so before finishing this book, my niece Hester – a Baggies fan, but I love her – dug out from a cupboard some old school books from my days at Moseley Church of England School. In one of the tattered exercise books she found a short composition, penned when I was six years old, in October 1961. This is what I wrote:

"Yesterday I went to Aston hall with mummy and my brother and sister. I saw villa park. it was a football ground. Aston villa play there. The flud lights have fourty two lights on them. they have them for at night when they play. the gardens were beautiful. We could not get in aston hall becuse it was shut. it was bilt a long time ago. there were swings. I played on them. children over twelve can not play there."

Six months later I was back, and although my spelling and punctuation had not improved greatly, this time I was able to enter the ground. The date was April 21, 1962. I was seven. I went with my brother Jonathan (Hester's dad), who was 11, and we sat in the Trinity Road Stand. I learnt my first swear word, while Villa beat Leicester 8-3. "It was a high football score," I wrote succinctly in my composition book.

By now I appear to have been hooked. The entry for May 15 has me back in Aston with persons unnamed. "We went to the park. We walked around the outside of Villa Park, and then we went to the suporters club."

"Aston Villa," I wrote, "started playing in 1872" – so I was not that clever. But I was clearly intrigued by the ground, for I added: "Villa Park will soon be a stadium, like Wembley. There is going to be a double-decker stand."

Reading these words, 35 years later, I can scarcely believe that at the age of seven I knew what a double-decker stand was. And yet I can easily understand how, unwittingly, I had become captivated by a strange collection of buildings in a far-off suburb, miles away from my home in Moseley.

For many people reading this book, Villa Park will have been a constant in their lives, too. Managers, players and directors have come and gone, but the ground has remained.

I know why I love Aston Villa. I love the very name. I love the colours. I love the idea of the club. But for many years during my adult life I have tried to persuade myself that I really fell in love with the Villa because of Villa Park. And now, the timely rediscovery of those primary school jottings has confirmed that this was indeed the case. And so, this tale of one hundred years has come to be written, this 'romantic tale, full of sporting and financial adventure'.

If this were merely a chronicle of bricks and mortar, stands and terraces, it might fill a useful, if somewhat esoteric niche in the annals of both the club and the city of Birmingham. But clearly, the story carries a much deeper and wider resonance, populated as it is by a cast of thousands: the famed and the nameless, the visionaries and the traditionalists, the champions and the chorus. And the little wide-eyed boys, of course.

More accurately, this is the story of a community, the claret-and-blue community of supporters, players, directors, officials, designers, builders, stewards, secretaries, turnstile-operators, hawkers, bandsmen, reporters, local residents, publicans, traders and many more besides.

Patently there exist other, equally apt metaphors for football grounds: the ground as a temple of worship, or as a garden of paradise, a haven in the city; the ground as a place of joy, or of hate; the ground as a symbol of pride, or as a blight upon the urban landscape. To some the football ground is a magnet. To others it is repellent. In the darkest days of hooliganism, during the 1970s and 1980s, the football ground was depressingly, but aptly, likened to a prison.

Villa Park has been all these things and, in its multifarious lights and shades, airs and odours; will no doubt continue to evoke different responses in us all for many years to come. Another century even? Why not?

Above all, Villa Park is redolent in history. To alight at Witton Station, to amble expectantly through Aston Park and past Aston Hall before kick-off, to meet pals by the Holte or at the church gates, to sink pints at the Aston Hotel or exchange banter in the McGregor Suite, is to participate, knowingly or not, in a century-long cavalcade of pilgrims.

The physical appearance of the ground might have changed beyond all recognition, not once but twice, within the last hundred years. Its approaches and surrounds have, in parts, been built up, pulled down, sliced through, cut off, widened or obliterated. Yet the sense of Villa Park's rightful place in this corner of Birmingham has barely altered at all.

Aston Hall endures. Aston Church is a familiar neighbour. Trinity Road and Witton Lane still exert their vice-like grip, with the Holte Hotel at the vertex. And for those who know where to look – guided, if need be, by the pages which follow – there are reminders aplenty of how Aston Villa's history is intimately entwined with that of the locality, and of how Villa Park came to attain those distinct architectural features which place it apart from all other grounds.

Amid the buildings and streets there are also private tales to tell. Several are told between these covers, for surely all of us who make that regular pilgrimage to Villa Park tread not only a well worn path through the century, but also through the winding roads of our own personal histories.

As we grow from childhood into adulthood, from sons and daughters into parents; as we change schools and jobs, even as we move from house to house, or town to town, Villa Park remains a constant; witnessing, and perhaps even helping to nurture, our passage through life, friendships, fads and fashion.

There we are one minute, wide-eyed, bobble-hatted and innocent, on the terraces with our dads or elder brothers, straining for a view of half-understood dramas, surrounded by giants and strangers.

Then suddenly we become independent; controllers of our own pre-match rituals, guardians of favourite spaces, members of inner-tribes, able to smoke, drink and swear to our heart's content, until... All too quickly we learn to walk but not run in Witton Lane, to look out for our children in the queues – the joy, the burden passed down from generation to generation – to dress sensibly in winter, to enjoy victories while we can, knowing that we must also accept defeat without tantrums, and finally, before we know it, to utter those words which come to us all in the end: "It wasn't like this in my day!"

Of course every football fan likes to imagine that their home ground is unique; that their club is special. And they are absolutely right to feel that way. But in truth, as I sincerely hope this book will show, Villa fans are luckier than most.

SIMON INGLIS, MAY 1997

# Chapter 1

# Aston and the Villa

**W**HAT'S IN A NAME? IN THE CASE OF Aston Villa, a great deal. To begin with, one need hardly be a dyed-in-the-wool devotee of the Villa to acknowledge that, amid the legions of Cities, Uniteds, Rovers and Albions, the name ASTON VILLA is still invested with a unique aura.

'A name to conjure with,' pronounced the VILLA NEWS AND RECORD in 1924. 'It is uncommon, and it is romantic.'

As many a reader would no doubt also testify, while football followers around the globe may not always appreciate that Aston lies in Birmingham, they invariably recognise 'the Villa' in an instant, and often follow that up with expressions of affection.

But to the club's pioneers – those four young cricketers who, legend tells us, gathered on one evening in 1874 under a gas lamp in Heathfield Road – the choice of 'Aston Villa' was no gimmick or astute piece of branding to catch the public's imagination. Rather, Aston Villa was already a familiar name in the neighbourhood.

Long before the small market town of Birmingham grew into one of the great industrial cities of the world, the parish of Aston (referred to as 'Estone' in the 11th century Domesday Book) covered a sizeable expanse of some 21 square miles, stretching from Erdington in the north to Bordesley in the south. Indeed, had these medieval parish boundaries survived until the modern era, Small Heath, home of Birmingham City, would have been part of Aston – a mischievous thought if ever there was to begin our tale.

Within this once-huge parish lay several manors, including those of Witton, Saltley and Castle Bromwich. But our focus will concentrate upon one in particular, the manor which also bore the name of Aston.

At the western edge of Aston Manor, where Heathfield Road and Lozells Lane (now Road) met, was built a house called Aston Villa, it is thought some time during the late 18th or early 19th century. For several decades the house served as a school for the 'sons of gentlemen' before being converted into the Villa Cross Tavern around the 1870s. (The building was finally demolished in the mid-1930s, to be replaced by a new pub, which in 1997 was serving as a job centre.)

Extremely modest compared with the likes of nearby Aston Hall or Heathfield House, Aston Villa appears to have been one of barely a dozen major buildings erected in the area during the period 1750-1835. Yet it was of sufficient importance that, by 1824 at least, the immediate vicinity around the house became known as Aston Villa, and later more formally as the Villa Ward. The junction in front of the house also became known as Villa Cross, from which Villa Road, as now, led to Soho Hill.

As parcels of the surrounding farmland were gradually swallowed up to house the massive influx of migrant workers from the 1850s onwards, there appeared a Villa Grove (now built over), Villa Cottages on Wills Street, an Aston Villa cottage on Park Lane (now Frederick Road) and, on Villa Street, the Villa Tavern and a Villa Cottage. Had it not been for the football club's intrepid founders, doubtless these names would excite little more than passing interest among local residents. But, crucially, there was another local institution to adopt the name Aston Villa, and that was a Wesleyan Chapel, founded in 1850 on the corner of Lozells Road and George Street, virtually opposite Aston Villa.

The ornate Aston Villa Wesleyan Chapel that we see today, with its curious blend of Gothic features and Italianate decoration – now home to a Pentecostal church – dates from 1865, and it was here in the adjoining Sunday school building that pupils followed the muscular Christian creed of the day by forming a cricket team, probably in 1872. That year the records state there were 301 scholars at the Sunday school, supervised by 30 teachers. Two years later four of those pupils, all members of the cricket team, saw other youths playing football on some waste ground off Heathfield Road and resolved, there and then, to extend their own sporting activities into the winter months. Thus was born the Aston Villa Football Club.

As previous club histories have stated, the would-be footballers conducted their first tentative kickabouts also on wasteland, approximately where the Westminster Road Church would later be built, off Heathfield Road.

Competitive games were rather harder to organise. Birmingham's first recorded club, Calthorpe FC (formed as the football section of the Birmingham Clerks Association in 1873), were probably too strong for the untried Villans to challenge. Otherwise, although football was already popular in places like Wednesbury and

Wolverhampton, this still developing sport had few adherents in the locality.

So it was that Villa had little choice but to make their public debut against a rugby team from the neighbouring church of Aston Brook St Mary's, probably in March 1874. According to one of the club's founding members, Jack Hughes – who also scored the Villa's first goal that day – this historic, but rather bizarre, half-soccer, half-rugby encounter took place in front of some 250 onlookers, on a field which would soon be swallowed up by houses on Wilson Road (again, just off Heathfield Road).

Aston Villa's roots were thus in a part of Aston Manor more correctly labelled Lozells or Birchfield, while it was only a coincidence, albeit a fortuitous one, that their name should also tie in closely with their eventual resting place in Aston Village.

More than twenty years would pass before the Villa finally settled in the heart of Aston, however, two decades during which the entire locality would be transformed.

To describe this change is important for two reasons. Firstly, despite the wholescale destruction of large tracts of late 19th century Aston in the 1960s and 70s, there remain a number of buildings and landmarks of significance to the history of both the club and Villa Park. Secondly, without the transformation of Aston from a small, almost sleepy rural village, into a densely populated suburb, in barely 40 years, Aston Villa would have had no constituency in which to grow and prosper.

It is, therefore, to the old heart of Aston which we now turn to gain a picture of the area in which the club would settle in 1897.

Until the industrial era, the area's two principle landmarks were the parish church – parts of which date back to the Norman period – and Aston Hall. Aston Hall, the grandiose Jacobean mansion, built between 1618 and 1635 on the rise overlooking the church, was the seat of a prominent Warwickshire baronet, Sir Thomas Holte, who inherited the estate from his father-in-law, and whose own Birmingham forebears had become landowners during the 14th century after profiting from the wool trade.

The name Holte has, of course, many echoes in modern-day Aston and Villa Park, although Sir Thomas was hardly a popular or admirable man. Oliver Fairclough's history of Aston Hall describes him as undeniably able, well read, and an accomplished linguist, but also 'markedly acquisitive, a builder of fortunes as well as houses, (who) was also aggressive, obstinate and vindictive.' Most seriously of all, in 1606 Holte was alleged to have attacked his own cook with a cleaver, splitting the man's head right down the middle.

He also disinherited his son for marrying the wrong woman, a ruthless action which even the king, Charles I, spoke out against.

Holte, nevertheless, had no choice but to back the Royalist cause. Thus the King spent a night at Aston Hall during the early stages of the Civil War. Then in December 1643, after the Hall had been bombarded

❖ This undated sketch shows a north-westerly view of the environs of Villa Park, as they might have appeared in the late 18th century. On the left, Aston Hall occupies the so-called 'upper grounds', now Aston Park. From Aston Church, two roads fork on either side of Dovehouse Pool (where the Villa Park pitch now lies), forming the triangular area known as the 'lower grounds'. The road to the right (or east) of Dovehouse Pool, Witton Lane, is marked as such on maps of the 18th Century, whereas the road on the left, Trinity Road, was strictly speaking not laid out formally until the 1860s.

❖ Built in 1865, the Aston Villa Wesleyan Chapel and its adjoining Sunday School building still serves as a house of prayer today, on the corner of Lozells Road and George Street.

by Parliamentary forces – around 24 men died in the ensuing battle – Sir Thomas was taken prisoner. Aston Church, which had been defended by 40 stout French and Irish mercenaries, was also overrun.

Fortunately for Holte he managed to regain his estates and former positions by squirming in front of his accusers and paying a hefty fine for 'delinquency' – that is, support for the King. Nor was the Hall badly damaged (though a part of the great stairs bears the scars to this day). Sir Thomas also managed to outlive several of his children before he died in 1654 at the age of 83, leaving a trail of debts.

For the next 160 years or so, Aston Hall was a rather more peaceful, happier home for Sir Thomas's heirs and their families, even if it never became fashionable or especially grand.

As was common in pre-industrial England, the Holtes' tenants and estate workers clustered around the church and a nearby mill on the River Tame. At the time Aston Hall was being built the local population was barely 1,800. By 1851 this had risen to nearer 7,000.

But by then the rural character of Aston was already under serious threat. At the time of the break-up of the Holte estates in 1818 – when the Hall and grounds were purchased by a firm of Warwick bankers called GREENWAY, GREAVES & WHITEHEAD – Aston Hall had fallen into disrepair. Indeed it might have been demolished had not a new tenant come forward. This was James Watt junior, son of the great pioneer of steam power, and himself an urbane bachelor and wealthy partner in his father's firm of engine-builders, BOULTON, WATT & SONS, based at the nearby Soho foundry.

In residence from 1819 until his death in 1848, Watt junior did a great deal to improve the remaining 156 acres attached to the Hall, but did not wield anything like the proprietorial powers exercised by the Holtes. For example, much to his ire, in 1837 the farmland to the north and east of the Hall was bisected by the arrival of the Grand Junction Railway, a product, ironically, of the age of steam.

The line – engineered by the famous George Stephenson to link London with the Manchester-to-Liverpool line at Warrington – sliced through the middle of a long avenue of chestnuts which extended from the Hall down to Lichfield Road. At first, Astonians could only watch from the fields as the puffing iron horses steamed past, en route from Birmingham's Curzon Street Station. But in 1854 Aston Station was opened, followed in 1876 by Witton Station. Both provided vital gateways to and from the rapidly expanding district, and would ultimately make the Aston Lower Grounds and its successor, Villa Park, highly accessible to vast and densely populated swathes of Birmingham and Staffordshire.

In this respect Villa were no different from the majority of great clubs, all of whom depended for support and mobility on the railway network and, in the late 19th century, the introduction of horse and then steam trams.

Nowadays, the majority of Villa fans choose to arrive by road, and it is to the club's main car park that our heritage trail now leads, bound by the Aston Tavern, church and vicarage on one side and the railway line on the other, but dominated by the brutish presence of the Aston Expressway, whose concrete stilts pierced through the heart of the old village in the 1970s.

Older supporters and local residents still know the car park as the Serpentine, so called because the area was formed by a looping channel from the River Tame and, until at least 1888, featured two irregularly-shaped ponds used for boating. After these were drained to form a rough expanse of ground, the Serpentine became the venue of the annual Aston Onion Fair, held in late September.

❖ *Aston Hall... built between 1618 and 1635, and home of the Holte family until 1817. Its red bricks, Dutch gables and Jacobean flourishes would be mirrored in public buildings throughout Aston during the late Victorian period and, in 1922, at Villa Park itself.*

This ancient fair had first been held in central Birmingham in 1400, at a time when people had only one chance to buy enough French onions to last throughout the year. But as the fair expanded and gradually drew crowds of up to 40,000, both overwhelming the city centre and disturbing Birmingham's more puritanical Victorian elders, the tradition was curtailed in 1875, only to re-emerge at the turn of the century at the Serpentine grounds. In its latter years the event was purely a fun-fair – run by the company of Pat Collins, as many local residents still recall with pleasure – while the Serpentine was otherwise used as an impromptu playground and as a car park by Villa's growing number of motoring supporters from the 1950s onwards. The last Onion Fair was held in 1969.

Where now lies the main entrance to the Aston Villa Sports and Leisure Centre (opened in 1979 in combination with an ASDA superstore, now demolished), in the 1880s there was a bowling green. Adjacent to the Aston Tavern (which was rebuilt at that time) there were two large houses. Opposite, on Aston Lane (now Aston Hall Road), stood the vicarage, public baths and the Holte Almshouses, built in 1665 and demolished in 1929. One can readily imagine the elderly inhabitants listening out for the roars of the crowd from Villa Park. Nowadays from this spot, only the roar of traffic can be heard, from the Expressway looming ominously above.

But if the village has all but been obliterated by the elevated motorway and sundry characterless industrial units, the parish church of St Peter and St Paul remains a resilient and familiar landmark. Many a photograph of Villa Park features its 200 feet tall tower and spire – both of which date from 1480 – peeking up behind the Holte End, while for generations of fans the churchyard walls and lych gate have served as trusty meeting places before and after games. Inside the church are several splendid monuments to various members of the Holte family, including Sir Thomas, but surprisingly none commemorate former Villa stalwarts. However, older fans do say that when the church bells peel for a Saturday wedding, Villa are destined to win. It was also said that the temporary removal of the spire's weather cock in the late 1960s presaged the club's relegation to Division Three.

Opposite the church stands an entrance to Aston Park, leading up to the Hall. As explained in Chapter 3, Aston Park occupies that part of the Holte's estates which were not sold off for building in the period between 1817 and the opening of the park to the public in 1858.

During the football club's first year in existence – before they settled at Perry Barr in September 1876 – Villa were one of several local teams to use Aston Park for their games.

Nowadays, the park's Witton Lane entrance is marked by a rather plain gateway, but for 200 years there stood a wonderful gothic stone arch, built in the 1750s and flanked by brick lodges, each topped by the Dutch gables which characterise the Hall and so

many other local buildings (including Villa's Trinity Road Stand). Sadly, the gate and lodges were torn down to facilitate road-widening in 1959. But this entrance, too, was a familiar landmark and meeting place for Villa fans, and yet another example of how Villa Park and its surrounds were quite unlike any other football ground in the land.

Another building which shows clearly how late Victorian architects in the area were seduced by Aston Hall's Dutch gables, red-brick detailing and Jacobean-style decoration is the Holte Hotel, on the corner where Witton Lane and Trinity Road meet.

In 1997 the pub was boarded up and in a poor state, having proved unable to sustain itself on match-day trade alone. But for thousands of Villa fans approaching from the south and the east, the Holte has always seemed like the gateway to Villa Park, and it was unfortunate that as the ground celebrated its centenary in such fine fettle, the Holte – its facade also 100 years old in 1997 – should have fallen on hard times. (Its rebirth has since begun, however, with the construction of a Villa merchandise shop in the former Witton Lane basement bar, hopefully to be followed by the restoration of the upper floors too.)

There had been a Holte Hotel on the site since the mid-1860s, before no doubt, in preparation for the arrival of thousands of thirsty Villa fans, in 1897 some £3,000 – a substantial sum at the time – was spent on creating the imposing frontage we know today, with its tapered central tower, Dutch gables (inevitably), and its prominent sandstone quoins, finials and sculpted flourishes.

The hotel's first manager was Henry Quilter, creator of the Aston Lower Grounds pleasure gardens. By 1897 the surviving rump of the Lower Grounds, and the Holte Hotel, were being run by Jimmy Lees, a rotund gentleman and director of Aston Villa. One of Lees' first acts after taking over was to invite the entire playing staff to the Holte for a social evening with members of the board. Regular adverts placed in the local sporting press (and later the VILLA NEWS AND RECORD) also invited fans to partake in luncheons, dinners and teas, and, of course, MITCHELLS & BUTLER's finest ales and stout.

❖ *The original Aston Villa... as painted by a local amateur artist, W. Green, probably around 1850.*

❖ *James Lees... managed the Holte Hotel and served as a Villa Director.*

There were billiard, concert and coffee rooms, a smoking club, and regular meetings of the local Masonic Lodge (which in the early part of the century counted amongst its members a number of Villa directors and officials). One Villa player, Andy Ducat (at the club from 1912-21), even married the landlord's daughter, and several Villa players have lodged there; for example, Johnny Dixon in the 1940s.

More recently, during the 1950s and 60s, Villa fans recall the Holte as the regular meeting place for the Supporters' Club, while many a fan returned to it after games to attend a Saturday night jazz club.

Immediately behind the Holte (where there is now a car park extending to the rear of the Holte End) lay the main entrance to the Aston Lower Grounds. For many years after that the area was covered by two bowling greens attached to the pub.

Having reached the gates of Villa Park, whose story will occupy most of the rest of this book, we now briefly slip off into the side streets around the ground, for further reminders of how Aston developed in the years before 1897.

The majority of roads to the south and west of Aston Park occupy land that was sold to speculative builders between 1850 and 1900, a period during which the population of Aston shot up from approximately 7,000 to 80,000.

Trinity Road was laid out during the 1860s between the church and Witton Road, cutting through the former Hall estate. The Lower Grounds pleasure gardens, on the site of what would become Villa Park, were developed between 1864-78, while a whole host of public buildings – halls, churches, public baths and libraries – sprouted up to serve the needs of the burgeoning ranks of Astonians.

Several such buildings, in addition to the Holte Hotel, would directly influence the design of the Trinity Road Stand (built in 1922); for example, Aston's own, if rather more compact Albert Hall, opened in 1899 on Witton Road (its round windows in particular are copied at Villa Park), and the Aston Manor Tramway Depot on Witton Lane which dates from 1903.

A building with a more direct link to the club was Florence Villa at 127 Albert Road. Even though situated some way from the Villa's ground at Perry Barr, this was the Villa's clubhouse and registered office during the 1890s.

The house had originally belonged to Thomas Vaughton, whose name will be recognisable to many readers familiar with Villa's history. Then, as now, Vaughton's company manufactured badges, cups and shields, and, from its Gothic Works in Livery Street, supplied the Football League with medals, a contract which it continues to fulfil to this very day. Thomas was also a director of the ASTON LOWER GROUNDS COMPANY and, more famously, father of Howard, an accomplished all-round sportsman who became a Villa regular during the 1880s and later joined the board.

Between 1892-97, 127 Albert Road must have been a hive of activity. Villa's offices were set up there, while other rooms were used for meetings, social gatherings and storage. The players used to play billiards in the converted coach house.

Once the move to the Lower Grounds site was completed in 1897, the building was sold to the ASTON JUBILEE FUND for £850, and a further £3,000 allocated to its conversion into a nurses' home and dispensary. Nowadays it serves as a home for the aged. Several other buildings in the area also have strong links with the Villa, as the following chapters will reveal.

And so to conclude this brief trail through the distinctive neighbourhood of Villa Park, the Aston into which the Villa moved in 1897 was, in certain respects, quite different from the Aston today. With its ancient centre around the old church, as it filled out from Aston Cross to Villa Cross, from Aston Station to Six Ways, it was, in parts, like so many late Victorian conurbations, an oppressive, soot-encrusted hive of lowly courts, monotonous terraces and cramped back-to-backs, alleviated by wide-open parkland, dignified civic buildings, leafy corners and bustling shopping streets, all served by horse-trams and railways. It was, in short, the perfect place to build a football ground.

❖ *The Holte Hotel... for many, the gateway to Villa Park. This photograph was taken in 1898, shortly after its grand frontage was remodelled. Most of the houses on Witton Lane (right) were demolished in the 1990s.*

# Perry Barr and the Pets

WHY BE COY ABOUT IT? THE FACT IS that professional football has proved to be one of the greatest and most enduring British cultural exports of the past one hundred years, arguably as influential as the railways, the English language and, maybe, even more so than the Beatles.

Lawn tennis, cricket, golf, hockey and rugby were all codified and developed by the British, and then spread around the world in the 19th century. But Association Football, with its roots in the industrial heartlands of Scotland, Lancashire and the Midlands, was the greatest export of them all.

When fans attending the European Championships at Villa Park in 1996 sang *Football's Coming Home* they were not merely mouthing the words of a catchy pop song. They were expressing a fundamental, historical truth.

As key players in the early development of the professional game, Aston Villa can rightly claim an honoured place among the pioneers. But was their contribution by luck or by design?

One of the most intriguing questions arising from the study of early football is this: what factors caused certain clubs to rise above the massed ranks of parks teams and become established professional outfits on the national scene?

In Birmingham, a number of clubs might have progressed further than the Villa or Small Heath. And

yet they did not. The likes of Birmingham Cricket and Football Club, Calthorpe, Saltley College, Aston Unity, Excelsior, Mitchell St George and Warwick County are all but forgotten names, recalled only as dim and distant contenders in a byegone age.

So what made Villa different? Clearly, the early involvement of competent administrators – most notably the Scottish duo, George Ramsay and William McGregor – was hugely important. So too was that timeless, unquantifiable asset which we call 'team spirit' and which permeates so powerfully from the dressing room to the touchlines, and lends all supporters good heart and a sense of loyalty. But without a home ground, and a well-placed home ground at that, no aspiring club ever stood a chance.

In the late 19th century a ground gave a club and its would-be supporters a focus, for sure. As we shall see with the Villa, it helped if that ground was close to a pub and to public transport. Most importantly of all, however, the club had to gain the permission of their landlord to erect a fence, because without a fence – as, for example, Calthorpe found to their cost – it was almost impossible to collect gate money.

Even in the days before professionalism was officially sanctioned in 1885, this was vital. Gate money meant that players of greater ability could be hired (albeit under the proverbial counter). It followed that better players allowed more attractive fixtures to be arranged, and thus that greater numbers of spectators would attend.

It is common for critics of the modern game to deride football as nothing more than a 'big business', a criticism which resurfaced in 1997 as Aston Villa (among several clubs) prepared to launch itself on the stock market. But in truth, professional football has always been a business. As one Birmingham journalist commented in 1888, the Football League was formed 'not for the purpose of encouraging football,' but 'so that the allied clubs may make more money than they already do.'

'As matters stand,' he added, 'many of our leading clubs are nothing better than circus shows.'

But if bread and circuses – *panem et circenses* – were the staple of the Roman masses two thousand years earlier, why should Britain's Victorian populace be any different?

After their initial game of two halves against the rugby players of Aston Brook St Mary's in March 1874, Villa's eager young founders trod a well worn path to Aston Park, already the favoured playground of many an aspiring local team. William McGregor called the park 'the football nursery of Birmingham'. (McGregor, famed for being the creator of the Football League, was a much-loved Villa committee member who ran a draper's shop in Summer Lane and lived in Witton Road.)

One of the club's founder members, Jack Hughes, recalled that Villa's first match in Aston Park was in 1875 against Wednesbury Old Athletic, on a pitch near to the Trinity Road side of the park. The team went on to play approximately 15 games in 1875-76, some of which were said to have attracted up to 1,000 onlookers.

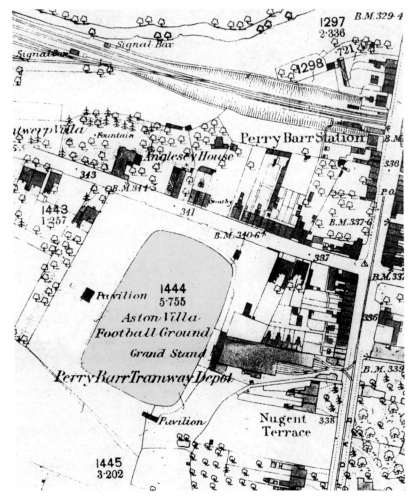

Even so, their continuing success was by no means guaranteed, particularly as there was a much greater draw only a stone's throw away, on the other side of Trinity Road. This was a ground quaintly named the Meadow, situated where Nelson Road now lies (just behind Villa Park) and forming part of the extensive Aston Lower Grounds' pleasure gardens. Between 1872 and 1888 the Meadow was by far the most advanced, multi-purpose sports venue in the Birmingham area.

We will return to that ground and its resident club, the Birmingham Cricket and Football Club, in the next chapter. But the very fact that Villa also played a few games there during 1875-76 suggests that the junior outfit had already begun to establish something of a local reputation.

One of the individuals responsible for this was George B. Ramsay, another Scot who had journeyed south to take up a clerical position with a firm of brassfounders in boom-town Birmingham. Ramsay encountered the Villa in Aston Park in early 1876. Whether he was actively seeking out Villa in particular, or came across them either by chance or in active pursuit of a game, only Ramsay himself knew. Whichever, having mastered the game in his native Glasgow, Ramsay set about enthralling the raw Villans with a dazzling display of skills. As McGregor would later describe, 'trimly built and firmly knit...' the 21-year-old Scot 'speedily gave those present an object lesson in dribbling' and there and then 'was literally compelled to accept the captaincy.'

On such chance encounters the fate of many a club has been decided. But after organising the team to his satisfaction over the following months, Ramsay understood that, without a ground of their own, Villa could never hope to progress.

Perhaps with this in mind, Ramsay and a Scottish friend, John Lindsay, were out for a stroll one Sunday when they came across some likely-looking grazing land. Situated on the borders of Birchfield and Perry Barr, the field lay just south of Wellington Road, barely a mile from Aston Park, and roughly the same distance north west of Villa Cross.

Compared with Aston the area was still markedly rural, being on the very outer edge of the city's development. The village of Perry Barr itself even retained an ancient toll-gate (whereas the one at Aston Cross had been removed in 1862).

Beyond a couple of detached houses and a blacksmith's (or 'smithy') on the north side of Wellington Road ran that same 1837 railway line which passed through Aston and Witton. Beyond the railway the River Tame meandered through farms and fields. To the east were detached houses on Birchfield Road – some quite grand – while to the south lay open grazing land and allotments.

William McGregor later recalled that when the Villa began renting the field 'there was a hayrick not far from the centre of the ground, a number of trees along the touch-lines, a pool not far away, and a nasty hill near the left-hand corner of the top goal.' It was, he admitted, 'not an ideal enclosure, by any means; but it was quite good enough for those days.'

It was also well placed for public transport. Within a few hundred yards was Perry Barr Station. In addition, soon after Villa moved in, a steam tramway depot was built on Birchfield Road, within a few yards of the east touchline.

Villa's first landlord was himself a tenant – a farmer, according to McGregor, a butcher according to other accounts (although he might well have been both) – who rented the field from the Bridge Trust. The Trust had originally been granted land in 1612 in order to raise funds for the building of bridges in the locality, but since 1862 had channelled a large part of its rents and income towards the upkeep of a school in Grove Lane (now Handsworth Grammar).

George Ramsay reportedly took an hour to persuade the farmer-cum-butcher to sub-let his field to the Villa for £5 per annum, a deal later described as quite a coup, as if the poor man had no idea of the impending popularity of his new tenants. But, in reality, even a rent of £5 was still a calculated gamble for a club as unestablished as the Villa. It was also fairly typical of what many clubs paid at that time. Small Heath, for example, also paid £5 to rent Muntz Street in 1877.

And so it was, only two years after their formation, that Villa made that all important first step towards securing a settled base.

Not that they could afford to be complacent. Their first ever 'gate', for a match against Wednesbury Town on September 30, 1876, amounted only to 5s 3d, or just over 26p. At 3d each for admission, this meant only 21 paying customers, although almost certainly there would have been other club members and friends in attendance. On other occasions, however, there were even fewer in the ground. William McGregor admitted, 'spectators were often few and far between at Wellington Road in the early days. I can recall more than one match where there were only two spectators; myself and George Ramsay's brother.'

But word must have soon spread, because when Villa went back to their landlord at the end of their first season he raised the rent to £8.

Football grounds in those early days of the 1870s and 1880s were almost all rough-and-ready compared with the new grounds which started to

*❖ The Perry Barr Stand, Saturday, September 2, 1893... In the days before action photos, the SPORTS ARGUS artist was at Perry Barr for Villa's opening game of what would prove to be a title-winning season, a 3-2 win over West Bromwich Albion, watched by a crowd of approximately 15,000. The kick-off had been delayed because, embarrassingly, the referee – a prominent League official and journalist, John Bentley – was late. Note the small stand to the left of the Grand Stand.*

*❖ An ORDNANCE SURVEY map of the late 1880s shows two pavilions and the new Grand Stand at Perry Barr. Willmore Road now covers much of the former pitch. Leslie Road runs along the former east touchline, and a council works depot occupies the site of the former tramway depot. The map also shows the 'smithy' where the teams used to change in the early days, on the north side of Wellington Road, behind the 'bottom goal'. It is possible that a single-storey brick building still standing on Wellington Road (almost opposite Willmore Road, next door to a garage) formed part of this smithy. The Old Crown and Cushion – now a large modern pub – is further along Wellington Road, on the corner with Birchfield Road.*

appear after 1890. The best were invariably those laid out at existing cricket grounds, such as the Oval, in London (where the Cup Final was staged from 1872-92), Bramall Lane in Sheffield, or Trent Bridge, Nottingham. But the majority were hardly more than roped-off fields with an assortment of wooden structures dotted around the touchlines, often supplemented by wagons and carts or, later, by earth and ash banks.

Perry Barr was no better and no worse. Indeed throughout their 21-year stay, despite their growing prowess and gates occasionally in excess of 20,000, Villa built no more than five or six relatively small, predominantly wooden structures at the ground, none of which would, nowadays, be regarded as permanent.

In the early days there were no dressing rooms, so the teams crossed Wellington Road and changed in the 'smithy'. This, of course, meant that after the final whistle players had to run the gauntlet of fans, not always a comfortable experience, particularly for visiting teams. But then most players were used to this from other grounds, too. (At St James' Park, Newcastle, for example, visiting teams had to be conveyed a few hundred yards to their dressing rooms in a city centre pub. At several other grounds the players simply had to walk along public roads, still in their muddy kit.)

Even when changing facilities were provided within the Perry Barr ground they remained fairly basic. In 1885 match reports were still referring to a 'dressing tent' rather than a 'dressing room' or 'pavilion'. Only in 1887 was a proper hut erected

behind one of the stands. This housed two dressing rooms, each measuring 16 square feet and fitted with two baths plus hot and cold running water.

The pitch was hardly more advanced, and seems to have been in constant need of dressing, filling or patching up. It was certainly never level, which explains why the ends were usually referred to as the 'top goal' (which was the south end) and 'bottom goal' (backing onto Wellington Road).

Nor did the groundsman, a Mr Williams, have much help other than a trusty pony. In common with most clubs, during the early period Villa allowed local butchers to fatten up their stock on the pitch, in order to keep the grass short. It must have tasted good because between 1880 and 1883 the income from grazing rights rose from £1.15s to £8 a year, at the time the equivalent of nearly 15 per cent of the club's total ground rent. Only in 1888 was Williams provided with a mower, and a second hand one at that, bought for under £3 from the Pickwick Cricket Club.

Meanwhile, a few doors along from the smithy, the club's unofficial headquarters became the OLD CROWN AND CUSHION, a coaching inn on the north west corner of Wellington Road and Birchfield Road, where, no doubt, the landlord, Walter Bowen, could not believe his luck in having all those thirsty young players, and a football crowd to boot, delivered to his door.

In fact the players' drinking habits were a constant source of worry for the Villa committee in the early years, particularly McGregor, a lifelong teetotaller. Certain individuals would be spied in pubs when they should have been training, or would arrive at training, or even matches, somewhat worse for wear. One or two were also caught brawling in pubs and had to be formally reprimanded.

To create a focus away from the tap room, therefore, in 1877 the committee rented a room at a coffee house in Aston High Street, where every Monday night during the season social gatherings, musical evenings and the like would be held. The club room would soon be switched to premises in Chain Walk, Lozells, then around 1878 to 'commodious premises' at Six Ways. (As mentioned in Chapter 1, in December 1892 the club took over an entire house at 127 Albert Road.)

As for catering inside the Perry Barr ground, at first Villa allowed horse-drawn refreshment vans to enter. Then in 1887 a Mr William Summers paid the club £4 for a five year lease to provide a Temperance Bar, serving 'tea, coffee, cocoa and eatables'. Another stall-holder complained that his takings had been affected by fans obstructing his counter.

Meanwhile, members of the press were left to their own devices. As described by McGregor, in the early days there were still trees lining the touchline (presumably on the ground's western side).

'I well remember the early reporters who used to have to trudge the touchlines,

❖ Stephen Gateley's membership card from Perry Barr in the 1890s. Membership then cost a bargain 10s 6d a season – the equivalent in today's terms of approximately £25 – and covered entry to all games at the ground.

finding a rest for their weary backs against these trees.' When spectators grew angry at having their views obscured, the trees also provided the pressmen with a loftier vantage point.

Unfortunately, few records and no photographs of the Perry Barr ground have survived, so we can only guess at its overall appearance from maps, etchings and reminiscences. One old regular recalled how 'fogs and the miasma' from the nearby River Tame 'used to gather so quickly on dreary November afternoons.' Other reports inform us that there was sufficient room on the site for a number of vehicles to be parked. These entered from a special gate on Wellington Road.

Before any stands were built, one of the most prominent wagons to be seen regularly at Perry Barr was that of another Scot, George Kynoch, who owned the ammunition works in Witton and later became Conservative MP for Aston. Described as 'a high-spirited sportsman,' Kynoch apparently took great delight in parking up along the touchline where, in the company of his invited guests, he probably felt jolly superior to the *hoi palloi* all around.

By 1887 there were at least three stands at Perry Barr. An ORDNANCE SURVEY map of that year shows there to have been two buildings marked as 'pavilion'. One, on the west side, may have been the structure referred to in the club's minute books as the Association Stand. The other may have been what was known as the Reporters Stand.

What we do know for certain was that the most imposing structure ever built at Perry Barr was the

Grand Stand, also erected in mid-1887, shortly after Villa's first ever FA Cup Final triumph, a 2-0 win over West Bromwich at the Oval in April 1887.

In order to raise the cash Villa set up a Pavilion Fund. This more than paid for the £383 costs of the construction, and guaranteed each individual subscriber a seat.

The stand itself measured some 30 yards long and was designed by Daniel Arkell, a local architect who had, that same year, finished a much grander edifice, the Victoria Hall on Victoria Road (now an Islamic study centre). Arkell advised the Villa for several years while they were at Perry Barr, and was later disappointed when the club chose another architect for the club's new home at the Lower Grounds. But in 1887 his neatly embellished Grand Stand was quite the most handsome stand in the Midlands.

Its proud opening took place before a representative match, Birmingham & District v Lancashire, on October 22 1887, watched by 11,000. Deemed by the BIRMINGHAM DAILY GAZETTE to be 'in every respect admirable,' the new stand had nine rows of seats, accommodating 700-800 spectators (who had to peer past no fewer than 14 slender columns), with a 'reserve promenade of ashes' along the front. This flat area, together with two sets of older wooden terraces placed on either side of the stand, held up to 1,500 standing.

As surviving etchings show, the stand was chiefly characterised by a central pedimented roof gable, on the front of which was a clock donated by a Mr Wray of New Street. Above the gable flew a large, pennant-

❖ George Kynoch was Villa's first wealthy patron. Born in Peterhead, Scotland, in common with Messrs McGregor and Ramsay, he came south to Birmingham in search of work, originally as a bank clerk. He then joined a munitions factory which, after an explosion killed 19 workers, he eventually took over and relocated to the more remote Witton, where his new Lion Works were opened in 1862. Business at Witton was soon booming, as it were, and in 1886 Kynoch was elected Conservative MP for Aston. Yet only two years later, pursued by his creditors, he absconded to South Africa, where he died in comparative poverty in 1891 at the age of 56. The Kynoch works stayed in business, however, expanded to cover over 200 acres, and eventually became part of IMI, the metals division of ICI.

❖ More running repairs at Perry Barr, in October 1890.

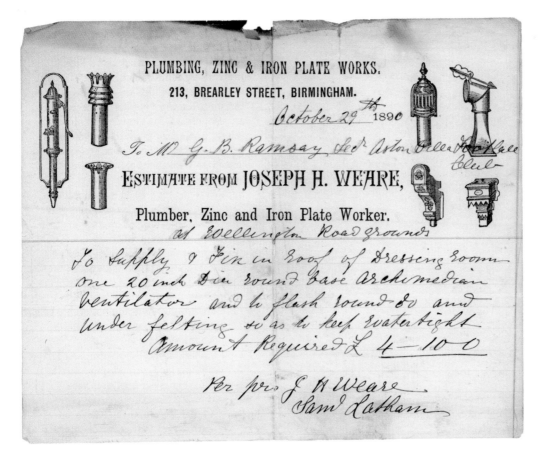

style flag with the initials AVFC. The ridge of the roof was lined by decorative ironwork.

Another admirable feature of the stand, according to the BIRMINGHAM DAILY POST was that 'it effectually hides the tramway sheds, which have for so long been an eyesore to visitors.'

Considering how basic the rest of the accommodation at Perry Barr remained throughout Villa's 21 years in residence, it is surprising how many people could be squeezed in.

Before the Grand Stand was built, the attendance record had risen dramatically within a matter of years. The gate of approximately 5,000 paying spectators – for a friendly against Lancashire Cup holders Darwen on January 12, 1881 (when Villa were holders of the Birmingham Cup, their first honour) – was described in the MIDLAND ATHLETE as 'the largest turn-out there has yet been for any football match in Birmingham.'

Yet only three years later a new record of 22,088 filled the ground for a Third Round FA Cup tie against West Bromwich Albion, on January 3, 1885. How many of those could actually see the game is open to question, as indeed is the actual figure, for this was before the days of turnstiles and strict controls.

The sharp rise in attendances also came at a time when 'rowdyism' was first witnessed at Perry Barr.

Mob violence was hardly a new phenomenon in Victorian Birmingham. As we shall learn in Chapter 3, there had been several outbreaks at the Aston Lower Grounds, not only at football matches but also at an athletics meeting of the Moseley Harriers in 1881, and after a Conservative Party rally held there in 1884 (the so-called Aston Riots). There were

reports of Villa and Albion fans clashing in 1883, and on May 9 1885 Perry Barr became the scene of one of the ugliest incidents yet seen at a British ground.

The fracas occurred at the end of a 'friendly' with Preston, in which Villa were humbled 5-1. According to the DAILY GAZETTE, among the crowd of approximately 3-5,000 were 'as usual, a large majority of the unruly population of the town and district.'

Enflamed by an incident during the game – in which a Villa player had retaliated after being kicked – a large group of these 'roughs' herded around the Preston team as they walked towards the dressing tent after the final whistle, hurling abuse.

'The Preston men, with commendable courage, turned round upon the crowd surrounding them and retaliated,' the GAZETTE reported. 'A free fight quickly ensued, during the course of which several aerated water bottles were hurled into the crowd and smashed, regardless of the consequences. The fight lasted but a few minutes, and the Preston team, with the assistance of the Villa men, made their way to the dressing tent. The roughs continued hissing and hooting, and it was a considerable time before they left the field, despite the efforts of the few constables of the Perry Barr division who were present.'

The GAZETTE later changed its story and claimed that there had been no policeman on duty at the ground at all.

But the most graphic account came from an eye witness, presumably one of the players.

According to him, a Preston player called Drummond, one of the last men to reach the tent, was apparently assaulted 'by a young, well-dressed fellow (who) gave him a half-hit and shove, saying "Oh, there's one of them."

Drummond was then 'hemmed in and most unmercifully kicked, struck at, and poked surreptitiously in the ribs with sticks.'

When they were finally ready to leave Perry Barr, the beleaguered Preston players were conveyed towards the exit in a horse-drawn vehicle, under a hail of 'earth, small stones, rubbish of all sorts,' only to find that a gang had closed the Wellington Road gates in front of them.

'We were thus brought to a standstill in the midst of 2,000 howling roughs. Thicker and faster came the stones, showers of spittle covered us; we were struck at over the side with sticks and umbrellas, and at last a big missile flew past my ear and caught Ross (a Preston player) on top of the head, smashing his hat and down he dropped.'

Eventually the visitors managed to break through. But they were followed by the mob for half a mile.

Villa somehow escaped censure for this appalling incident, perhaps because similar outrages had occurred elsewhere. But they were less fortunate three years later when Preston were again the visitors to Perry Barr, despite the fact that on this occasion

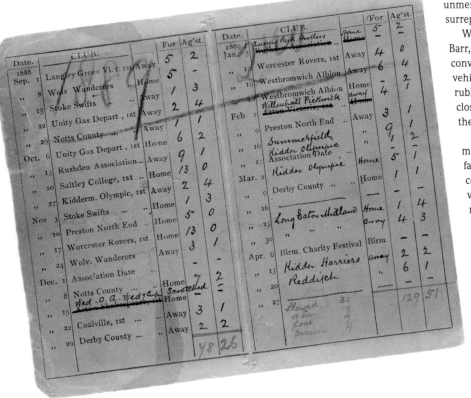

❖ *Despite a regular fixture list, George Ramsay still placed occasional adverts in the sporting press for extra games for Villa's reserves. It is possible that Ramsay himself filled in the results on this card from 1889-90.*

no violence occurred at all. Instead, the ground was simply overwhelmed by thousands of eager spectators wanting to witness the clash of the season: Aston Villa – the so-called *Perry Barr Pets* and FA Cup holders – against the *Invincibles* from Preston, in the fifth round of the Cup on January 7, 1888.

Apart from any fears Villa's committee may have harboured about further violence, their main concern was how the ground would cope with the anticipated hordes. As a result, as soon as the draw was made, several detailed planning meetings were held, meetings which provide us with an unusually detailed insight into life at Perry Barr.

The first sensitive issue, naturally, was that of seat allocation. Accordingly, at a Special General Meeting held at the Grand Hotel nine days before the match, some 150 members were asked to 'relinquish their right to occupy the Grand Stand' so as to allow the club to make the maximum profit from the occasion. Surprisingly, the proposal was unanimously agreed, leaving the committee a free hand to set admission prices. These were later agreed at 6d for unreserved and 1s for reserved areas (double the usual prices) and, for seats in the Grand Stand, no less than 5s, or 10s for the best three rows. This last figure was later said by William McGregor to be 'quite unheard of in connection with football of that day.'

One local newspaper even claimed that stand seats usually reserved for the press were sold at £1 each, the equivalent of £50 today. If true, never before had any football match, other than a Cup Final, been so highly priced. And yet, as later reports confirmed, even the highest prices were 'cheerfully paid'.

In those days there was no official ticket office at Perry Barr, so tickets were to be sold from the business premises of various committee members on the three days preceding the game. Interestingly, one of the chosen outlets was in Small Heath.

While the team prepared at their favourite retreat, Holt Fleet in Worcestershire, Daniel Arkell was delegated to look after arrangements in the Grand Stand. The Association Stand was moved back

and raised at a cost of £5. A temporary stand (probably no more than a set of wooden bleachers) was hired for £18 and placed behind the 'top goal'. Extra duckboards loaned by a Mr Mitchell were also placed around the touchlines, to keep spectators' feet dry.

Elsewhere in the ground new pay boxes were hastily erected, and a number of garden seats were hired, presumably to provide more accommodation in front of the Grand Stand. Another committeeman, Philip Clamp, went to West Bromwich to seek a police superintendent's advice on the deployment of extra officers. Permission was also sought from the Handsworth Local Board to position extra barriers outside the entrance gates.

No detail was too small. For the Reporters Stand six stewards were allocated and refreshments organised by William McGregor. Sawdust was also to be laid on the floor. Could this also have been to keep patrons' feet dry, or was it to absorb splatterings of ink from the journalists?

Six more stewards would assist committee members Isaac Whitehouse and Tom Vaughton in the Association Stand (which was to be partitioned for use by members on the day). Another eight stewards and committeeman, John Vickerstaff, would organise the parking of vehicles on the ground. Charges were set at the following rates: 2s 6d (25p) for two-wheeled traps, 5s for four-wheelers, and 10s for brakes and horse-drawn buses, all prices being exclusive of occupants. Two other committee members, Joshua Margoschis and Arthur Albut, took care of the Wellington Road entrance. To counter fraud, all season tickets were to be punched on entry and forfeited if presented twice. McGregor also agreed to provide rosettes; white for committee members, and ones in the club colours of chocolate and blue for each steward.

Behind the scenes, George Ramsay would look after the Preston officials while, in his absence, a lad would be stationed to guard the office. Mr Williams, the groundsman, was asked to ensure that only Dr Jones and Joe Gorman (the trainer) were admitted to the dressing room before kick-off. Villa's Scottish

*❖ No photographs survive of Villa's 21 years at Perry Barr, and like this one from 1886-87, most of the sketches showing Villa in action were only loose representations.*

*continued on page 22*

# Still counting after all these years

❖ Just think, the very same turnstile you nudged through on your last visit to Villa Park might well have been one of original cast-iron turnstiles installed at Perry Barr in 1895!

Not only that but in its 102 years of trusty, but seldom rusty service, that turnstile will almost certainly have admitted well over two million people – more than the entire population of Birmingham!

Throughout all the changes at Villa Park during the last century, these amazingly solid and yet still delightfully-crafted turnstiles are, without doubt, the only fixtures to have survived the test of time, so much so that the current stadium management actually prefer them to several hydraulic models installed in the 1970s. Seldom has the club obtained such incredibly good value, and all for the princely sum of £7 12s 6d each.

The man generally credited with introducing turnstiles to Villa was the ubiquitous 'FWR' – Fred Rinder. But the circumstances in which he ordered them were not entirely happy.

Until late 1895, entry to Perry Barr had been via simple pay-boxes, either by ticket or cash. Since no-one actually counted spectators as they entered, the 'gate' was then calculated on the basis of the

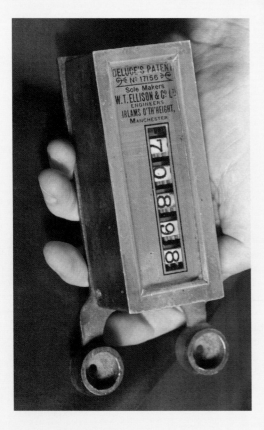

❖ This lovingly preserved brass mechanism may well be one of the counters attached to the 1895 Rush Preventive turnstiles at Perry Barr. ELLISON'S told Villa's committee in 1895 that each turnstile could admit up to 4,000 people per hour, or 3,000 if change had to be handed over. This compares with today's recommendations (from the Taylor Report) that there should be sufficient turnstiles at each ground to admit the entire capacity within one hour, at a rate of no more than 660 people per turnstile. How times have changed, even if the old RUSH PREVENTIVES look like outlasting us all!

takings handed over by each gateman. As Villa and several other clubs found to their cost, here was a system perfectly designed for corruption.

In Villa's case the need for a more secure entry system became paramount in September 1895. Already suspicious of fraud, Rinder had made doubly sure that all the fences around the ground were secure, while Joshua Margoschis hired detectives to watch out on a match day, particularly for touts. The sleuths found no evidence. But then George Ramsay discovered that 2,017 tickets had been unaccounted for following a match against Small Heath on September 7. This was in the same week as the FA Cup was stolen from Billy Shillcock's shop in Newtown Row, so Villa's committee were understandably more security conscious than ever before.

Suspecting that the gatemen were pocketing a portion of the receipts, Rinder organised a visit to Bramall Lane to study a new type of metered turnstile, the *Rush Preventive*. Always a stickler for details, Rinder also visited the manufacturers, W. T.

ELLISON & CO, at their works in Irlam o' th' Heights, near Manchester.

Within days, Villa ordered a dozen turnstiles, then six more after further overcrowding was reported in a 20,000 attendance against Sunderland in October 1895. The club also decided to rent a house on Wellington Road, to be used on match days for counting the receipts.

The turnstiles were unpopular with fans at first, possibly because Villa decided that, instead of handing out change at the actual turnstiles, separate 'change offices' would be provided – a practice which certainly did not continue for long.

Angriest of all were the gatemen. Furious at the insinuations of dishonesty, some of them threatened libel action. Rinder diplomatically responded that no allegations had been made against any individuals, but, according to various club histories, gate receipts shot up from £75 to £250 on the first occasion the turnstiles were used. Although the receipts may well have risen, these oft-quoted figures are hardly credible, however, since receipts for games during this period were regularly in excess of £200. For example, for the aforementioned match against Small Heath – one of the last home games before the turnstiles were installed – the receipts from an estimated crowd of 13,000 amounted to £327.17s.

Similarly, although average gates rose from around 8,700 in 1894-95 to around 13,150 the following year, Villa did win the First Division title that season, so a rise in receipts was only to be expected. All the same, Villa's new turnstiles gave the club much needed security and peace of mind, and have continued to do so ever since.

Since they were brought over to Villa Park in 1897, the hardy old turnstiles have been moved around, knocked around, patched up and, more recently, modernised with electronic counters. Some of the Perry Barr originals may well have been among 34 turnstiles borrowed by the AUSTIN MOTOR COMPANY during the Second World War, presumably to increase security at their works. AUSTIN paid Villa £400 for the loan.

At the last count in 1997, a total of 12 ELLISON'S 'RUSH PREVENTIVE' turnstiles are still in use at Villa Park, in the Trinity Road Stand, Doug Ellis Stand and Holte End. Although some were ordered after Villa moved to the Lower Grounds in 1897, Ted Pearson of the turnstile company GUNNEBO MAYOR (which took over ELLISON in 1963) believes that at least four date back to the original order of 1895.

And what service they have performed! Imagine the infinite variety of fans, young and old, home and away, who have preceeded us through those well-worn barriers. And for so many, after a lengthy, uncomfortable and uncertain queue outside the ground, the familiar sound of that turnstile clanking has meant one thing, and one thing only: entry to the promised land!

❖ In June 1992 the old turnstiles from the Witton Lane stand were taken out for yet another thorough overhaul. Fans entering the ground today can tell whether their turnstile is one of the originals from either 1895 or from the period immediately after. A brass plate in the centre of the counter clearly states ELLISON'S RUSH PREVENTIVE, made in Irlam o' th' Height. Later ELLISON models were marked as being made in Salford or West Bromwich. Other old turnstiles at Villa Park, dating from the 1920s, were made by SIR W.H. BAILEY & CO., at the Albion Works in Salford.

captain, Archie Hunter, was put in charge of the footballs. Never before had Villa planned for a match so meticulously. And yet on the day it all went horribly wrong.

The invasion of Perry Barr began long before mid-day. Queues started forming at 10.30am. Tightly packed steam trams tottered up and down the Birchfield Road. Archie Hunter recalled that it was 'just like Derby Day' as the Villa team emerged from a dining room in town, only to find themselves bogged down in slow-moving traffic on Birchfield Road.

'We were soon recognised, and amid the exciting hubbub could be heard the encouraging and familiar shout of "Play Up, Villa!" Once arrived at the ground,' said Hunter, 'the crowd was a source of amazement to us all,' and particularly to the police superintendent. 'An hour before the game... it seemed impossible to crush any more onto the ground; yet the stream still rolled on.'

Eventually, the barriers on Wellington Road gave way, leaving the fifty or so West Bromwich constables on duty powerless to control the queues. At around

*❖ Villa's hugely admired Scottish captain and centre forward, Archie Hunter, died from consumption in a hotel room near Six Ways, Aston, on November 29, 1894, at the age of just 35. He had collapsed while playing against Everton in January 1890 and never fully recovered. The proceeds of this benefit match went to his family, while the Old Villans Society paid for a memorial at his grave in Witton Cemetery.*

2.30 the police tried to close the gates but, as the BIRMINGHAM MAIL reported, so determined were the crowds still outside 'that it would have been sheer madness to have carried the order into execution.'

Nor were latecomers dissuaded from entering when warned that they had no chance whatsoever of seeing any of the game.

Inside the ground an extraordinary scene unfolded. While every stand was packed to the brim at least an hour before kick-off, so, too, every charabanc, brake, wagon, lorry and trap parked along the touchlines strained under the weight of hangers-on, some of them reportedly paying the owners or drivers an extra half-a-crown for the privilege.

All the surrounding trees and rooftops were covered by fans, with 'a dozen heads' peeping out from every available window. Several more energetic individuals managed to climb onto the roof of the Grand Stand, including one bold fellow who was described as 'looking wonderfully at home with his legs turned around the flagstaff.'

Inevitably something had to give. As yet more fans tried to push their way through from the entrances, or strained for even a glimpse of the pitch, the flimsy barriers lining the touchlines gave way, sending hundreds of people spilling onto the field.

Somehow the fans were forced back, so that when the two teams finally emerged from the dressing rooms 'amid a storm of cheers', as Archie Hunter recalled, they hardly imagined that there would be any further problems.

For the first fifteen minutes or so, that was the case. Villa happily took the lead through Hunter, at which point, as was the custom of the day, a flight of homing pigeons was released from the ground in order to convey the news to coffee shops, tobacconists and newspaper offices all over Birmingham and the Black Country. At first, the pigeons 'circled round and round, and didn't seem to understand it all.'

But even as they gained their bearings and took flight, down below, Villa's joy was about to be stymied. Once again, the crowd had spilled onto the pitch, rendering further play impossible.

Archie Hunter's account continued: 'The Preston team gathered in a group and sat on the ground while our players were told to assist the police in clearing the lines. I myself, having some influence with the populace in those days, was particularly requested to speak to the people and induce them to return to their places. I went forward and begged of them to withdraw, pointing out that there was an empty space of a dozen yards or more at the back. But they would not be reasoned with, and I next tried to push the multitude back, with the help of a posse of police, and I never worked so hard and so ineffectually in my life. I might as well have tried to move a mountain. All my efforts were unavailing.'

It was at this point that Hunter approached his Preston counterpart, the legendary Nick Ross and, together with the umpires and referee (who was, incidentally, a lawyer), agreed that if

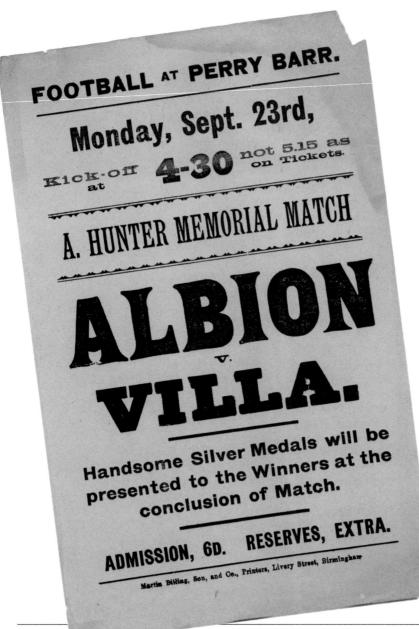

FOOTBALL AT PERRY BARR.

Monday, Sept. 23rd,

KICK-OFF at 4-30 not 5.15 as on Tickets.

A. HUNTER MEMORIAL MATCH

ALBION v. VILLA.

Handsome Silver Medals will be presented to the Winners at the conclusion of Match.

ADMISSION, 6D. RESERVES, EXTRA.

Martin Billing, Son, and Co., Printers, Livery Street, Birmingham the game was to continue, it should be played only as a friendly. Few in the crowd would have known of this decision, but then most informed spectators would have guessed that Preston would lodge a protest anyway.

George Ramsay, meanwhile, ordered some mounted police to help restore order. Some reports say he telegraphed the nearby Great Brook Street barracks, where the Hussars were stationed. Others say he contacted the local police. Confusingly, McGregor wrote, many years after the event, that Ramsay 'telephoned' for assistance. But a telegraph was more likely. Certain national newspapers also confused the issue by using the dramatic headline – *Military Called Out!*

But the reality was rather more mundane. When the mounted police failed to appear in time, two uniformed soldiers, who had been spotted in the crowd, were each saddled onto cab horses unhitched from their vehicles. Hunter described the men as Hussars, who 'careered round as wildly as their dashing steeds would allow them.'

Off-duty Hussars they may have been, even if the cab horses were unlikely to have been very dashing. But the ploy seemed to work. As the crowds were forced back behind the touchlines, the first half was allowed to restart, and only ten minutes of the second half remained by the time the real mounted officers arrived. By this time, however, there was not much for them to do. Although there were still signs of unruliness, many people had given up and gone home, thus relieving the pressure. In addition, Villa ended up losing 3-1. According to Hunter, the first-half decision to play out the 90 minutes as a friendly 'had a depressing effect upon the Villa players; they would not exert themselves.'

Thus the day of Perry Barr's record crowd also turned out to be the Villa's single greatest embarrassment to date. Officially, the gate was put at 26,849. McGregor reckoned there were 35,000 actually in the ground. True, there had been no actual violence, while much of the blame was attached to the police – nothing new there, then – particularly the West Bromwich superintendent, who had deliberately chosen not to deploy mounted officers at the ground, because, he said, he did not approve of their use. THE ATHLETIC JOURNAL went further by describing the police on the day as a 'pack of idiots' who 'pushed and kicked about, seemingly enjoying the struggle.'

But for Villa there were two bitter pills to swallow in the aftermath. Firstly, the FOOTBALL ASSOCIATION refused to let the clubs replay the game, awarded the tie to Preston, and threw Villa – the Cup holders, no less – out of the competition for failing to maintain order at their ground. This in itself was a major scandal at the time, and was discussed and argued over in Birmingham for many a year after.

Secondly, the chaotic scenes strongly suggested that, despite all Villa's careful efforts and planning, the Perry Barr site might not be as suitable as was thought to cope with the club's rising popularity and long term ambition. With hindsight the Preston

# BRUM DISGRACED

Since it has been our lot to frequent football matches we have never been witness of such disgraceful scenes as occurred this afternoon at the conclusion of the match at Perry Barr. It was feared by the Birmingham officials that one or two episodes which took place between the players would lead to an unpleasant finish, as a great deal of hostility was loudly expressed by a section of the spectators during the process of the game.

Still none of them for one moment supposed that the more unscrupulous of the Villa partisans would behave in such a blackguardly manner. On the North End team leaving the field, they were mercilessly attacked by a band of–if appearances go for anything–bona-fide Brummagem roughs, who mobbed them, and used sticks, stones, mud, and every available missile with which to wreak their vengeance on the visitors.

It need scarcely be said that the Villa men exerted themselves to the utmost to protect the North Enders. If the dribbling game is to be marred (as it has been of late) by such cowardly exhibitions as that of this afternoon, the sooner football is consigned to oblivion the better for all concerned. Brum, go to the bottom of the class until you can learn better manners.

❖ *Preston North End had good cause to be wary of visiting Perry Barr in the 1880s. Although the scene depicted above, when mounted soldiers were called into action at the Cup-tie in 1888, arose largely because of overcrowding, three years earlier the Preston's players were the targets of outright hooliganism. The Birmingham weekly, SATURDAY NIGHT, placed a black border around its shocked report and wondered if the game could survive such incidents. Fortunately, Villa fans have since proved to be rather more sporting and mild-mannered.*

fiasco may even be described as a major turning point.

Life, nevertheless, soon returned to normal, as Villa, and William McGregor in particular, prepared for the inauguration of the FOOTBALL LEAGUE in September 1888. But, apart from a worrying lack of success on the pitch after Villa's first League season, it soon became apparent that the club's committee were becoming a tad too complacent.

Cometh the hour, cometh the man. It was time for a much-needed shake-up and, fortunately for Villa, one of the members proved to be just the man for the job.

As other accounts have shown, from 1893 until his sensational removal from the chairmanship in 1925, and from 1935 until his death in 1938, Frederick William Rinder was to play a dominant, often dictatorial role in the Villa's affairs, as well as proving a dogged campaigner in FOOTBALL LEAGUE and FOOTBALL ASSOCIATION circles.

But in the context of our tale, Rinder's most salient characteristic was his absolute passion for ground developments, a passion which at times bordered upon obsession and rightly earned him the sobriquet of the 'architectural agitator'.

Rinder was typical of Villa's early stalwarts in that he had arrived in the city as a stranger. Unusually, however, he was not Scottish. Instead, he had been born in Liverpool in July 1858, reared in Leeds – where he was a useful rugby player, runner and pole vaulter – then, after a spell in Battersea, London, had arrived in Birmingham in 1876 at the age of 18.

Rinder's first contact with Villa was in the late 1870s, after which he became a member in 1881. But he remained fairly anonymous for several years, and only became more closely involved in 1887 as a willing aid to the committee set up to build the Grand Stand. Rinder was, by then, working as a surveyor for

Birmingham City Corporation, a profession which, no doubt, reflected his love of construction and also enabled him to provide Villa with free advice and useful contacts.

He would, nevertheless, have been a relative unknown when he called a Special General Meeting of members in early 1893, to hammer out a number of issues which he and others felt were damaging the club's stability and prospects. Held at the New Gallery in Barwick Street on February 24, 1893 – the eve of Perry Barr's first and only international fixture, England v Ireland – the meeting was to prove a watershed in the club's history.

In a long, detailed and scathing speech that night, Rinder defiantly declared that Villa were in a 'deplorable state' owing to the 'utter mismanagement' of a 'well-meaning but hopelessly incapable' committee.

Their policy of signing players purely on the recommendations of agents was suspect, he argued. The lack of discipline within the club was now acute. Most worryingly of all, stated Rinder, several of the eleven serving committee members were exacerbating the situation by drinking openly and frequently in the company of players. This laxity, he suggested quite pointedly, had been a root cause in the team's 3-0 defeat to West Bromwich Albion in the previous year's Cup Final at Crystal Palace. (A few weeks before the meeting Villa had also been knocked out of that season's Cup, by Second Division Darwen.)

Faced with such a frank onslaught, followed by an overwhelming vote in support of Rinder, the committee resigned en bloc, and although certain individuals (including McGregor, Josh Margoschis, Dr Jones and Joe Dunkley) were re-appointed to a provisional committee, and George Ramsay kept his post as Secretary, the Barwick Street meeting patently signalled the dawn of a new era.

Whether Rinder alone initiated the coup, or merely acted on behalf of other anxious committeemen, or even Ramsay, is not known. But it is clear that, from that moment onwards, Villa began to assume a much more disciplined, businesslike approach; an approach which helped transform the club's fortunes over the next decade and reach a high point in 1897 when the Double was won and, weeks later, the new ground in Aston was inaugurated. Much of that achievement was credited to Rinder's stern, and sometimes 'coldly logical' leadership. He may not have been universally popular, but no-one doubted his almost puritanical dedication and devotion to the Villa.

Eulogising Rinder after his death in 1938, the club programme said of him, 'Only a big man, a man with a powerful brain and a large mind could have rescued Aston Villa from the slough from which he extricated them.'

In fact, after the Barwick Street showdown, Rinder did not join the committee until the following Annual General Meeting in June 1893 and, even then, for his first two years he seemed content to prove himself behind the scenes, particularly regarding financial matters and the general upkeep and development of the Wellington Road ground.

Rinder fussed over every detail; the stands, the pitch, the dressing rooms, the boundary fences. But the one aspect of his work which seems to have attracted the most public attention was his introduction of turnstiles to Perry Barr, as explained on page 20. Before we follow those trusty turnstiles on their journey with Villa to the Lower Grounds in 1897, a few last words on Perry Barr.

Apart from Villa's games, Perry Barr hosted a number of events. In 1890 and 1896 there were FA Cup semi-finals; Bolton v Sheffield Wednesday and Derby v Wolves. (Earlier semi-finals in 1884 and 1886 were staged at the Lower Grounds Meadow – not at Perry Barr).

As mentioned above, the day after the Barwick Street showdown there was an England v Ireland international at Perry Barr, watched by 10,000. To this were added three international trial games and a number of representative matches involving the Birmingham and District Association. From 1878 onwards Villa also staged popular annual sports days, in which players such as Charlie Johnstone, Howard Vaughton and Tom Pank displayed their prowess as athletes. (Pank was also a member of the Birchfield Harriers, who shared Villa's base at the Old Crown & Cushion and held many a meeting at the Lower Grounds.)

Perry Barr was also busy during the summer months. In the first year or two at the ground the club maintained their cricketing activities, but apparently with little success. Thereafter, they earned much needed revenue by hiring out the ground. For example, Aston Grammar School paid £7 for three months rental in 1888, which, on the eve of Villa's debut League season, left the pitch in desperate need of returfing. The following summer

saw the American sport of baseball staged at Perry Barr, charged at a minimum rent of £10 per game. The players left behind a set of bats and balls in the hope that interest in the game might continue, and were back the summer after, this time paying a minimum of £25, with two further guarantees: that the pitch would be restored at their expense and that they would not engage any of Villa's players without the club's permission.

This second condition was necessary because the baseball club was now playing under the name of ASTON VILLA, in a summer league which also included the likes of Derby County, Preston and Stoke. Two Americans played in Villa's colours, and when a national baseball association was formed in July 1890 William McGregor was elected Honorary Treasurer.

The baseball craze certainly lasted for several years, at least until Villa's final summer at Perry Barr in 1896. But, by then, Villa hardly needed either the extra rent, or the distraction. They had just secured a second League title, having won the FA Cup for a second time the year before. Their turnover had leapt from £3,368 in 1889-90 to £8,857 by 1894.

Still uncertain of their lease, however, only basic improvements were made to the ground. In 1889 a company was permitted to place 'automatic closets' at Perry Barr, in return for which Villa took 30%, presumably of every penny spent! A number of small stands were added. One was called the Gazette Stand – an early example of sponsorship – another was called the Press Stand, and a third was mysteriously referred to as the Skeleton Stand (perhaps because it was no more than a bare frame).

Certainly, none were particularly sophisticated, as shown in March 1895 when gales toppled and wrecked the Gazette Stand. (Ever mindful of resources, Rinder ordered the timber to be stored for future use.) Then, at the beginning of August 1895, Rinder proposed a new stand holding 800 spectators behind 'the bottom goal', to cost all of £35. By the end of the month he reported its completion! Another contract was to patch up the old dressing room roof, which had grown so unsafe that policemen had to make sure no fans sat on it during games.

Occasionally, fans did come a cropper. One asked for recompense after ripping his overcoat in the Gazette Stand. More seriously, in September 1894, an accident resulted in a supporter losing an eye. Villa denied all responsibility, but still offered him two guineas and a season ticket. Villa were also pursued on a regular basis by a Mr Lane, apparently for the non-payment of damages to his garden seats during the Preston debacle in 1888. They finally settled at 30s, nearly nine years after the event.

By early 1895, Villa seemed firmly committed to leaving Perry Barr. A number of niggling difficulties had arisen with access to the ground, including the closure of a passage leading to the members' enclosure by an irate neighbour. Another neighbour wrote to the HANDSWORTH HERALD in November 1890 that 'residents are in constant terror on big (match) days.'

❖ *Villa advertise their assets in BICYCLING NEWS, on March 17, 1897*

❖ *Villa reject! When Villa left Perry Barr, Small Heath (now Birmingham City) bought the old Perry Barr Grand Stand for £90 and turned it into a terrace cover behind the goal at Muntz Street.*

More importantly, as far as the club was concerned, Villa were still unable to obtain a long term lease from their landlords, the Bridge Trust.

As noted earlier, Villa's first landlord, the butcher-cum-farmer, had sub-let the field for £5 in the first season, rising to £8 in 1877. The rent then rose to £10 for Villa's third season. But as many other clubs found, annual agreements provided no security. For this reason, in around 1880, the club paid £26 in order to purchase the 'complete rights' for the Perry Barr site – that is, they became direct tenants of the Bridge Trust. (The £26 was paid to a Mrs Hall, who may have been the wife or widow of the former landlord.)

Clearly aware of the game's growing profitability, the Trust now demanded £60 per annum for a three year lease. Villa signed the deal, but as the years passed this rose to £120 in 1891 and, finally, by the mid 1890s, to £200.

Contemporaries at the club, including the normally mild-mannered McGregor, came to regard the Trust's demands as exorbitant, although, in truth, the rent was hardly onerous when compared with the club's income. Other clubs had received similar or, in some cases, much higher demands from their landlords.

But the plain truth was obvious. Aston Villa could not continue to dominate their rivals as long as they remained at a ground which was both constricted and under-developed. Just as the 1990s have seen the construction and modernisation of dozens of grounds all over Britain, so too there was a building boom in the early 1890s, a boom which left Villa in serious danger of falling behind. Perry Barr was certainly no match for the likes of Ewood Park, Blackburn (opened in 1890), Burnden Park, Bolton (1895), or the best ground in the country at that time, Goodison Park, built by Everton in 1892.

Hence, in 1894 Villa's committee entered negotiations with the owners of the finest sports ground in the district, the Aston Lower Grounds.

These negotiations would take nearly two years to conclude, and would be followed by another 16 months of preparations, during which time a few Villa members would fight tooth and nail to keep the club at Perry Barr.

Fortunately, for the future of the club these traditionalists were outvoted, and Perry Barr saw its last action on April 16, 1897, the day before Villa kicked off at the Lower Grounds. A low-key reserve game v Shrewsbury brought down the curtain on 21 eventful years, watched by a mere 500 spectators. According to legend, the last man ever to kick a ball on the ground was George Ramsay, who also claimed to have been the first to grace the turf at Villa Park.

Within a few years a speculative builder called Thomas had erased all memory of Perry Barr. Where the pitch had been, Willmore Road and Leslie Road were laid out, both of which remain today.

As for the landlord of the Old Crown & Cushion, the redoubtable Walter Bowen – 'a sportsman of the first quality' – and indeed the owners of the neighbouring tramway company, life would never be quite the same again. Nor would it be for poor old Williams, the groundsman, who Villa left behind, together with the club's pony, which was deemed too slight to cope with the more onerous duties likely to crop up at the new ground.

But for more sentimental Villa fans in search of nostalgia, a reminder of the happy days at Perry Barr was not too far away. As Villa prepared to depart they invited offers from neighbouring clubs for all their stands; £100 for Daniel Arkell's Grand Stand, £60 each for the bottom goal stand and both wing stands, £10 for the dressing rooms, £10 for the referee's hut and the press box, and £5 for the one turnstile they did not take with them to Aston.

Mr Thomas duly offered a derisory £50 for the job lot. Mitchell St George's successfully bid £25 for the bottom goal stand. West Bromwich Albion asked for more time, Warwick County did not reply and, in the end, the Grand Stand found its way to Small Heath for a knockdown £90.

It took the Heathens another eight months to pay up, but it has to be said that the stand looked as grand as ever when re-erected as a terrace cover behind one of the goals at Muntz Street. There it would remain for another nine years (before Small Heath moved on too), during which time no doubt the sight of it caused many a visiting Villa fan to break out in a wry smile, and maybe shed the odd tear or two, in fond memory of a much-loved home.

# The Lower Grounds and its Magnificent Meadow

THE ASTON LOWER GROUNDS AND ASTON Villa were made for each other. So much so that, on the surface, it might seem curious that the club took so long to move there and that, once the decision was finally taken, a determined minority of club members should have objected so strongly.

To explain this in full – and with all due apologies to those readers now anxious to read about 1897 and all that – requires us to take one more leap back in time to the very beginnings of the Lower Grounds. But the story is a fascinating one and, once again, serves to remind us not only of Aston's rich heritage, but also of the unique pedigree of Villa Park.

In addition, long before Villa Park was opened in 1897, Aston Villa played several important games at the Lower Grounds. These took place on the Meadow, the ground which formed the main sports arena of the Lower Grounds until it was swallowed up by housing on Nelson, Jardine and Endicott Roads in 1888. Indeed, Villa won their first ever trophy – the Birmingham Senior Cup – at the Meadow in April

❖ *Yet more of the Holte estates go under the hammer in 1851. Notice how, with uncanny foresight, the auctioneers declare the area to be suitable for Villa!*

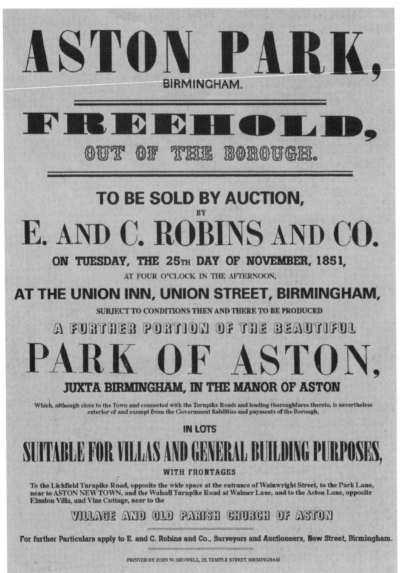

1880. By chance, they also played in the last ever football match staged there in August 1888.

This chapter tells the story of the Lower Grounds in the period between 1864 and that final match. The following chapter covers the period between 1888 and 1896, when there was a new Meadow in use, exactly on the site of the current Villa Park.

The development of the Lower Grounds as a separate entity began in the mid-19th century. It will be recalled that the Holte family estates began to be sold off, bit by bit, from 1818 onwards, mainly for housing, leaving Aston Hall and its grounds in the hands of James Watt junior – the Hall's last long term tenant – from 1818 until his death in 1848. Thereafter, those tracts of the estate which would survive the relentless onslaught of bricks and mortar, broadly fell into two portions, one on either side of what would become Trinity Road in around the 1860s.

The upper grounds, which had once formed the Holte's deer park, together with the Hall's formal gardens, largely survived to become Aston Park in 1858. This area comprised 43 acres.

The lower grounds, covering just over 31 acres, essentially formed a large tongue of flat land between Trinity Road and Witton Lane, and were developed from 1864 onwards into the Aston Lower Grounds.

During their heyday in the 1870s and 1880s, the Aston Lower Grounds formed, probably, the most sophisticated sporting and leisure complex outside London. Villa Park, its car parks and associated buildings, now cover roughly half of their former expanse. But to understand how and why the Lower Grounds developed as they did, we must first consider the upper grounds.

In 1856, eight years after the death of James Watt junior, Birmingham Town Council made its first efforts to take over Aston Hall and preserve the upper grounds for the benefit of the rapidly expanding populace (even though Aston Manor was then outside Birmingham's boundaries and would remain so until 1911).

Meanwhile, also in 1856, two charitable fetes held in the grounds were successful enough to suggest that there might be a demand for a permanent place for public gatherings and entertainment. Already in Birmingham the enthusiasm for exhibitions and annual shows had helped launch Bingley Hall in 1851, while, no doubt, a further inspiration was the recently-held, exceptionally popular and morale boosting Great Exhibition in London's Hyde Park (centred upon Joseph Paxton's famous Crystal Palace).

So it was that Aston Hall and its upper grounds, now renamed Aston Park, were purchased by the specially created ASTON HALL & PARK COMPANY, before being opened to the public with great pomp and circumstance by Queen Victoria in June 1858.

The clerk of works who helped organise that Royal visit and supervise the grounds on behalf of the new company was one Henry G. Quilter.

In several respects, Quilter was a quite extraordinary character, and yet he may also be

❖ This is the earliest known view of the Lower Grounds, after they had been split from the upper grounds in 1864, but before more substantial development took place in the 1870s. The watercolour was painted in order to show where George Kynoch's new ammunition works (shown lower left), were built in Witton (lower right), in 1862. But it also tells us a great deal about the Lower Grounds in their formative years. The Holte Hotel and Dovehouse Pool can be seen on the left, with the newly laid-out Trinity Road now dividing the pool from the slopes of Aston Hall (at the top of the picture). The cricket ground can also be seen (top right), as can the area which became a bowling green on Trinity Road, with what appears to be a small pavilion. In the foreground the curve of the River Tame is just visible below the train steaming along towards Witton Station. Notice, also, the footbridge over Witton Road, linking the main Lower Grounds with the boating lake (far right).

described as a fairly typical Victorian self-made man. A Cockney by birth and an orphan at the age of 13, like thousands of other young hopefuls from around the country, in 1842 Quilter had moved to Birmingham in search of work. After several years as a grocer in New Street and then Constitution Hill, he became the managing cashier of a firm of builders in Aston, a job which, as a later profile explained, uncovered hidden talents and changed his life absolutely. Above all, it brought Quilter 'into relation with buildings, plans, architecture etc., and thus instilled in him a love of the beautiful. Being of an enquiring, ambitious and energetic temperament, he soon added to his many acquirements those of landscape and ornamental gardening (and) floriculture.'

Anxious to implement these new-found skills, Quilter became so immersed in the local campaign to save Aston Hall – a campaign in which many ordinary working people were active – that he soon found himself appointed as general superintendent of the whole grounds, with rent-free living quarters in one of the hall's wings, no less. As mentioned earlier, he was also put in charge of arrangements for the Royal visit in 1858. (To a more modest degree Quilter's rise to prominence thus echoed that of Joseph Paxton, who was also a working-class, self-taught horticulturalist and designer.)

Unfortunately, within a few years the ASTON HALL & PARK COMPANY collapsed in debt (and with a haughty rebuke from the Queen herself when she learnt that a female tightrope walker had been killed during a fete in the park). All was not lost, however. In 1864 both the hall and park were again saved from redevelopment, this time thanks to private donations of £7,000 and a hefty £19,000 grant from Birmingham Town Council (City status was not granted until 1889).

The hall itself became Britain's first municipally-owned stately home to be opened to the public, and later served as Birmingham's first museum. Aston Park, meanwhile, as already noted, soon became a

magnet for the area's rapidly growing number of soccer enthusiasts, among which Aston Villa were regulars. Cricket historian, Robert Brooke, has discovered that the park also staged the earliest recorded first-class cricket match in Birmingham. This was a three-day encounter in September 1861, featuring a North XI (captained by George Parr) against a South XI (led by John Lillywhite).

But if the hall and park were now saved, the Lower Grounds were not part of the council's purchase in 1864. Instead, they remained in the hands of the heirs of the Warwick bankers, GREENWAY, GREAVES & WHITEHEAD, who had bought the estate from the Holte family in 1818. After 1871 the ownership passed to Edgar Flower, the son of Selina Greaves and a member of the well-known family of brewers in Stratford. Flower would later be responsible for leasing the Lower Grounds to Aston Villa in 1896.

The Lower Grounds were dominated by three main features.

Firstly, almost exactly where the Villa Park pitch is now, there was an ancient fishpond called Dovehouse Pool. According to Oliver Fairclough's history of Aston Hall, in 1827 James Watt junior, a keen angler, had drained the pool, taken out 3,700 brace of carp, 700 brace of tench, as well as eels and other freshwater fish, and then refilled and restocked it for both his profit and pleasure.

Just next to Dovehouse Pool, roughly where the Holte End is now, there had been a large barn-yard. Once this was cleared in the 1760s, and before Trinity Road was laid out, uninterrupted parkland sloped gently down from Aston Hall to Dovehouse Pool. Witton Lane, a much older thoroughfare – it is clearly shown on a map of 1758 – ran along the eastern edge of the pool.

The second main feature of the Lower Grounds lay to the immediate north of Dovehouse Pool, on land now straddled by the North Stand, car park and Stumps (Villa's cricket school). This was an extensive, walled kitchen garden which dated from

❖ As shown on page 27, Victorian-style virtual reality at the Lower Grounds thrilled the crowds using a combination of scenery, live figures, fireworks and moving props. This sketch from the BIRMINGHAM GRAPHIC in 1883 shows Iroquois Indians taking on the locals in a display of lacrosse, somewhat incongruously against the backdrop of a tableau depicting what appears to be the Bombardment of Dover, or was it Alexandria? Other tableaus featured The Last days of Pompeii, complete with erupting volcano, and the opening of the Forth Bridge, which featured a moving train. Model ships on the ornamental lake added to the illusion.

the 1760s and provided an abundance of fruits, vegetables and herbs for the inhabitants of the hall. Again, this part of the grounds was to benefit considerably from Watt's assiduous estate management and his passion for horticulture. Like the fishpond it, too, became wild and overgrown after his death in 1848.

Finally, walking north from the kitchen garden there were limes, exotic trees and shrubs leading to a fishing lodge and a large expanse of water known as the Staffordshire Pool (where Emscote Road is now, north of Witton Road).

Amid the tarmac, traffic and hard edges of the urban landscape today, it is difficult for us to imagine the carefully nurtured beauty and verdure of this private haven. Although the estate was far from the rolling splendour of a Chatsworth or a Blenheim, and like all great estates derived its lushness from the toil of many and the wealth of few, its almost complete obliteration within the course of half a century must nevertheless have been a painful transformation for Astonians to witness.

On the other hand, if any man was likely to appreciate its finer points, that man was Henry Quilter.

So impressed were the Warwick bankers with Quilter's stewardship of the hall and park that he was offered a trial tenancy of the entire Lower Grounds site, with virtual *carte blanche* to turn the area into whatever sort of public attraction he deemed appropriate.

Not only did this demonstrate an extraordinary faith in his abilities, but it also prevented the Lower Grounds from being submerged by yet more speculative housing development. Those who love Villa Park today thus owe Quilter an indirect but, nevertheless, considerable vote of thanks.

Quilter started work in 1864, and by 1868 had done enough to persuade the owners to grant him a proper lease. As a local journal, THE DART, recalled, 'Those who remember the wild, rugged, overgrown, neglected condition of the grounds when (Quilter) took possession, may well wonder at the magic transformation he has effected. Bit by bit, and acre by acre, the wilderness has been reclaimed.'

Records are sketchy as to whether the Lower Grounds were entirely accessible to the public during the 1860s and, if so, how developed they were. Several sources suggest that the grounds were not formally opened until 1872.

We do know, however, that a cricket pitch – the Meadow – was one of the first areas to be laid out, in the western corner of the site, bound by Trinity Road and Bevington Road.

The first recorded event there was a three-day game in July and August 1865, between a United All England XI and a team from Aston comprising 22 players. This form of invitation match was common at the time, and was supposed to give local players a chance against their more talented opponents. Results suggest that the contrivance seldom succeeded.

But Quilter's real passion was horticulture rather than sport, hence one of the first major events at the Lower Grounds being the Royal Horticultural Show, opened in June 1872 by Prince Arthur, the 22-year-old son of Queen Victoria. An early chronicler of Aston, H. A. Botwood, noted dolefully that the party of local gentlemen which bowed and scraped before the royal personage – including Quilter, William Bloore (the Lower Grounds builder) and Joseph Ansell (a prominent solicitor, member of the brewing family and later president of the Villa) – were dressed, head to foot, in black and looked more like mourners at a funeral.

Yet the Aston Lower Grounds, as they were now officially titled, were far from sombre.

Rather, they were an artfully designed series of formal gardens, centred around the Dovehouse Pool and the walled kitchen gardens where, every year, according to the ASTON CHRONICLE, Quilter – the grocer turned master gardener – would exhibit 'his celebrated Spring and Summer floral displays.'

These displays, it was reported with pride, 'combined with the ivy festooned walls, the ornamental wirework, covered with choice creeping plants, and the lawns planted with costly specimen shrubs, have been pronounced by competent judges, and are acknowledged on all hands, to be the grandest exhibition of ornamental gardening to be found in the kingdom.'

To the original walled garden had been added a large conservatory, filled to the brim with luxurious ferns, rare foliage and fountains.

The main entrance to the Aston Lower Grounds was located at the Aston Village end of the site, behind the newly built Holte Hotel, which became the Lower Grounds' business headquarters and social centre. Clubs using the Meadow would regularly hold their post-match gatherings there. Visiting teams and sportsmen would often stay in it, and for many years the hotel was the base for a bowls club and a Masonic lodge (Quilter being an active Freemason). In effect, the Holte formed the gateway to the Lower Grounds.

From the rear of the building an entrance path into the Lower Grounds skirted a bowling green on the Witton Lane side and led to the so-called 'Main Walk.' This ran within a few yards of, and parallel to, Trinity Road. The boundary fence along Trinity Road was fronted by 'a magnificent belt of rhododendrons of a most choice nature.' On the other side of the Main Walk was a 'neatly trimmed lawn, handsomely interspersed with numerous beds of flowers,' with the Dovehouse Pool occupying the remaining area up to Witton Lane.

Dovehouse Pool had been given the full Quilter treatment. No longer an irregular, slightly unkempt pond, it was now a neatly landscaped 'ornamental lake' with its own rustic bridge and a small man-made island on which were placed nesting boxes for a variety of swans, Canadian geese, and Muscovy, American, mandarin and whistling ducks. Alongside the lake, backing onto Witton Lane, was a 'profusely-planted sub-tropical garden admirably laid out as a cool promenade for the summer.' (That same area is now covered by the Doug Ellis Stand.)

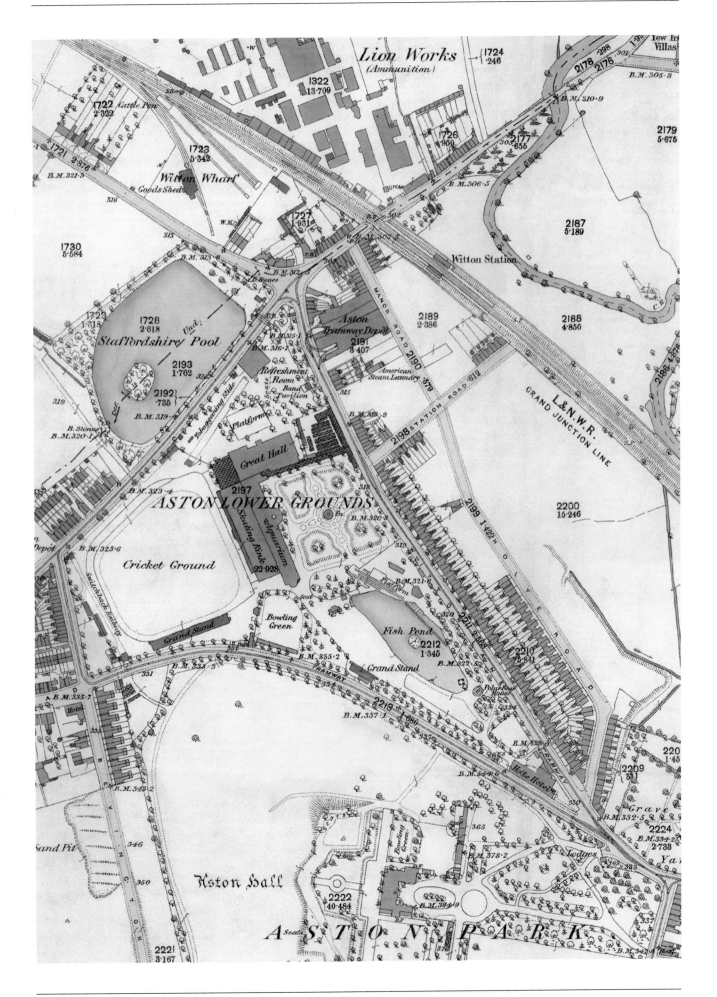

❖ *This view, also from the 1880s, was taken from the balcony of the dining rooms, and overlooks the area which had once formed the Holte's kitchen garden. The fountain on the right is clearly marked on the map on page 31. To the left is the Great Hall, with Henry Quilter's beloved conservatories lining the far side of the gardens. Beyond these, on the right, can be seen a row of houses, on the corner of Witton Lane and Station Road (where there is now a coach park for visiting supporters). The lawns in the lower right foreground correspond almost exactly with the eventual site of the Witton End banking (now the North Stand).*

But then the entire Lower Grounds seem to have been designed with a studiously romantic air. Visitors were never far from a shaded bench or, as the guidebook put it, a 'retired nook'. Another favourite rendezvous was 'a noble old oak, a monarch of the forest, a relic of the Warwickshire Ardennes.' This was decorously smothered in clinging ivy and abounded 'in numerous holes and fissures' which afforded 'pleasurable abodes for many feathered songsters.' No doubt these warblers witnessed many Brummagem lovebirds exchange stolen kisses on a moonlit evening.

Still in the bucolic vein – and perhaps even in a conscious attempt to remind the industrial labourers of their recently relinquished rural roots – a 'Rustic Cottage' was built on Witton Road, complete with first and second class refreshment rooms. This was on the site of where a billiard hall would later be erected, next to the Aston Hotel pub. The pub itself was built (in 1910) on the site of the Lower Grounds' northern entrance, which faced Witton Circle and thus formed the most convenient entry point for excursionists arriving at Witton Station.

Between this entrance and the Rustic Cottage, a wooden footbridge spanned Witton Road and led to the Staffordshire Pool, now redeveloped as a boating lake, with its own island resplendent with rhododendrons. The lake, it was emphasised, was perfectly safe for both boating, and in winter for skating, being a uniform four feet deep across its

seven acre expanse. Circling the lake was another sheltered promenade which the proprietors were only too happy to call 'The Lovers' Walk'.

For the Lower Grounds' more sporting patrons, apart from a skating rink, there were also two bowling greens. One, as mentioned earlier, was behind the Holte Hotel. The other backed onto Trinity Road, between the Main Walk and the cricket ground (and would survive long after Aston Villa's arrival, until finally covered by the Lion's Club in 1966). Both greens were also later used for lawn tennis when that game started to become fashionable in the 1880s.

But by far the most important focus of sporting activity at the Lower Grounds was the Meadow.

We have already noted that cricket had been played on this ground from at least 1865. To increase its usage for athletics (and cycling after 1879), during the 1870s a distinctive red-ash running track was laid, measuring 501 yards and one foot in length. Presumably this awkward distance only came about because Quilter was anxious to retain a reasonably sized cricket pitch, which would have been impossible with a standard quarter-mile track. Certainly, the distance caused no end of problems for the organisers of athletics meetings. Both pitch and track were also on a slight gradient, which hardly helped its reputation, either.

Nor did the quality of the actual cricket pitch. While Quilter quaintly called his ground the

Meadow, others called it 'execrable' or 'simply disgraceful'. After a Staffordshire v Warks & Worcestershire cricket match in May 1881, the sporting weekly, MIDLAND ATHLETE, fulminated that there were enough holes 'to justify one in mistaking the pitch for a bagatelle board.' Nor was there a pavilion, as such, so the players and athletes had to change in tents.

For all its faults, however, for 20 years the Meadow was still the only cricket ground in Birmingham capable of accommodating reasonable crowds. And it was by far the best track, too, its only rivals being a private ground belonging to King Edward's Grammar School on Portland Road, and the Bournbrook Grounds on Bristol Road.

A number of cricket teams used the Meadow on a regular basis during the 1870s, including Aston Unity, before they established their own ground further up Trinity Road, and the Lower Grounds' resident club, the Birmingham Cricket and Football Club (of which more later).

There were also some illustrious visitors. The famed Gloucestershire and England all-rounder, W. G. Grace, appeared at the Meadow on several occasions, the most notable being in July 1878, when he led his touring team, the United South of England XI against a local team of 22 players. All but one of them lost their wickets to Grace's expert bowling.

But what of football?

When the Meadow was first laid out it is true to say that cricket and athletics still formed the staple diet of local sport. Although the first English Cup Final was contested at the Oval in 1872, the first record of football being played anywhere in Birmingham was not until 1873. Thereafter, however, the game became a major attraction at the Lower Grounds.

Villa, as already noted, formed in 1874, and played occasional games at the Meadow in season 1875-76. But the ground's resident club, and perhaps the leading local club of the period, was the aforementioned Birmingham Cricket and Football Club. They were nicknamed 'The Quilters', not only because they played regularly at the Lower Grounds, but because Henry's two sons, Charles and George, were in the team.

The former, known as 'Kid', was over six feet tall and was quite an all-rounder. Apart from playing in goal for the Birmingham club, he was a reasonable cricketer – appearing, for example, in a Birmingham XI which played at Lord's in 1875 – and also performing the odd stint as a referee, once at a Villa v Blackburn game at Perry Barr in 1881. In March of that year he also guested for an Aston Villa reserve team in a friendly against Nottingham Wanderers at Trent Bridge.

Albeit indirectly, Villa owe the Quilters a much greater debt, however. When William McGregor started watching football in Birmingham, a few years after his arrival in the city, it was the Quilters who

first won his attention. The only problem was that they kicked-off too late for him to see the whole game and get back to his shop in Summer Lane, in time for Saturday evening opening. According to his own memoirs, he therefore wrote to a local newspaper to urge earlier kick-offs – a letter which he reckoned might well have been the first published complaint against a football club. McGregor then began watching Calthorpe, who played on Bristol Road, before news of Villa's Scottish connections finally, and happily, took him to Perry Barr.

Apart from the Quilters, with a range of other football, cricket and athletics events being staged on a regular basis throughout the 1870s, it is no exaggeration to state that the Meadow was as well-used as any leading sports ground in the country.

George Kynoch – the Scottish ammunition manufacturer whose huge Lion Works lay north of Witton Road (now forming part of IMI) – called it 'the Magnificent Meadow', and with good cause. Businessmen like Kynoch (and the Cadburys at Bournville, and numerous others) recognised only too well that the swelling mass of workers pouring into Birmingham sorely needed an outlet on their precious days off. The Lower Grounds not only provided such diversion, away from 'the demon drink,' but by promoting sport and outdoor pursuits they also encouraged the workers to maintain a healthy body as well as a healthy mind. This was no small matter. In 1871 the Aston area had been devastated by a smallpox epidemic.

As we shall soon learn, the Magnificent Meadow's hey-day was to follow during the 1880s. But, before then, significant developments at the Lower Grounds were to have crucial consequences.

From 1864 until 1878 it is probably fair to conclude that the Lower Grounds offered a comparatively unsophisticated fare, depending to a large extent upon the success of the Meadow, the novelty value of the boating lake, and the horticultural splendours of Quilter's gardens and greenhouses.

But, despite its continuing popularity, Quilter could not afford to be complacent. Even in Victorian England tastes and fashions changed rapidly. At sometime during the mid-1870s, therefore, he decided (or at least was persuaded) to acquire the freehold of the site with a view to enhancing its facilities and thus keep abreast of the times.

In order to achieve this, however, he desperately needed additional investment.

For this reason, in 1877 Quilter agreed to turn over the whole enterprise – valued at the time at £93,700 – to a specially-formed ASTON LOWER GROUNDS COMPANY LIMITED. This was set up with a capital of £100,000 in January 1878, with five directors. In addition to Quilter, who now became Managing Director, there was Mr T. Bragg, a local jeweller; Mr C. T. Brook from south London, who was a pyrotechnist – that is, a specialist in firework displays – then working for the Crystal Palace complex in Sydenham; Mr J. Neale, a Birmingham lamp manufacturer; and Thomas Vaughton, the father of Howard and well-known local manufacturer of medals, badges, cups and shields.

In return for selling the Lower Grounds Quilter was to receive a 50 per cent share in the new company, plus £20,000 in cash, to be paid in instalments, but without interest. At the same time, the company took out a mortgage of £35,000 on the site and planned a further £25,000 worth of improvements.

The aim of these improvements was to lend the Lower Grounds a more populist appeal, particularly by providing a range of modern, indoor facilities which might attract extra custom throughout the year, come rain or shine, day or night.

Just as nowadays, any self-respecting, state-of-the-art leisure complex would automatically include a multiplex cinema, ten-pin bowling alley, fast-food restaurants, theme pubs and hi-tech arcades (virtual reality, laser games and so on), so in the late 1870s there seems to have been a shopping list of *de rigueur* attractions. In this respect, the involvement of Mr Brook was, no doubt, crucial, as was the advice the Lower Grounds' directors sought from William Alford Lloyd, a naturalist who had worked in both Paris and Hamburg, and was currently managing the Crystal Palace Aquarium. (Crystal Palace was then the country's leading leisure development, having been moved from its original site in Hyde Park to Sydenham in 1854. Another model to follow was that of Alexandra Palace, which had been developed in north London between 1873-75.)

Construction of the new facilities began in early 1878, and within a year they had transformed the Lower Grounds into the single greatest attraction in the Midlands.

Essentially, there were three main elements – a skating rink, the Aquarium and the Great Hall – forming an L-shaped central block between the Meadow and the formal gardens.

Designed by Birmingham architect, Thomas Naden, outwardly the new buildings bore the scale and proportions of an Oxford College, but with a rich array of more playful details, such as Flemish-style, stepped brickwork on the numerous gables, Byzantine-style lustred tiling, tinted glazing, and a procession of self-important, neo-classical arched and circular windows (such as were to be found in public buildings all over Victorian Birmingham).

The new building's central focus was a tower,

ASTON PARK.
Lower Grounds Ticket,
FOR SUNDAYS ONLY.
2d.
Admit One          2412

❖ *An etching from the Lower Ground's guidebook of the 1880s shows that, in the days before aerial photography, the artist had no choice but to use his imagination in order to provide a 'bird's-eye' perspective. The Meadow (left), for example, was more square than oval-shaped. Notice the train in the top corner. Henry Quilter and the railway companies combined to offer cheap excursion tickets from all points around the Black Country, including admission to the Lower Grounds.*

topped by a French-influenced tapered roof and wrought-iron embellishments, inside of which, incongruously, was located an ultra-modern Engine Room and Electrical Room. The former contained an engine supplied by the ATLAS COMPANY of Birmingham, capable of generating 20 horse power. The latter housed two pairs of alternating current dynamos, each pair of which could power 20 Jablochkoff arc lights, mainly for use in the Great Hall. (This particular brand of electric light was absolutely state-of-the-art, having been invented only two years earlier in Russia.)

These advanced systems, alone, cost £5,000 and because anything electrical was then deemed to be a major attraction – gas lighting still being the norm – the equipment was proudly displayed for all to witness in operation.

The Great Hall opened in 1879 and was claimed to have a greater capacity than the Birmingham Town Hall. It was, furthermore, a wonderful example of how Victorian engineers – already practised in the art of designing churches and railways stations – borrowed freely from Classical and Gothic forms to create genuinely elegant and spacious public assembly rooms. Bathed in natural light, and with raised galleries along each side, the hall would host a wide variety of events. Regular programmes were provided by the newly formed HOLTE THEATRE COMPANY and HOLTE CHORAL SOCIETY, but there were also visiting opera companies, orchestral concerts, tea-dances, music hall-style entertainments, and even Punch and Judy Shows during the day.

When the stage was not in use the floor was cleared and soirées held – card tables and all – as if in a conscious effort to make the inhabitants of this corner of Birmingham and Staffordshire feel quite as sophisticated as any of the gentlemen or ladies of Edgbaston or Leamington.

But even the most fashionable denizens of the Midlands could not help but be captivated by the aquarium. This occupied the west flank of the new building, between the formal gardens and the skating rink, and was the first of its kind in the area. Inside its richly tiled interior, huge glass tanks were recessed between yet more Byzantine-style arches. The Lower Grounds management were particularly proud of the fact that, rather than transport gallons of sea-water to Birmingham, a team of chemists had successfully treated ordinary water in such a way that 'no marine animal, and no chemist' could possibly tell the difference. Not only did this save the company £1,200 on 300,000 gallons, but the water was said never to need replacing.

Within the same building were dining rooms, from where a balcony provided an overview of the gardens. (When Aston Villa took over the site in 1897, the dining rooms were converted into offices and eventually the aquarium into a gymnasium. Indeed, for many years thereafter, fans standing at the Witton End could still see the fading word 'Aquarium' on the side of the building.)

One of the most popular parts of the new Lower Grounds complex proved to be the covered, gas-lit roller skating rink, sandwiched between the cricket ground and the Aquarium. Opened in 1878, this measured 300 x 80 feet and was modelled on rinks already popular in Brighton and at the Prince's Grounds, Knightsbridge. One of the reasons for their appeal was that they provided a safer form of skating than on ice. But they also offered a rare opportunity for young men and women to mix freely and without inhibition – a notion which the Lower Grounds management were happy to encourage in their publicity material (even though the rules of the rink urged 'gentlemen without ladies' not to 'trespass upon the time or space' set apart for unattached women, or couples.)

While the skating rink, Great Hall and Aquarium were built, the new company was careful to make improvements to the Meadow also.

On the stating rink side was added a low, narrow covered walkway, which was later converted into a reserved seating area. Opposite this was built a wooden grandstand holding 1,500 spectators, backing onto Trinity Road. No raised banking was ever built, but on the other sides there was plenty of room for hired stands and vehicles, thus creating a capacity of approximately 15,000.

Elsewhere in the Lower Grounds a number of other new attractions were laid on.

One innovation was a mineral water manufactory, where visitors could see aerated water and ginger beer being produced. 'The water used,' spouted the guidebook, 'is obtained from an artesian well of great depth, and is of absolute purity.'

❖ *Until Thomas Naden's 1878 building was demolished in 1981, bemused Villa fans on the Witton End could still make out the word AQUARIUM on the side of the old offices.*

In time there would be a polar bear house at the southern end of the lake and, elsewhere in the grounds, a monkey house, where mandrills and macaques cavorted in front of wide-eyed excursionists from all over Birmingham and the Black Country. Over at the aviary, macaws, parakeets and slender-bill cockatoos – one of them, apparently, an accomplished talker – no doubt added their voice to the general hubbub and, in the case of the East Indian Mino birds, maybe threw back the odd nasal expletive, to the delight and astonishment of all. Sharing the aviary were two opossums. (Appropriately enough, some might say, the aviary stood roughly where the managers' dug-outs are now situated!)

As would be expected, the new-improved Lower Grounds won lavish praise from all quarters. THE DART commented effusively in February 1880:

'Little by little, but always growing in beauty, the desert has blossomed into grounds only surpassed by those two "palaces for the people" in London. The taste for the beautiful and the orderly, which seems inherent in Mr Quilter, has prevented him, in the management of these grounds, from pandering to vulgar tastes, and has enabled him to present to his visitors such rare combinations of floriculture, landscape-gardening, good music and general amusements, as have not only gratified their appetite for pleasure, but have elevated their tastes. (Quilter) often says that no one is more astonished than himself at the marvellous development of the place.'

Another local report described the newly completed complex as 'the largest and most elegantly-fitted block of buildings, dedicated to public amusement' and 'the most *recherché* place of resort in England today.'

And for the first two years of the new facilities' operation the public turned up in their thousands, particularly during the Easter holidays and summer months. Excursion trains from all over the Midlands delivered thousands of day-trippers to Witton and Aston stations. Tramway companies thrived. The Aston Tavern was rebuilt to cope with the influx. In 1879 and 1880 attendances totalled nearly 900,000.

But for all the novelty of the Great Hall, Aquarium and skating rink, some of the most popular attractions continued to be those of a sporting nature.

Moreover, one of the first of these to be arranged by the new company, on October 28, 1878, was a truly historic event – the first ever football match played in Birmingham under electric light.

Electric light! The words alone seemed to bear a magical glow of their own. But football under electric light? This was an entirely new prospect, so new, in fact, that the match at the Meadow was to take place only two weeks after the world's first such experiment, conducted at Bramall Lane, Sheffield. (Highly successful it had been, too, attracting over 20,000 spectators; the first gate of over 10,000 recorded for any football match outside Glasgow.)

Of course, the proposed match also provided the LOWER GROUNDS COMPANY with the perfect

opportunity to show off its expensive new generators and Jablochkoff arc lights.

As the reports on page 41 indicate, on the night the technology worked perfectly well. Cruelly, however, the whole event was completely ruined by hurricane force gales – ill winds indeed – and 'a pitiless and an uncompromising downpour.' But the experiment was an intriguing development, nevertheless, and was followed two days later by an evening of gaiety and music in the Lower Grounds skating rink, again 'Illuminated By The Electric Light!' (as the adverts never failed to emphasise). From then on, hardly a major event at the Lower Grounds, whether in the gardens or the Great Hall, would be complete without electricity.

But to return to the Meadow. As can be seen, the floodlit game had taken place between the Birmingham club – the Quilters – and Nottingham Forest, one of the leading outfits of the period. At that time Aston Villa were still relatively junior, and would not enter the FA Cup until the year after, in 1879. But as the Birmingham club started to fade from the scene Aston Villa's star was most definitely on the rise. Not only that but, as noted earlier, the Aston Lower Grounds were the venue for Villa's first ever trophy win, the Birmingham Senior Cup in 1880.

The background to this apparently modest, but still significant triumph, reveals a great deal about the changing ethos of the Lower Grounds management, once the new company took over in 1878.

In the days before the FOOTBALL LEAGUE, regional competitions such as the Birmingham Senior Cup – and those staged also in Lancashire and London – were second only in importance to the FA Cup. Because of this, the BIRMINGHAM AND DISTRICT FA decided that after the first round, all Birmingham Cup ties should be staged at the Meadow, which was still by far the finest neutral venue in the city.

To begin with, the chances of this coming about were not encouraging. For example, when the local FA approached the new company in January 1878, in the hope of staging a representative game at the Meadow against a London XI, they proved unable to negotiate favourable terms. Instead, the game went to Aston Unity's ground on the other side of Witton Lane (long since built over).

During the ensuing months the new company proved equally obstructive over the issue of the Birmingham Senior Cup games. Apart from arguing over the rental, the company was concerned that existing season-ticket holders, who were supposed to enjoy access to all events at the Lower Grounds, should not be displaced by incoming supporters.

❖ *The Great Hall, like an iron and glass church, flooded by light through the east window and clerestory windows. In November 1887 Buffalo Bill's native Indians set up a mock encampment here. Concerts and recitals continued to be staged in the hall until several years after Villa took over the site in 1897. The building was eventually demolished shortly before the First World War.*

The football authorities were not alone in meeting such obstacles. As the MIDLAND ATHLETE warned in January 1881, 'better terms will have to be made with the ASTON LOWER GROUNDS COMPANY if they wish our local (athletic) clubs to patronise their grounds.'

Given the enormous costs incurred in developing the site in 1878 it was understandable that the company should wish to maximise their income. But in trying to drive too hard a bargain they were in danger of alienating the entire sporting fraternity.

As the negotiations continued during 1879 Villa offered the BIRMINGHAM FA the use of Perry Barr instead. However, a deal was eventually struck and so began a regular schedule of local cup ties at the Meadow. This culminated at the end of the first season with Villa winning the Birmingham Senior Cup on April 3, 1880, courtesy of a 3-1 win over Saltley College, watched by around 5,000 spectators.

Thus, Villa secured their first trophy, little knowing that 17 years later the ornamental gardens which lay next to the Meadow would one day be transformed into a stadium fit for the winners of both the FA Cup and the League. The 1880 Birmingham Cup Final would also represent a watershed in the career of captain George Ramsay, for it was both the last time he scored and the last time he played in a competitive game.

Over the next few seasons Villa played many a Birmingham Cup game and friendly at the Meadow. In March 1881, for example, their fourth round tie against Wednesbury Old Athletic attracted a bumper crowd of 12,226 paying spectators, plus hundreds more perched on every available wall, roof-top and tree, and no fewer than 157 carriages parked around the touchlines. That match alone raised nearly £100 for local charities, from total receipts of £360.

Villa would return a few weeks later for their semi-final against West Bromwich Albion while, during the interim, Small Heath Alliance faced Aston Unity in a friendly. Also in March 1881, the FOOTBALL ASSOCIATION chose the Lower Grounds for an international trial match. In short, the Meadow was now the undisputed sporting mecca of the Midlands, and would remain so for a least the next five years.

Yet, no sooner had it achieved this enviable status, than the splendid edifice of the Lower Grounds started to show serious signs of cracking. Despite a packed schedule of events, the extravagant sums expended on the Great Hall, Aquarium and skating rink forced the LOWER GROUNDS COMPANY into liquidation in April 1881, after a mere three years and four months in business.

The reasons were simple enough. Instead of spending £25,000 on building projects, as predicted in 1878, the company had shelled out nearly £68,000. In addition, the cost of maintaining all the lavish new buildings and equipment, not to mention the burden of feeding and caring for all the various birds, animals and exotic marine creatures, meant that the deficit could never be bridged. It was also suggested that a particularly elaborate staging of the pantomime *Sleeping Beauty*, in the Great Hall, had resulted in losses of £2,000.

For Henry Quilter the liquidation was a personal disaster. He lost his home in the Holte Hotel, his work and, most painful of all, one suspects, his beloved gardens. He would also lose all the money owing to him from the sale of the site in 1878, while the value of his shareholding was now worthless.

All that effort, all those dreams... maybe his own *naiveté* and romantic idealism had been partly to blame; maybe he had been too easily seduced by smooth-talking developers; or maybe he was just allowed too much power when he should have remained as a landscape gardener.

Whatever, Quilter could clearly not bear to hang around to see the consequences of the collapse. His romantic haven now branded as a commercial folly, he quit the Lower Grounds and Birmingham, so strapped for cash, it was later reported, that he even had to mortgage his family vault in Aston churchyard for £25. With him departed his two sons, George and Charles. (The latter had only just taken on Henry's role as managing director of the Lower Grounds and must have been doubly devastated by the company's failure.) It was a reversal of fortunes worthy of a Thomas Hardy epic.

Yet, as befitted this extraordinary individual, this self-made entrepreneur and aesthete, Henry Quilter was soon back in business. He took his family to Felixstowe where the management of the Bath Hotel would allow him and his sons to restore the Quilters' fortune, if not their fame. He died there 13 years later, at the age of 69, and never lived to see the last of his gardens submerged under the terraces of a football stadium.

He was fondly remembered, too. In fact, it was repeatedly stated in valedictory articles that had the company not undertaken the construction of the Great Hall and Aquarium, the Lower Grounds would have continued to thrive. On the other hand, such was (and is) the nature of the leisure industry that success has always hinged upon the relentless pursuit of new and ever more sophisticated attractions.

For a few months in the spring of 1881 the Lower Grounds entered a state of limbo; too popular with the public to be written off completely, yet not profitable enough to pay its debts. Not unlike the majority of football clubs, in fact.

As far as the public was concerned, however, apart from occasional reports in the local newspapers, the Lower Grounds show went on, courtesy of the creditors and another group of investors who hoped that a new management team with ever brighter ideas might yet make a commercial success of the new facilities. At the same time, after the bad blood of the late 1870s, the new proprietors clearly needed all the help and support they could glean from local sporting interests.

The summer of 1881 provided exactly that opportunity – and what an opportunity it was too!

We all know about the 1966 World Cup and the 1996 European Championships at Villa Park. But as reported more fully on page 42, for a few heady days in July 1881, the Aston Lower Grounds were at the very epicentre of world athletics, as the venue for the AMATEUR ATHLETICS ASSOCIATION's second annual Championships.

Nowadays the appearance of American athletes in Birmingham would hardly raise an eyebrow outside the sporting world. But in 1881 the participation of two world famous Yankee runners – Lawrence Myers and E. E. Merrill – was sufficient to move some local scribes to bill the AAA Championships as the *Olympian Games*. (Remember, the first true modern Olympics did not take place until 1896.) Nor did it escape their attention that when the inaugural Championships had been held the previous year at Lillie Bridge in London, only British athletes had entered, and there had been a paltry attendance.

So it was, during that balmy summer of 1881, that Birmingham became temporarily obsessed with the visiting Yankee runners; their prowess, their habits, their travel plans and, most of all, how they would acquit themselves against the two great English runners of the age, Walter George and William Snook, both of whom, coincidentally, were members of the local Moseley Harriers.

Meanwhile, those among the inner-circle of Birmingham athletics started to question whether, in

the midst of the liquidation crisis, the Lower Grounds management would be up to the task of hosting such a prestige event. To mess up this one great opportunity – the first Championships outside of London – would cast a terrible blight upon the city, especially as the provincial associations had insisted a year before that the Championships should be strictly rotated between the South, the Midlands and the North.

A further worry was that the Meadow had an unsavoury reputation for attracting unruly betting rings, which were then the curse of many an athletics meeting. For this reason, in March 1881 a faction campaigned for the AAA Championships to be held at the more respectable headquarters of the Birmingham Athletic Club in Portland Road. Even though the Meadow had the superior track and was being offered at a lower rent, the pro-Edgbaston lobby insisted haughtily that the Lower Grounds were nothing more than 'a sort of tea-garden business' and a speculation which had 'proved an ignominious failure.' Gangs of low-life riff-raff had caused such disgraceful scenes, it was claimed, that some competitors feared for their lives if they upset the predictions of the bookmakers.

In the end, the trustees of the Portland Road

ground refused permission for the Championships to be staged there, so the Lower Grounds won by default.

But the superior gentlemen of Edgbaston had a point. Only a week before the AAA Championships, Moseley Harriers staged their annual meeting at the Lower Grounds and were delighted when both Myers and Merrill agreed to travel up from London and make the occasion their first ever appearance on English soil. No doubt the new management at the Lower Grounds was excited, too. A double dose of Yankee fever was bound to yield a midsummer bonanza at the turnstiles, not to mention in sales of iced mineral water.

Sure enough, an excitable crowd of 12,000 packed the Meadow for the Moseley meeting, anxious to see what all the fuss was about. (This compared with only 3,000 for Birchfield Harriers' equivalent meeting, also at the Lower Grounds.)

But just as the Edgbaston men had warned, Aston proved to be no place for the faint-hearted. Halfway through the afternoon the judges controversially disqualified a Midlands' favourite, H. Whyatt of Nottingham, during the course of the one-mile walking event. This should have left the field clear for Merrill to win comfortably, except that the incensed crowd – many of whom no doubt stood to lose bets on the outcome – blocked the track and forced the poor American to rush for cover in the dressing tent. There he joined his trembling compatriot, Myers, while outside, according to one report, baying youths disdainfully invited the pair to come out fighting with their Bowie knives and pistols.

Of course, they did no such thing. As the MIDLAND ATHLETE reported, 'they beat a hasty retreat from the scene and repaired to London by the next train, utterly amazed and bewildered to understand why the "Brums" had so disgraced themselves.' Myers said later that he had never encountered a more frightening mob, while Merrill was all for heading back to America on the next steam packet.

But a week later both were back in Birmingham for the main event and, as reported on page 42, the Championships were held without a hint of crowd trouble. Furthermore, the Lower Grounds impressed all those who visited from around the country, drawing many compliments about the gardens, the lakes and even the monkeys on view.

So was this the beginning of a brave new era for the Lower Grounds?

At first the signs seemed favourable, especially when the newly appointed secretary of the Lower Grounds, Mr Smedley, promised all local clubs 'fair and reasonable terms' to use the Meadow.

One club which took the bait was Moseley FC, the rugby union club based at the Reddings. Like most clubs, including Villa, in order to raise funds and provide an enjoyable day out, Moseley held invitation sports meetings every summer. Between novelty races and events featuring their own players, serious competitions would be staged, usually with invited professionals to boost the gate.

*continued on page 43*

# Football by the Electric Light

❖ On October 14 1878, at Bramall Lane, Sheffield, a local pioneer of electric light called John Tasker staged the world's first ever floodlit sporting event, a football match between two representative teams. So successful was this, both in terms of the technology and the gate (officially 14,000, unofficially over 20,000), that rival electrical companies around the country immediately started planning their own night-time spectaculars. Over the ensuing eleven days two further games were staged; a rugby match at Salford and a football match at Cathkin Park, Glasgow. (A third attempt at Chorley failed when the lights refused to function in the rain.) Having only just installed its own expensive electricity generators, the Aston Lower Grounds Company wasted no time in organising a floodlit experiment for Monday, October 28 - only the fourth match by electric light in the world.

ELECTRIC LIGHT.   ELECTRIC LIGHT.
—
Aston Lower Grounds,
MONDAY NEXT, OCTOBER 28,
Grand Football Match
BY
Electric Light!
BIRMINGHAM V. NOTTINGHAM FOREST.

The following are the Teams :–

BIRMINGHAM
C. H. Quilter (Captain)
T. Bryan
F. Bill
G. B. Ramsay
C. Durban
R. C. Knowles
J. R. Riddell
C. Allen
R. Evans
B. W. Stevens
T. Butler

NOTTINGHAM
S. W. Widdowson (Captain)
A. H. Smith
W. Luntley
E. Luntley
C. Caborn
J. P. Turner
M. Holroyd
A. C. Goodyer
A. J. Bates
E. Earp
J. Sands (Goal)

The Company have made arrangements with Mr Maccabe to LIGHT UP THE GROUNDS with Jablochkoff's Patent Electric Light.

KICK-OFF AT 7 PM

Admission, 6d each; Reserved Seats 1s
Further particulars in bills and future advertisements.

9922

❖ *Despite the billing, Charles Quilter did not play for Birmingham on the night. But Villa's George Ramsay did, and may well have regretted the fact. A later profile of Ramsay in the* VILLA NEWS AND RECORD *claimed that the Villa captain sustained a severe injury that night, as a result of which he rarely played for the first team between then and his retirement in April 1880. Another of the Birmingham line-up that night, T. Bryan, may have been the Thomas Bryan who later played for Villa in 1882. For the record, Birmingham won 2-1, before stormy weather stopped play during the second half.*

❖ An exhibition of the electric light, by the agency of Jablochkoff's now celebrated candle, could not have taken place under more adverse circumstances than it did last evening at the Aston Lower Grounds. The complicated contrivances which are required in exhibiting the new light had been carefully arranged and placed in position yesterday afternoon, when a storm assuming the proportions of a hurricane, and accompanied by a pitiless and an uncompromising downpour, completely nullified every preparation by shattering most of the globes which enclosed the lights, and upon which so much depends for the radiating power of the invention. To remedy the effects of the disaster was a work of no small magnitude, and the various glass establishments of the town were applied to with a view of supplying the deficiency so inopportunely created. With such a sensitive light the ordinary glass globe necessarily produces a dimness which must ensure the failure of the exhibition, and when it is considered that the familiar street lamp was resorted to in respect of two or three of the lights, the unfortunate position of Messrs. Maccabe and Sutton, who have brought this power-

ful illuminating medium into our midst, will be readily sympathised with.

Twelve lamps were employed to supply the light requisite for the occasion. Each light represented the power of 1,200 candles, and the electricity was supplied by two engines of six-horse power, stationed some 250 yards apart. The line of play was brilliantly indicated by the lamps, which, despite the heavy rain, cast a clear and mellow light across the field, the only dark spot being a narrow mirage in the centre. Shortly after eight o'clock the dozen lights were in full glare, and the spectators, limited in number by the exigencies of the weather, had a splendid view of the field. It was a wretched night for football, cold and damp, and with a keen biting wind blowing across the ground... but the novelty of the situation, and the strong test which the light was undergoing, induced the spectators to remain until a heavy storm which came on a few minutes after the last goal (forced) both players and spectators (to make) a speedy retreat.

It is to a certain extent unfair to judge of the power of Jablochkoff's patent by last night's experiment; but the severe ordeal which it so satisfactorily underwent must

assure the public that it is capable of greater achievements in the future.

BIRMINGHAM DAILY GAZETTE, OCTOBER 29, 1878

❖ A novelty is generally more pleasurable by anticipation than in actual reality. On a calm night thousands of spectators may derive a peculiar pleasure from the sight of a football match played under these novel conditions, but with the temperature almost at freezing point, a strong, biting east wind beating persistently about you, the rain coming down in torrents, and the earth ankle deep in mud, the pleasure of the on-looker, unless like Mr. Dumbs, he took a sinister delight in witnessing the misery of other people, is very small indeed. There can be no doubt, however, that with favourable conditions, the spectacle of a football match played by the electric light would be very picturesque, and it is one which is almost certain to become popular.

BIRMINGHAM DAILY MAIL, OCTOBER 29, 1878

❖ *In fact the next floodlit match to take place in Aston would not be for another 80 years, when Villa Park's first floodlights were switched on in August 1958.*

# The Olympian Games come to Aston

❖ On a glorious Saturday in July 1881, the world of athletics – which then essentially encompassed Britain, Ireland, the USA and Canada – turned its attention to the Lower Grounds' Meadow, venue for the second Amateur Athletics Association Championships. After the unsavoury incidents at the Meadow the week before (see page 42) policemen lined the track, but in the event the visiting Americans, Myers and Merrill, were cheered heartily by the 10,000 crowd.

The Lower Grounds looked splendid for the occasion. The gardens had been spruced up, the lawns trimmed, and a bright scarlet awning was draped across the stand on Trinity Road.

A wonderful programme of athletics followed, with the Irish brothers, Patrick and Maurice Davin, setting records in the high jump, long jump, shot and hammer, and the enigmatic Lawrence Myers from Manhattan showing in the 440 yards why he had won virtually every race in previous championships in both the USA and Canada. The only real disappointment was the poor form of the two Brummie favourites from Moseley Harriers, Walter George

(the reigning one mile record holder) and William Snook (the two mile champion). George made up for it, however, when the AAA Championships returned to the Meadow on June 21, 1884. Although the event was generally more low key than 1881, George created a sensation by beating his arch rival Snook in the mile, in an official world record time of 4 minutes, 18.4 seconds.

Such great feats, such characters, such a pageant of sporting excellence! And yet barely five years later the Meadow was lost to the 'jerry builder' and not a single memorial was erected, nor a road named in honour either of the great athletes of the 1880s or of the Meadow's hallowed place in the history of sport.

❖ American champion, Lawrence 'Lon' Myers, strides home to win the 440 yards in front of the main stand on Trinity Road in 1881, so far ahead of the English favourite – the towering old Etonian, William Page Phillips – that before crossing the line Myers turned back and goaded his opponent into catching him up. Even then, he beat the English 440 yard record of 50.4 seconds by a full 1.8 seconds, only to be told later that his achievement would not count officially because of the slight gradient of the Aston track.

❖ A dramatic moment during the 1881 AAA Championships, as the American, E. E. Merrill, lies prostrate on the track in front of the skating rink enclosure, unable to finish the seven mile walking race. John Swein's somewhat idealised portrayal of the Lower Grounds shows the dressing tents to which Merrill and Myers had escaped only a week before, with Aston Hall in the background.

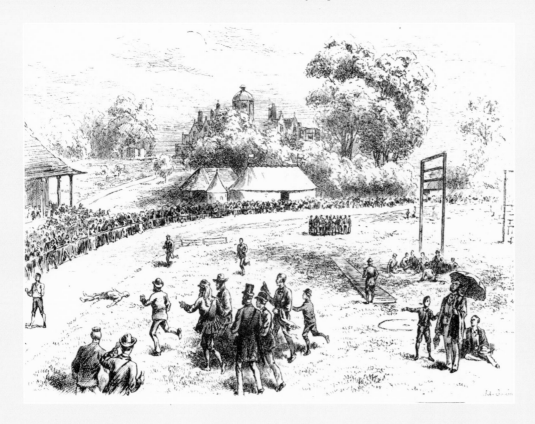

But only 4,400 attended the Moseley gathering at the Meadow, leaving them 'disgusted' with the poor return once the Lower Grounds took their cut. The Moseley officials – among them E. B. Holmes, the future architect of Villa Park – were additionally appalled at the scale of betting being carried out quietly, but still openly, at the ground, 'in spite of bills and notice boards threatening all the penalties of the law.'

Another disgruntled club was Small Heath Harriers, who complained that the Meadow's dressing tents had no flooring or benches. Instead, a few bales of mouldy straw had been scattered around the tent. In damp and confined conditions, they complained, this was likely to make athletes ill.

There were also regular gripes about the length of the track. As if measuring 501 yards and one foot was not awkward enough, the Lower Grounds management never bothered to provide permanent markers to establish correct lengths for specific races. They also left it to race organisers to hire their own surveyors to mark the distances.

Local cricketers remained equally critical. In April 1881 one of their number commented, 'I was surprised and excessively annoyed the other day, on making a visit to the cricket ground at Aston, to discover the absolutely neglected and consequently deplorable condition in which it is to be found at the commencement of a season... The new company will do well to set a ground man on without delay.'

But perhaps it was a lost cause. The Meadow staged two matches featuring the touring Australians,

in June 1880 and on May 26, 1884. On the second occasion a match against an England XI, which had been scheduled to last three days, ended ignominiously after just over four hours, courtesy of an appalling pitch and a lethal bowler, Fred 'The Demon' Spofforth. Incredibly, considering the number of established players taking part, Spofforth managed to take 14 English wickets for 37 runs. This included a devastating second innings spell of seven wickets for just three runs!

Predictably, the English came up with all kinds of excuses. The pitch, which had clearly been watered liberally the day before, was virtually bereft of grass, they complained. The constant movement of crowds in and around the surrounding Lower Grounds was also blamed as a distraction. Whether these criticisms were justified or not, the England defeat had a far more lasting consequence.

Warwickshire County Cricket Club had formed two years earlier and were apparently intent on finding a permanent home somewhere in Birmingham. The Lower Grounds management must therefore have been quite encouraged when the club chose the Meadow for their first ever trial game in 1882. Several more games followed, but the dreadful state of the wicket for that Australia game in 1884 was enough to persuade the county members that Aston was not the promised land after all, and in 1886 they opted for the more wide open spaces and refined air of Edgbaston. Another reason why the Meadow lost out, it is thought, was that the ground lay on the border with Staffordshire.

❖ This was the view from Aston Park in 1886, looking towards the houses on Witton Lane. The ornamental pool – once Dovehouse Pool, now the site of the Villa Park pitch – can be clearly seen, with scaffolding being erected on its far side as a mount for one of the Lower Ground's giant tableaus. Just visible on the far left are the branches of the 'noble oak' also pictured on page 45.

❖ *All the fun of the fair in the north-eastern corner of the Lower Grounds. This photograph was taken just inside the entrance from Witton Circle.*

Imagine for a minute, though, how different might have been the fate of the Lower Grounds – and possibly of Aston Villa – had Warwickshire opted for the Meadow instead of Edgbaston. Villa Park might never have been built, or might have even evolved like Headingley, where the rugby and cricket grounds are back-to-back.

But, alas for Aston it was not to be, and although cricket would continue to be played on the Meadow until 1888, after 1884 it was clear that its days as a first class venue were over.

Not so for athletics or cycling, however. In 1884 the AAA Championships were staged a second time – with a little less hype – and as the decade wore on the Meadow also became a regular venue for the increasingly popular sport of cycle racing. Many of these races were sponsored by a new Birmingham publication called SPORT AND PLAY which, as we shall learn, later developed a close relationship with both the Lower Grounds and Aston Villa.

As for football, the Meadow continued to stage regular games, both senior and junior. But the relationship was not always easy.

After all the arguments over terms for the Birmingham Senior Cup in 1879, further friction arose during 1881-82 when, without the BIRMINGHAM FA'S approval, the Lower Grounds' new management, rather foolishly, tried to stage a local knock-out competition, with eleven silver cups worth a total of £100 to be awarded to members of the winning team. The inference was quite plain. At a time when professionalism was still strictly taboo, here was a blatant inducement to play for profit.

The company was duly excoriated in the sporting press for this attempt to work outside the aegis of the local association. Yet the national association happily chose the Meadow in both 1884 and 1886 as the venue for FA Cup semi-finals. Here again was a considerable honour which might have led to greater things, but never did.

The first semi-final, on March 1, 1884, was an unseemly encounter between Blackburn Rovers and Notts County. Local elements among the estimated 14,000 crowd 'hooted and chaffed' County, partly for their rough approach on the day, but also because many in the crowd remembered earlier Cup encounters between County and the Villa. This may explain why some of them turned up with small packets of yellow ochre to throw at the Notts players. Others, less well-prepared, simply threw clods of turf.

Two years later, on March 6, 1886, Small Heath and West Bromwich Albion were the semi-finalists, and although cold weather kept the derby crowd down to 10,000, tempers became overheated just before the end. Albion were 4-0 up when, according to ATHLETIC NEWS, 'a gang of the great unwashed element (began) to snowball a contingent of Black Country people who occupied one of the vehicles, and in a very short time a complete bombardment was going on, which resulted in the crowd breaking onto the field of play, and here hostilities were carried on with renewed vigour.'

So, depressingly, ended one of the last major football matches to take place at the Lower Grounds. But if the Meadow was not destined to survive as a sports venue, there were signs that, in every other respect, business at the Lower Grounds was as busy as ever.

The man generally credited with this short-lived 1880s revival was George Reeves-Smith junior, whose father, a former manager of the Brighton Aquarium, had taken over as manager of the Lower Grounds in April 1882. George senior had a rocky start in the job, and just over two years later was forced to file for bankruptcy when receivers took over the grounds (which were then £10,000 in debt). But his son stayed on, and although he could be haughty and obstinate, George junior, or Master Smith as he was also known, was by all accounts a popular man. The VILLA NEWS AND RECORD later described him as 'a very handsome man of distinguished presence, but without an atom of "side" and always approachable.' No doubt it helped that he also let local sportswriters play the odd game on the precious Meadow.

Apart from having plenty of friends, George junior never seemed to lack ideas. He restocked the aviary and created a bear-pit at the Lower Grounds. Mechanical models were displayed in the aquarium entrance, past which ran a new switchback mini-railway skirting the Meadow. There would also be a tobogganing slide and, as one former visitor recalled, 'a Crystal Cave with the worst-tempered hermit we ever saw.' Was he an example of the then popular form of freak show? If so, perhaps *Sylvia the Mystery* – to be seen in the pavilion by the skating rink – provoked an equally ghoulish allure.

Another fascination of the modern age was a camera obscura. 'For a trifling charge' this mirrored device allowed viewers to see 'live' moving images from around the grounds, projected onto a flat surface. Nowadays, such images might seem as interesting as watching a CCTV monitor. But in the 1880s they were deemed little short of a miracle.

But the Reeves-Smith innovation which seems to have been highlighted the most in later descriptions of the Lower Grounds was a giant tableau, painted on boards erected along the Witton Lane side behind the ornamental lake. The work of 'the celebrated artist, Mr L. Hart of London,' the tableau depicted the *Eruption of Vesuvius* and the *Last Days of Pompeii*.

Ostensibly, the purpose of this huge work of art was to serve as a dramatic backdrop for the increasing number of outdoor spectaculars and firework displays staged around the lake. Apart from the simulation of an erupting volcano, one spectacular in 1884 depicted the Forth Bridge, with a moving train. Others recreated the bombardment of Dover and the opening of the Eiffel Tower.

To offer a prime view of these night-time extravaganzas, a small wooden grandstand was erected on the Trinity Road side, almost exactly where the southern flank of the current Trinity Road Stand is now situated.

But the tableau may also have had a secondary purpose, and that was to mask the row of new terraced houses which had sprung up on the opposite side of Witton Lane. Perhaps it was felt that their roofs rather detracted from the illusion of the Lower Grounds as a place of escape from the grinding hardships of everyday life. Or, maybe, Reeves-Smith simply wanted to stop people in the upper windows of the houses from gaining a free view of the entertainments. Certainly, these entertainments became ever more ambitious during the 1880s as the company sought to attract greater audiences.

Apart from increasingly sophisticated firework displays, there were balloon ascents, one of which – Richard Branson-style – promised to take its intrepid occupants the North Pole.

❖ *This was the small wooden grandstand erected on the Trinity Road side of the Lower Grounds, facing the giant tableau which depicted the Eruption of Vesuvius and the Last Days of Pompeii. Entrance cost an extra sixpence. Could the wizened tree on the left have been the 'noble old oak' described on page 32?*

In the Great Hall, meanwhile, variety acts performed day and night during the Easter and summer seasons. These included the Cruikshank Family (demon jugglers), and Monsieur Dusoni, with his troupe of trained dogs and monkeys. More high-brow entertainment came courtesy of the ENGLISH OPERA COMPANY, who performed in the Great Hall for twelve nights in 1884.

Music was provided outdoors too, for those who could not afford the extra sixpence to enter the Great Hall but who wished to enjoy a twirl or two on the specially-erected dance platform by the ornamental lake. One outdoor performance, by one of the great singers of the days – billed politely as Mrs Wheldon – drew an audience of over 5,000.

Entertainments were also regularly staged on the Meadow. There was the American Dan Canary, billed as the *Champion Bicycle Trick Rider of the World*, and a succession of marching bands, including the Lower Grounds' own Military Band. Another attraction was Menotti, the *Stockholm Wonder*, a high-wire artist who carried a man on his back and performed amid a riot of brightly coloured flares and fireworks.

Three other events at the Lower Grounds during this period deserve a brief mention.

On October 13, 1884, the Lower Grounds were hired for a large garden party in aid of the local Conservative Association. Lord Randolph Churchill and various local worthies were in the Great Hall when a number of local 'roughs' stormed the building and forced the leading delegates to rush for cover in the Holte Hotel. Horrified opinion blamed the incident – which became known somewhat dramatically as the Aston Riots – on Radicals opposed to the Government. But while it was true that inflammatory speeches were made on the platform, and that political unrest was generally rife in the poorer quarters of Birmingham (as it was also in the likes of Manchester, Glasgow and Liverpool), there may also have been an element of hooliganism. At least that was the impression various honourable members in the House of Commons tried to create. They even named the rowdies said to have started the fracas – the so-called Harding Street Gang – whom William McGregor knew only too well, since they were said to have terrorised Summer Lane for a period during the 1880s.

Another, rather more sedate garden party at the Lower Grounds was held in 1887, this time to celebrate Queen Victoria's Jubilee. Eight hundred of the district's more elderly residents were invited for a dinner of roast beef, plum pudding, ale and mineral water, with free tobacco handed out for the smokers.

Hundreds of children, meanwhile, gathered in Aston Park, before they, too, descended on the Lower Grounds, marching behind a police band down Frederick and Bevington Roads. Once there, the boys had an athletics competition on the Meadow before joining the girls for a slap-up tea in the skating rink.

Undoubtedly, many of those children would have returned a few months later for surely the greatest and most spectacular event ever staged at the Lower Grounds – Buffalo Bill's legendary *Wild West Show*. This arrived in Birmingham on November 3, 1887, and played for four weeks at the Meadow, often with two shows a day.

Wild West fever gripped the entire Midlands throughout the run. 'By night our dreams are haunted by visions of deadly combats between the redskins and the palefaces,' wrote one bemused sufferer. Nor was the mania restricted to small boys. The Hon. W. F. Cody, as Buffalo Bill liked to be known, found himself 'feted like a prince, petted and lionised by society's leaders.'

But Cody was no mere showman. A battle-scarred hero of the American west and the star of a hundred or more dime novels, he was truly a living legend. Here was a man who had fought in the Indian wars, ridden for the Pony Express, sat with Sitting Bull and done goodness knows what with Annie Oakley when she wasn't out gettin' her gun. And now here he was with Annie, in person, turning the Aston Lower Grounds into a Wild West staging post. Annie herself

❖ Changing times, changing cultures – over a century separates the bill posters, but the location is almost the same. In the late 1880s (below) the hoardings line the Lower Grounds' boundary fence, with the Holte Hotel and church clearly visible on the right. In the 1990s (left) Meat Loaf and Asian delights brighten up the forlorn Holte.

BIRMINGHAM.

## Aston Lower Grounds.

TWELVE DAYS ONLY,
COMMENCING MONDAY, SEPTEMBER 7TH.
Return to England of the Original and Only

## BUFFALO BILL'S

(Colonel W. F. Cody)

## WILD WEST.

REPRESENTATION of INDIAN and FRONTIER Life.

200 INDIANS, MEXICANS, COWBOYS, SCOUTS,
BUCK RIDERS, RIFLEMEN, &c.,
In animated Tableau and Vivid Scenes.

VISIT THE PICTURESQUE INDIAN VILLAGE AND
FRONTIER CAMP.

THE MOST COLOSSAL AMUSEMENT ENTERPRISE
THAT EVER VISITED WARWICKSHIRE.

COL. W. F. CODY (BUFFALO BILL,) WILL POSI-
TIVELY APPEAR AT EVERY PERFORMANCE.

FOR TWELVE DAYS ONLY.
Two Performances Daily, at 3 and 8 p.m.
RAIN OR SHINE.
Doors open at 1.30 and 6.30.  Prices, 1/-, 2/-, 3/-, and 4/-.
Nights Brilliantly Illuminated.
Seats for 15,000 People.  5,000 One Shilling Seats.
GENERAL ADMISSION, 1/-.  Seats for all.
SATURDAY, SEPTEMBER 19TH.
POSITIVELY LAST REPRESENTATIONS.

was hired to advertise Kynoch's ammunition.

Also with Buffalo Bill travelled an enormous cast of some 800 performers, many of whom were real cowboys and American Indians. The latter set up a mock encampment in the Great Hall where awed visitors could study their living quarters and habits. Over at the skating rink, meanwhile, a herd of 250 performing horses, ponies, mules, burros, assorted buffalos and elks, were tended by staff from BARNUM AND BAILEY'S CIRCUS. Other animals were stabled up at Aston Hall.

Another major attraction in the show was the absolutely gen-u-ine, original – claimed Cody – Deadwood Stagecoach, the very same one Calamity Jane had ridden across the prairie between Cheyenne and Deadwood, and which bore the pockmarked evidence of real gun battles!

Already, it was claimed, over two million 'delighted patrons' had seen the travelling show. To cope with the expected rush, therefore, an extra grandstand, seating 4,000 people, was erected on Trinity Road while, for added dramatic effect, a huge black backdrop was hung in front of the rink. Truly, the Lower Grounds had seen many a spectacular, but here was, possibly, the greatest show of them all.

Except that George Reeves-Smith had overlooked one thing. Buffalo Bill's first show was to take place on the afternoon of Saturday, November 5. That same afternoon there was the small matter of a football match taking place, a second round Cup tie between Small Heath and Aston Villa at Muntz Street.

Over 12,000 saw the Villa rout the Heathens 4-0, while rather less than a third of that number watched Buffalo Bill and was reported to have been rather less than impressed with what they saw.

But as the days went by the show started to attract rave notices, and it was not long before the Lower Grounds' electric arc lights were brought out to enable the company to stage two shows a day. After all, if they could play football under electric light then

surely an eagle-eyed cowboy could lasso a tame buffalo.

Eventually, in early December the Wild West circus packed its bags and headed off back for London, and reality returned. And when it did George Reeves-Smith did not like what he saw. For all the packed houses watching Buffalo Bill, and for all the success of his other entertainment programmes, his board of directors concluded that the Lower Grounds had to become a tighter, more compact operation, and that it needed a rapid injection of funds. The HOLTE THEATRE COMPANY had already closed down, and in yet another effort to attract more visitors the celebrated aquarium was converted into a menagerie. For a short period lions and tigers were among the residents, until they too proved too expensive to keep. An elephant was tried, too, but died after only a year or two.

The only choice left to the management was to sell some land. The first and most obvious parcel was the boating lake, across Witton Road. This was quickly submerged by Nelson, Emscote and Dunsink Roads. But the second, and most controversial decision, was to dispose of the Meadow.

The first inkling most people had was the placing of an advert in the local sporting press in mid-August 1888, offering for sale various fixtures and fittings from the ground, as from September 1. These included 'the best and largest' Sports Telegraph Board in England, 550 yards of first class posts and railings, and the entire dressing room block which had only been erected the year before.

These new dressing rooms and other improvements to the track had, no doubt, been part of a final attempt by the management to restore local faith in the Meadow as a decent venue. But the improvements were either too late, or not enough, as was shown by the fact that, for first time, in 1887, the LOWER GROUNDS COMPANY had actually been forced to place adverts offering their facilities for hire.

SPORT AND PLAY magazine railed against the closure. If only sponsors would come forward with £2,500, it urged, the Meadow could be saved, and a four-year lease secured to guarantee that Birmingham would not be without a prime cycling and athletics venue. But their pleas appear to have met with a deafening silence.

As the September 1 deadline approached, SPORT AND PLAY lamented: 'It is a cogent sign that amateur sport is on its last legs when an event of this kind takes place without a sign of regret. Nobody cares – if we are to judge from outward appearances – a tinker's curse about the matter.'

Not even the attendance of over 15,000 spectators for the annual Birmingham Charity Sports on August 18 could sway the Lower Grounds management.

After all, they probably argued, the crowds had not turned up for the athletics, but to see the first football match of the season. (This, it should be noted, was only a few weeks before the first ever matches in the newly formed FOOTBALL LEAGUE.)

And what was this final football match at the Meadow? Appropriately enough, from our point of view, it was a game between a Birmingham XI and Aston Villa. Not only that, but Villa emerged as 1-0 winners, with centre forward Tom Green claiming the dubious honour of scoring what would prove to be the ground's last ever goal.

A few days after the game it was reported that a last-ditch meeting might be called to save the Meadow from 'the jerry builders'. But it was to no avail. On Saturday, September 1, over two decades of Birmingham sporting history came to an end with a meagrely attended, damp squib of a meeting, held by the Midland Athletic Club.

But this was not quite the final act. Two days later, quite literally, the balloon went up at the Lower Grounds, and there to see it happen was probably the largest crowd to assemble in Aston since the visit of Queen Victoria thirty years earlier.

The object of such intense interest was yet another intrepid American, a showman who went under the unlikely name of Professor T. S. Baldwin. Baldwin's speciality was to ascend rapidly into the air by balloon, and then drop from a harness and parachute back to earth. Ballooning was then a huge attraction, particularly as it was still a risk-laden business. (The Wright brothers' first powered flight was still 15 years away). But parachuting was even more of a novelty and, despite the Professor having already made 10 successful jumps in London, the most recent of which had been at Alexandra Park a few days earlier, the people of Birmingham had never before witnessed such a feat.

Accordingly, around 10,000 people paid the shilling entrance fee to the Meadow to watch Baldwin and his assistants prepare for the jump, while much to the chagrin of George Reeves-Smith, another 50,000 or so crowded onto the slopes of Aston Park and into the surrounding streets to gain a free view. Bevington Road and Trinity Road, reported the BIRMINGHAM DAILY GAZETTE were 'literally alive with human beings.'

Eventually, the balloon was ready. Baldwin kissed his wife, put on his harness, gave the signal and, seemingly in an instant, the balloon shot up to a height of 1,000 feet, at which point a cruel wind – for those inside the Lower Grounds, at least – directed the Professor right over Aston Park, thus providing those who had not paid with a perfect view.

And then, as thousands of eyes peered upwards into the rapidly darkening skies, Baldwin was seen to release himself from the harness.

For three agonising seconds the daredevil American plummeted downwards, head first, towards the horrified hordes, dropping at least 300 feet before – to gasps of relief and wild cheers – his parachute unfurled. But where would he land? On the roof of Aston Hall? In the ornamental lake? In the graveyard of Aston Church?

Unfortunately for Baldwin it was none of these. As his balloon fluttered down onto the railway embankment on the other side of Witton Lane, he landed slap-bang in the middle of the throng in Aston Park, some 30 yards

from Trinity Road, where he was immediately set upon by hundreds of admirers, all eager to shake his hand, slap his back or grab a piece of his parachute.

It was, he remarked later after making a tortuous escape back to the awaiting guests in the Great Hall, 'a rude kind of hero worship,' made worse by the fact that his assailants had not even paid for the privilege, and had torn his parachute into the bargain.

Nevertheless, as a finale for the Magnificent Meadow there could hardly have been a more tumultuous end to 24 years of highs and lows.

And as the park and surrounding streets cleared on that early September evening, not far away a local building contractor called John Little prepared to lower the final curtain.

'Alas for the Aston track,' bemoaned SPORT AND PLAY a week later, 'Its doom is sealed. On Wednesday last the work of desecration commenced, the turnstiles being removed and several loads of bricks being carted onto the green. The turf, too, on which so many historic contests have been witnessed, is in the course of removal. Possession will be formally given up on the 29th inst. and then goodbye Aston.'

So ended another eventful chapter in the history of the Lower Grounds. Within months the Meadow had all but disappeared under the bricks, mortar and cobbled stones of three new streets, Nelson, Jardine and Endicott Roads, leaving not a single remembrance of the great deeds once performed by Dr Grace, George Ramsay, 'the Demon' Spofforth, Lon Myers, George and Snook, Buffalo Bill and the flying Professor Baldwin.

But, emotion apart, if the directors of the Lower Grounds were now better able to face their bank manager, the fact remained that, for the first time in nearly 20 years, the city of Birmingham found itself without a single first-class athletics or cycling track.

Clearly, something had to be done.

❖ *The Magnificent Meadow, 1864-88, with the skating rink, Aquarium and Great Hall on the far side.*

# Farewell to the Magnificent Meadow

❖ Apart from comments in the Birmingham weekly magazine SPORT AND PLAY the only local newspaper to even mention the demise of the 'Magnificent Meadow' was the BIRMINGHAM DAILY POST. The following article was published on the day of the Meadow's final sporting event, staged by the Midland Athletic Club on Saturday, September 1, 1888.

## ASTON LOWER GROUNDS

A very important alteration is about to be effected at the Aston Lower Grounds. For several years past the athletic sports which have been held on the meadow have resulted in a loss to the company. The general public did not patronise the gatherings in sufficient numbers to make them a financial success, their abstention being mainly due to the great decline in the public interest in amateur athletics. A few years ago the receipts from the running-track were sufficient to make the whole of the grounds a paying concern, and this was the case even when Messrs. Reeves-Smith and Son entered upon their management, although then the public interest in athletics was already on the wane. The suddenness and completeness of the collapse of that interest may be judged from the fact that, four years ago, at the sports held by the Speedwell Club, the sum of £260 was divided between the management and the club as the profits of the afternoon, while in the following year, with precisely the same attractions and precisely the same weather, a loss of

£50 had to be divided. The result was that the sports rarely, if ever, paid and last year the company lost £500 by one meeting alone. This year only two meetings have been held – namely, on Whit Monday and August Bank Holiday, and in respect to these there was a balance on the right side; but this success, the directors have discovered, can only be achieved on Bank Holidays. The directors have consequently come to the conclusion that it would be advisable to abandon athletic sports altogether, and as this would enable them to dispose of the meadow and running-track, which comprise an area of eight acres, there would not only be a saving in rates and taxes, but no actual loss on sports would be incurred. The meadow was sold about a month ago for building purposes, and after the 29th inst. it will be cut off from the buildings and gardens by means of a boundary wall, and the work of building will be almost immediately commenced. The sports telegraph-board, the posts and rails, and the buildings, dressing-rooms, etc, which are situated on the meadow, and within the area disposed of, are advertised to be sold, and the running-track, which is a very fine one, is to be broken up. The gardens are to be continued as a pleasure resort. A suggestion has been made that a running-path should be laid down round one of the pools, but it has not been favourably entertained.

In the heyday of success and popularity the Lower Grounds meadow and track were second to none in the world, and perhaps more champions in all varieties of sport have competed there than on any other ground. It was the home of football – its very cradle and nursery in the district, for here came the celebrated Notts Forest Club in its palmy days to teach the young Birmingham players the very rudiments and alphabet of the sport. Here, too, all that was best in cricket was to be witnessed when North and South, All-England elevens, and the flower and pink of English cricket were to be seen season after season on the meadow, which the champion himself once described as one of the best grounds in the kingdom. Old cricketers to this day speak with affectionate remembrance of the glorious games which were witnessed there, and the great players of the past – some gathered long ago to their fathers, and others who are still amongst us – have been seen on the greensward which is now threatened with the ruthless reign of the jerry-builder. It was the paradise of amateur athletes for many years, and it undoubtedly holds a record for athletic sports absolutely unapproached by any other place of resort in the country. The track was one of the best and fastest in the country. Owing to the slope down the 'straight' it was not accepted as a record for less than a quarter of a mile, but except for that disadvantage it had scarcely an equal in the country. Last year it was better than ever. It is stated that during the last three years between £1,500 and £2,000 have been spent upon it, and, with the exception of the Long Eaton track it is certainly the best in the kingdom. Two of the most successful championship meetings were held there, the first of which – that in 1882 – stands unique as being the occasion of the finest gathering of athletes ever known, when three or four new records were established, one at least of which has never been

❖ Henry G. Quilter (1824-93) – the grocer-turned-gardener, and creator of the Aston Lower Grounds.

broken – that of the American, L. E. Myers, for the quarter-mile. That meeting will be long remembered, for amateur athletics were then at their best, and proficiency in the dexterous art of 'roping' was not a part of the equipment of the amateur sportsman, and the 'gentle voice of the bookmaker' was unheard in the land. To a very great extent the amateur athlete committed deliberate suicide, for the public sickened on the flagrant proceedings of a good many of the *soi disant* amateurs who fattened on the proceeds of their dishonesty; and from the decadence of these sports, which were at one time admirably conducted and managed by some of the best and oldest of the athletic clubs of the district, may be traced to a very great extent the decline in popularity of the Lower Grounds. To those who remember the place in all its beauty and freshness, when it used to be the rendezvous and delight of all who took a part or interest in matters pertaining to outdoor sport and pastime, its decay and fast approaching doom must be a source of very keen regret.

The 'champion himself' mentioned above was, of course, W. G. Grace, while the practice of 'roping' referred to the commonplace practice of athletes deliberately holding back in a race in order to influence the betting odds. The reporter clearly had his rose-tinted spectacles on when he suggested that all cricketers recalled the 'greensward' with affection, or that bookmakers were not prevalent at athletics meetings in the early years. He was wrong too in dating the famous 1881 championships as taking

place in 1882. But one fact he did not mention was that, on the very same day as this article appeared, the DAILY POST also reported that George Reeves-Smith and his father had been given the go-ahead to build the CENTRAL RESTAURANT in Corporation Street, at the considerable cost of £19,100. Was this venture the reason why the Meadow had to go?

If so, it was not this, nor indeed any of the financial or sporting issues which aroused the ire of one noted correspondent to the DAILY POST, in a bitter, yet deeply poignant letter published five days later.

*Sir – a friend in Birmingham has sent me your 'paper of Saturday last, in which I read an article on the Lower Grounds, Aston – a spot you and all your Birmingham readers must know I held an important position in, and in which I naturally feel some degree of interest; and I must say I feel very much surprised that after raising that place, and spending the best part of my life in doing so, and losing the whole of my money there, any writer of an article in your paper on that subject would finish on such pathetic terms without any mention of the name of the man who is both well known to yourself and the Birmingham public as having made the place, and been the chief promoter of everything mentioned in your article, it seems hard that after doing all I did for Birmingham, and the benefits derived by the town, that no allusions should be made to me.*
H. G. QUILTER
BATH HOTEL, FELIXSTOWE, SEPTEMBER 3

❖ *The Magnificent Meadow, viewed from the Bevington Road end of the pitch. The covered walkway in front of the skating rink was converted into a reserved seating area, while on the left is a large square conservatory, whose windows must have been extremely vulnerable to stray clearances or the odd six hit from W. G. Grace. To take this shot, the photographer would have stood on what is now roughly the corner of Witton Road and Endicott Road, pointing due east towards the North Stand.*

THE ENTIRE AUSTRALIAN CRICKETING TEAM.

R. Thoms (L.S.&P.C.LTD.)  Mc. Ilwraith  Trumble  Jarvis  Bruce  Jones  Palmer  Spofforth  Farrands (COPYRIGHT)
Wardill  Blackham  Evans  Scott  Bonnor  Garrett  G. Giffen

The London Stereoscopic & Photographic Company, Limited. 54 CHEAPSIDE, E.C. & 110 & 108, REGENT STREET, W.

❖ *Local cricket-lovers must have trembled with anticipation when the demon Australian bowler Fred Spofforth (pictured on the back row) arrived at the recently opened Edgbaston in August 1886. Two years earlier on the Lower Grounds Meadow Spofforth had claimed 14 England wickets for just 37 runs.*

# Milestones at the Meadow

**1864** Aston Lower Grounds become separate entity under Henry Quilter's stewardship. Meadow laid out for cricket.

**1865** July & August... Cricket: United All England XI v 22 of Aston.

**1870s** Resident Birmingham Cricket & Football Club – the Quilters – becomes one of leading outfits in the city.

**1878** January... New company takes over Lower Grounds.

**1878** July... United South of England v 22 of Birmingham. W.G. Grace takes 21 wickets.

**1878** October 28... Football: First floodlit match, Birmingham v Nottingham Forest.

**1879** June 21... Athletics and cycling: First Birchfield Harriers meeting.

**1880** April 3... Football: Aston Villa beat Saltley College 3-1 to win their first honour. George Ramsay's final first team match.

**1880** June 21-23... Cricket: first visit of Australians, v 18 of Birmingham.

**1881** February 5... Football: Birmingham & District v London. A crowd of around 8,000 see match of the season, won 2-0 by visitors.

**1881** March 5... Football: International Trial Match; England XI v Birmingham & District.

**1881** July 16... Athletics: second annual AAA Championships

**1882** Summer... Cricket: Warwickshire CCC play trial games with a view to making the Meadow their permanent home.

**1884** March 1... Football: FA Cup semi-final, Blackburn Rovers v Notts County.

**1884** May 26... Cricket: England v Australia finishes in just over four hours.

**1884** June 21... Athletics: fifth annual AAA Championships. Walter George breaks world record for the mile.

**1886** March 6... Football: FA Cup semi-final, Small Heath v West Bromwich Albion.

**1887** October... Programme of improvements to track and field completed in attempt to increase profitability of Meadow.

**1887** November 5... Buffalo Bill's Wild West Show starts a four-week run.

**1888** August 18... Football: final match on Meadow; Aston Villa v Birmingham & District, as part of Birmingham Charity Sports day. Villa's Tom Green scores last goal in 1-0 win.

**1888** September 1... Athletics: Midland Athletics Club stage final meeting at Meadow.

**1888** September 3... Professor Baldwin performs his parachute jump from the Meadow, watched by 10,000 in the Lower Grounds and up to 50,000 on the slopes of Aston Park.

**1888** September 5... The first bricks are delivered and the turf is dug up.

# Sport and Play at the New Meadow

*in which a Birmingham sports weekly saves the day* ❖

*Dovehouse Pool makes way for the New Meadow* ❖

*cycle mania hits Brum* ❖

*ladies' cricket proves more popular than athletics* ❖

*the Eiffel Tower lights up Aston* ❖

*Mr Winchurch eats a marathon meal* ❖

*Villa try out their future home for size* ❖

NEWSPAPER HEADLINES FROM September 1888 may not have paid much heed to the loss of the Magnificent Meadow, but they seem uncannily familiar to modern day readers.

Just as in the 1990s the National Exhibition Centre in Birmingham would press its claims to rival Wembley as the home of the national stadium, so in 1888 was launched a major local campaign to promote Cannock Chase as the venue for the National Rifle Association's prestigious annual tournament (in succession to Wimbledon).

In the 1990s a string of horrific murders has provoked a national debate on crime and punishment. In 1888 a so-called 'murder epidemic' was sending shudders through Victorian Britain; from the back-streets of Whitechapel, where the infamous Ripper was on the prowl, to the back-to-backs of Summer Lane, where two children aged 10 and 12 were on trial for the murder of a six-month-old baby.

Then there was the Irish question, in 1888, as now, a hugely divisive issue, which had sent the opposition Liberal leader, Gladstone, on a series of passionate lectures around the country, advocating his commitment to Home Rule. Further afield, there was civil war in Serbia and Albania, just as there would be in the 1990s.

There were parallel concerns in the sporting world too. Athletics, its critics now complain, has become a travelling circus of overpaid prima donnas. In the late 1880s the lament was that the sport had lost its integrity to an ever-increasing number of professionals who, in turn, were becoming hopelessly compromised by the activities of illegal bookmakers. And where football in the 1990s has been characterised by the breakaway of the Premier League, in 1888 William McGregor's newly-formed FOOTBALL LEAGUE was denounced as a money-making stunt which threatened to divide an elite of clubs from the mainstream.

One week after the last race at the Lower Grounds Meadow, the FOOTBALL LEAGUE kicked-off for the first time, without the merest hint of a fanfare or firework, let alone mini-skirted cheerleaders. Aston Villa were away on the opening Saturday, drawing 1-1 at Wolverhampton. Only 2,500 spectators attended. A week later, Villa's first home League fixture at Perry Barr would draw even fewer fans for an emphatic 5-1 win over Stoke.

Not that the apparent lack of interest would have been too surprising to the founders. One of the motivating factors behind the League's formation had been the public's flagging enthusiasm for meaningless games, a trend hardly reversed during the first season when Villa's three largest gates (of between 10-12,000) were all against familiar foes of old; Blackburn Rovers, West Bromwich Albion and Preston North End. One fixture – a 4-3 win over Accrington in October 1888 – drew a gate of only 600 to Perry Barr, the lowest crowd ever to see Villa at home in the League.

Apart from feeling their way in the new competition, Villa were also experiencing a few growing pains in their own administration and constitution, a phase which would ultimately lead, via Barwick Street in February 1893, to the formation of a limited liability company in January 1896.

In short, with so much happening and so many challenges to meet at Perry Barr, whatever problems the management of the Aston Lower Grounds may have been facing, they were almost certainly, and quite understandably, of no concern to the officials or supporters of Aston Villa.

Not so for the athletes and cyclists of Birmingham, however, and, in particular, not for Charles Wheelwright, the influential honorary secretary of the MIDLAND COUNTIES AMATEUR ATHLETICS ASSOCIATION, and his friends, the editor and proprietor of the weekly magazine, SPORT AND PLAY. Their collective response to the loss of the Meadow was to have an absolutely crucial bearing on the future of the Lower Grounds. Indeed, it is no exaggeration to assert that had it not been for SPORT AND PLAY, Villa Park might never have been built.

In the context of modern sport such a claim might seem rather exaggerated. After all, how could a local weekly possibly have so much influence? But in the

❖ *Edwin Cox (pictured below) one of the team at* SPORT AND PLAY, *and in 1906 destined to become the first editor of the* VILLA NEWS AND RECORD.

*A regular contributor to the programme was Cox's former collaborator at Lucifer House, John Urry (opposite), known as Jack to his friends and as* LEATHER STOCKING *to his readers.*

late 19th century the sporting press was almost as powerful in its own way as television and satellite broadcasting are today.

For example, with its weekly circulation of some 230,000 by 1897, the hugely successful, Manchester-based ATHLETIC NEWS was virtually the official organ of the FOOTBALL LEAGUE. Its editor, John Bentley, was not only a regular reporter and columnist, but also President of the League from 1894-1910, a League referee, and a senior official of Bolton Wanderers (before becoming chairman of Manchester United). Not even Rupert Murdoch has managed to dip his fingers in that many footballing pies.

In the Midlands there were several influential titles. THE MIDLAND ATHLETE was launched in January 1879 under the editorship of H. M. Oliver, a prominent figure and race official in local athletics circles. Its main football reporter was the Scot, John Campbell Orr, who, as a co-founder member of the Calthorpe club, has often been credited with introducing football to Birmingham in 1873. Orr wrote a regular column called *Chasing the Leather* under the pseudonym of *Don Juan*. One of the MIDLAND ATHLETE'S first subscribers was George Ramsay.

In 1881 a rival publication appeared, called the MIDLAND ATHLETIC STAR. Run by John Urry and Edwin Cox, this survived only two years. But in February 1886 the same pair and Charles Wheelwright launched a second title, SPORT AND PLAY. Produced first from Edmund Street, then from an office in Lucifer House, Lionel Street, this title eventually took over the MIDLAND ATHLETE in 1887, and then the Coventry-based title, BICYCLE NEWS, in 1895.

The personnel behind SPORT AND PLAY would become intimately involved with both the Lower Grounds and Aston Villa. It was SPORT AND PLAY which organised and sponsored all the major cycling events at the Lower Grounds between 1889 and 1914, that is, both before and after Villa took over the site. After deciding to devote SPORT AND PLAY purely to cycling in November 1894, Urry and Cox also launched a general sports weekly called THE GRASSHOPPER, which during its two years in print covered Villa's affairs in so much detail that it sometimes read like an in-house magazine. But then, the SPORT AND PLAY company also had the contract to print Villa's fixture cards.

This close relationship eventually culminated in the company producing Villa's first ever official match programmes – the VILLA NEWS AND RECORD – from September 1906 onwards. Edwin Cox was the programme's first editor (in season 1906-07), while John Urry (known as Jack to his friends and *Leather Stocking* in SPORT AND PLAY), was a regular contributor until the 1920s.

But to return to September 1888. As quoted on pages 50, when the old Meadow at the Lower Grounds finally succumbed to the 'jerry builders' the BIRMINGHAM DAILY POST reported that although the gardens were to be continued as a pleasure resort, a suggestion 'that a running-path should be laid down

**SPORT & PLAY.**
**Whitsuntide, 1889.**
OPENING OF THE
NEW CYCLING TRACK AT ASTON.
——o——
GRAND INTERNATIONAL
**Cycling Tournament**
(Under N.C.U. Rules), for
**AMATEURS AND PROFESSIONALS**
(*Promoted by the Proprietors of* SPORT AND PLAY),
ON
**MONDAY & TUESDAY, JUNE 10 & 11,**
AT THE
**ASTON LOWER GROUNDS;**
BIRMINGHAM.
**£220 in Prizes!**
HANDICAPPER—MR. C. WHEELWRIGHT,
(*Sport and Play,*)
REFEREE—MR. W. COOKE, Wolverhampton.

❖ *SPORT AND PLAY announce their new venture on the site of the current Villa Park. Note the offer of £220 in prizes, not cash.*

round one of the pools' had not been 'favourably entertained' by the Lower Grounds management.

At some point between then and April 1889 they were clearly persuaded to change their minds, thus launching an entirely new, and ultimately decisive phase in the development of the Lower Grounds.

It has frequently been claimed in various histories of Aston Villa and the Lower Grounds that the club itself was responsible for both filling in the ornamental lake and laying down the first pitch, cycle track and stands, during the period 1896-97.

Emphatically, this was not the case.

Firstly, the ornamental lake was in fact drained and filled in during the first half of 1889.

Secondly, a cycle track was opened on the site in June 1889, and from then until Villa's arrival in early 1896, the so-called 'New Meadow' at the Lower Grounds was a well-developed and popular sports ground in its own right, staging almost as wide a range of sports events and entertainments as ever the old Meadow witnessed.

But thirdly, and perhaps most intriguingly of all, Aston Villa actually played on this ground at least three times between 1893-95, before they moved there permanently.

In other words, when Villa took over the lease of the Lower Grounds in 1896 – although they would not actually make it ready until April 1897 – the sports ground was already seven years old, and Villa's officials and fans would have been quite familiar with the place, as indeed would have sporting enthusiasts from all over the Midlands.

Unfortunately, very few details survive of how the all-important transition took place in 1889. Nor can there be traced any detailed maps or photographs showing the 'New Meadow' between 1889 and 1897.

Various snippets of information do, however,

provide some significant clues as to why the all-important transition took place.

We know from SPORT AND PLAY, for example, that despite the decision to dispose of the old Meadow in August 1888, the Lower Grounds manager, George Reeves-Smith, had 'tried his very hardest' to preserve it, and that 'the regret which was felt by all sportsmen when its beauty and comeliness were destroyed was as keen with the debonair manager as any body.' When SPORT AND PLAY and a number of sporting lobbyists tried to persuade the LOWER GROUNDS COMPANY to lay a new track on the site, therefore, they clearly had an ally on the inside.

It must also have helped that most of the entertainments now being staged at the Lower Grounds were centred upon the Great Hall and Aquarium complex, whereas the gardens and lake *per se* would only have had limited earning potential. Nor would their replacement by a sports ground prevent the management from continuing to stage the sort of outdoor spectaculars and firework displays which had become so popular during the 1880s.

But perhaps the most persuasive argument of all was the fact that, after football, cycling was now patently the fastest growing craze in English sport.

This was true not only in terms of road or track racing but also for ordinary leisure seekers, for whom the new generation of 'safety' cycles formed a relatively cheap but liberating form of transport. First produced by the Coventry firm of Rover, in 1885, the safety cycle – that is, with two wheels of the same size and a chain – allowed lords and labourers alike to become kings of the road for no more than a tenner, payable in instalments if necessary. It even opened up the highways to women, who had previously been excluded from cycling because the 'ordinary' model (or penny-farthing) was deemed too dangerous and unfeminine. Novice riders gained further comfort when J. B. Dunlop patented pneumatic tyres in 1888.

Furthermore, although the boom started in Coventry, Birmingham rapidly became an important centre of bicycle manufacture. In the Aston area alone there were several factories – for example BAXTER's in Loveday Street and BOWN's in Summer Lane (followed later by famous names such as HERCULES and NORTON) – plus countless smaller workshops turning out ever more innovative accessories: lamps by JOSEPH LUCAS in Little King Street, MILLER's in Miller Street or POWELL & HAMMER in Aston Road; chains by PERRY & CO in Lancaster Street; sprung saddles by BROOKES of Great Charles Street, not to mention tyres, badges, spanners, springs, ball-bearings and so on. By the peak of the boom in around 1896 it was thought that production nationwide reached 750,000 cycles a year. By 1914 nearly 10,000 Brummies were employed in the industry.

Small wonder then that SPORT AND PLAY should campaign for the city to have a first class cycle track.

The first confirmation that a deal had been struck with the LOWER GROUNDS COMPANY was a surprise announcement printed in the SPORT AND PLAY issue of April 9, 1889.

## A SURPRISE PACKET
### *Good News for Cyclists*
### *Sport and Play to the Rescue*

Last week we intimated that we had an important announcement to make which would be welcoming news for Midland athletes and cyclists  Knowing the necessity that exists for a first class athletic and cycle track in Birmingham, and seeing that all other efforts to provide one have failed, we have taken the whole responsibility on our own shoulders.

The announcement added that the track would measure the regulation 440 yards, with banked up curves for extra speed, and would be laid by Messrs LEWIS & CURRALL, 'the famous road contractors of Birmingham.' No costs were mentioned, but the going rate for other new tracks being laid around the country, at places like Herne Hill and Nottingham, was then around £400-500.

By the end of May SPORT AND PLAY had gone into full publicity overdrive.

'All the world knows by this time that the cycling meeting to be held at the Lower Grounds on Whit Monday and Tuesday will be absolutely the best ever held in the history of cycling. Already some of the finest wheelmen in the country, both amateur and professional, have entered, and fine weather is all that is required to make the meeting a phenomenal success. The track is being prepared and finished in a style that does the contractors credit, and promises to be one of the fastest, if not the fastest, in the country. Intending competitors had better send in their entries at once, as Saturday is the last day; and they will regret, in the event of being too late, that they did not take part in what undoubtedly will be one of the most memorable sporting events in the history of the Midlands.'

For their part, the Lower Grounds management laid on their own Easter entertainments in the Great Hall, including one stuntman specifically hired for the interest of all bicyclists. This was Mr A. H. Minting, whose act was to ascend a spiral ramp, 50 feet high, on a monocycle.

As May turned to June the clearance work between the Great Hall and the Holte Hotel continued. Away went Henry Quilter's neatly tended lawns, his flower beds, the sub-tropical garden and the Main Walk. Away, too, went the rustic bridge, as the ornamental lake – the last vestige of the centuries-old Dovehouse Pool – was finally drained and infilled. In its place was laid the cinder cycling track and an inner grass track for athletics. The centre area was also levelled in readiness for a pitch, although this would not be turfed over for several months.

London and North Western Railway.

# CHEAP BOOKINGS
## TO
# ✳ ASTON ✳
# LOWER GROUNDS
### BIRMINGHAM.

**HENRY C. CRAWFORD - Secretary and Manager.**

# EASTER MONDAY and TUESDAY,
## March 26th and 27th, 1894.

### ✳ OPENING OF NEW TRACK. ✳
## GREAT
# Cycling & Athletic Carnival

### (PROMOTED BY "SPORT & PLAY.")

# Prizes £225 Prizes

## IMMENSE PROGRAMME! SPECIAL PRIZES FOR RECORDS!
# A MEETING OF CHAMPIONS!

# VARIETY ENTERTAINMENT
### In the Great Hall, Afternoon and Evening.

# MISS NANA GILFORT
Will execute the most daring feat of ascending a Wire the distance of 600 feet, suspended only by her teeth, and perform in various positions at the height of 93 feet, the top of Aston Tower. She will also Descend the Wire in the time of 30 seconds, representing the Shooting Star.
**This feat has never been performed by any other Lady or Gentleman in the World.**

# MONS. LE BLONDE
Sensational Aerial Trapeze Act and Parisian Ring Act. Two distinct Acts.

# MISS CISSIE TRENT
The Captivating Transformation and Queen of Quick Change Artistes, introducing the different National Costumes and Dances.

# BARTON AND HART
Negro Sketch Artistes, in their most amusing Act with their BLONDIN ELEPHANT.

# 2–THE LOYALS–2
Lady and Gentleman Acrobats, Chair Pyramidists, One Hand Balancers, A1 Tumblers, and Staircase Experts. Splendid Dresses and Bright Appliances.

# 3–THE ASHLEY TEAM–3
American Pantomimic Skaters, Three in Number. One Lady Artiste, Two Gentlemen Artistes.
**MISS MARIE.** "The Great Lady Skater," in her Marvellous Toe and Bottle Work.
**MR. C. M. ASHLEY.** in his Original Creation, THE JUMBO POLICEMAN.

### MAGNIFICENT WORLD'S FAIR. Fun and Frolic
Cavern of Mysteries, Electric Bars, Camera Obscura, and Polar Bear Pit.
THREE BANDS. DANCING on Great Platform and in Great Hall.

# Admission Monday, 1s., after 6 p.m., 6d.
## TUESDAY, ALL DAY, 6d.
REFRESHMENTS in Bars, Tea Rooms, and Holte Hotel.

❖ From 1889-95 the New Meadow and its cycling track – on the exact site of Villa Park today – was the scene of a number of memorable sporting events after Henry Crawford had taken over as secretary and manager of the Lower Grounds. This poster from 1894 shows a typical annual Easter programme, with the added attraction of a newly re-laid cinder track.

As for spectator accommodation, there are few clues as to the new arrangements, other than that there was definitely a small grandstand on the Trinity Road side, which may have been either the same small one erected in the 1880s for the night-time fireworks displays (pictured on page 45), or even the 1,500 seat stand originally built at the old Meadow.

Certainly, there must have been some form of rudimentary accommodation constructed around the other sides of the track – perhaps shallow earth banks or wooden bleachers – because when the new sports ground was proudly opened on Monday, June 10, 1889, an estimated crowd of 15,000 attended.

Even SPORT AND PLAY could not deny that conditions were hardly ideal, however.

'It cannot be said that the meteorological conditions were of the best; in fact, from early morning till close of day it blew great guns, and ever and anon a few drops of rain would fall just to let us know there were more to follow when the proper moment came; how it howled and roared among the tree-tops and scudded the clouds across the sky as though they, too, were trying to beat a record: and how cold and bleak and cheerless it was everywhere. Great coats and mufflers that had been put by, it was fondly hoped, for months, were requisitioned for the occasion and though there was a lot of grumbling – and worse – we had to put up with it, and make the best of a bad time.'

But at least there was plenty of exciting action, with the pick of professional cyclists making sure that there was 'not a tame finish' to be seen. Among the stars on show over the two days were top cyclists from France, Holland and Ireland, together with leading English riders such as Fred Wood, Bob and Tom English, Jack Lee, and the English champion, R. Howell, who, as usual, turned up in his 'loud "national" knicks.'

For the record, the first winner on the new track was Bob English, in the one mile heats, with a time of 2 minutes, 57 seconds. His prize for this modest honour was £10. But not £10 in cash, you understand – for that would have been tantamount to admitting the riders were professional – but £10 in the form of some desirable trinket or other. As was the customary hypocrisy of the day, English would then have traded this trinket through a special broker, for the not surprising sum of £10, thus preserving his amateur status!

In such a fashion over £200 worth of 'prizes' were offered for this inaugural meeting. As SPORT AND PLAY freely admitted, 'Good prizes fetch good men; good men attract good gates.'

The second day of the tournament was a much greater success, not only for SPORT AND PLAY but for the Lower Grounds management. This time the sun shone, the crowd was estimated at around 18,000 and, according to SPORT AND PLAY, it was 'like one of the rare old meetings of by-gone times'.

'The grounds were crowded with sightseers the whole of the day, and the best of order prevailed. The appearance of this popular resort recalled the palmiest of the "Lower" and it seems quite probable that it will again become the attraction of the Midlands.'

In between races the holiday crowd witnessed some daring feats by the De Colmar aerial-wire bicycle troupe, while Captain Dixon, the renowned shot (ably assisted by his clever dog, Black Prince) managed to shatter 100 balls in 7 minutes and 10 seconds, without a single miss. And after dusk settled on the Lower Grounds, the glow of electric lamps lit up the Great Hall and busy pathways, as, on the so-called New Meadow, a 'brilliant display' of fireworks was orchestrated by Messrs JAMES PAIN & SONS. The centrepiece of their display was a sparkling rendition of the recently completed Eiffel Tower.

Only one incident marred the day, a pile-up of four riders in the five mile event. Otherwise, noted SPORT AND PLAY with barely disguised pride, 'we may conscientiously flatter ourselves on having given the public the best tanners' worth of sport they ever had placed before them.'

But was this just self-congratulatory hype? Not according to the ATHLETIC NEWS correspondent, who reckoned that the Lower Grounds now boasted the finest track in the kingdom, an opinion reportedly shared by all but one of the leading riders who had participated in the opening. Other commentators rated the Aston track as least as good as the best, which they considered to be at Paddington.

The BIRMINGHAM DAILY MAIL was less effusive.

## Training at the Aston Track.

The following moderate Tariff has been fixed for Training Tickets at the new Aston Track:—

|  | Cyclists. | | | Athletes. | | |
|---|---|---|---|---|---|---|
| Whole Season | £1 | 1 | 0 | £0 | 10 | 6 |
| One Month | 0 | 7 | 6 | 0 | 4 | 0 |
| One Week | 0 | 2 | 6 | 0 | 2 | 0 |
| One Day | 0 | 1 | 0 | 0 | 0 | 6 |

Friends and Assistants (other than Professional Trainers) are admitted to the Ground on payment of 3d.

Sports promoting bodies who desire to engage the Grounds must apply to the Manager, "Sport and Play," Lionel Street, Birmingham.

The following dates are already filled :—

June 7 and 8—Whit-Monday and Tuesday—Sport and Play Tournament.
June 21—Aston Villa F.C. Sports.
June 22—(Jubilee Day)—Midland C. and A.C.
July 17—N.C.U. Championships.
Aug. 2 and 3—Bank Holiday—Sport and Play Tournament
Aug. 28—Birmingham Charity Sports.

Track Superintendent—FRED HUGHES, to whom all questions must be referred.

Dismissing the two-day event as 'a speculative meeting got up purely as a matter of business' the MAIL would only concede that the races had been organised 'as thoroughly as any amateur club could have done.'

Damned by such feint praise, SPORT AND PLAY responded indignantly, 'Faugh! What miserable rot is all this twaddle which journalistic jackasses bray about the doings of amateurs!'

Not that they had any need to be on the defensive. The new track soon became a hive of activity, particularly on the long summer evenings, as experienced riders and novices alike gladly paid to train at the Lower Grounds.

Eleven days after the opening they were joined by the athletes of Birchfield Harriers, for their Annual Amateur Festival. After the old Meadow had been cleared the Harriers had talked of transferring their events to the Bournbrook Grounds, on Bristol Road, Selly Oak (since the only other track, at Portland Road, Edgbaston, was private). But clearly the Lower Grounds were more convenient, and now much more advanced.

There were also plenty of familiar faces around from the old Meadow; Billy Branston, the dressing room attendant, Fred Hughes, the former professional runner who had been the Lower Grounds starter for many years (and who had once finished a race by turning three hand springs to prove his fitness), and Roberts, the groundsman. (Groundsmen in those days never seem to have been accorded the courtesy of being referred to by their full name.) On the day of the Birchfield meeting, Roberts was said to have uttered quite a few curses when athletes, crossing onto the running track in their spiked shoes, had messed up the cycle track which he had so lovingly worked to get 'as smooth as a proverbial billiard table.' And, of course, George Reeves-Smith was still around, although now that he was more involved with establishing his new CENTRAL RESTAURANT in Corporation Street he had an acting manager at the Lower Grounds, a Mr Edgar Lane.

All summer the mood remained resolutely upbeat. SPORT AND PLAY promoted a second cycle event, billed as *Enterprise v Sentiment! Another Cracker!* And so it proved. Apart from the participation of riders from Australia and the United States, in a race justly described as 'one of the most exciting ever seen,' the veteran Englishman, Fred Wood, won a thrilling ten mile event by just half a yard at the death, and then promptly retired from the sport. Much quaffing and back-slapping followed that evening at the Holte Hotel.

On August 31, the new track also staged the annual Birmingham Charity Sports which, despite not including a football match for the first time (because the new pitch was still not ready), managed to draw a 15,000 crowd, with the grandstand and reserved enclosure 'crammed to excess.' Approximately £300 was raised, as reported triumphantly, of course, in SPORT AND PLAY:

'Where would the Charity Sports Committee

have been this year but for the spirited enterprise displayed by the proprietors of SPORT AND PLAY in providing Birmingham with a new cycling and athletic path after the old meadow was handed over to the builder?'

Every summer for the next six years the new ground had a busy programme of events, some more successful than others. On July 12 1890 the AMATEUR ATHLETICS ASSOCIATION returned to stage their annual championships. This was their third time in Birmingham (after 1881 and 1884 at the old Meadow), but it would also be their last. Despite a strong turn out of first-class athletes and the attendance of several celebrity runners from the past, barely 2,000 spectators attended, deterred partly by the grey, drizzly conditions and partly by a breakdown of the tram service. Apart from resulting in a loss for the AAA, the poor turnout must have been equally disheartening for James Kibblewhite, a local Birchfield Harrier who managed the astonishing feat of winning the mile, four mile and ten mile races, all in one afternoon. The only other achievement of note in an otherwise enjoyable, if hardly compelling day, was Harry Curtis's record of 52 minutes and 28.4 seconds in the seven mile walking event.

Just how much athletics had slipped in the public's estimation was further exemplified a week later, when the Lower Grounds laid coconut matting on the centre field in order to stage a *Ladies Cricket Match*. For this novelty event, featuring a troupe of professional players 'who play and do not burlesque the game,' the crowd approached 6,000. 'It is wonderful what a powerful attraction petticoats and pretty faces are,' noted SPORT AND PLAY wryly, adding that during the post-match entertainments in the Great Hall 'the ladies appeared to much greater advantage than they did on the cricket field.'

Perhaps, SPORT AND PLAY concluded in 1892, the proprietors of the magazine would have to do for athletics what they had already done for cycling.

'If SPORT AND PLAY can bring about the renaissance of athletics in the Midlands and enable our dear, dirty old Brum to take its proper place in the world of sport and once more turn out its champions on foot and wheel alike, we shall feel proud of having been engaged in a glorious task and amply rewarded for our pains by having permitted to take even a small

❖ *In the days before match programmes, SPORT & PLAY, was happy to call itself the official organ of the three Birmingham clubs. The company that published the magazine also printed all Villa's tickets, and, as the advert opposite shows, organised the cycle track at the Lower Grounds.*

share in a big effort to restore the lost prestige of the district.'

But the returns from meetings promoted at the Lower Grounds suggests that the task of reviving athletics was too much, even for the mighty SPORT AND PLAY. Attendances were only good when the weather was fine or when football was part of the programme. Thus, rain kept the annual Charity Sports crowd down to an unprecedented low of 2,000 in September 1892, while presumably apathy prevented more than 1,000 turning up for the AAA ten mile championship in March 1893.

Cycle racing, on the other hand, remained incredibly popular. Nearly 9,000 turned out in 'bitter winds and blinding snow' for a race meeting in March 1891, while SPORT AND PLAY's Whitsuntide event that year pulled in almost 21,000 over two days. The National Cycling Union Championships in June 1894, attracted 15,000 for one day alone.

This latter meeting took place shortly after the track had been relaid in order to bring it up to the standards of other, more modern tracks – such as Herne Hill in south London – and came at a time when the Lower Grounds had come under new management.

George Reeves-Smith left in late 1892, after ten years in Aston. Maybe his lavish restaurant in Corporation Street had failed. Maybe he simply wanted an easier life. In any event, like Henry Quilter before him, he returned to the south, handing over the Lower Grounds management to one Henry Crawford, of whom very little is known. (Reeves Smith was not entirely forgotten, however, since his sister remained in Birmingham and married the Villa player, Howard Vaughton).

# A remarkable recipe for victory

❖ One of the last cycling events to take place at the Lower Grounds before Villa took over the site was a 24 hour marathon held on August 6-7, 1895. In later years such events would be completed by teams of two riders, cycling in relays. But in the Lower Grounds' event – the first of its kind ever run in the Midlands – each rider raced for himself, taking short breaks as and when needed.

Staged under a glowing necklace of electric lights, slung around the track, the race began at 8.15pm on the Tuesday evening. Each rider was spendidly attired in brilliant white, with a lamp on his bike to add to the drama. It is not known how many of the large crowd stayed at the track all night, but when the majority reconvened the following evening the winner was the remarkable Ben Winchurch of Birmingham, who managed to cover 421 miles and 1,380 yards in the allotted time, at an average of 17.6 miles per hour.

Remarkable? Most certainly, when you consider the quite enormous, stomach-churning quantitites of food and drink Mr Winchurch apparently consumed during his 24-hour stint on the saddle.

According the the BIRMINGHAM DAILY MAIL, this was Winchurch's 'very remarkable' recipe for victory:

Six chickens, two stewed shins of beef, 6 lbs of tomatoes, 5 lbs of grapes, 4 lbs of pears, a basket of apricots, 50 bananas, plus sundry eggs, jellies, custards and chocolate, all washed down by two 16 oz. jars of Bovril, a pint of port wine, a pint of sherry, champagne and milk.

Because Aston Villa would soon take over the Lower Grounds, and because so many accounts of its latter years paint a picture of steady and inexorable decline, it is tempting to conclude that the final years before 1897 must have been fairly grim.

Certainly, it is true that the Lower Grounds' golden era had passed, and that the gardens and buildings had lost much of their gentility and novelty. In both Aston and Birmingham were also many more theatres, music-halls and places of entertainment than had been the case in the 1870s and 1880s.

Yet, there continued to be full programmes of activities in the grounds and Great Hall right up until Villa's arrival in 1896, and in the Great Hall for some years after. If the LOWER GROUNDS COMPANY was losing money, therefore, it was losing it on a stubbornly regular and persistent basis.

Nor were the programmes any less varied. In March 1894, visitors saw Miss Nana Gilfort, suspended only by her teeth, slide on a 600 feet long wire from the top of the aquarium tower down to the gardens, 60 feet below, while representing a shooting star. 'This feat,' the audience was assured, had 'never been performed by any other lady or gentleman in the world.' And one could understand why.

In September 1896 – while Villa Park was being laid out – visitors to the Great Hall were also able to see Professor J. Bracken dive from the roof into a small tank, just like in the comics.

Henry Crawford appears to have put new life, if not new money, into the Lower Grounds. He maintained the weekly Sunday evening concerts which had begun in the early 1880s, despite occasional complaints of 'unseemly rowdyism' and, throughout 1893 and 1894, a long running dispute with the licensing authorities over Sunday trading laws. But the battle was well worth it. The concerts regularly drew astonishingly large audiences of 3-4,000, right up until at least 1896.

Crawford planned a cricket team at the Lower Grounds, which never materialised. He tried novelty games, such as ladies football, in March 1895, and a number of charity events, including a Salvation Army festival, and a football match between Aston Postmen and Aston School Board Officials in April 1893, which managed to bring in a crowd of 4,000. At another charity event, a sports day in aid of the Aston Poor Children's Holiday Fund, in July 1895, a ten-year-old boy, called Charles Summerfield, was knocked down and killed by a horse and trap. (Sadly, as we shall later discover, he would not be the last fatality at the ground.)

In short, the Lower Grounds may have ceased to be financially viable as pleasure grounds alone, but they were still an active and important part of both the Aston community and the Midlands sporting scene, right up until the moment that Aston Villa became the new tenants in 1896.

They were also, as mentioned at the beginning of this chapter, quite familiar to football fans, and to Villa fans in particular.

Reports suggest that the 'New Meadow' (as the ground was sometimes called during this transitional period of 1889-96) was not used for football until at least 1891, either because the turf was not in a playable state, or because Reeves-Smith, or even SPORT AND PLAY, were not keen on having the ground used other than for cycling or athletics.

This may explain why the 1890 Birmingham and District Cup Final – once a regular fixture at the old Meadow – was played at Perry Barr, even though Villa were the finalists (against West Bromwich Albion). Similarly, in April 1891, when Villa and Albion met again in the Birmingham Cup semi-final, the match was played at the County Ground, Edgbaston. The game itself ended in a draw, but so chaotic were the arrangements that the BIRMINGHAM FA was urged in the press to stage the replay at the Lower Grounds. Whether there were still doubts concerning the pitch, the facilities or, maybe, the rent, is not certain. But, in any case, the replay went to Molineux instead, as did the second replay.

(Incidentally, Molineux was very much the Wolverhampton equivalent of the Lower Grounds, being a former pleasure garden with a hotel attached, and which was now used primarily for cycling, athletics and football. Wolverhampton Wanderers had started renting it in September 1889, with a friendly against Villa.)

The first evidence of regular football being played on the New Meadow – that is, on the very same site as the current Villa Park pitch – comes in season 1891-92.

After the end of the cycling season in August 1891, for 12 days in September 1891, Buffalo Bill came back for his second *Wild West* stint at the Lower Grounds, together with the still sharp-shootin' Annie Oakley. Thereafter until the end of the season, a little-known Birmingham League team called Aston Victoria played their home games there on a regular basis. Although the Birmingham League would soon consist mainly of professional clubs or their reserve teams – including Singers (later Coventry City) and Aston Villa's second eleven – in 1891 there were still relatively minor clubs involved. So minor, in fact, that no record exists of how many spectators ever went to watch Aston Victoria's games.

In season 1893-94, another local club seems to have used the Lower Grounds on a reasonably regular basis. This was Lozells, who played in the Birmingham Junior League. There is also a report of a rugby match in March 1892, between Water Orton and St Mary's, who were, coincidentally, Aston Villa's first ever opponents back in March 1874.

But of course in the context of our story, the most intriguing matches to be played on the New Meadow concern the Villa.

Their first recorded appearance on the ground was for a *Theatrical Sports Day*, on February 16, 1892. Before the main match various Villa players competed in a 440 yards handicap race, won by the Scottish half-back James Cowan.

(Students of Villa's history will know that Cowan won another famous race, four years later. While the directors thought he was recuperating from a back injury, Cowan won the Powderhall Sprint in Edinburgh under an assumed name. For this he won £80, but for his duplicity he was then fined and suspended by the club for four weeks, although the board later relented.)

After winning his race at the Lower Grounds in 1892 Cowan then joined the rest of the Villa team to play a farcical match against a team of some 30-40 pantomimists, drawn from among the Birmingham theatrical set and dressed 'in a most comical fashion,' according to the ASTON AND EAST BIRMINGHAM NEWS. Fortunately for the Villa men the 'boisterous fun' was brought to an end after thirty goalless minutes.

Thus, bizarrely, began Villa's career on the site of what was soon to become their home, playing against an inept bunch of clowns and pantomime dames.

Small Heath were Villa's next opponents at the ground. This was for another charity match – the final of the Lord Mayor's Charity Cup – on May 6 1893. Villa won 3-2. The two rivals were fated to meet again in the same event two years later. But this time the circumstances were rather unusual.

# Main events at the New Meadow

❖ The following are some of the main events at the new Lower Grounds sports meadow, not including the annual Easter and Summer cycle meetings organised by SPORT AND PLAY, or numerous charity sports events.

1889    June 11-12... Cycling: new track opens on the site of the current Villa Park. 33,000 attend over two days.
        June 22... Athletics: first meeting on new ground, Birchfield Harriers.

1890    July 12... Athletics: 11th annual AAA Championships. James Kibblewhite wins three distance races. Harry Curtis breaks seven mile walking record.

1891    September... Buffalo Bill's second Wild West Show

1891-2  Football... first regular matches on New Meadow; Aston Victoria in the Birmingham League

1892    February 16... Villa make their first appearance at the new ground, in theatrical sports.

1893    March 18... Athletics: AAA 10 mile championship.
        May 6... Football: Aston Villa make their full debut at the ground, beating Small Heath 3-2 in Lord Mayor's Charity Cup Final.

1894    March 26... Cycling: re-laid track inaugurated.
        June 9... Cycling: NCU Championships, attended by 15,000.

1895    April 27... Football: Villa beat Small Heath 5-3 in Lord Mayor's Charity Cup Final.
        April 29... Football: WBA beat Villa 1-0 in Birmingham Cup Final, attended by 16,000.
        August 6-7... Cycling: 24 hour floodlit cycle race.
        August 31... Charity Sports: final major event before Villa move in.

1896    January... Lozells junior team play at ground as Villa's contractors move in. Easter cycling programme cancelled.

Villa cognoscenti will be aware that April 1895 was a hugely significant month for the club. On the field, Villa had an arduous programme.

On April 20, Villa made their third Cup Final appearance in nine years, at the newly opened Crystal Palace ground.

By an extraordinary coincidence, as in their previous two Cup Finals, both at the Oval, Villa's opponents in 1895 were yet again their neighbours from West Bromwich. As in 1886 Villa won, this time by just one goal, scored by John Devey.

The following Wednesday, Villa completed their League programme with a 2-2 draw at Perry Barr against Everton, thus confirming a final placing of third in the First Division. Three days later there then followed a repeat of the May 1893 game, the final of the Lord Mayor's Charity Cup, once again v Small Heath at the Lower Grounds. A tired, but happy Villa eleven won 5-3.

That gave them Sunday off, before on the Monday they were back at the Lower Grounds for their fourth game in eight days. This was the final of the Birmingham and District Cup when, lo and behold, who were they to face but the old foe from across Handsworth, West Bromwich Albion.

For the record, Albion won a dreadful game 1-0, while for Villa's exhausted players consolation came from a share of the £325 gate divided between the teams.

But the irony of this, Villa's third full game at the New Meadow, was that it was also the last time they would play there before the club's committee and members would meet for the most important decision in the club's 21-year history – whether or not to form a limited liability company and, if so, whether to move from Perry Barr and buy their own ground.

That historic meeting is fully covered in the next chapter. But for those committeemen already committed to the idea of moving into the Lower Grounds, the two games Villa played at the New Meadow in April would have served as a sobering reminder of just how much work would be necessary if the ground were to be made into a home fit for the holders of the FA Cup.

For the first game, against Small Heath, only three payboxes were opened to admit a crowd of several thousand, thereby causing havoc in the surrounding streets. Whatever arrangements SPORT AND PLAY usually made for the cycling fraternity, the football press were shocked to find their accommodation consisted of a table on the track. Kick-off was then delayed because the Lower Grounds management could not find a ball and then, to cap it all, the Small Heath players returned to their sparce dressing hut after their 5-3 defeat to find only one handbowl of water between them, and no soap! Villa's players were more fortunate. They were directed to changing quarters in the Holte Hotel.

Scenes of even greater chaos greeted the Villa on the following Monday for the game against Albion. This time some 16,000 fans turned up at the Lower Grounds, to see the previous week's Cup finalists do battle one more time. Once again, the entrances could not cope. Fences were broken down in the crush, thousands entered without paying (thus reducing the Villa players' share), but most seriously of all, boarding at the back of a small wooden stand at the Holte Hotel end gave way under pressure and sent several fans tumbling backwards on to the ground, ten feet below. Happily, none were seriously hurt 'beyond a severe shaking.' But it had been a close shave, and only confirmed that, if Aston Villa were to make the ground their new home, a considerable amount of reconstruction would be absolutely vital.

That summer would be the last for the New Meadow under the management of the Lower Grounds. The usual programme of cycling events took place, as always under the auspices of SPORT AND PLAY, and while Villa negotiated with the Lower Grounds owners in late 1895, the junior team, Lozells, continued to use the pitch, usually watched by a mere twenty or so onlookers.

Villa's hired contractors moved in a few months later, in early 1896.

A later resumé of the Lower Grounds' history, sketched in an issue of the VILLA NEWS AND RECORD in December 1924 – presumably by one who remembered the place in its prime – would make this comment upon Henry Quilter's once-proud pleasure resort.

'If the history of the big plot of land on which the Villa teams play and all its many "accessories" are included ever comes to be written, it will form quite a romantic tale, full of sporting and financial adventure.'

And so these opening chapters have proved. There are not many sports grounds which can claim to have been graced by champions in the field of cycling, athletics, cricket and football, nor even by the real heroes of the *Wild West*, or by opera singers, sharp-shooters, parachutists, acrobats, balloonists or pyrotechnists. And did we mention the Iroquois Indians who once came to the Lower Grounds to demonstrate their native sport of lacrosse? Alas not, nor, indeed, countless other daring acts and memorable events which could comfortably fill a volume all of their own.

To we world-weary, sophisticated consumers of the late 20th century – sated as we are by computerised imagery, digitised sound systems and hi-tech wizardry – much of what was on offer at the Lower Grounds during its hey-day might be regarded as tame, and even rather touchingly innocent.

But to the people of Aston, Birmingham and the Black Country, the 'Lower' was a place of fun and frolics, of high and low art, of modern marvels and ancient mystery, of repose and romance. It was both Alton Towers and the Botanical Gardens. It was a bit of Music Hall and a bit of Town Hall. It was a village green for Aston, and yet also the Wembley of the Midlands.

But then we should not grow too maudlin, for the Lower Grounds were by no means finished in 1896. Far from it; their most famous days had yet to come.

# Chapter 5

# Villa hire
# the Lower

WHENEVER THE GREATNESS OF ASTON Villa is expounded – and that can hardly be too often from our point of view – one can be fairly certain that the praise will be gilded by at least one reference to the Victorian splendour of Villa Park, even though precious little of the ground's Victorian legacy has actually survived into the modern era and the Queen's long reign would end within four years of Villa moving in. And yet the association is entirely understandable, for without doubt the 1890s were years of unparalleled success for Aston Villa.

One hesitates to say that Villa were the Manchester United or Liverpool of the day, since we naturally admit no sense of inferiority to these latter-day giants. But following on from the *Invincibles* of Preston in the late 1880s and Sunderland's *Team of All Talents* in the early 1890s, the Villa were unquestionably the first club in England to earn widespread fame for their achievements both on and off the pitch.

Held in particular awe as a powerful business entity, by all accounts Villa were also widely respected for their espousal of a stylish approach and a commitment to fair play. To put it crudely, at a time when professional football could often be rough and ready, and carry with it some fairly unseemly associations, Aston Villa had class.

Above all they also had a cupboard full of silverware. After losing in the 1892 Cup Final to the Albion, Villa went on to become League champions in 1894, 1896, 1897, 1899 and 1900, and were Cup winners in both 1895 and 1897. They also dominated the local competitions, in particular the Birmingham and Staffordshire Cups.

For a decade or so no England team was complete without a Villa man. The likes of Charlie Athersmith, Jimmy Crabtree, John Devey, Denny Hodgetts, Howard Spencer, Howard Vaughton, Fred Wheldon and Albert Wilkes all sported the three lions of England. James Cowan won honours with Scotland, while John Reynolds managed to earn caps for both Ireland and England.

From 1895-98 Villa drew gates larger than any other League club apart from Everton, and from 1898 until 1904 average crowds at Villa Park were consistently the highest in England.

Yet, at the outset of the 1890s, none of this could possibly have been foreseen. At the end of their second League season Villa were only saved from having to seek re-election by a technicality. The year after they were not so fortunate and had to enter a ballot with the likes of Accrington, Darwen and Newton Heath.

Recognising the need to put Villa onto a more businesslike footing, in January 1889 William McGregor proposed that the club be converted into a limited liability company. Small Heath had been the first club to take this step a few months earlier, and most of the major clubs would follow suit within the decade.

But in 1889 a majority of Villa's 382 members sided with the club president, James Hinks, and flatly rejected the idea. So opposed was the silver haired Hinks – who also sponsored Warwickshire CCC and Birchfield Harriers – that he even threatened to resign if Villa, as he put it, abandoned the principles of sport and turned themselves into a business. But while it was all very well for a wealthy man such as Hinks to decry McGregor's intentions, the fact remained that while the club remained tenants at Perry Barr on a short-term lease, and had precious few assets of their own, the strain and responsibility falling on the shoulders of committee members – all of whom were either small businessmen or men of limited means – was simply too much of a burden. Nor did the *status quo* allow the club to advance.

There was another setback for the modernisers in mid 1892, when an apparently innocuous motion at the Annual General Meeting was put forward to increase the yearly membership fees from 7s 6d to 10s 6d. The idea was to start a fund for the purchase of a new ground. Yet even this proved too radical for many members, and after a dead heat in the vote – 228 for and 228 against – the proposal was dropped.

Within a few months the cracks in the Villa set-up had widened into a chasm, leading to Fred Rinder's coup at Barwick Street in February 1893. But it was not only the ground issue causing divisions. For months, reported the BIRMINGHAM SPORTING MAIL, 'it had become quite evident that the affairs of the club

❖ *Villa President and prominent solicitor Joseph Ansell steered the club through the difficult negotiations with both the Bridge Trust School and Edgar Flower.*

were at sixes and sevens.' Other reports suggest that a clique of bar-room regulars among the twelve strong committee was disrupting activities and threatening indiscipline among the players.

After the Barwick Street showdown the committee was culled to a more manageable half dozen, with Rinder joining the committee and Josh Margoschis, the dapper little tobacconist, becoming chairman. An equally important change was the election of the much respected Joseph Ansell as club president.

Ansell would prove to be a formidable ally for the Villa. The son of the founder of the ANSELLS brewery, Joseph junior was an experienced solicitor, active in both the family business and in local political and social circles. Apart from offering legal skills and connections, Ansell's main contribution was to act as a negotiator between all the various parties with whom Villa would have to deal over the ground issue. Frustratingly for the committee, he was often far too busy to be at Villa's beck and call – hence the negotiations often took longer than they would have wished – but when it came to the crunch his diplomacy and legendary sense of humour must have soothed many a furrowed brow. In this respect he was the perfect foil for the more reticent and straightlaced Rinder.

Together, Rinder and Ansell would spearhead the two main thrusts of club policy between 1893 and 1896; namely, the formation of a limited liability company and the signing of a lease for the Lower Grounds.

In order to pursue both aims, a special Full Scheme sub-committee was set up under Ansell's chairmanship in June 1894, two months after Villa had secured their first League Championship.

At that stage, whatever the private hopes of the protagonists, it was by no means certain that Villa would leave Perry Barr or, if they did, whether the Lower Grounds would be their destination.

The latter option largely depended on the outcome of protracted talks with the owner of the Lower Grounds, Edgar Flower, who had recently become chairman of the family firm of FLOWERS & CO, the famous brewers of IPA in Stratford-upon-Avon. (There was, however, no actual business link between the brewery and the Lower Grounds. Rather, as explained in CHAPTER 3, Flower had inherited the property from his mother.)

The first indication that Flower was anxious to offload the property came in December 1894, when he invited the Villa committee to dine with him at the Royal Hotel in Birmingham. Thereafter, discussions continued on and off for over a year.

Meanwhile, similarly drawn-out talks were taking place with the BRIDGE TRUST SCHOOL over the club's lease at Perry Barr. Villa, it will be recalled, were unhappy, both at the annual rent of £200 and the fact that the Trust would not offer them a long term lease. (Incidentally, acting on behalf of the Trust were a Birmingham firm of solicitors, EDGE & ELLISON, who are not only still going strong in Edmund Street but have also acted for Aston Villa since 1971.)

As the negotiations with Flowers and the BRIDGE TRUST dragged on throughout 1895, Fred Rinder came increasingly to the fore. Clearly revelling in his new role he personally drew up minutely detailed plans of both the Perry Barr ground and the Lower Grounds site – sadly neither of which have survived – briefing the committee on the advantages and disadvantages of each. Not for nothing was he dubbed 'the architectural agitator'.

The first major hurdle to overcome occurred on May 24, 1895, a few weeks after Villa had won the FA Cup at Crystal Palace and played their two end-of-season games against Small Heath and West Bromwich at the Lower Grounds (referred to in the previous chapter).

This was the occasion of a Special General Meeting at the Masonic Hall in New Street, attended by around 260 of the club's 900 or so members.

By now, it would seem, most opposition to the idea of forming a limited liability company had fallen away. Nowadays we might say that the dissenters were swung by the 'feelgood factor' – Villa having just won the Cup – but there were compelling business reasons too.

Firstly, Villa had become, in the words of former president, James Hinks, 'a gigantic trading concern'. The balance sheets showed that their turnover had shot up since 1890 from £3,368 to £8,857, of which £7,603 derived from gate receipts alone. At the same time, however, expenses had in some cases doubled or even trebled, including the players' and staff wages, which now ate up 41 per cent of the club's total income. Providing the best team possible, it was reiterated, 'could only be done at enormous cost.'

(How little changes! In season 1995-96 total staff costs, including pensions and directors emoluments, amounted to just under 43 per cent of Villa's total income.)

Hinks now wrote an open letter to the meeting endorsing the incorporation scheme. Joseph Ansell, who took the chair, admitted that he too had once been opposed, but was now also strongly in favour.

But it was the Full Scheme Committee's report which made the strongest case. Essentially, this report stated, Villa had to take steps to secure their own ground as soon as possible. Other clubs had done so, and now Villa had to follow suit. Furthermore, not any ground would suffice. The Villa's new home would have to be 'worthy of our great club and the champion team of England.' It would also, said Rinder – no doubt with an eye on his potential detractors in the audience – need to offer much better facilities for the members than they currently enjoyed at Perry Barr.

None of this could come about unless a limited liability company was formed. Moreover, even if Villa remained at Perry Barr, the present committee members would find it hard to conclude a deal with the BRIDGE TRUST. This was because the Trust, rather than accept the club's seal as before, wanted individual committee members to act as personal guarantors of all rents and rates. That, clearly, was no longer a tenable arrangement for such a large

❖ Although Villa chairman Fred Rinder, a surveyor, would later claim much of the credit for planning Villa Park, its design was drawn up and its construction supervised by the architect, Edward 'Teddy' Holmes, who was already thoroughly familiar with the Lower Grounds as a senior official and regular judge for the Midland Counties AAA. He was also a keen cricketer and croquet player. But Holmes was best known as one of the leading lights of Moseley RFC, and for being a prominent rugby referee until he reached the age of 50, in 1909; this, despite his 'portly and aristocratic' stature and a lifelong penchant for 'a glass and a cigar.' Holmes was in practice with his architect father, and although they designed several substantial houses, offices and other public buildings in Birmingham, Villa Park - probably the least sophisticated commission in his portfolio - is the only work for which he has ever been remembered.

❖ Teddy Holmes submitted his plans for the Witton Lane Stand to the Aston Manor Urban District Council on January 4, 1897. This pitch side elevation shows the intricate detail of the three, arched central roof gables, a feature quite unique to Villa Park (although several other grounds, such as Ayresome Park and Anfield would later have one such central gable). The inspiration for this roof detailing might well have been Joseph Paxton's Crystal Palace, the glass and iron exhibition hall which stood next to the Cup Final ground inaugurated by Villa and Albion in April 1895. The stand would hold 5,500 seats on its rear tier, with a covered paddock for 4,500 standing in front. The clock on the central fascia board was fitted in August 1897. It measured 6 feet in diameter and cost 18 guineas, plus another guinea a year for the clockmaker to wind it up.

organisation. Thus the way forward to incorporation was agreed, but with one important proviso. The members were unhappy. Would they, or would they not, continue to enjoy the privileges to which they were currently entitled in return for their annual subscription (which now stood at 10s 6d)?

One can almost hear the impatient sigh emanating from the top table as the subject came up, a sentiment the GRASSHOPPER weekly newspaper echoed in its own report of the exchange.

'So, the Aston Villa members have agreed to accept the principles of a limited liability company, and now the committee are cudgelling their brains as to how best please about the most rapacious set of folk it has ever been our agony to listen to in an affair of this description.

'The value (members) want for a half-a-guinea is nothing short of stupendous,' scoffed the GRASSHOPPER. Whereas most ordinary fans paid their tanners week in and week out, any members attending all the matches to which they were entitled for 10s 6d would pay no more than about twopence a time on average.

But if the GRASSHOPPER considered the members' demands to be niggardly, nor was it impressed by the Full Scheme Committee's proposal for setting up the new company. This was, in brief, to launch a new Aston Villa company with a capital of £5,000, to be made up of 1,000 shares of £5 each.

First of all, complained the GRASSHOPPER, 'The details given are meagre in the extreme. Its looseness of language, its inconsequent ramblings, and vague generalities, are not calculated to draw money from the pockets of investors.'

To limit the new company to £5,000, the newspaper argued with uncanny prescience, would only require that even more money be raised in a couple of years. Instead, it recommended that the share capital should be upped to £20,000, with a further £10,000 raised in the form of debentures. That way Villa could buy the whole Lower Grounds and build a new ground all in one go. 'Besides, the Lower Grounds may not always be available as they are now,' it warned, adding that 'Why, the profits from the Holte Hotel would quickly pay off the debentures.' (In that respect, alas, times have changed.)

Only part of the criticism was heeded. Instead of issuing 1,000 shares of £5 each, the number was doubled to 2,000, thereby raising the capital to £10,000. But even that seemed a big enough challenge to be getting on with. In addition, the committee had other obstacles yet to overcome, not least of which were the continuing demands from the members.

On June 10, another Special General Meeting was convened to formally agree upon the winding up of the old club and the formation of a new company. This time only 70 members turned up, but those who did insisted that, regardless of any future share-holders' rights, their membership fees must be pegged at 10s 6d, and that, furthermore, they should be allowed entry to any part of the ground for which

an admission price of 1s 6d or under was charged.

After wearily consenting, the committee members then concentrated upon their next major meeting, to be held in private on June 26. Intriguingly, it would appear from the minutes of this meeting that the Lower Grounds was not the only site under consideration. Rather, there were several options, all of which the committee now reviewed.

For the benefit of our more fanciful readers – who may now enjoy a brief moment to ask 'what if?' – these were the sites vying for the honour of becoming Villa's permanent home:

OPTION ONE: Villa could still not rule out the existing ground at Perry Barr. However, Joseph Ansell reported that the BRIDGE TRUSTEES would not agree to the terms Villa had requested, that is, a 14 year lease at £200 per annum, plus an option for 21 years. When asked what terms they would approve, the Trust's response had merely been to offer a seven or nine year lease at £300. Ansell then asked them to state a purchase price for the site, to which the response was, he reported, 'a distinct negative.' In short, even if Villa were forced to stay put, Perry Barr was unlikely to offer a long term solution.

OPTION TWO: This was a site in Handsworth, described as being next to 'the old cricket garden' (or perhaps the Crick Lane gardens, since George Ramsay's handwriting and spelling were somewhat erratic). Its most likely location was an area to the east of the railway line which cuts through Handsworth Park (then called Victoria Park), just north of Holly Road. Josh Margoschis and Fred Rinder had been to assess the site and explained that it measured 206 x 130 yards, was convenient for both trams and rail, and was ready to be built upon straight away. The expected rental would be £300 per annum.

OPTION THREE: Four months earlier Villa had been approached by a Mr Martin, who had a site in Cuckoo Road. This had been rejected. But now another site in the vicinity was on offer, also at around £300 per annum. Fergus Johnstone reported back on this. It was, he said, 'a bit out of the way at Gravelly Hill,' was next to the canal – he did not specify which one (since there are two) – and the soil seemed both very damp and almost impossible to drain. If it was at the east end of Cuckoo Road Villa fans can be thankful this option was not chosen. A short distance away lay a huge sewage farm.

OPTION FOUR: The Aston Lower Grounds. Fred Rinder once again pulled out detailed plans and reported that Edgar Flower was now willing to grant a 14 or 21 year lease to the sports ground section of the grounds (that is, excluding the Great Hall, the bowling green on Trinity Road, the Holte Hotel and its two bowling greens). The proposed rental was £300 per annum, but in return for Flower

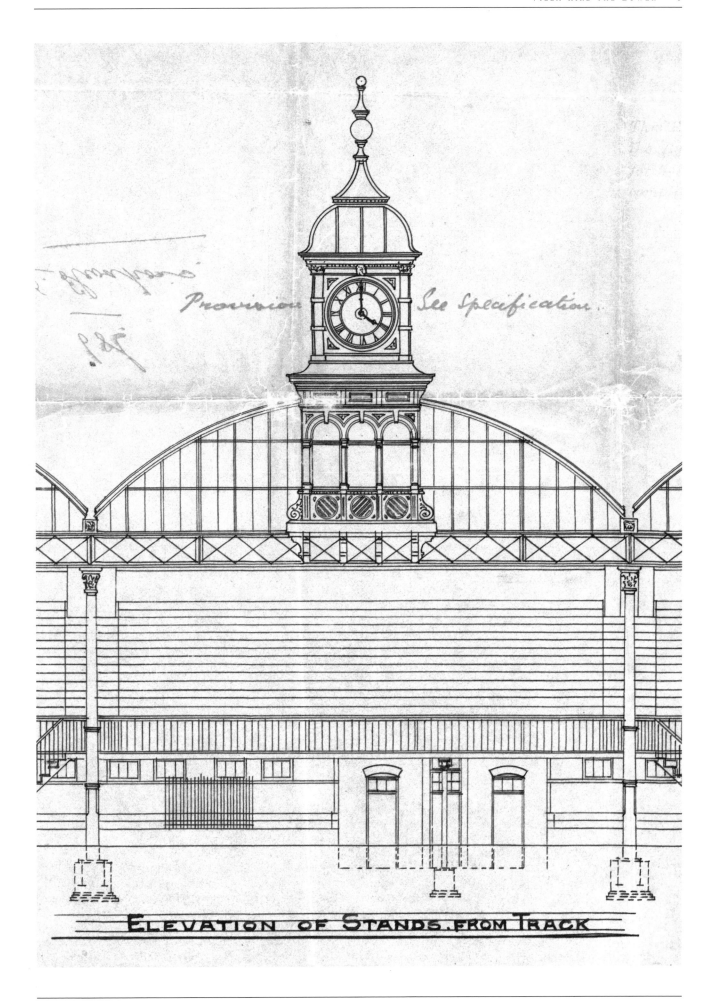

*Provision* ......................... *See Specification*.

ELEVATION OF STANDS. FROM TRACK

continuing to pay all rates and taxes, he would want to retain all rights to refreshment sales at the ground. An alternative offer was for Villa to buy the ground outright for £10,000. Rinder calculated that in order to accommodate around 50,000 people Villa would have to spend a further £4-5,000 on improvements. Another committee member, Isaac Whitehouse, said that if the Villa went to the Lower Grounds he had already been promised several donations.

OTHER OPTIONS: Three other sites had been considered but ruled out immediately and therefore not reported upon. These were said to be in the vicinity of Witton Lane, Bristol Road, and the Birmingham Racecourse, which had only opened twelve days earlier in Bromford. (The course lay just south of the River Tame, where Reynoldstown Road is now, and remained in use until 1965.)

There are no prizes for guessing which of the options was favoured. Accordingly, Edgar Flower was invited to meet the committee once again to hammer out the details of a lease, while at the same time, just in case, Ansell was asked if he would try to extract better terms from the BRIDGE TRUST. Clearly, no-one expected matters to move too quickly, however, because that same month Rinder was authorised to go ahead with the construction of another wooden stand at Perry Barr.

Poor Edgar Flower. Every time he or his son, Archibald, met with the committee the Villa officials appeared to bargain with him over every detail of the proposed lease. Would he lower the annual rent? Would he grant them an option to buy at a fixed price? Would he let them have an extra bit of the site? Would he concede full rights to sell advertising around the ground?

In most instances, happily, Flower did seem prepared to accord with their wishes, and within a month a detailed draft had been drawn up. He even agreed to advance the club a loan of £4,000 in the form of a debenture, in order to fund some of the necessary groundworks. All he asked in return was that Villa take full responsibility for any drunkenness at the ground – a bit rich that, coming from a brewer! – and do all within their powers to prevent gambling.

Thus the enticing path to the Lower Grounds was all but cleared by early September 1895. Surely no-one could stop the move now. Or could they?

For reasons which have never been explained, Joseph Dunkley – an otherwise active and willing Villa committee member since 1891 – spent the next four months doing everything he possibly could to prevent the deal with Flower going through.

Of course, one can understand that, like many fans, Dunkley was emotionally attached to the Perry Barr ground. Nor can he have been alone in fearing that Villa might be biting off more than they could chew. But can this really explain his persistence in the face of all odds? Even the usually well-informed GRASSHOPPER was baffled by his behaviour.

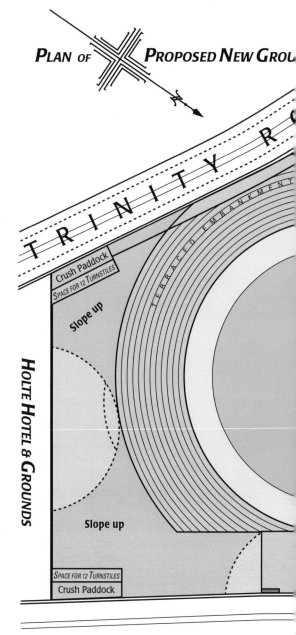

PLAN OF PROPOSED NEW GROU

'We don't quite know what to make of Mr "Joe" Dunkley, nor can we understand what motive it is that actuates him in his persistent opposition to the Villa going to the Lower Grounds. If he were the owner of the present land at Perry Barr or had a pecuniary interest in the surrounding pubs and shops, we could understand him using all his persuasive eloquence to induce the Villa to stop at Wellington Road.

'Why then this "thusness"? It seems to us either that he is troubled with a chronic liver complaint, and consequently, becomes so irritable that he can't agree with anything or anybody.' Either, speculated the GRASSHOPPER, Dunkley was 'a very much disappointed man' or, more likely, he had simply become 'impressed with his own importance.'

A balding, bearded man, little is known about

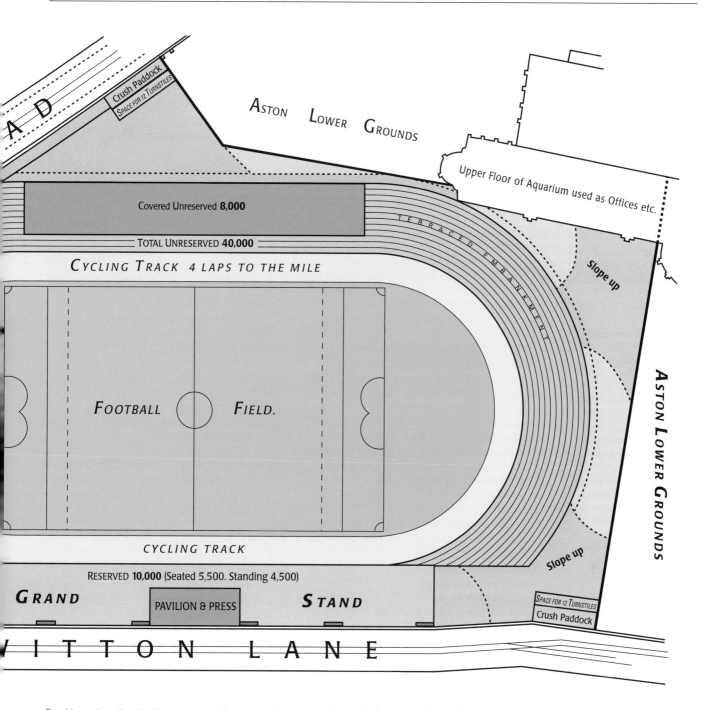

Dunkley, other than that he was an auctioneer, and appears to have had the support of only one other committee member – J. Kent – and a small but vociferous group of members.

His first intervention came in August, just as the final draft agreement with Flowers was being considered. Before it was finalised, he insisted, two other sites must be considered; the Aston Unity Cricket Ground in Trinity Road, and another unnamed site close by, owned by a Mr Bragg. On further investigation neither proved remotely suitable owing to covenants restricting their use. But his intervention wasted at least a week.

Undeterred, Dunkley next proposed that Villa should offer the BRIDGE TRUST an extra £100 per annum rental so that they could stay at Perry Barr. But if a few eyebrows were raised around the

committee table (accompanied by a few muttered oaths perhaps), surely Dunkley and Kent got the message when his motion was defeated by seven votes to two.

By October, Perry Barr's fate was all but sealed. Despite the ongoing installation of the ground's new ELLISON turnstiles, the committee ignored a late, but vague offer from the BRIDGE TRUST for slightly improved terms. Instead, Messrs Rinder, Margoschis, McGregor and Johnstone were delegated to complete the deal with Edgar Flower.

Yet once again Dunkley interceded. Armed with a letter of support from 26 members, he called another meeting at the Colonnade Hotel in New Street (where most committee meetings were then held), during which he demanded that the committee organise one further gathering of all the members to

❖ *Taken from the Holte Hotel end (as it was then known), this is the earliest known photograph of Villa Park, reproduced in the GOLDEN PENNY magazine of October 23, 1897, but clearly taken shortly before the April opening. When Villa Park opened, the Witton Lane Stand roof (right) was not yet completed, and nor would it be for some weeks, as the BIRMINGHAM DAILY MAIL reported on May 8 1897: 'Nothing is complete now without a strike of workmen, and the Aston Villa's new ground was the scene of one of those interesting little disputes. The men who were engaged in the task of putting the zinc roofing sheets on the top of the grand stand, hearing, doubtless, of the fabulous wages paid to footballers, and of the magnitude of the bonus to be received by members of the Cup team, were suddenly seized by a contempt for their humble earnings, and stopped work. The dispute was settled in a few hours, and the process of roofing went on, but to this day those roofers are regretting the choice of employment they made. There is not a man amongst them who doubts but that he would have been a Crabtree, a Cowan or an Athersmith, had he elected to kick a ball instead of wielding a roofing hammer.'*

vote on the new terms being offered by the BRIDGE TRUST.

By now the likes of Rinder and Ansell must have been holding themselves back from throttling Dunkley. Not even the members' representative on the committee saw fit to support him. Could he not see, McGregor explained, that the BRIDGE TRUST were 'playing with us?' They had only improved their offer after realising how intent the club was on moving to the Lower Grounds, and in any case, they were still refusing to give Villa an option to buy Perry Barr.

This time the vote against Dunkley was 13-2, at which point he refused to sign the agreement with Flower.

Seven weeks later he was still holding out, and also refusing to become a director of the new limited liability company. Even as the prospectus for the new company was being printed, he tried one more time to put Perry Barr back on the agenda, at a committee meeting in early December.

A weary Joseph Ansell said that he thought they had gone through all this before. But, ever the diplomat, he allowed a vote, which now totalled 15-2. And what did Dunkley do? He stormed out in protest of course, followed closely by Kent.

'We should have like to have had a snap shot of Mr Dunkley when he took up his hat and walked out of the room because he could not have his own way,' commented the GRASSHOPPER. 'He must have felt like a whipped child.'

But he clearly had not given up. Imagine therefore the reaction of the other committee members when, three days later, Dunkley turned up at their next meeting, waving a new letter from EDGE & ELLISON, which repeated the BRIDGE TRUST's offer of a seven year lease for Perry Barr at £300 per annum. In other words, no better or different than before!

George Ramsay's summary of the subsequent 'discussion' was a triumph of understatement.

Mr Dunkley, he wrote, was informed that he was obstructing the time of the meeting. He obviously had nothing new to report. Joseph Ansell did not wish to discuss the matter further. Mr Dunkley then retired, defeated at last.

So ended a curious, but time-consuming episode in the run-up to Villa's big move, although that was not quite the end of Dunkley's involvement. Clearly forgiven for his stubbornness, he was later elected a vice president of the club before he eventually emigrated to Australia. More than that we cannot add, other than to be grateful, over a century later, that Joe Dunkley's 'thusness' did not succeed.

On January 20, 1896, a new chapter in the history of the club began, with the first ever board meeting of the ASTON VILLA FOOTBALL CLUB LIMITED.

Nine men were present on this historic occasion. In addition to the secretary of the new company, George Ramsay − an associate of the Villa since its days in Aston Park − there was the newly elected chairman, Fred Rinder, plus the two former chairmen, William McGregor and Josh Margoschis, joined by the schoolmaster Charlie Johnstone (the former player and son of an early committee man, Fergus), Jimmy Lees (who became the new manager at the Holte Hotel), Isaac Whitehouse, Fred Cooper and a Mr F. W. Lloyd, who sat in as a representative of the members. Now, at last, the real business of moving could begin.

Firstly, it was agreed that once £1,000 worth of the shares had been purchased the agreement with Edgar Flower should be signed. This would not be far off, since 1,698 of the 2,000 shares had already been applied for. The actual terms of the agreement were excellent. Villa were to rent the Lower Grounds for £300 per annum, with a 21-year lease and an option to buy the site within that period at a cost of just 5s per square yard (or roughly £10,000 overall). If that seemed like a bargain in 1896, by the end of the 21 years it would surely be even better value.

Secondly, it was agreed that in order to make the Lower Grounds ready for action as soon as possible, rather than invite designs in an open competition, an architect should be appointed immediately. Two names emerged from the list of recommended men; Daniel Arkell, who had designed the Perry Barr grandstand, and Edward B. Holmes, who was based at Cobden Buildings, Corporation Street, and had designed several offices, houses and factories in the city (none of which have survived). The latter won the vote, even though, as far as we know, he had no experience of designing football grounds and had no previous connections with the club. On the other hand, everyone in local sporting circles knew Teddy Holmes. He was a prominent official of the Moseley Rugby Club at the Reddings, a rugby referee, president of the MIDLAND COUNTIES AAA, and as such, a regular judge officiating at athletics events at the Lower Grounds.

By March 1896 Holmes had drawn up his first set of plans, which, it was now agreed after anxious representations from SPORT AND PLAY, would include the provision of a new cycle track. Although this would add £1,000 to the overall costs, the potential rental would easily recoup this within a few years. In addition, by maintaining cycling at the Lower Grounds Villa could not be accused of breaking its longstanding traditions, or of depriving the city of a much needed facility.

It was also agreed that in order to accommodate the track the pitch would have to measure only 110 x 71 yards, which was smaller than at Perry Barr. (The current Villa Park pitch is 115 x 75 yards.)

One other decision was much less fathomable. Then, as now, the majority of sports ground designers would locate the most expensive seats on the west side of a ground, so that patrons do not have to face the afternoon sun. Villa, however, decided to build their main stand on the east, or Witton Lane side. On the Trinity Road, or west side, there would only be a simple cover over the banking. This banking would be continued around both ends of the ground, in front of both the Great Hall and the Holte Hotel.

Having approved Holmes' plans, the next step was to invite tenders for the first phase of the works; the relaying of the pitch, and the raising of the embankments for the track and terracing. This would cost £3,350 and be carried out by a building company called W. V. HOPKINS, based in Thorp Street. The same company had recently worked on the new Birmingham racecourse at Bromford.

At first all went smoothly, as reported by the ASTON AND EAST BIRMINGHAM NEWS, on May 30 1896, a few weeks after Villa had won their second League championship.

'The alterations to the Aston Lower Grounds are being pushed forward with vigour and despatch, and in the course of the next fortnight the drains will be laid down and the playing space re-turfed.'

The new ground's capacity would be approximately 50,000 (compared with around 16,000 before), with 12-15,000 in 'a huge stand' on Witton Lane and 7,000 under a cover on the opposite side.

The cycle track was to measure exactly 440 yards in length, as did the previous one, but would be banked more steeply on the bends and have a cement, rather than a cinder surface, which would consequently make it 'very fast indeed.'

The only drawback of all this work was that there would be no cycling or athletics during the summer

# Easter Saturday

❖ ASTON VILLA v BLACKBURN ROVERS

After winning the Cup a week earlier Villa were expecting a bumper crowd to witness their first ever game as tenants of the Aston Lower Grounds, v Blackburn Rovers, on Saturday, April 17, 1897. Unfortunately, the heavens opened, and refused to close all afternoon, sending the majority of a disappointing 14-15,000 crowd home drenched to the skin, including many who had made the trip from Blackburn. Nor did it help that the ground was clearly not finished, there being large sections of the stand roof not yet sheeted over.

But at least Villa kicked-off their new era with a flourish. Although there were no formal opening ceremonies – since Villa still hoped to stage a high-profile official opening – the eleven players who had won the Cup seven days earlier entered the field from the new Witton Lane Stand to an enormous roar from the crowd. This was shortly before four o'clock in the afternoon.

George Ramsay (pictured above) would later claim that he was the first Villa man to kick a ball on the new turf (which had been laid with help from Warwickshire CCC). There was also apparently a considerable rivalry between the players to see who would score the first goal. In the end this honour fell to another Scot, John Campbell (pictured below), who scored a fine individual effort early in the first half. His fellow countryman, John Cowan, added a second, to which a third was added after a break, an own-goal by the Rovers defender Edward Killean.

Apart from the 3-0 win, the local press was suitably impressed with the new Lower Grounds (as they would continue to be called officially for some

time). 'If it is ever finished,' commented the BIRMINGHAM DAILY MAIL, 'there will be no ground to equal it, save only the great enclosure at the Crystal Palace.'

But there were a few brickbats too. 'Many of the members have an uneasy suspicion that the excellence of the playing portion has been somewhat sacrificed for the sake of the cycling track.' This would be recurring complaint over the next decade, not only concerning the narrowness of the pitch but also the proximity of the hard, cement surface to the touchlines. The new drainage also came in for criticism, the pitch being covered in pools of rainwater.

And what of the fans? In those days, alas, the view from the terraces was seldom recorded. But we can readily imagine how strange, grand and yet alien the new quarters must have seemed – particularly owing to the distance of the terraces behind each goal and along the side lines – after the familiar intimacy of Perry Barr. Such is progress.

of 1896, the first time the Lower Grounds had been without a summer programme since Henry Quilter took over in 1864. Nor did it seem likely that Villa themselves would be able to move in until the end of the following season.

Why so long, when most of the preparatory work was finished by August 1896?

For a start, it would seem that the directors, but particularly Fred Rinder, as the only building professional on the board – he was a surveyor – had grossly underestimated the likely costs. When Teddy Holmes presented his plans for the next stage of works, essentially the building of the stands and the final fitting out of the ground, the estimate of some £9,000 was double what the board said they could afford.

None of this was aired at the first AGM of the new company on June 30, at the Masonic Hall. But it was clearly a matter of acute concern over the ensuing months, particularly when Hopkins priced up Holmes' plans at a total of £10,485, if all the work were to be completed 'in best style'.

Fred Rinder was the last man in Birmingham to accept anything less than best style, and so with

## Stabbing affray at Aston Lower Grounds...

❖ For two men in particular the opening match of the Lower Grounds was an afternoon they would both deeply regret. As reported in the ASTON & EAST BIRMINGHAM NEWS, after 20 minutes of the game 'a cry was raised among the crowd in the sixpenny enclosure' when it was realised that someone had been stabbed in the face. As a man was quickly taken out and conveyed to the General Hospital, bleeding profusely, two constables managed to wade into the crowd and arrest the assailant, whom they found lying on the ground being kicked and punched by indignant witnesses to the assault.

Identified later as Jabez Jackson, a painter who lived in Wheeler Street, it turned out that the attacker had been blind drunk and had not known or even spoken to his victim, a Mr Thomas Hodges of Berner Street. He had simply produced a broken pocket knife, turned round and stabbed indiscriminately at Hodges, lascerating his cheek and facturing his jaw.

When Jackson woke up in his police cell the following day, himself bruised and bloody after his mauling by the crowd, he claimed not to remember anything of the incident. He was, nevertheless, found guilty and charged.

several weeks now having been wasted, he and Holmes went on a spying trip to Bramall Lane. Their aim was to compare Sheffield United's costs of £2,250 for a stand holding 5,300, with Hopkins' projected costs for the Witton Lane Stand, priced at £3,820 for 4,800 spectators.

This visit convinced both men to proceed with the more expensive option. In their opinion the Sheffield stand did not represent good value, did not function well, and had 14 columns restricting views, compared with only six in Holmes' plan.

On his return, Rinder raised the idea of Villa seeking an additional loan from Edgar Flower of £7,500. Exactly as the GRASSHOPPER had predicted, the new company had been under-capitalised. At the same time, no fewer than 19 contractors were invited to submit tenders for the stand construction and for its roofing.

Once again Hopkins came in with the lowest tender for the construction, as one would expect of a company already on site and with a close knowledge of the club. Or was it just an extraordinary coincidence that their bid of £7,698 was exactly £1 lower than their nearest rivals? Even then Villa still managed to haggle them down another £48! They did the same to the successful roofing contractor, E. S. KEAY, who were asked to round down their price of £3,265 to £3,000. KEAYS compromised at £3,165. Clearly, every penny counted.

So the final phase of works began, just as the winter of 1896 set in, while the Villa directors called an Extraordinary General Meeting to persuade the shareholders to sanction the borrowing of extra funds. This vital meeting took place at the Colonnade Hotel on January 20, 1897.

Assuring the large assemblage of shareholders and members that the Lower Grounds would be 'one of the finest football and cycling enclosures in the kingdom,' Fred Rinder explained that unexpected difficulties had been encountered. When he went on to say that the final estimate for the work would amount to around £14,000, there were cries of 'Oh' and 'Phew' from around the hall. As well there might be. That was double the original estimate.

'Originally it was intended to erect only wooden stands and structures on the ground,' said the report of Rinder's speech in the BIRMINGHAM DAILY GAZETTE. 'But after due consideration, and in the possible event of their purchasing the freehold, the directors thought it better to build more substantial structures of wood and iron, especially as they were providing accommodation for between 40,000 and 60,000 spectators.'

Rinder went on to explain that when work on the new ground had started in early 1896, the building trade had been going through a lean time (as indeed had the whole British economy). But now things had picked up, so prices had risen. There had also been several unforeseen expenses, such as the necessity of erecting much thicker and stronger brick retaining walls than had originally been envisaged.

One of the new directors, Charlie Johnstone, added that delays to the building work – and the

Views of the New Track at Aston.    Scene of the Great Easter Tournament

opposition they had encountered (by which he must have meant from Dunkley) – had meant that rather than opening the new ground the previous August, the likely inauguration would now take place on March 13, for the Villa v Liverpool League match. This loss of potential income had cost Villa as much as £3,000.

Coming to the point, Rinder proposed that in order to cover all these extra costs, the shareholders agree to allow the directors to borrow an extra sum of up to £10,000 to finish the job.

One or two of the shareholders were not best pleased by this. The sum of £10,000 represented the exact value of the company, barely a year after its launch! Thus they demanded precise figures and an explanation of why they had not been consulted before the extra work had been authorised. But by the end of the evening every question had been answered and every temper cooled, leaving Rinder and Co to breathe a huge sigh of relief as the resolution was 'enthusiastically carried'.

There would still be disappointments and more delays to come, nevertheless. Apart from continuing bad weather, a new Clerk of Works had to be appointed after the first one could not be persuaded

to stay by an offer, from a clearly anxious Holmes, of an extra ten shillings a week (to be paid out of his own pocket).

The directors were also miffed when the FA refused to grant Villa the right to stage the England v Scotland game on April 3, 1897. The FA argued, with some justification, that it was too important a fixture for a ground which had never been used before.

One important matter was resolved, however. After meeting with various interested parties, Villa signed a seven year deal to rent out the new cycle track to their old friends at SPORT AND PLAY, at £200 a year, plus a percentage of receipts. Thus Villa would recoup most of their rent, and there would remain a strong link between the New Meadow of old, as it were, and the Villa Park of the future.

Meanwhile, as Villa prepared to pack up their bags at Perry Barr, progress at the Lower Grounds continued to be slow. Officially the delay was down to bad weather. But behind the scenes Villa were now clearly furious with Holmes. Every few weeks the board would despatch a letter, urging him to speed up. One missive asked him to stop the building workers walking all over the new turf.

But to the majority of Villa fans, excited or anxious

❖ 'The enclosure now resembles nothing so much as the crater of a volcano, the green meadow, bounded by the broad grey band, forming the bed.'
So enthused BICYCLING NEWS on the day of Villa Park's opening. These photographs show how the Witton Lane Stand was almost completely open to the elements, while those fans under the Trinity Road's barrel-shaped roof could 'gather like chicks beneath the wings of their mother.' The cycle track, though apparently smooth, had actually been brushed by a domestic broom as it set, in order to improve the grip. For the terrace fans, six miles of timber footings had been dug in to create the steps.

though they may have been about the move, events on other pitches proved far more compelling.

By a glorious coincidence, the 1896-97 season was turning out to be Villa's best ever, with a scintillating – and highly profitable – run of games reaching a climax as the new ground's opening day approached. Already in a commanding position at the top of the League, on March 10 the team beat their old rivals from Preston in a second replay of their Third Round Cup tie, at Bramall Lane. Three days later, on the afternoon the new ground had been scheduled to open, Villa drew 0-0 with Liverpool in the League at Perry Barr, followed a week later by another meeting of the teams for the FA Cup semi-final, again at Bramall Lane. This time Villa cruised home 3-0, to reach their fourth Final. Oh happy days!

But then a slightly misty-eyed one. On March 22 Perry Barr staged its last ever League match. With the game being played on a Monday and Villa now virtually guaranteed the title (being several points clear of their nearest rivals, Sheffield United and

Derby), only 8,000 or so fans bothered to turn up, compared with their average that season of around 13,000. Bolton then prepared to ruin Villa's farewell by defending a 2-0 lead until the last half hour. But Villa were not Double contenders by chance, and in a devastating finish they pounded the Bolton goal relentlessly, to end their 21 years at the ground with a crushing 6-2 win.

After beating Bolton again in the return League fixture five days later, Villa then sent a weakened XI to inaugurate the new Eastville ground of Bristol Rovers on April 3, before heading off to Crystal Palace for their crowning moment, the Cup Final against Everton.

No need to dwell here on the magnificence of that epic Final. Other volumes have done it much greater justice. Suffice it to say that on a cold day and in front of a record Final crowd of 65,891, Villa emerged as 3-2 winners, and were thus able to return to Brum as both League champions and Cup winners – the first team to secure the Double since Preston in 1889 (and the last to do so until Tottenham's triumph in 1961).

No scriptwriter, other than perhaps one with experience of working on *Roy of the Rovers*, could have conjured up a greater build-up to the opening of the new Lower Grounds. And so, at long last, the great day dawned.

Strictly speaking, the ground was being re-opened, rather than used for the first time, since it had already been in use for cycling, athletics, football and other events between June 1889 and early 1896.

But try telling that to the likes of Fred Rinder, William McGregor, George Ramsay, Joseph Ansell and, lest we forget, even Joe Dunkley.

Until April 1897, Aston Villa had been a great club playing on a cosy meadow with a handful of wooden stands. Now they were about to take possession of one of the most advanced sporting arenas in Britain, and therefore in the world.

Aston Villa were about to become an institution.

❖ *The BIRMINGHAM MAIL advertises Villa Park's first games and the very last one at Perry Barr.*

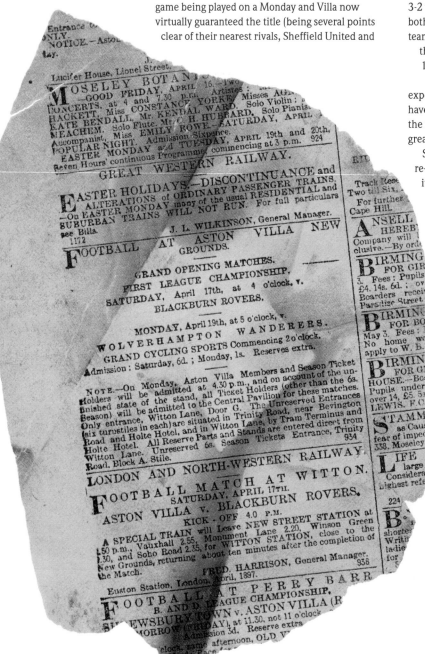

# Easter Monday

❖ Two days after the opening match against Blackburn, the Lower Grounds staged its first major double-header; a SPORT AND PLAY cycling tournament, followed by Villa' s final League match of the season, against Wolves. For the cycling fraternity the day signalled not so much the opening of a football ground as the re-opening of an already well established venue.

This time the weather was fine, though windy, as a crowd, variously estimated at between 30-40,000, started arriving long before the start, clearly undeterred by the admission price of one shilling (which was double the usual sixpence charged both at Perry Barr and Villa Park for ordinary games).

'What a magnificent re-opening of the Lower Grounds! What splendid reward for much work, waiting and anxiety,' declared BICYCLING NEWS (which now incorporated SPORT AND PLAY).

'Thirty thousand spectators lined the athletic enclosure, whose equal Great Britain cannot produce, and cheered with unbounded enthusiasm the grand programme of sport placed before them. Never before has the famous old ground, whose transformation is compete, witnessed such a soul-stirring scene.'

BICYCLING NEWS reckoned that the attendance of around 35,000 (paying receipts of £1,375) was the 'largest that has ever been known at any meeting held in Europe.' If true, it was also by far the largest ever to have watched a Villa home match, which must surely have given Messrs Rinder and Co. a warm glow of satisfaction after the long wait to move from Perry Barr.

(They might also have noted that for the following day's cycle racing, when there was no football to be seen, only 15,000 attended. But even that compared extremely favourably with cycle meetings held elsewhere in Britain during 1897.)

The day's proceedings began at 1.00pm, with the first winner on the new track being Ellis Bradshaw, a member of the Midland Cycling and Athletic Club. But this was no local affair. Such was its importance in the cycling calendar that riders came from all over Britain, and from Belgium, Holland, New Zealand and France. All were said to be full of praise for the speedy new track, even if an early tumble by one of the riders suggested they would need time to adjust to its cement surface and banked-up corners.

But whether the track was to blame for the worst accident of the afternoon is almost impossible to determine.

The final race of the day, begun about 45 minutes before Villa and Wolves kicked off at 5.00pm, was the ten-mile event for professionals. Sixteen riders started, but only six finished. Three riders fell during the 26 minute race, each of whom was shaken but suffered only minor injuries. Tragically, the popular Aston born rider, Bert

## Renewal of the 'Sport and Play' Tournaments

## Record Gate at the Aston Lower Grounds

## 30,000 Spectators Present

## BAD ACCIDENT TO A. W. HARRIS

Harris, then based in Leicester, was not so fortunate.

As the riders sped round the banked-up corner between the Trinity Road enclosure and the Witton End, with only ten or so of the 40 laps completed, Harris's front wheel clipped the rider in front. His tyre burst, became entangled in his forks and Harris was sent headlong onto the track.

'A sharp shout of apprehension and horror ascended from that immense throng,' reported BICYLING NEWS, followed by a 'huge sob of sympathy and shock which welled up from thousands of throats when the writhing form of Harris was recognised.'

Blood was now pouring from the fallen rider's right ear, and as the race continued – to be won eventually by Paul Nossam from Paris – Harris's limp, unconscious form was conveyed to the General Hospital in a private vehicle. (Appallingly, the organiser had not arranged for a single ambulance to be on duty that day.)

Fifteen minutes later, Villa and Wolves kicked off. Villa scored five, and yet again kept a clean sheet on their new home turf. But as the crowds dispersed that sun-baked evening, many of them no doubt weary after standing on barrier-less terraces for nearly seven hours, there could be no doubt that the chilling image of Bert Harris, laying bloodied and lifeless on the track, had cast a dark shadow across the entire afternoon.

When the next issue of BICYCLING NEWS hit the news stands on the following Wednesday, Harris was reported to be in a critical condition. But he had in fact died that very morning. Since the accident he had regained consciousness only momentarily. Seeing him stir in his hospital bed, his friend and fellow cyclist Will Jordan had chided him gently, 'Pull yourself together, Bert.'

Harris apparently murmured, 'Will, I am beat.'

# Bert Harris... racing hero

❖ The fatal accident of young Bert Harris at Villa Park on Easter Monday, 1897, was arguably one of the most traumatic event to beset British sport in the late Victorian era. Considering its inherent dangers, cycling had a reasonably good track record, with three fatalities recorded during the 1890s, hardly fewer than for football or rugby. But Harris was widely acknowledged as a model sportsman. His boyish enthusiasm and generosity towards other riders had won him friends all over Europe, and particularly in Birmingham.

Indeed, he had grown up only a stone's throw away from the track where, as chance would have it, he both started and ended his career.

Born in Aston in April 1874, only a month after Aston Villa were formed, Harris's first public race had been on the old Meadow in 1888, when he sensationally won a handicap race as a precocious 14-year-old. He remained a regular at the Lower Grounds' new track during the early 1890s – by which time he had moved to Leicester – until a controversial crash in Cardiff, blamed on other riders, nearly terminated his career in 1895. Since then he had suffered from bouts of dizziness and had not yet returned to form. The Easter Monday meeting was therefore an ideal opportunity to revive his professional career in front of friends and family.

The day brought him mixed fortunes. He nearly missed his first race, and had to be called by telephone from the dressing rooms to the starting line-up. Arriving on the track in his unlaced pumps he then proceeded to win his first heat comfortably. Then in his second race he burst a tyre, and had to ask around for a spare wheel so that he could enter the fateful ten mile event. How the unfortunate rider who lent Harris that wheel – the one whose tyre burst – must have rued his generosity.

But as it transpired the true cause of the accident was never established. One possible explanation was that Harris had only recently switched to a more highly-geared BEESTON HUMBER, and was perhaps unused to its feel in tight situations. He was certainly not known as a reckless rider. It was even possible that he had suffered a blackout – the legacy of his Cardiff spill.

Might Harris have survived had he fallen on a cinder, rather than on a cement track? THE BIRMINGHAM GAZETTE clearly thought so, because on the very day of the accident its football correspondent warned, 'I see the possibility of a rather serious accident should a player be thrown violently onto the track.' But the coroner said nothing of the track, and instead gave a verdict of accidental death. And certainly it was true that no further serious accidents would occur, and that most of the tracks being laid around Britain in 1897 – at Celtic Park and Herne Hill for example – were of a similar design and made of cement.

Nevertheless, a day which should have been the cause of so much celebration was forever tainted by this painful, and all too public tragedy. A local lad now lay buried in Leicester and, for once, the life-affirming joy of sport found itself humbled by the fleeting whim of fate.

# Chapter 6

# Early Days at Villa Park

BIRMINGHAM DURING THE 1890s WAS truly a city to behold; not only 'the workshop of the world,' but thanks to the creed of Municipal Socialism fathered by the great Liberal Mayor and MP, Joseph Chamberlain, also 'the best governed city in the world' (according to one American visitor at least). And now, in Aston Villa, the city could boast the greatest football club in England – the Double winners – and at the Lower Grounds, one of the best football grounds also.

Apart from this new beginning for Villa, other events in 1897 suggested that great change was on the horizon. Amid the lavish celebrations of Queen Victoria's Golden Jubilee lingered a recognition that, at the age of 78, the old Queen would be unlikely to lead Great Britain far into the new century. Nor was the future of her Empire guaranteed. There were threats from Afghans on the North West frontier, and from Boers in South Africa.

Closer to home, many of Aston's leading citizens were still fighting to retain the area's identity, and although in 1903 they succeeded in attaining the status of a borough, independence lasted only eight years before Aston was finally absorbed into the body politic of metropolitan Birmingham.

Meanwhile, no border could halt the spread of a new publication called the SPORTS ARGUS. This hit the streets in February 1897 and has been out there ever since. A couple of weeks earlier, in the Burlington Hall on Aston's High Street, a pioneer of cinematography put on the area's first ever film show (featuring three shorts on the Henley Regatta, the 1895 Derby and 'Rough Seas at Dover'). Many locals

also saw their first motor cars in 1897, exhibited at Bingley Hall and paraded around the city centre streets to a mixed reaction of amusement and amazement. Little did anyone realise then just how overwhelmingly the economy and geography of the city would be shaped by these curious horseless carriages.

The opening of Villa's new ground also came at a time of developing social provision. The new General Hospital in Steelhouse Lane was opened in July 1897. The first public conveniences for women were opened in Old Square. Plans were drawn up for a lunatic asylum at Rubery. Yet such was the homeless problem that the Birmingham Workhouse had to be extended to accommodate the growing number of male and female 'tramps', as they were then termed. There were debates too about the numbers of children leaving board schools without a proper education.

Villa's own domestic problems were, of course, of a rather more mundane nature; packing up their belongings from Perry Barr and spending the summer getting their new home ship-shape for the following season. Apart from having to finish the construction work, this meant setting up new offices.

As mentioned earlier, since Christmas 1892 the club office had been located at 127 Albert Road, where there were also meeting rooms and a billiard room for the players. These would remain in use until July 1897, while new offices and club rooms were made ready in the Lower Grounds' main aquarium block, now split into two sections. The northern half of the building, plus the skating rink, the Great Hall, the formal gardens and Rustic Cottage remained the property of Edgar Flower, who continued leasing them to the ASTON GROUNDS COMPANY as the LOWER GROUNDS COMPANY was now called. Villa rented the upper storey of the southern half of the complex, mainly consisting of the former dining rooms and verandah nearest the Witton End terracing.

Though undeniably grand and spacious compared with their former quarters, Villa's new club rooms must have filled their new tenants with a mixture of awe and dread; awe at the thought of how mighty an organisation Aston Villa must now have become in order to occupy such a splendid, if incongruous set of buildings, yet dread at the prospect of making them seem like home after the club atmosphere of Albert Road and Perry Barr. It is also possible that many a Villa man recalled visiting those same rooms at the height of the Lower Grounds' popularity, perhaps to dine, take tea, or simply to stroll through with friends to the balcony overlooking the gardens and the Magnificent Meadow of yore. As they surveyed their new surrounds did they, perchance, fancy they could hear the echoing sounds of laughter, chinking plates and glasses, or even the ghostly roar of one of the lions which, only a few years earlier, had been caged in the aquarium below?

Partly palatial, partly forsaken, never were there football club headquarters quite like it. As the VILLA NEWS AND RECORD would later describe the scene so poignantly, the Lower Grounds had become

❖ *Never were there football club headquarters like it. This was the southern entrance of the former Aquarium building into which Villa moved their offices (onto the upper floor) in August 1897. Behind this frontage was the MINERAL WATER MANUFACTORY (which was converted into a ticket office in 1969) and the 200 foot long promenade which once housed the aquarium and later became Villa's gymnasium. The skating rink lay immediately behind the single-storey extension to the left. After the building was demolished in 1981, the wall on the right was the last remnant of the Lower Grounds to survive, just in front of the west flank of the North Stand.*

'unkempt and a little unholy as if "Ichabod" had been written over the portals.'

But not all the glory had departed, at least, not just yet. Even if Henry Quilter's gardens and greenhouses in front of the Great Hall were now sadly threadbare, the Hall itself remained in use, as of course did the Holte Hotel.

Nor had the ASTON GROUNDS COMPANY thrown in the towel entirely. Villa director and long-time club activist Jimmy Lees – a rotund man who apparently reacted to any Villa defeat like a sulking child – became the company's new manager, and, following in the footsteps of Messrs Quilter, Reeves-Smith and Crawford, moved in to the Holte Hotel.

A new-look Holte it was too. At the same time as Villa Park was being developed, £2,000 was spent on upgrading the hotel's frontage and improving its facilities. Lees also continued the tradition of Sunday concerts in the Great Hall, and for the summer season of 1897 built a large new dancing platform in the gardens (even if the once romantic vista over the ornamental lake was now replaced by the earthen rear of the Witton End banking). As the ASTON NEWS optimistically reported in June 1897, 'There is no doubt that Mr Lees intends to still popularise the already popular Lower Grounds as a resort for holiday makers.'

Behind the new boundary walls of the football and cycle ground, meanwhile, Villa started to settle down. They built a strongroom within the new office area, to contain a safe and, following the embarrassment of 1895, their precious League and Cup trophies (which a bank stored in the interim).

The directors also authorised the purchase of a horse-drawn mower and heavy roller for the pitch. Having decided that the old Perry Barr pony was not up to it, they then bought a new horse, for £10. Since the old groundsman Williams had been left behind at Perry Barr as well, and the Lower Grounds turf had been laid and tended so far by advisers from Warwickshire CCC, it was also necessary to place advertisements for a new groundsman, one preferably with a wife who would be willing to keep the offices clean. An incentive to prospective applicants was that Fred Rinder proposed to build a small house for this couple. According to the ASTON NEWS, hundreds of people applied for the job, including many unemployed clerks and post office

*❖ A studious George Ramsay sits at the board room table, in part of the former restaurant above the aquarium. The ornate, dark mahogany cupboard on the right is still in the club's possession, as is the framed photograph of the 1896-97 Double winners, seen here above Ramsay's desk.*

workers who 'knew as much about managing a football ground as a city banker or a draper.' In the end the job went to a Mr Ruben Leeson.

Fred Rinder was constantly on the go throughout the summer, checking this, measuring that, always finding faults and suggesting remedies. But it was just as well Villa had such an expert to hand, because after the best part of 15 months on the site, the contractors had still not finished. A board minute of June 1897 summed up the mood of impatience. It read, 'Resolved (that) a strong letter of complaint as to the laxity and procedure be sent to Mr Holmes.' How old Teddy, the arch amateur sportsman himself, must have cursed Villa's urgency when he was back among his cronies at the Reddings, especially after Rinder tried to speed up matters by inviting tenders for some minor works from other contractors – a practice which Holmes complained haughtily was 'a breach of etiquette' while HOPKINS were still on the site.

Yet the sheer amount of basic work still to be done suggests that between them, Holmes and HOPKINS were either incompetent or painfully slow, or equally possible, that Holmes' or Rinder's original specifications were just plain inadequate. (In defence of all parties, however, it should be remembered that ground design in Britain was still very much in its infancy in 1897, so there were hardly queues of experts waiting to be consulted, as there would be a century later.)

Whatever the excuse – and bad weather seems to have been the favourite one – as late as mid August, a fortnight before the new season, Rinder was still ordering apparently routine tasks to be completed; the fixing of locks on external doors, glazing the ends of the stand, attaching fascia boards along the stand

roof, putting signs up on all entrances and installing more ELLISON turnstiles (in addition to the 18 already brought from Perry Barr).

To complicate matters, while all these tasks were being attended to, the ground remained in regular use for cycling and athletics meetings throughout the summer. Indeed 1897 was something a golden year for cycling in Britain. Apart from Villa's new track there would be major cycling races staged at Burnden Park, Crystal Palace and Wood Green, and at brand new tracks at Celtic Park, Nottingham, Herne Hill and Putney.

After the inaugural Easter Monday and Tuesday events, there were at least ten further race meetings at Villa Park during the summer of 1897, enough to amount almost to over-exposure. Predictably, attendances varied. An estimated 13,000 saw the prestigious annual National Cycling Union championships on July 17, and on August 28 there were 10,000 for the annual Birmingham Charity Sports, at which there were more fearful spills on the track, but fortunately no serious injuries. Other meetings drew only a few thousand, however, including one double-header on September 11 which featured a SPORT AND PLAY race card from 2.30pm to 5.00pm, followed by Villa Reserves v Worcester Rovers in the Birmingham League, watched by 4,122. An even smaller crowd turned up to see Villa's own annual cycling and athletics carnival, an event which had been firmly established at Perry Barr, and in 1897 would yet again be dominated by the athletic prowess of former player and now director and schoolmaster, Charlie Johnstone.

Apart from these public events, the new track was also in use almost every day, since, as was the custom

❖ *A mixed crowd of mainly girls and boys gather on the Holte End for a sports day in mid 1898.*

❖ *In common with most clubs of the period, Villa faced a constant battle to keep their more errant players out of the pub for as long as possible. These recreations rooms were their answer, although the club still had to ban all card games in 1906 after a heavy bout of gambling. George Ramsay asked members and shareholders to donate books and magazines for the enjoyment of the team, but quite how many of them were read when the billiard table was only a few feet away is another matter altogether.*

before 1896, cyclists could buy a summer's training season ticket (now priced one guinea). As before, Fred Hughes, the old starter from the days of the Magnificent Meadow, was appointed to superintend the track on a day-to-day basis.

In short, the new ground was in constant use from day one, which though excellent in terms of its profile and profitability – especially to Villa, who earned £500 from cycling over the summer – cannot have helped the contractors to complete the construction work nor allow the turf time to settle.

Nevertheless, the club continued to enjoy a close and fruitful relationship with their new sub-tenants at SPORT AND PLAY.

Although the magazine SPORT AND PLAY had merged with the long established BICYCLE NEWS in 1895, the Lionel Street printing company which produced it – SPORT AND PLAY LIMITED – was at that time going from strength to strength, having been launched as a limited liability company a few weeks before Villa Park's opening. Villa bought £10 worth of shares, while one of the company's new directors was the club president, Joseph Ansell.

Connections with the club were further strengthened in September 1897 when SPORT AND PLAY LTD started printing 'an interesting bijou newspaper' called the VILLA TIMES. Costing one penny, the weekly publication was probably an early form of match programme. Sadly, only a small fragment from one issue has survived, so we know precious little of its 'bijou' content, and it would not be until September 1906 that the club began producing match programmes as we know them today.

Just as important as the business relationships were the personal and local connections. Nowadays Villa's directors, players and personnel all drive to Villa Park from addresses scattered around the city and the West Midlands. But in 1897, before the age of the motor car and the motorway, the focus was very much upon Aston. Villa's chairman Fred Rinder lived in Aston Lane, George Ramsay in Trinity Road, and William McGregor in Witton Road. Most of the players lived locally too, as did several leading sports writers. For example, John Urry of BICYCLING NEWS lived in Frederick Road, Edwin Cox in Sycamore Road, and Charles Wheelwright, one of the co-founders of SPORT AND PLAY and a leading official in cycling and athletic circles, lived a few doors down from Villa's former office in Albert Road. Almost opposite was the house of the NATIONAL CYCLING UNION's local representative.

For these men, who ate, drank and celebrated together (many of them as fellow Freemasons), passed each other both in the streets and in committee rooms, railway stations, hotels and sports grounds across the country, the wonderful new ground now in their midst must have seemed like the centre of the universe. It was, in a very real sense, the hub of their existence.

After the summer of cycling and athletics, Villa returned to action there on September 1, netting five against Sheffield Wednesday – including the

ground's first hat-trick, by Fred Wheldon – but conceding two, the first opposition goals to be scored at Villa Park in a senior game. It had been hoped to invite the FA President Lord Kinnaird to perform a ceremonial opening for the ground on the following Wednesday, when West Bromwich Albion were the visitors. But Kinnaird was not available, and so missed another Wheldon hat-trick in a thrilling 4-3 victory, watched by just under 21,000.

Not that the good Lord was ever likely to do the honours, at least not after October 1897, when Villa flouted certain FA regulations in order to sign a new goalkeeper, Billy George; a misdemeanour which earned them a £50 fine, a severe ticking off, and month-long suspensions for the player, for George Ramsay and for Fred Rinder. But then Rinder was

often in trouble with the authorities during this period, particularly for his vociferous opposition to the concept of a maximum wage for players.

(As for the 'Diamond' Wheldon, who was otherwise famed for playing in tartan golf socks and being an ace batsman for Worcestershire, he clearly loved his new home turf so much that he scored in every one of Villa's first nine home matches of the season, ending up with a remarkable tally of 23 goals in 26 appearances.)

Having failed to lure Lord Kinnaird, the board then considered organising a celebratory dinner to mark the opening. But this too failed to materialise, which was probably just as well for the overworked George Ramsay.

To Ramsay fell the considerable challenge of bringing the club's administration into line with their modern new quarters, no easy task given the numerous teething problems cropping up almost every week. Nor could it have helped when his

request for a pay rise was flatly rejected by the board during the summer. They did, however, ease his workload, by employing an assistant named Horner, in September 1897.

One of the most contentious issues for Ramsay to deal with in those early months was the pricing of tickets in the main stand, and the fraught question of members' privileges. Terrace prices were held at the same level as Perry Barr, at sixpence per admission. But with the stand seats divided into three price bands – 1s, 1s 6d and 2s – a barrage of complaints soon arose about overcrowding in certain areas, who could sit where with their membership cards, and how this might conflict with the rights of shareholders. Not surprisingly one of the chief complainants was Joe Dunkley's pal, J. Kent.

To assuage the aggrieved, a number of fans were offered a 5s refund on their 15s 6d season ticket holders, the 1s 6d category was dropped and a shareholders' turnstile was introduced.

Another problem was that the customary practice of handing out free passes to soldiers, sailors, police and firemen was getting out of hand. Suddenly there were hundreds of self-styled off-duty men claiming their rights, forcing Villa to restrict free entry to those serving in Aston Manor or turning up in uniform.

These issues were of course symptomatic of a wider trend. Villa were now in command of a large, sophisticated stadium and had to be commensurately businesslike. To many Perry Barr old timers, this transition was clearly painful.

When not sorting out tickets and fans Ramsay had to wrestle with the new fangled telephones, not just for his office but for the ARGUS and MAIL. He also had regular run-ins with various souvenir sellers and publications, all of them eager to cash in on Villa's new status as lords of the manor.

For his part, Fred Rinder continued to find problems with the ground. The roofs leaked. The new flags kept tearing in the wind. The players complained about the proximity of the cement track to the touchlines. Amazingly, it was only realised two months into the season that Villa's female patrons

Aston Villa Football Ground, Birmingham

Valentine's Series

might need more than one toilet! (This was soon remedied in the Grand Stand but, as was common at the time, not in the rest of the ground.)

In almost every other respect, however, the new ground was proving to be a huge success. Before Christmas attendances were, at an average of approximately 17,000, the highest in England along with those of Everton, and were roughly 30 per cent up on the previous season at Perry Barr. But then Villa were the defending champions and were, as yet, unbeaten at home.

Unfortunately a disappointing run of four consecutive away games followed, before the League leaders Sheffield United – who had beaten Villa 1-0 on the previous Saturday at Bramall Lane – arrived at Villa Park on January 15 for what would prove to be Villa's crunch match of 1897-98 season. It would also provide the new ground's first major test.

The ASTON NEWS marvelled at the scenes. 'Who shall say after this, that football enthusiasm is on the wane? So eager were some of the visitors to see the match that they wended their way to the ground as early as ten o'clock in the morning, while from twelve until two there was nothing to be heard in the Witton, Whitehead, Birchfield, and Park Roads but the hurried tramp of men and boys, broken occasionally by the rattle of a cab or tramcar. One might almost have imagined that an army was being hurried to the battle front.

'At the ground, too, the spectacle was a never-to-be forgotten one in the history of football. Not only were the stands covered with a sea of human beings, but quite a crowd of youngsters had clambered to the top of the Trinity Road stand, and upwards of fifty still more daring spirits were to be seen perched up on the top of the advertisement hoardings.'

(These hoardings had been erected in the corner between the Trinity Road stand and the Holte Hotel End, as it was then known, to block the view from Aston Park.)

In the end the crowd was believed to have been around 42-43,000, a record not only for Villa but almost certainly for the entire FOOTBALL LEAGUE. There were also record receipts for a single League match, of £1,310 18s.

Best of all there were apparently no serious organisational problems. Praising the performance of the local police, the ASTON NEWS correspondent reported, 'Notwithstanding the endless string of cabs, char-a-bancs, and other vehicles, there was, I believe, from first to last, not a single hitch or blockade of the traffic. Inside the grounds not an accident occurred, while it is also a noteworthy fact that no case of pocket-picking was reported at the police station. Of course there was a fine array of torn garments, and one young man came out of the ground at the conclusion of the match minus his collar and tie, while his shirt front was reduced to ribbons. But such things are minor details on a field day at the Villa Ground, and only add a finer flavour to the general excitement.'

Perhaps the young man's mother took a rather dimmer view when he returned home. So too may

## Villa Park? Ugh!

❖ When did the Aston Lower Grounds become known as Villa Park? Surprisingly, there is no simple answer. Rather, the name Villa Park seems to have crept into use during Villa's first few years at the ground, until eventually, around 1907, it seems to have stuck. There was certainly never any official decision by the club.

As far as can be ascertained, the first recorded usage of the name Villa Park was in the 'Football Gossip' column of the BIRMINGHAM DAILY MAIL, in August 1897, five months after the opening.

But then the MAIL and most other newspapers referred to the 'Lower Grounds' far more often, and for many years after 1897. Other titles used by the press were 'the Villa Grounds,' the 'Aston Grounds' or simply 'the Lower.' For their part Villa gave their new registered address as 'the Aston Villa Grounds,' while even the VILLA NEWS AND RECORD stuck faithfully to the 'Lower Grounds' throughout its first season of publication, in 1906-07, and did not start to mention Villa Park until August 1907.

There have been suggestions that the name Lower Grounds had negative connotations, hence the name change. But not all fans were keen on the alternative, as this pseudonymous letter to the BIRMINGHAM DAILY MAIL in September 1897 suggested:

*Sir, - While perusing my* MAIL *a week or two ago, I suddenly came across the term "Villa Park." On finding that it referred to our beloved sports arena, the historic Lower Grounds, I turned sick, and have recovered to find that the Villa have lost two matches and that Haydock has refused to come. And Mr Editor, can you wonder at it? Villa Park! Ugh!*
*Yours truly, A. Chirl, Handsworth*

Jimmy Haydock of Blackburn Rovers never did sign for Villa. But no-one else seemed to share this correspondent's dislike of the name Villa Park, and so it became known.

Still on the subject of names, nowadays we all refer to the Holte End, but in the early years it was known variously as the City End, the Church End, or more fully as the Holte Hotel End. Similarly, where now stands the North Stand was banking called variously the Great Hall End (before 1914), the Witton Road End, and then later simply the Witton End. The original Witton Lane Stand was also called the Main Stand or Grand Stand until the opening of the Trinity Road Stand in 1922.

most of the home fans, for the afternoon ended in bitter disappointment. Apart from the usual Wheldon goal, Villa lost 2-1, thereby ending their unbeaten run at Villa Park and effectively killing any chance of catching the Blades in the race for the championship. They would suffer a further blow when Villa were also knocked out of the Cup, two weeks later at Derby.

But if the club's first full season at Villa Park was turning into a major anti-climax after the heroics of the year before, the huge, milling crowds at the Sheffield United game also exposed one major problem with the ground's lay out. There was not a single crush barrier on the terraces.

Quite why these had not been part of the original design is baffling, at least to modern eyes. But immediately after the game Fred Rinder ordered this to be corrected, and over the ensuing months wooden barriers started to appear around all three sides of the terracing.

And so came to an end Villa's first year at their new home; a mixed year in many respects. Finishing only sixth in the League had led to a sharp drop in attendances towards the end of the season, so that the average gate ended up at only 16,300 or so. This was still Villa's best ever, and was bettered only by Everton's average of around 17,500. But such was the fans' disillusion with the team that the final match, against Nottingham Forest, pulled in a mere 4,000 diehards – the second worst in Villa Park's 100 year history.

The end-of-season financial figures confirmed this late slump. Gate receipts at the new ground were actually slightly under those of the previous season, at £9,742 compared with £10,001. However, to this could be added another £855, which was Villa's share of the cycle track earnings and other event receipts. On the debit side, however, the outlay on ground developments had now reached the worrying total of £16,733, way above the original estimates. To balance the deficit, £7,000 worth of debentures therefore had to be called upon.

There would be more worries that summer as it seemed possible that the cycling boom in Birmingham had passed its peak. Indeed attendances during the race seasons of both 1898 and 1899 – when they were doubly affected by the outbreak of the Boer War – were so far reduced for SPORT AND PLAY to seek a humiliating renegotiation of their five year lease.

By then, however, much to everyone's relief, Villa were emphatically back in the clover and could, for the time being at least, afford to be patient with their cycling friends. Season 1898-99 proved to be a bonanza year, not only for the team but also for Villa Park.

For a start, the ground had already been chosen for its first major representative match, featuring the Football League v Scottish League, on April 9, 1898. At the time this was regarded as an important event on the calendar. Three Villa men were chosen for the League XI: Charlie Athersmith, Fred Wheldon and Stevie Smith, none of whom could prevent the Scots

inflicting a 2-1 defeat. But the attendance was a reasonable 22,000, and all went well enough for Villa Park to be selected, almost exactly a year later, for the greatest prize of all – bar the Cup Final, that is – the England v Scotland international.

This match truly signalled Villa Park's arrival in the big time, for not only was it the ground's first major international but also the first for the city of Birmingham. (True, Perry Barr had staged the England v Ireland game in 1893, but those fixtures were regarded as only of secondary status.)

On the momentous day, April 8, 1899, a combination of wind, sleet and snow conspired to make conditions tough, which no doubt explains why the gate was lower than might have been expected. The exact figure is unclear. One source puts it as 22,000, another at 37,000. But the most precise, and therefore the most likely total, according to one newspaper, was 25,590. Just as importantly, England secured a well earned victory, with Villa's own Charlie Athersmith setting up the second goal

in a 2-1 win. (One other Villa man played for England, Jimmy Crabtree.)

As far as Villa fans were concerned, however, the best was yet to come. Two weeks later, with Villa now faltering slightly in their pursuit of the League championship, only 8,000 turned up to see Notts County trounced 6-1. Two days after this, a mere 10,000 were at the ground for the derby against West Bromwich Albion. This time Villa went one better by recording their second 7-1 rout of the season.

But their finest performance of all was reserved for the last Saturday of the campaign. This followed five days after the Albion game, when, still unbeaten at home, Villa faced Liverpool, with whom they were now level on points at the top of the League. A seasonal best of 41,000 crammed into Villa Park for this, the championship decider, with the trophy itself on tantalising display in the Main Stand for all to view. And how the Villa men responded to the bait! They thrashed the Reds 5-0, to win their fourth League title in emphatic fashion.

With a record breaking average crowd of some 21,000 (23,000 according to one source), Villa were now comfortably the best supported team in the land. And with the coffers now full to brimming, all the anxieties of the previous summer melted away.

Moreover, the club was now in a position to afford two much needed ground improvements.

The first stage was to provide additional cover for terrace fans on the Trinity Road side, with curving wings added to each end of the original corrugated, barrel-roof. This work was carried out during the summer of 1899 at a cost of £887. The second stage, also beginning in 1899, was to re-lay all the terracing.

The reason for this appears to have been yet another flaw in the Holmes-Rinder design. When the ground opened, each terrace had been wide enough for fans to stand two deep. But this was hopeless for sightlines, and had the effect of reducing the comfortable capacity of the ground. After only two full seasons, therefore, every bit of banking had to be dug up and reprofiled, so that each terrace was now

❖ *An early action shot from behind the Holte End goal. Notice how the goalnets are held up by extra posts and guy-ropes, a system almost identical to the one favoured nowadays instead of fixed stanchions.*

❖ *Nowadays most senior football grounds are sealed off from the public on non-match days and the pitches carefully protected. But in its early years Villa Park was a hive of activity during the summer. Following on from the tradition at Perry Barr, Villa used to put on their own annual sports and athletics carnivals, or, as these pictures show, rent out the ground to local clubs, schools and charities. For several years tug-of-war teams competed for the NEWS OF THE WORLD Cup.*

half the width of the original. This work cost roughly another £1,300, and was completed, section by section, by early 1900.

Just in time, as it happened. For season 1899-1900 turned out to be another wonder year for Villa; their fifth League championship in just seven seasons proving to be a glorious antidote to the dismal news flowing in from the Boer War. (The infamous battle of Spion Kop, for example, forever commemorated at so many English football grounds, took place on January 24, 1900.)

Villa's main rivals throughout the season were Sheffield United, who, for the second time since Villa Park's opening, managed to attract a new record attendance, on March 3, 1900. This time the estimated total reached 50,000, with receipts of nearly £1,500

The 1-1 scoreline proved to be fairly inconclusive, but the game was memorable for other reasons. Present at the match was a photographer from the

BRITISH MUSICSCOPE AND BIOGRAPH COMPANY, whose action images – possibly the first ever captured at the ground – would be projected in larger-than-life fashion in front of an audience at the Theatre Royal on the Monday night.

None of these images appear to have survived, but if they had, would they have showed us something of the chaotic scenes which preceded the game?

In order to increase the ground's capacity, the directors had decided to erect temporary wooden bench seats on the cycle track (as they had done for the previous year's international v Scotland). But just as the Villa and United players emerged from the dressing rooms, the crush behind the Witton End goal became so intense that the track seats collapsed 'with a crash'.

Thankfully, what could have been 'a terrible disaster' according to the SPORTS ARGUS, ended up as only a minor incident with no serious injuries. Nor was there any disorder, largely thanks to the exemplary behaviour of the fans, who, in a matter of minutes, managed to salvage sufficient timber from the wreckage to make themselves 'as comfortable as possible for the kick off.' Their coolness, declared the ARGUS 'was something for Birmingham sportsmen to be proud of.'

Villa's directors were far from impressed however, especially when Fred Rinder discovered that Leeson, the groundsman, had not followed the usual instructions when he erected those particular seats. The board also had to deal with various letters of complaint, and dispatch a doctor to check on all those who were claiming to be injured.

But despite the collapse, Leeson appears to have kept his job and the seats remained in trouble-free use for many years to come. In 1902, they even earned Villa ten guineas when Warwickshire CCC hired them for the visit of Australia to Edgbaston. But the cycling fraternity was not happy with them. Apart from risking damage to the track, the seats

were often left in position for long enough to prevent cyclists using the ground for daily training.

Nor were the seats always needed, particularly as Villa's increasingly inconsistent form during the first decade of the century drew gates smaller than the bumper year of 1898-99 (although individual gates of 40-50,000 were still occasionally recorded).

While the team struggled to emulate the achievements of the 1890s, behind the scenes George Ramsay and the Villa directors had their hands full with a succession of thorny and often time consuming problems, most of which revolved around the ownership of the neighbouring parts of the Lower Grounds.

Ramsay himself was now well settled into his new quarters. He was, at last, given a pay rise in September 1899, to £300 a year, plus the same win bonuses as the players. He could also now count on a reliable and popular assistant in the person of Wallie Strange, a former half-back who had played only two games for the first team before being forced to retire with a knee injury. (Strange served as Ramsay's assistant until his death in 1925, and was best remembered for managing the reserves to eight championships in a row in the Birmingham League between 1902-10.)

Yet no sooner had Ramsay and Strange sorted out the club offices and made sure the players' rooms were comfortably equipped and furnished than Edgar Flower tried to persuade Villa to vacate the building altogether! Or rather, his company did.

Since his failed attempt to sell the entire Lower Grounds site in 1898 (see page 90), Flower seems to have turned all matters concerning the property over to his son, Archibald, and to the family firm of brewers in Stratford. In 1900, FLOWER & SONS informed Villa that they now wished to build a road and new houses on the northern part of the Lower Grounds, between Villa Park and Witton Road, and would therefore prefer the club to vacate the aquarium building and construct new offices elsewhere on the site.

Fred Rinder responded as he usually did in such situations. He drew up plans. He then worked out how much it would cost to put these plans into practice – £2,000 – and then advised that Villa ask FLOWER & SONS for £2,000 compensation.

Maybe this demand frightened off FLOWERS, or maybe they simply failed to gain permission for their plans. But in the end no new roads or houses were built, which is just as well as far as the current Villa Park is concerned, since the area on which the road was proposed in 1900 would have effectively squeezed Villa into a much smaller island site, and certainly prevented any future expansion beyond the North Stand.

The road proposals did contain a warning, however. It was now patently clear that the remaining parts of the Lower Grounds had no future as a place of entertainment or leisure. The Holte Hotel could easily stand alone. The football ground was proving a great success. But the rest – the bowling greens, the Aquarium building, the Great

Hall, the Rustic Cottage and the land between the Witton End terrace and Witton Road – might easily be redeveloped or sold off to speculators.

And if that were to be so, as seemed increasingly likely after 1900, it was clearly in Villa's interest to be kept informed. This was not just a question of making sure that the club did not end up with hostile neighbours. Villa were keen to extend their own boundaries, and had good reason to suppose that FLOWERS would give them first option on any land which might come up for grabs. After all, the company did pretty well from sales of refreshments at Villa Park, while in general they seemed like fairly amenable landlords.

For example, in 1901, they agreed to lower Villa's rent from £300 to £187 per annum, provided that Villa took on the responsibility of paying all the relevant rates and taxes. Then in 1904 Villa decided they would like to convert the former garden area by the Great Hall into a small training pitch, since the Villa Park pitch had been suffering from over-use for

several years. FLOWERS agreed to let the area, but at first insisted on no less than £60 per annum. Two months later they happily agreed on £35. It was almost as if they just wanted to wash their hands of the whole place.

(The training pitch, incidentally, only just reached minimum dimensions, and was used for Villa's newly formed third team.)

Yet FLOWERS could also dig in their heels, as happened over the issue of the cycle track.

The cycle track was proving to be both a blessing and a curse to Villa. As far as cycling was concerned, the sport was already being eclipsed by the new breed of motorcycle racers – some of whom first appeared at Villa Park in 1902 – while income from the usual Easter and Whitsuntide meetings dropped off so badly that in one year SPORT AND PLAY's rental cheque to Villa bounced.

But in public, at least, Villa's directors did seem to genuinely approve of the track remaining, for the good of sport in Birmingham overall and for the general prestige of the ground and club in particular. All they wanted was to change the surface from cement to cinders.

Their reasons were twofold. Firstly, cinders would have made it easier for Villa to put seats on the track during the football season and then remove them and make good for the summer racing season. Secondly, the club received several complaints from visiting teams that the proximity of the cement track to the touchlines was dangerous. These complaints would eventually lead the FOOTBALL LEAGUE to warn Villa formally in December 1903.

The local press was not surprised. 'It has been more by sheer good luck than anything else that there have not been lamentable, if not fatal, accidents caused by players tumbling onto the track,' commented the MIDLAND EXPRESS. 'The narrow strip of cocoa nut matting which runs along the track close to the turf is absolutely useless – nay, it but adds to the danger, for I have seen many a player tripped up by it and sent sprawling.'

Someone suggested an alternative form of protective grass matting then popular in theatres, whenever performing animals were on stage. But this would have cost £400, enough to wrap all 22 players in cotton wool three times over. Villa also wrote to other clubs who had tracks, including Wolves, Bury and Nottingham Forest, to see if they ever had any problems. But the conclusion was always the same; that cinders would solve all their problems.

Accordingly, George Ramsay wrote to FLOWERS to seek permission to resurface the track. But the track, responded FLOWERS, represented their only form of income from Villa Park during the summer months, besides which, all the leading cycling organisations wanted the cement to be retained, since it was the only such track in the entire Midlands.

After Villa passed on that blunt message the League seemed to lose interest, and Villa decided to let the matter rest too. No player had ever been seriously injured, after all. But the cement versus cinders dispute seemed to surface with

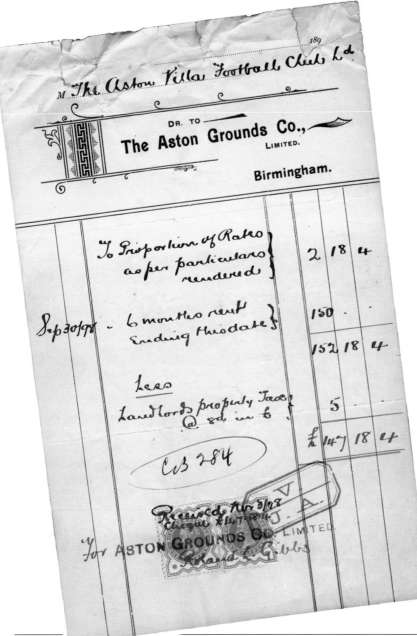

❖ Villa get the bill for six months' rent and rates from their landlords.

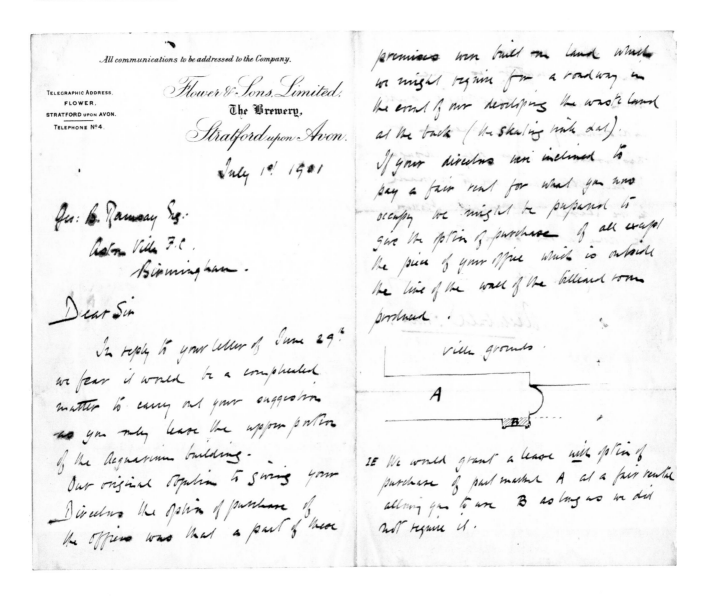

All communications to be addressed to the Company.

TELEGRAPHIC ADDRESS.
FLOWER.
STRATFORD UPON AVON.
TELEPHONE Nº 4.

*Flower & Sons, Limited,*
*The Brewery,*
*Stratford upon Avon.*

*July 1st 1901*

*Geo: B. Ramsay Esq.*
*Aston Villa F.C.*
*Birmingham.*

*Dear Sir*

*In reply to your letter of June 29th we fear it would be a complicated matter to carry out your suggestion as you only lease the upper portion of the Aquarium building.*
*Our original objection to giving your Directors the option of purchase of the offices was that a part of these premises were built on land which we might require for a roadway in the event of our developing the waste land at the back (the skating rink &c).*
*If your directors were inclined to pay a fair rent for what you now occupy we might be prepared to give the option of purchase of all except the piece of your office which is outside the line of the wall of the billiard room produced.*

*villa grounds.*

*A*

*B*

*IE We would grant a lease with option of purchase of part marked A at a fair rental allowing you to use B so long as we did not require it.*

*But this matter is one which must be dealt with quite independently of the question we discussed the other day though if any alterations are to be made in the lease they might perhaps be done at the same time.*

*Yours truly*

*Archibald Flower.*

monotonous regularity, until Fred Rinder must have grown heartily sick of discussing the matter.

But not half as sick as he was shortly before Christmas 1907, when Rinder discovered that contrary to everything he had been led to believe, FLOWER AND SONS. had gone behind his back and sold the rest of the Lower Grounds – including Villa's offices, club rooms and gymnasium – without so much as a nod or a wink in Villa's direction.

With landlords like that, what on earth could Villa do? Could they be evicted from their offices? Had they lost the chance of extending their boundaries? How could they trust FLOWERS again if this was the underhand way in which they were prepared to act?

Clearly, Villa needed some legal advice, and who better to give it than Villa's own club president, the learned solicitor Joseph Ansell.

So off went Fred Rinder to the president's city centre office, and what did he find? He found that the people to whom FLOWERS had sold the land were none other than the brewers, ANSELLS.

❖ Archibald Flower responds to another rental dispute raised by Villa's directors. The tone suggests an uneasy relationship at the time.

# Lower Grounds for sale

❖ Barely a year after moving in, Villa expected to find themselves with a new landlord when Edgar Flower put the entire 16 acre site of the Lower Grounds up for auction at the Grand Hotel, Colmore Row, on July 21, 1898. The particulars drawn up for the sale, by FLOWER'S Birmingham solicitors, F. H. PEPPER & TANGYE, tell us a great deal about Villa's environs in this early period.

Extolling the site's virtues as 'probably the most important and extensive Free-Licensed Premises at present to be obtained in the Midlands,' the sales pitch accentuated the profitability of its various outlets, the popularity of the football ground and the density of the surrounding population. Within a 12 mile radius there were 1.25 million people, all within cheap and easy reach of the Lower Grounds by tram or train.

The site's total income in the year 1897-98 was £14,035 (which, considering the place was supposed to be in the doldrums, was still higher than Villa's gross receipts). Of this, £101 came from the Villa Park tea bars. The rest was made up of rents and £12,088 worth of sales at the Holte Hotel and other bars. The MINERAL WATER MANUFACTORY had also earned £2,525 in the previous year.

The Holte Hotel, stated the brochure, 'stands in a commanding position' and had been 'entirely reconstructed and remodelled in 1897 at a great cost.' Former regulars of the Holte may well recall some its listed features. These included a smoke room fitted expensively with American walnut, high dados, cosy corners and a valuable old oak mantlepiece which had once been fitted in Aston Hall. Other rooms consisted of a manager's sitting room (with a telephone), the Trinity Road Bar, the lower level Witton Lane Bar (now Villa's new merchandise shop) and a 'capital Music Hall or Assembly Room' at the back, with its own stage and room for 400 people. This was used regularly for Smoking Concerts and Entertainments.

On the Holte's upper floors was a billiard room, a coffee and dining room (which was often used for post-match celebrations, such as after the 1905 Cup Final win against Newcastle), and ten hotel bedrooms, where many a Villa player, visiting cyclist and athlete stayed. Outside there was also a stable for eight horses, on the Witton Lane side, and behind the hotel, two bowling greens. These were served by two summer houses and rented by the LOWER GROUNDS BOWLING CLUB. (The greens would survive right up until the 1960s and were on the area now occupied by the car park, behind the Holte End.) Also by the bowling greens was an Artesian Well and pump house, which supplied the water for the MINERAL WATER FACTORY on the northern side of the site.

The football ground was then described, it being noted that all rights to refreshment sales within the ground resided with the owners of the Lower Grounds and that the outlets themselves were run by the manager at the Holte (the Villa director Jimmy Lees).

In front of the football ground's Trinity Road enclosure was a third bowling green. This had its own small pavilion, and, confusingly, was rented by the HOLTE BOWLING CLUB. (The green survived until 1966).

Next, at the end of a driveway, was the MINERAL WATER MANUFACTORY which, only the year before, had won a gold medal for its ginger beer at an exhibition in Scarborough. This was housed at one end of Thomas Naden's former Aquarium block, whose ground floor retained its 200 foot long, arched and richly decorated promenade, and still featured eleven large tanks from the old aquarium, eight wild beast cages from when it had been converted into a menagerie, plus a polar bear pit, aviaries and a monkey house. The adjacent skating

rink also survived, although it too appears not to have been in use.

Above the promenade, a full-length verandah provided views over the gardens, while the rooms were now being rented for a nominal rent by Villa as their offices, club house and gymnasium. (In 1958 Villa would move the gym to the former aquarium downstairs). Also still standing was the lofty tower, from which extensive views of Aston Park and the city of Birmingham could be obtained.

Next there was the Great Hall, 'one of the finest buildings of its kind in the Provinces' and well known as the venue for promenade concerts, held every Sunday throughout the year and at holiday times. Attendances at each of these concerts, it was stated, averaged an amazing 4-5,000 people.

Outside the Great Hall was the dancing platform Jimmy Lees had constructed the year before, a bandstand, a gardener's cottage, and Henry Quilter's greenhouses, which, it was admitted, were 'now much out of repair,' as were the adjacent formal gardens.

Finally, the particulars described the Rustic Cottage, which still stood on Witton Road, at the northern edge of the grounds. This consisted of first and second class bars, tea and refreshment rooms, and on the upper floor, eight bedrooms.

The ASTON NEWS expressed surprise that Edgar Flower should be anxious to sell the Lower Grounds, especially since takings at the Holte alone had more than doubled because of the football crowds. The auctioneers, WALTER LUDLOW & BRISCOE, also believed that the rest of the site could easily flourish again, given an injection of fresh capital and the expenditure of perhaps £10,000 on restoration works.

But it would appear that few people agreed. Before the sale it was reckoned that the Lower Grounds would fetch between £60,000 and £100,000. Bidding started briskly, until it stuttered to a halt at £48,500 and the auctioneer had no choice but to withdraw the lot.

So the Lower Grounds remained in the hands of Edgar Flower, and Villa kept their reluctant landlord.

# Freeholders
# at last

THE UNEXPECTED SALE OF VILLA'S offices and training pitch to ANSELLS could hardly have come at a more anxious time for the club. An injury-ridden start to the 1907-08 season had been followed by weeks of maddening inconsistency. At one point, in October, Villa had been fifth from bottom. In March, only 8,000 turned up for the home game v Notts County. True, Villa had won the Cup in 1905, but it was now eight years since their last League title, and five since they had even been considered as challengers.

Nor was this certain to be a temporary blip. That small clique of teams over which Villa had ruled so triumphantly in the 1890s had now grown into a much larger phalanx of monied clubs. Chelsea, formed only in 1905, had the powerful backing of the property developer Gus Mears. Blackburn had just been taken over by an immensely wealthy textile baron. Both Manchester clubs were being bankrolled by breweries, while Newcastle United had emerged as the best supported team in the land.

For their part, Villa had no especially wealthy directors and could count on a hard core of fans hardly greater than 20,000. And now it turned out their own club president had been the one to personally negotiate ANSELLS purchase of the remaining Lower Grounds site from FLOWERS.

Joseph Ansell later told Villa's shareholders that neither he nor FLOWERS had possessed any inkling – 'not even a hint' he said – that the club might have been interested in the property. But in an official statement to supporters in the club programme on January 11, 1908, Fred Rinder claimed that the directors were 'greatly surprised' by this and had 'always been led to understand that, in the event of the landlord desiring to sell, the club would have first opportunity to purchase.'

On its own this communication breakdown

would not have mattered much. After all, what did it matter if Villa paid rent on their offices and training pitch to ANSELLS rather than FLOWERS?

But unfortunately for Villa it was not quite as simple as that. No sooner had ANSELLS taken over the site than the brewery was approached by the TERRITORIAL ASSOCIATION. The Territorials were keen to rent or purchase a considerable slice of the former Lower Ground site, including the training pitch, the Great Hall and the old aquarium building, in which Villa's new offices and club rooms were located.

As a result of this approach, ANSELLS were thus torn between a desire to help the Villa and what they saw as their patriotic duty.

The new year of 1908 therefore brought with it a series of critical challenges for Villa, both on and off the field. Any wrong move or loss of nerve in either the dressing room or the boardroom could yet prove disastrous, potentially sending Villa the same way as others from among the former elite, for example, Preston, Bolton and even West Bromwich Albion, all of whom, since the turn of the century, had tasted life in the Second Division.

But, as is so often the case, a jolt to the system often turns out to be the best cure for complacency. After losing 3-2 at home to Birmingham in January 1908, Villa's newly blooded youngsters put in a remarkable run of performances; so remarkable that by the end of the season the team managed to finish as runners-up in the League, their best placing since 1903. And although the club would struggle to match the achievements of the 1890s, there would still be much to shout about over the next few years; most notably, a sixth League Championship in 1910 and a fifth FA Cup triumph in 1913.

Otherwise, the period between 1908 and 1914 would prove to be absolutely pivotal in the overall context of Aston Villa's history. For this was the period in which the club – no doubt stung by the pressures building up in their backyard – finally harnessed their resources to purchase Villa Park. The story of how this came about is complex, no less so for modern readers than it must have seemed to ordinary supporters at the time. However, the train of events was essentially as follows.

At some time during 1908 ANSELLS bowed to joint pressure from the ASTON MANOR BOROUGH COUNCIL and the WAR OFFICE and agreed to sell roughly half of their holding to the TERRITORIAL ASSOCIATION. Villa thus lost access to the training pitch, and even had to give up the use of the players' recreation room. It was also made clear that once Villa's lease ran out, in 1917, the TERRITORIAL ASSOCATION would press for the club to leave their offices altogether.

As pressure from the military pushed Villa increasingly into a corner – both metaphorically and literally (for by 1909 they found themselves squeezed into just two rooms) – Fred Rinder's inclination was that Villa should seek to buy part of the aquarium building, the bowling green on Trinity Road and other small parcels of the site, so as to give them enough room for at least modest training facilities and improve the club's frontage along Trinity Road. But

❖ *The SPORTING MAIL caption said it all - RISKY! As the two Cup Finalists, Villa and Sunderland, met again for a top-of-the-table clash, on April 23, 1913, desperate fans scaled the advertisement hoardings on Trinity Road for a view of the action. One report claimed that 38,000 people were locked out!*

he also believed that the purchase price of £4,000 being suggested by the Territorials' representative, Colonel Ludlow, was quite extortionate. Half that would have been more appropriate, in his professional opinion as a surveyor.

Certainly it was true that Villa could not afford to buy both this extra land and the ground all in one go. This was, it should be remembered, in the days before football clubs derived any income from commercial sources. Unless they had wealthy backers, clubs lived and died by their gate receipts, and football was, as it always has been, a notoriously fickle business (as shown all too clearly by the club's decreased income in 1907-08). Nor should we forget that since the 1870s, men like Rinder, Ramsay and McGregor had seen Villa through some fairly rough periods. They were naturally cautious, and with good reason.

Allied to the ownership question was that of ground development. Rinder recognised that Villa Park was now in danger of falling behind its rivals. It had fewer seats than many other leading grounds, while the presence of the cycle track imposed a crucial constraint on expansion.

But here was the catch. Until Villa bought Villa Park they could not develop the ground. Yet the cost of purchasing the ground would leave them very little, if any surplus funds to do just that. Just to get the ground into the state it was after ten years in occupation had required the club to pay off £9,000 worth of debentures.

Meanwhile, all around them the world was changing. As one of Rinder's many speeches on the issue would argue, the much greater mobility of the local populace meant that for Villa to compete with

their rivals – in Small Heath, West Bromwich, and even further afield – the ground had to be capable of accommodating as many people as possible. Electric trams, which had been introduced in January 1904, (and were based at the nearby depot on Witton Lane, now the transport museum) now ran along both sides of the ground on Witton Lane and Trinity Road. Combined with the railway stations at Witton and Aston, this made Villa Park easily accessible to vast tracts of Birmingham and the surrounding areas. In short, Villa could not afford to squander this advantage for long, simply because the ground was too small or too uncomfortable.

Nor did Rinder wish Villa Park – or indeed the city of Birmingham – to lose its status as a venue of national repute. After the initial England v Scotland game in April 1899, the ground had staged the same fixture three years later. In 1901, 1903 and 1906 Villa Park was also selected to stage lucrative FA Cup semi-finals. To maintain that number of important neutral matches, Villa had to offer better facilities, more seats and a larger capacity. (The facts bear out Rinder's concern in this respect. Villa Park waited another 20 years before it hosted its next international, in 1922, while between 1906 and 1929 it staged only one semi-final.)

Negotiations with ANSELLS and the TERRITORIAL ASSOCIATION dragged on throughout 1909. But in the end, the delays worked to Villa's advantage, because by 1910 both their finances and morale had improved considerably. No need to explain why. The results said it all: 5-1 against Arsenal on the opening day of the 1909-10 season; 5-0 against Sheffield Wednesday, six games in which the team scored four goals, and best of all, a 7-1 rout of Manchester United.

❖ *Winning their sixth League Championship in 1909-10 gave Villa's board extra confidence to undertake the purchase of Villa Park a year later. Winger Charlie Wallace, who played in every game that season, later acted as dressing room attendant, steward, scout and a general handyman, and was known for wearing claret and blue workclothes at all times. Contrasting fortunes saw his team-mate, centre half Chris Buckley, join the board in 1936 and serve as chairman from 1955-66.*
*The line-up shows:*
*Back row standing: Lyons, Layton, Logan, George, Cartlidge, Miles, Kearns, J. Grierson.*
*Second row standing: G. Ramsay, W. Bate, J. Devey, F. Cooper, Jack Jones, F. Rinder, H. Spencer, J. Margoschis, I. Whitehouse, Dr H. Jessop, E. Strange.*
*Seated: Gerrish, G. Hunter, Eyre, Bache, Tranter, C. Buckley, Hall.*
*Ground: Walters, Jones, Hampton, Wallace.*

In winning their sixth League Championship, in April 1910, Villa had remained unbeaten at home and drawn average gates of approximately 22,000, their second highest since moving to Villa Park and worth £2,000 more in gate receipts than the previous season. As a result, the club could now show a healthy profit of £3,318 overall.

Even more satisfying was the strength of the playing squad. Incredibly, all but a few of the 18 players who figured in the first team that season were young, local lads who had come up from the club's junior ranks. And to cap it all, Wallie Strange's reserves won their eighth Birmingham League title in succession.

It was therefore just like the good old days at the club's AGM held at Fletcher's Cafe, Corporation Street, in June 1910, with vice-presidents and shareholders almost falling over each other to offer up hearty congratulations to the directors and players. Even Fred Rinder seemed taken aback by their protestations of loyalty, especially after some fairly frosty gatherings in the past.

As usual, Joseph Ansell delivered the keynote address, and soon earned a few guffaws with a sideways dig or two at their mutual acquaintance, Colonel Ludlow. (Despite the events of December 1907, it would appear that the president was still held in high esteem at Villa, and certainly never lost his sense of humour.) After praising the efforts of the team, Ansell then turned to the matter of the ground.

Villa, he reminded everyone, were currently paying FLOWERS & SONS the sum of £187 per year for the ground, plus rates and taxes, and had an option to purchase at 5s per square yard. Given the ground's existing boundaries, this required the club to raise the sum of £8,487. So far, various stocks and shares which Villa had bought specifically for the ground fund, were worth approximately £4,300. (These shares were in BIRMINGHAM CORPORATION and various railway companies.) If the club added a further £1,500 from the year's profits, as was proposed by the board, this left some £2,700 still to find.

Yet however tempting it might be to go for the freehold now, Ansell counselled patience. The club still had several years before their lease ended, and in that time they could steadily build up more funds without having to borrow. (Modern readers may note, wistfully, that Ansell warned that the bank rate for borrowing £2,700 in 1910 would have been at least 4 per cent!)

William McGregor – now a vice president and very much the elder statesman of the club – was persuaded by this argument too, although he confessed that a few years earlier he had been all in favour of buying the freehold there and then. But he advised shareholders that buying Villa Park would not be enough. The ground was now, he freely admitted, out of date, particularly compared with Goodison Park, for example (where an awesome double-decker stand had recently been completed for the staggering sum of £28,000, more than Villa Park had cost in its entirety).

❖ As the British Expeditonary Force prepared to do battle in Mons during the summer of 1914, building contractors started carving up Villa Park to implement the first phase of Fred Rinder's masterplan. These Albert Wilkes photographs show the track being cleared and the banking on both sides of the ground being reprofiled for new terraces.

❖ One of the most significant alterations effected during the summer of 1914 was to bring both end terraces much closer and parallel to the goal-lines, thus changing the ground from an oval to a rectangular shape. The new banking here at the Holte Hotel End (or City End, as Rinder called it) can just be made out on the left, with part of the old banking and refreshment hut visible behind it. The half-time scoreboards were first used for the game against Blackburn, on September 1, 1906, on the same day that the VILLA NEWS AND RECORD was first issued.

Fred Rinder agreed. Although no-one connected with the club was more anxious than he for Villa to own their own freehold, he saw little point in paying interest charges, simply for the sentimental pleasure of saying 'We own the ground.'

Thus the issue was settled for another year, and after further votes of thanks, cheers and loud exclamations of 'hear, hear!' Joseph Ansell (who was re-elected unanimously as club president) declared that the meeting had been one of the most harmonious he had had the pleasure of attending for some time.

A year later the directors reversed their ground policy completely!

They did so for the best possible reasons, however. The 1910-11 season turned out to be another bumper year. No honours were won, but the still developing team only missed out on the Championship by one point, finishing runners-up to Manchester United in a thrilling finish. Furthermore, in the meeting between the two front-runners on the penultimate Saturday of the season, a new Villa Park attendance record was established, with a packed house of 50,885 seeing the Lions confirm their challenge thanks to a 4-2 win.

In the end Villa lost out on the title by failing to win either of their remaining two away games. But once again the mood amongst shareholders at the AGM, in June 1911, was triumphant (even if they could hardly drink to this success, since the venue was the Temperance Hall in Temple Street). Nearly £15,500 had been taken at the gate, with profits reaching an unprecedented high of £5,924. This was a breathtaking 75 per cent improvement on the club's previous record profit, recorded in the Cup-winning year of 1905.

But these impressive returns were not the sole reason for Villa's *volte-face* over their ground policy.

During the preceding season there had been two significant changes in circumstances.

As explained to the AGM by Ansell, the first change was a small but vital one, relating to a 10 feet wide pathway linking the Great Hall and Trinity Road. Edgar Flower had insisted on excluding this from Villa's original lease in order that the Hall could be kept stocked up with food and drink from the Holte Hotel. However, since ANSELLS had purchased the Great Hall in late 1907 and then, only a few hundred yards away, built the Aston Hotel three years later, there was no longer any need to keep the pathway. That was one legal obstacle out of the way. (Three cheers for the Aston Hotel therefore!)

The next concerned the TERRITORIAL ASSOCIATION. It transpired that the WAR OFFICE had, in the end, been less than willing to fund the Association's plans for the Lower Grounds, and had suggested a cheaper scheme for barracks instead. This was wonderful news, and a huge let off for ANSELLS, since it meant that the Territorials would no longer need to impinge on the areas wanted by Villa. Instead, they were now willing to sell Villa a substantial portion of the former aquarium, and also its adjacent forecourt (where the skating rink had been), for a total of £1,500.

But that was not all. For the shareholders were told of yet another unexpected bonus. Now that the way seemed clear to Villa finally becoming freeholders, Joseph Ansell's brother, Edward, who ran the brewery, had generously offered to donate £500 towards the cost of buying a third plot of land, the bowling green on Trinity Road. Together with the southernmost sections of the former aquarium building, also being sold by ANSELLS, this was now being offered to Villa for £2,000.

Was Edward Ansell's largesse motivated by guilt over what had occurred in December 1907? Possibly, but then he was also generous enough to subsidise the building of the nearby Victoria Road baths, and to donate the land required for a public library at Aston Cross. What was certain was that the bowling green area was sorely coveted by Villa, because one side of it could now form the basis of a much-needed entranceway to the club offices (which would later be known rather grandly as the Carriage Drive).

Taking into account Edward Ansell's gift of £500, the three extra plots now on offer would cost Villa £3,000, a good deal less than the £4,000 being asked for a smaller area of land only three years earlier. (Thus Joseph Ansell's advice for Villa to be patient had been completely vindicated.)

The price for Villa Park itself, of course, had never altered. Thanks to Fred Rinder's hard bargaining back in 1896, it was still available for 5s per square yard. Measuring up the whole therefore, it was found that the ground occupied 33,000 square yards, resulting in a purchase price of £8,250.

Thus Villa had to find a total of £11,250 if they wished to assume Edgar Flower's mantle as the largest single landowner of the Lower Grounds since the Holte family in the early 19th century.

After their pleas for caution only a year before, the Villa directors, the president and vice-presidents, were now all unanimous. Now, assuredly, was the time to grasp the nettle.

'But were they going to issue debentures to borrow money from their bankers?' Joseph Ansell asked the gathering rhetorically.

'No such thing!' he retorted, to enthusiastic cries of 'Hear, hear!'

After two successful seasons, the club had £7,091 in the bank, plus £1,000 on deposit. To this they could add a further £4,867 worth of stocks and shares.

Not only could Aston Villa afford to buy all the land now on offer, therefore, but they would still be left with some £1,800 in the bank, enough to keep the club running throughout the close season. But even if it were not, smiled the president, once the club had become freeholders 'five or ten minutes interview with their bankers would surely overcome any difficulty of that sort.'

As Ansell concluded this highly gratifying analysis, mighty applause erupted around the hall, to which loud cheers were added when Fred Rinder – in a very real sense the architect of the entire scheme – stood up to address the assembly.

There is no need to report Rinder's speech in full. Everything had gone so well that season that he could do little more than heap further praise on all concerned. Regarding the purchase of the ground, he believed the price being put before the shareholders represented tremendous value. If Villa had been forced to build premises similar to the buildings currently on offer they would need to spend at least £5-7,000. And with the extra land now at their disposal, Villa would own an overall site which would be 'very valuable in the future, if the ground was not wanted for athletics or football.' (Fortunately this last assertion has never been tested.)

If they, the shareholders, hesitated one moment to clinch the bargain in front of them, declared Rinder, they did not possess the business acumen for which he gave them credit.

And so the die was cast. After 37 years in existence, Aston Villa were about to become freeholders for the very first time. Truly, another momentous phase of their history was about to begin.

But before we turn the pages to discover what Fred Rinder was already planning for this new

❖ Before the Territorial Army squeezed Villa out in 1908, this was the player's gymnasium, in one of the first floor rooms of the aquarium block, next to the offices. Villa were starting to take the fitness and health of their players more seriously at the time. Apart from buying new X-ray equipment and various other electrical devices with magical properties, in 1906 they also decided to hire a former athlete called Platnauer to conduct compulsory weekly exercise classes for all players. Platnauer charged £25 for the season, or £32 with music! In 1958 a more substantial gym would be set up in the former aquarium on the ground floor.

❖ *William McGregor – the Father of the Football League and a towering influence at the Villa. The genial Scot is remembered today by having the Mcgregor Suite at Villa Park named after him, and McGregor Close, off Station Road.*

chapter, a few words concerning two old friends.

Immediately after the ground question was settled at the 1911 AGM, more thunderous approval was given to another proposal, that George Ramsay be granted a testimonial match to reward his 25 years as club secretary. In fact Ramsay had been associated with Villa for 35 years overall, longer than anyone then still actively involved. As many old hands recognised, he had in the early days, been instrumental in saving the club by managing to attract a crack Scottish XI to Perry Barr, when the coffers had been empty.

He was also credited with introducing to the club at least two of Villa's most influential Scottish protagonists; the late, great centre-forward and captain, Archie Hunter, and the genial administrator and draper from Perthshire, William McGregor.

So Ramsay was awarded his testimonial, to more loud cheers. But the man who had put forward the idea, McGregor, was not there to see it.

Owing to another footballing commitment, McGregor had been unable to attend this momentous AGM. And nor, sadly, would he attend any more. After the death of his wife Jessie, in 1908, old Mac's health had deteriorated, and although he continued to be active in League and FA affairs, he died shortly before Christmas, 1911 in Miss Storer's Nursing Home, on Newhall Street, at the age of 65.

There would be several memorials to the avuncular McGregor.

Villa endowed a bed in his name at the General Hospital, while the BIRMINGHAM COUNTY FA commissioned an ornamental drinking fountain to be fixed in the wall of the MIDLAND BANK at Six Ways,

Aston, close to his former home and to the Wheeler Street chapel where he had worshipped for many years. Unveiled by the Lord Mayor in 1913, the fountain narrowly escaped destruction during the Second World War blitz, and was later removed to Villa Park, where it can still be seen today, appropriately enough, in the club's McGregor Suite restaurant. Next to this in the suite there is a fine oil portrait of the man who did so much to enhance Aston Villa's standing, and who is of course best remembered as the 'Father of the Football League.' Finally, just around the corner from Villa Park is McGregor Close, off Station Road.

McGregor was undoubtedly a giant among men, and thoroughly deserved to be remembered. Yet curiously, and some might say regrettably, no such memorials exist for the man who might well be dubbed the 'Father of Villa Park'.

According to several contemporary profiles of Fred Rinder – none of which he ever sought to contradict – Rinder was said to have laid down every level and line when Villa Park was being laid out in 1896-97. 'Levels, drainage, roofing, banking, fencing – all were set out by the chairman,' stated the BIRMINGHAM SPORTING MAIL in 1906.

Even if this were an exaggeration, the essence was undoubtedly true. For no-one, surely, was ever more passionately devoted to Villa Park than Frederick W. Rinder. From negotiating the original lease, to fussing over light bulbs in the dressing rooms; from drawing up plans with Teddy Holmes to selling advertisements for the stand roofs – Fred Rinder did the lot. It is a wonder that he ever managed to hold down a full-time job, let alone fit in time to serve as club chairman or as a regular and often strident member of various League and FA committees.

But if the early years of Villa Park had been busy and eventful, the period which followed the purchase of the freehold in 1911 would see Rinder absolutely in his element. At long last he enjoyed a virtual *carte blanche* to develop the ground as he saw fit, an opportunity which, one senses, he had been awaiting for a very long time. The result of his near obsession was there for all to see, for at least until the beginnings of chairman Doug Ellis's revolution in 1968, the Villa Park with which so many supporters would be familiar was indubitably the Villa Park of Fred Rinder. The Trinity Road Stand and the massive Holte End were his principal legacies, but so too was the shape, and shall we say, the unmistakable style of Villa Park.

Yet it should also be remembered that Rinder was equally responsible for the lay-out of the ground as it appeared in 1897, a lay-out which, as time would prove, was hardly ideal for a football ground of the early 20th century. The Witton Lane Stand, though distinctive, was cramped and uncomfortable. The terraces had to be completely reprofiled after only two years, while the pitch and its surrounding cycle track were the constant targets of criticism. Having been regarded as a marvel in 1897, by 1911 Villa Park was already in need of a serious rethink.

As the VILLA NEWS AND RECORD reported just weeks after that year's AGM, the purchase of the ground was only the beginning.

'The scheme commits the club no further at present than the purchase of the freehold; but when there are sufficient funds in hand Mr F. W. Rinder will propound a scheme of alterations and improvements which will make the Villa Ground the largest and most up-to-date football arena in the kingdom. Mr Rinder's proposal will include widening the playing area by several yards, and extending the present unreserved stand above the present banking, covering it, and thus making that section of the ground (which has already accommodated 35,000 spectators) capable of holding over 100,000 people. The acquirement of the land will also enable the club to break up the present cement track and replace it with a cinder track, on which spectators can stand in the winter, and in the "close-season" cyclists will have the benefit of an excellent training surface. There is no ground in the kingdom so excellently situated for ingress and exit. At each of the four corners there is plenty of room, and sufficient accommodation to deal with a crowd of final Cup-tie dimensions; on two sides of the triangle formed by the site there are tram lines, and when the greater Birmingham scheme is accomplished the tram supply will be efficient and regular; it will then be possible for people from the Black Country to journey by tram to Villa Park without change of car, whilst other important suburbs of the city will be linked up. Mr Rinder has devoted years of study to this magnificent scheme, and when the club realises that gentleman's ambition it will have a football arena perfect in every detail, and capable of holding something like 150,000 spectators.'

Something like 150,000 spectators! Well, at least no-one could accuse Fred Rinder of lacking ambition.

Two other points in the article are just as revealing, however. Firstly, the idea of Villa Park staging Cup Finals was not as far-fetched as it might seem today. There were various press reports during the Edwardian era hinting that representatives from the FA had visited the ground with a view to assessing its suitability for the Final. If true, none of these ever came to anything. By 1911, however, the issue was very much back on the front burner, and for reasons which many readers with experience of Wembley will appreciate only too readily.

Since 1895, Cup Finals had been staged at the vast open bowl of Crystal Palace, which was now patently lagging far behind many of the leading grounds in the League. Indeed, apart from its historical associations and novelty value, the ground's only real asset was its enormous capacity. Villa fans experienced this at first hand in both 1905 and 1913, when the official Cup Final attendances were respectively 101,117 and 120,081. In each case it is doubtful whether more than half that number could actually see all of the game.

For that reason a queue of alternative venues vied for the right to take over from the Palace. Stamford Bridge was the favourite, but both Arsenal and Manchester United also entertained hopes, as did Villa with Fred Rinder's now grandiose plans for a capacity of 150,000. (In the end Old Trafford was tried once, in 1915, while Chelsea hosted three finals after the First World War. But after Wembley's opening in 1923, no other ground got a look in.)

The second issue of note in the above article concerned Rinder's reference to the cycle track.

Despite the declining interest in track and field events, and the inevitable drop-off in rents earned by Villa for the summer meetings, as mentioned in the previous chapter, the board was subject to regular lobbying from local cycling and athletics organisations, always urging Villa not to remove the track and to keep the existing cement surface. Fred Rinder's response to this lobbying in January 1908, as reported in the VILLA NEWS AND RECORD, summed up his view.

'There seems to be an idea abroad that we desire to abolish the track altogether; this is not so, but we do wish to break up the present cement surface and replace it with a high-class cinder surface. By doing so we should remove any danger to players which may be either imaginary or real, and at the same time we could also use the track to greater advantage for the accommodation of spectators during the football season. We are as anxious as anyone to keep up and improve the usefulness of our ground as a sports enclosure, and desire to keep it what it has been in the past – the best and most useful in the Midlands.'

As we have seen above, Rinder repeated this commitment to a cinder track in his article of 1911. He then spent the following months studiously honing his masterplan, waiting only for the moment when Villa's finances might be robust enough to put

# Interesting figures

❖ In 1911 Fred Rinder presented readers of the club programme with some unusual information concerning Villa Park.

'To give an idea of the vast proportions of the present arena the following figures may be useful:-

❖ UNRESERVED SIDE. There are fourteen and a half miles of single terraces. Sixty terraces of an average length each of 420 yards give a total length of 25,200 yards – fourteen and a half miles.

❖ GRAND STAND. Here there are 17 tiers (each with seats) of 150 yards each; total length 2,550 yards – One and a half miles. On the terrace in front of the stand there are seven tiers of 150 yards each – total 1,050 yards – nearly three-quarters of a mile.

❖ TRACK SEATS. Pavilion side (5 rows), goals (7 rows at each), unreserved side (4 rows); total length, 3,890 yards – two and a quarter miles.

❖ Thus the total length of accommodation for the public at Villa Park aggregates seventeen and a half miles; roughly speaking, the terraces, tiers, and seating, put end to end, would reach from the Bull Ring to Coventry.

❖ There are 54 turnstiles, 42 separate public entrances, 24 exit gates, each ten feet wide; altogether over 300 separate doors.'

❖ *This is the plan presented to Villa's shareholders at the club's AGM on June 16, 1911, showing the extent of the areas which Villa now wished to purchase. The areas in yellow represent those parts of the ground leased from FLOWERS & SONS, amounting to 33,000 square yards. The pink area, totalling 7,404 square yards, was to be purchased from ANSELLS brewery. The blue area denoted the 1,784 square yards to be bought from the TERRITORIAL ASSOCIATION.*

*The building shown on Witton Road was the old Rustic Cottage, which in 1911 made way for the Pavilion Electric Theatre, Aston's first ever custom-built cinema. This building still stands, although in recent years it has been used as a snooker club. Next to this, but not shown on the plans, was the Aston Hotel, built by Ansell's in 1910 on the corner of Witton Lane and Witton Road, and a firm favourite with Villa fans ever since.*

*From this plan it can be seen that where the Great Hall stood is now the car park between the North Stand and the Villa Village. The grand old Hall itself was demolished during the First World War in order to extend the Territorials' drill ground.*

*One other major difference from today is the narrowness of the ground on the east side, since remedied in 1993 by the realignment of Witton Lane, in order to make room for the Doug Ellis Stand. Thanks to a series of land acquisitions since 1990, Villa have come to own almost the entire former Lower Grounds site, from the Holte Hotel right up to the back of the houses now on Witton Road.*

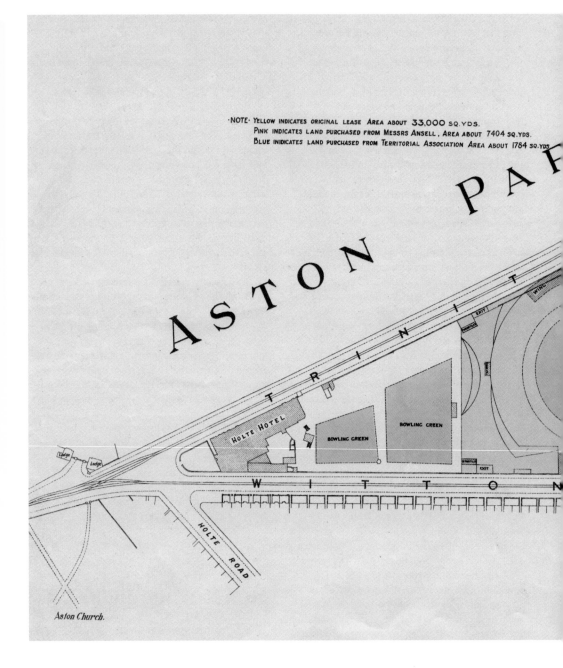

·NOTE· YELLOW INDICATES ORIGINAL LEASE AREA ABOUT 33,000 SQ.YDS.
PINK INDICATES LAND PURCHASED FROM MESSRS ANSELL, AREA ABOUT 7404 SQ.YDS.
BLUE INIDICATES LAND PURCHASED FROM TERRITORIAL ASSOCIATION AREA ABOUT 1784 SQ.YDS

it into practice. That moment came sooner than perhaps even he might have expected.

Season 1912-13 turned out to be – oh happy days – yet another wonderful year for Villa; so much so in fact that just three more wins in the League and they would have won their second Double. Instead, they won the next best prize, and that was to beat Sunderland 1-0 in the Cup Final in front of that record crowd, mentioned earlier, of over 120,000. Four days after the Final the two teams met again in the League at Villa Park. Sunderland were then top of the First Division, four points ahead of Villa, who were third. That alone guaranteed that there would be a huge crowd, but no-one imagined quite how big, especially considering that the game was played in mid-week and kicked-off in the early evening. According to the BIRMINGHAM GAZETTE there were an estimated 38,000 people, and that was just the

number locked out! Actually inside the ground there were 59,740 – thereby establishing a new Villa Park record. Small wonder Fred Rinder could not wait to start on his expansion plans.

Unfortunately for Villa they could only draw against the Rokerites, thus ending their title hopes and dreams of a Double. And just to show how fickle fans could be, for their final home match of the season, a now meaningless game against Sheffield United, only a measly 4,850 turned up, one of the lowest crowds ever known at Villa Park. Never before or since, surely, has the ground witnessed such contrasting scenes in just five days.

Still, the season's average of nearly 27,000 was the best ever in the club's history, with profits of £5,617 to add to another £9,000 in the bank. Fred Rinder therefore deemed that the time was ripe to ask the shareholders, 'should the club go ahead and

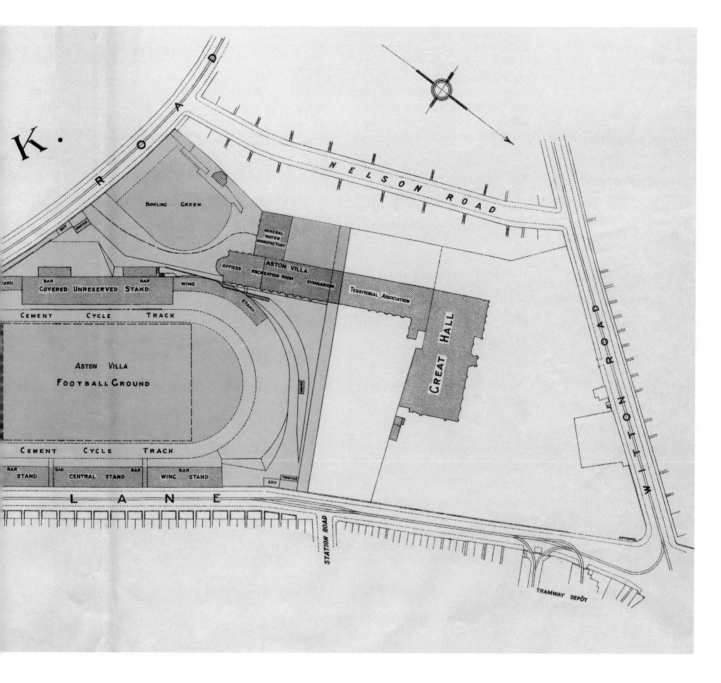

start drawing up detailed designs for the redevelopment?'

Overall, he told the 1913 AGM, the total scheme would cost in the region of £20,000, including the cost of a new stand on the Trinity Road side, and would be ready for their final approval in time to start the work during the following summe,r for completion a year or so later in 1915.

This approval having been duly given – but with the condition that the scheme should cost no more than £20,000 – the usual series of summertime cycling and athletics meetings proceeded at Villa Park, in the certain knowledge that although the ground would be out of commission in 1914, it would be back in use with a new track – albeit a cinder one – for the year after.

The final meeting of the summer was, as tradition dictated, the Birmingham Charity Sports, staged on

Saturday, August 23, 1913. A fair crowd of 7,000 saw a busy schedule of events, including cycling, gymnastics, a tug-of-war contest for the NEWS OF THE WORLD CUP and a 14 miles walking contest. And when it was over, apart from a few nostalgic comments in the press about the passing of the cement track, the only real matter of concern was where local cyclists and athletes would be able to perform in 1914, while Villa Park was undergoing its redevelopment.

As the following season passed by, behind the scenes Rinder continued drawing up the redevelopment plan in detail. But as the time for the contractors to move in approached, in March 1914 the cycling magazine SPORT AND PLAY AND WHEEL LIFE (as BICYLING NEWS was now known), reported worrying misgivings. Were Aston Villa about to renege on their promise of a new cinder track?

❖ *Archibald Leitch's detailed rendition shows how, in 1914, he and Fred Rinder intended to create the new Villa Park. A full description of this scheme appears on pages 104-108. It will be noted that the Trinity Road Stand was not originally designed with a central stairway or a pavilion-style entrance. Nor was the Witton End ever built up, as illustrated. But the Holte End was, in 1939, even though neither Leitch nor Rinder would live to see it in all its vastness. Had the masterplan ever been completed, Villa Park would theoretically have held 104,000, making it the largest stadium in England.*

According to the report, representatives of the NCU were to seek urgent talks with the club to find out, but the prospects did not look good. Nevertheless, in a forlorn bid to remind the Villa chairman of his earlier promise, the magazine printed the following poem, penned, it was said, by a contributor to the VILLA NEWS AND RECORD who was 'evidently fond of summer sport'.

**THE LOST TRACK**

Alas! I look around and see
A wrecked and hopeless Aston Track.
Think when 'twas all a track should be,
And cycling was a game that we
Enjoyed, my friends, a few years back.

How many times have I seen fought
Those battles royal between the pros.
And "makers' amateurs" who sought
The gold, but didn't like the thought
That they were paid – beneath the rose?

And now these gath'rings all are done,
And wheelmen, dreaming of their speed,
Must find another place to run
And garner all that youthful fun
Which once was theirs on Villa's mead.

But stay, a still small voice repeats:
"You'll have a track, but 'twill be cinder;
Go, tell it to the crowded streets,
Where athlete or the cyclist meets" –
It was the voice of Mr Rinder!

Alas for the poet, but, it has to be said, fortunately for whole generations of Villa fans, his plea fell on deaf ears. Fred Rinder and his fellow directors had decided, or had perhaps always known, that there would be no track after all – cinder, cement or otherwise – in the new-look Villa Park.

Thus it was that the August 1913 Charity Sports proved to be the last of their kind ever to be staged at the ground, thereby ending a tradition of cycling and athletics at the Lower Grounds which had started on the site of Villa Park in 1889 (and before then went back to the 1870s at the Old Meadow). Furthermore, by an extraordinary coincidence, the man who had organised the 1913 Charity Sports was Ellis Bradshaw, whom eagle-eyed readers might recall was the first cyclist ever to win a race on the cement track, back in April 1897.

Final confirmation of Rinder's change of heart came at Villa's AGM in June 1914, when the detailed plans were placed before an excited gathering of shareholders.

A full report of Rinder's speech appears on the following pages and needs no further comment, other than to explain two matters.

Firstly, after the club's less-than-happy experience with the well-meaning but hardly-expert Teddy Holmes, Fred Rinder had decided to turn for guidance to the most tried and tested ground expert of the day. That man was Archibald Leitch.

Now to those readers familiar with the development of British football grounds in the period

PLANS AND PARTICULAR

from 1900 to 1939, Archibald Leitch will need no introduction. A Scottish engineer whose first football engagement had been at Ibrox Park, Glasgow, in 1899, thereafter his firm popped up all over the country; at Bramall Lane in 1902, at Hampden and Ayresome Parks in 1903, at Fulham and Chelsea in 1905, followed rapidly by Ewood Park, White Hart Lane, Anfield, Goodison Park (where Leitch designed the colossal double-decker mentioned earlier), and many more grounds besides. Leitch it was who first laid out Old Trafford in 1910 and Highbury three years later.

In all, it is thought his firm was closely involved in the design and layout of no fewer than 27 grounds

# F PROPOSED ALTERATIONS TO ASTON VILLA FOOTBALL GROUNDS.

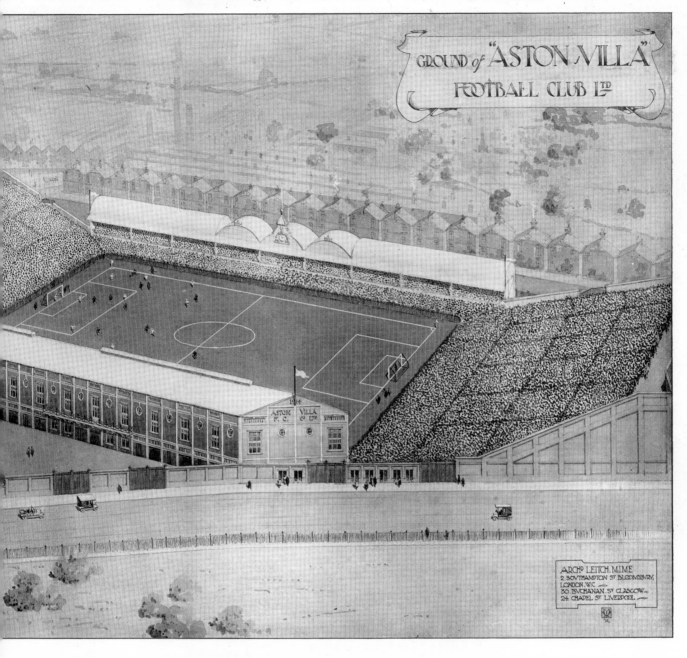

GROUND *of* "ASTON VILLA"
FOOTBALL CLUB L^{TD}

ARCH^D LEITCH. M.I.M.E
2. SOVTHAMPTON S^T BLOOMSBVRY,
LONDON .W.C.
30. BVCHANAN S^T GLASGOW
24. CHAPEL S^T LIVERPOOL

across Britain, an involvement which no modern designer can even hope to match.

But although Leitch was an accomplished engineer who clearly understood the principles of crowd movement, circulation and sightlines, he was not, despite being described by the Villa as such, an architect. Many of his stand designs were therefore quite simple and formulaic, as one would expect of a man whose other great speciality was shipyard and factory buildings.

Only when he was working with a visionary client did he produce buildings of genuine architectural quality. One such building was the now-listed South Stand at Ibrox Park, opened in

1929. The other was the Trinity Road Stand at Villa Park.

The final comment to make on the plans for the redevelopment of Villa Park concerns their timing.

Villa's AGM took place on June 18, 1914. Ten days later, as the contractors started work on digging up the cement track and shifting hundreds of tons of earth at both ends of the ground, a 19-year-old Serbian student fired two shots at the Austro-Hungarian Archduke, Franz Ferdinand and his wife, as they made a state visit to the town of Sarajevo. On August 4, with Villa Park now looking as if a bomb had hit it, Britain declared war on Germany. Fred Rinder's dream was about to turn into a nightmare.

# The New Ground Scheme

## Interesting Speech by Mr Rinder

### Full Details

THE CHAIRMAN (Mr Jos. Ansell) called attention to the undertaking given by Mr Rinder on behalf of the Directors some few years ago. You will recollect, he said, that he (Mr Rinder) intimated to the then annual meeting that his Directorate would not embark on any large scheme of expenditure without first consulting the shareholders at an annual or special meeting assembled for the purpose; and it was in accordance with that undertaking that the Directors last year submitted a general scheme for the enlargement of the ground. A resolution was then passed to the effect that the Directors and honorary officials be authorised to formulate a scheme at an approximate expenditure of £20,000, and to proceed with the work in accordance with the terms of their report and recommendations. The equitable and legal interpretation of that resolution was and is that the honorary officials and Directors had ample power to proceed with the work, bearing in mind that they were limited as to cost – viz., £20,000. During the recess many meetings have been held by this committee, and in the end they came to the conclusion that Mr Archibald Leitch, who had had considerable experience in this class of work, was the man to carry out their scheme. A plan has accordingly been made, and we are of the opinion that the time has arrived when it is desirable to proceed with some of the work at once. We have, by arrangement, left it to Mr Rinder, with his large and expert knowledge of such matters, to move the resolution I am about to read to you. But it is impossible, in my judgment, to over-rate the importance of the vote you are going to take. Already you will see that the estimate is exceeded by something like £7,000, and, therefore, the matter requires earnest and grave consideration. This it has had at the hands of the Committee, who have unanimously come to the conclusion that it is desirable to proceed with the scheme. But, in view of the financial aspect of the question, we have – wisely, as I think – made it clear to the architect that, whilst approving of the plans of Mr Leitch, we reserve our right to proceed with the scheme as and when the financial and other circumstances justify. In the discussions which have arisen on the question as to whether this big expenditure would be wise, we have considered the possibility of the popularity of football ever being on the wane. I don't know what you think about that, but as far as some of us are able to judge it will be very many years hence before you find any outdoor pastime to supply the place of the ever-increasing popularity of football. ("Hear, hear," and applause.) It is the game of the masses, and there is more interest put into an hour and a half's football than in any other game you can imagine, unless you happen to be hunting a fox "well in the run and well at the tail of the hounds." And, having considered that matter, the next question was as to the popularity and traditions of the team. It had been said that it did not always follow that the Villa would maintain their position in the football world in the future as in the past. Need you hesitate in that respect? ("No" and "Hear, hear.") You are one of the richest and most powerful clubs to be found in the football world, and I venture to say, without too much extravagance of speech, no club in the past has maintained such traditions in the football world as Aston Villa. ("Hear, hear," and loud applause.) And, therefore, in asking Mr Rinder to submit the resolution we have drafted, I only want to say this – the resolution, if passed, pledges you to adopt the scheme and such modifications as may from time to time arise in the discretion of the Executive Committee. You also empower the committee to raise money as and in accordance with the memorandum and articles of association, and to proceed with this work when the finances and other circumstances render it in our judgment fit and expedient to do so. The resolution which Mr Rinder will submit is as follows: –

### The Resolution.

*"That the scheme for the enlargement and the extension of the grounds, as prepared by Mr Leitch and now submitted by the Committee for*

*adoption, be approved, and the Directors and honorary officials be and they are hereby authorised and empowered to carry the same into effect with such modifications as they may from time to time deem necessary; and for this purpose the Directors be authorised to raise or borrow such sum or sums of money as shall be necessary, and to secure the repayment of the same in such manner as may be desirable, in accordance with the memorandum and articles of association."*

It may be said, added Mr Ansell, that this is a sweeping resolution to pass, but you will see the inconvenience – amounting almost to impossibility – of doing the work piecemeal. ("Hear, hear.")

## Mr Rinder Describes the Scheme.

Mr Rinder, who met with an encouraging and enthusiastic reception, commenced by observing that the Committee had wished to give the shareholders a longer period for considering the details of the scheme. They thought they could not do better than supply each and every member with a perspective view of the ground as it was intended it should be after the alterations had been made, together with a plan and a few brief details of the accommodation that was suggested. Unfortunately, the printers were not able to get them done so that members could have them earlier in the week, but he hoped they had all had an opportunity of looking at them and studying them. Proceeding, Mr Rinder said: So far as the plans go, I think they will very clearly explain to you what the whole of the ground will be like when the alterations are completed – if you approve of them. ("Hear, hear.") It is intended that the playing pitch as it at present exists shall remain exactly the same. I may tell you that our playing pitch, whilst perhaps a yard or yard and a half narrower from side to side than some of the other grounds in the kingdom, is at least three or four yards longer in length. As a matter of fact, our ground is of international size – 115 yards from goal to goal and 70 yards from touch-line to touch-line. The ground is so laid out that no matter what may be the match – whether it be a cup-tie or a League match, an Association match or an International match – the playing pitch as laid out is able to take any one of these matches. Many of the other grounds in the kingdom could not take an International match because they are short in length.

The cement track is to be entirely removed; the turf margin where now only one and a half yards wide will be increased – at the sides to 18 feet between the chalk line and the nearest spectator, whilst behind the goals the distance will be 24 feet. That means that the spectators behind the goals will be brought considerably nearer than they are at the present time; and, instead of the oval shape of the ground as at present, it will be more of an oblong. The first row of terracing all round the field of play will be sunk 2ft 8in. below the level of the surface of the playing pitch, the object of this being twofold: The first and important reason is that it saves all round the ground 2ft 8in, and in sinking that below the plane level you prevent the necessity of having to go 2ft 8in higher at the back. When you remember the retaining wall carrying the terraces is intended to be something like 50 feet above the roadway, you will quite understand the value of saving 2ft 8in at the bottom. It means a very considerable saving in the expense. ("Hear, hear.") The other reason is that by putting the players on a higher level than the lowest spectators you get for every spectator on the ground a very much better view of the actual play that is taking place.

## The Old Stand and Pavilion to Remain.

The present stand and pavilion it is intended to retain as at present – so far as the seating is concerned. It is intended that in front of this shall be an enclosure with narrower steps than at present, with a verandah 15 feet in length from the front of the present stand, so that there will be a projection running the whole length of the old stand covering the people standing in front and extending 30 feet in width. On that side of the ground, and particularly at the close of the matches, there is a great congestion caused by the people coming down the steps from the seats on the stand and meeting the people coming from the terracing in front; and to obviate that difficulty the idea is to reserve the present staircases for the use of the people occupying seats, and to construct entirely new entrances from Witton Lane direct through the bottom of the stand to the enclosure in front for those who prefer to stand, so that there will be no necessity for their mixing and crowding with those going up and down to the seats on the stand. I may say the necessity for this provision has been pointed out to us more than once, as that is the spot where most the pocket-picking takes place. It is to avoid that that we propose this alteration ("Hear, hear.") The terracing at either end will be brought within 24 feet of the back of the goals as they at present stand, and the terraces will be extended right away back to the full extent of our boundary. They will be separated at various points as shown in the plan by sunken distributing passages 4 feet in width – the object being to prevent anyone standing in those passages being able to see the play, so that they will make every endeavour to get out of those passages as quickly as possible, and seek some favourable position from which they can see the play. The result would be that those passages, interspersed all over the terracing, would, during the matches, always be kept clear, so that late-comers would be able to walk along them to find a suitable position to view the game in one of the numerous sections. ("Hear, hear.")

In calculating the accommodation of the new ground a very liberal estimate has been taken – no account has been taken of the possibility of anyone standing in any of those sunken passages – and we are quite sure there is ample provision for 104,000 – I think the number can be exceeded – but we say that under this scheme that number will be able to take their places and see the game. That is not a statement that the ground will hold that number, and then, when tested, be found to come very much short of that accommodation. I feel perfectly confident that, if these alterations are carried out, the ground will hold the number of people mentioned.

## The New Stand.

On the opposite side of the ground to the present stand the suggestion is to erect an entirely new stand. This is intended to seat 6,500 persons, with a minimum allowance of 1ft 6in to each person, the centre portion having 1ft 8in in width for each seat; and it is worth while remembering that there are very few people in this world, however big they may be, who are 1ft 6in between one shoulder and the other. I may tell you the recognised measurement in

an omnibus or railway train is 1ft 3in (Laughter). In that stand it is intended to construct a new suite of dressing rooms for the players, for the referee, for the trainer; whilst a new feature will be a special room for the doctor. This latter, it is suggested, should be fitted up in the most approved style of a surgical room in a hospital, and fitted with X-rays, radium, heat, and other modern appliances – the object being not only to get injured players attended to as quickly as possible, but to obviate the possibility of the recurrence of an incident like that at the end of last season, where our much-respected player, Freddie Miles – instead of the true nature of his accident being ascertained at once by proper examination, was allowed to play three-parts of the game with a broken small bone in the leg. ("Hear, hear," and applause.) Pointing to the plan, Mr Rinder (continuing) said: About level with the white line of the back elevation, there is what we term a distributing passage 15ft above the level of the ground. The spectators, by ascending a flight of steps, will reach this distributing floor, which is about 35ft in width, and runs the whole length of the stand. It is well lighted by windows, and from the floor there are flights of steps to the various sections of the stand. On that floor there will be constructed, in convenient positions and for every section of the stand, suitable refreshment and tea rooms and all the other necessary conveniences for those attending the matches. It has also been suggested that we should equip that floor with all sorts of social conveniences for those who attend our matches. The stand itself it is intended shall be divided into six or seven different sections – each, of course, at different prices, with the centre portion the highest-priced. In that centre portion it is intended to allot a particular section to the shareholders, and maintain it for their special use. (Loud applause.) The whole of the stand, it is suggested, shall be fitted with tip-up chairs – the reason being to afford the easiest possible passage for those desiring to get to their respective seats. It is further suggested that each person applying should be able to have a definite seat allotted to him. ("Hear, hear.")

With regard to the suggested new dressing-rooms, they are to be placed in the corner of the stand nearest the present offices – the object being to enable those dressing-rooms when built to act as training quarters during the week for the players.

At the present time the dressing-rooms are on the Witton Lane side, and the players have to use the field for one portion of their training, and to cross the field or use the terracing to reach the offices, gymnasium and recreation rooms on the other side. The object of placing the dressing rooms in that corner of the stand is to have everything compact and close together. Underneath the offices there is a space which it is suggested should be turned into a cinder track; whilst on the other side of the office building there is a plot of land 70 yards in length, which it is suggested should be turfed and made into a small practice ground, so that players will be entirely in that one corner of the grounds for training purposes, and be kept off the playing pitch. The training quarters and recreation rooms would then be under the easy control and supervision of the trainer without his having to walk to the opposite side of the ground to see how things are going on. ("Hear, hear.") There is also a suggestion that part of the building known as the old mineral water factory should be converted into the groundsman's house, so that we should have him living on the grounds and able to exercise proper control over them.

On the Witton Lane side there are under the present stand a number of rooms which have been used for storing the seats, etc, used on the track. As there will be no track in future, these rooms will be available for some other purpose; and we have, at the present time, one fitted as a cycle store room. We have been asked to provide accommodation for motor cycles and motors; and it has been suggested we shall be able to adapt these rooms for that purpose. ("Hear, hear.") The general construction of the new stand will be of steel and concrete.

The design is simple, but it will be as pleasing as possible. We shall endeavour to make it a credit to the club, and not an eyesore to those who have to pass along. ("Hear, hear," and applause.) It is our intention – always providing that you shareholders approve – that the whole of the work shall be advertised and open to free and local competition, and to get the best and cheapest we possibly can. The holding capacity is explained approximately on the plan as follows:-

| | |
|---|---|
| New Grand Stand (Seated) | 6,500 |
| Enclosure in front, part covered in by roof of Grand Stand | 11,000 |
| Existing Grand Stand (Seated) | 4,500 |
| Enclosure in front, part covered in by roof of Stand | 12,000 |
| Terracing – City end | 40,000 |
| Terracing – Witton end | 30,000 |
| Total | 104,000 |

It is intended – continued Mr Rinder – although it is not shown on the plan, to remove the existing covers on the unreserved side of the ground, and place a portion of them on top of the embankments at either end, behind the goals. (Applause.) At present that accommodation extends to about 15,000, and it may be possible to increase that covered accommodation. Personally, I feel that the covered accommodation on particular days is the backbone of our support – ("Hear, hear.") – and I should be very loth to see the covered portions of the 6d accommodation reduced in size. I would much rather see it increase from 15,000 to 30,000 ("Hear, hear," and loud applause.)

## The Earning Capacity.

I will endeavour now to give you the earning capacity. The old stand as at present existing is able to earn £387 per match at our usual prices; the new stand, at similar prices for the main portion and very moderately increased prices for the better portion, will realise £756. The enclosures in front of the two stands, partly covered, at 1s. will realise £1,200, and the portions at either end at 6d will realise £1,800 – a total of £4,143 – or, roughly, an earning capacity with a sixpenny gate of £4,000 per match. (Applause.) The present ground at similar prices is able to earn – (present covered seating, £387; uncovered track seats, £275; other parts, £1,150) – at the utmost £1,650; so that the difference in the two capacities is more than doubled.

As to the necessity for the improvements, one of the worst features of the existing arrangements is the fact that there are only 4,500 seats under cover. To my mind it is apparent that it is absolutely insufficient. There is not a First Team match we play, even of the smallest importance, and against the team doing worst in the League, and in the vilest weather in which we play, but what the seats on the stand are overcrowded. They could be filled two or three times over, if covered seats were available; and in that respect we are miles behind other clubs in the kingdom. ("Hear, hear.") I think it is essential that increased seated accommodation under cover should be provided, and I am sure if you were to erect the stand now your expenditure would be easily and quickly justified. ("Hear, hear.") You would only need to have the new stand a quarter full at each First Team match we play during the season to have an income of £3,750. You would earn money which at present you have no means of earning, and on the lines indicated the stand would pay for itself in five years. ("Hear, hear," and applause.)

During the past season we have had on the ground over 40,000 people on four occasions; over 50,000 on two occasions; and on one occasion 58,000. ("Hear, hear.") It has been demonstrated the ground will hold that number of people, but I think you will all admit that when thirty to thirty-five thousand are on the present ground, it is most uncomfortably crowded; and, if you can provide more room, I feel perfectly satisfied in my own mind that you would on such occasions very greatly increase your attendances. At First League matches during the past season, the average attendance has been 30,000. (Applause.) I know, and you must have seen, a number of times when the ground, particularly in the 6d and 1s portions, has been most uncomfortably crowded. It is most essential that we should endeavour to provide increased and better accommodation for those who wish to patronise us. There are a large number of people desirous of attending our matches who come from districts as far away as Coventry, Worcester, Walsall, Kidderminster, and different parts of the Black Country. The railway people will tell you that at our First League matches it is rarely they bring fewer than 1,000 people from Coventry alone; and it is the same with regard to the other places to a corresponding degree. Well, you just imagine an important match being played at Aston, and people at Coventry, Kidderminster, and other places a

distance away, all anxious to come, and not leaving work until 1 o'clock and the kick-off at 2.15 pm! They have to get to Birmingham first of all, and then get down to the ground. What chance have they got to get a decent place? ("Hear, hear.") I am confident a large number of those people stay away because of that, whereas they would be perfectly satisfied to come down and pay their admission money if they knew they could get a comfortable view of even one-half of the game ("Hear, hear.")

### A Bogey.

I have been told by a number of members of the club that if the scheme is carried out the ground at ordinary matches would look very bare, and more like a half-empty theatre. Gentlemen, don't you believe it! (Laughter.) You can take it from me, the people will spread themselves out in the most comfortable positions, so that it will look fairly full. ("Hear, hear.") I will tell you an instance. A member of a club that had just been successful in getting into the First Division was making his first appearance on our ground. Just before the match he said to me: "How many have you got here?" and I said, "About 12,000." He said, in amazement, "What? Why, you say your ground will hold 50,000! Well, where do you put the others, then?" (Laughter.) Well, the match had been going on about half an hour when it came on to rain; and suddenly there was a scamper to get under cover, and in a very few minutes the covered part of the sixpenny side was full and the rest bare. I said. "What do you think about it now?" And, of course, the gentleman could only express his astonishment. (Laughter.) I think you would find that our regular crowd would spread themselves out so that the ground would look comfortably full. ("Hear, hear.")

# War, Peace and Squandermania

SET AGAINST THE PAIN AND SUFFERING endured by nearly a million British and Empire servicemen, civilians and their families between 1914 and 1918, the War-time woes of Aston Villa were of but trifling importance. No football club, yet alone any football ground, could ever be worth more than one life.

There can be little doubt, however, that the outbreak of war and the changes it wrought upon the national economy drastically upset Fred Rinder's plans for Villa Park.

As already noted, during the summer of 1914 the first phase of Rinder and Leitch's masterplan was nearly finished, in that both end terraces were completely rebuilt, closer to and parallel with the touchlines, thereby giving the ground its present-day rectangular shape (as opposed to the oval lay-out of before). The terraces on both the Trinity Road and Witton Lane sides were also extended, to take up the space created by the removal of the cycle track. By the time the board called a halt in September 1914, with some sections of terracing yet to be finished off, £3,261 had been spent.

Had war not erupted, the intention had been to carry out almost immediately the second phase of the redevelopment, the building of the new Trinity Road stand. Overall, this had been costed, in June 1914, at around £27,000.

At that time the omens looked extremely positive. The team had just finished second in the League and reached an FA Cup semi-final. Profits for season 1913-14 had amounted to a record £6,777, giving Villa a total accumulated surplus of nearly £19,000, more, probably, than any other club in the land. If the new stand was built, reckoned Rinder, it would be comfortably paid off within five years, as had been the experience of several other clubs who had recently completed two-tier stands (such as Blackburn and Sheffield Wednesday, both of whom also employed Archibald Leitch).

Yet four years later the outlook could hardly have been more different.

For the first year of the War professional football carried on, with the FOOTBALL LEAGUE defiantly insisting that that was what the public and the troops serving overseas would have wanted. But once it was realised that the bloody conflict would not, as some senior generals had predicted, be 'over by Christmas', the League's position became increasingly untenable, and the game effectively shut itself down in July 1915, its image tarnished amid accusations of selfishness and disloyalty to the cause of victory.

(Incidentally, during that controversial, and rather unreal campaign of 1914-15, Villa Park witnessed its lowest ever gate for a first team match, when just 2,900 turned up for a game against Bradford City on February 13, 1915. Only a few days earlier, as if in judgement, a geyser in the dressing room exploded.)

In fairness, Villa could hardly have done more for the War effort. Villa Park itself was offered to the army for billeting (to supplement the Territorial's facilities behind the Witton End). All Villa players were kitted out with special uniforms and given strict military training by ex-army sergeant-majors, at the club's expense. The board even purchased 30 service rifles so that a shooting range could be established (although in the end this plan fell through and some of the rifles were later sold to, of all people, Archibald Leitch. Perhaps he wanted them to chivvy along his contractors.)

Regular appeals for volunteers from Lord Kitchener appeared in the VILLA NEWS AND RECORD, while the board, having promised to support the Middlesex Regiment's efforts to establish a Footballers Battalion, offered to carry on paying half wages to any player who enlisted, so that their wives and children could be looked after.

According to Fred Rinder, over the course of the four year conflict, 22 of the 30 or so players registered with Villa in 1914 entered the services, with the majority of the others being engaged in munitions work at KYNOCH'S in Witton. Of the 22, five were wounded, including Tommy Barber, scorer of Villa's goal in the 1913 Cup Final (who never played again) and Frank Moss (who recovered to make 283 appearances and bring up two future playing sons, Frank junior and Amos).

Three Villa men were killed − only Clapton Orient lost as many − among whom was one player who had featured in the first team; a half back called Arthur Dobson, who made seven senior appearances between 1912-15 and who died in action in Germany in 1918, at the age of 25.

Other than occasional trial games played behind closed doors, there would be only 13 official matches at Villa Park between April 1915 and the resumption of League football in September 1919. Played mainly by juniors, against West Bromwich, Wolves and Derby, these games raised over £4,000 in receipts, all of which was distributed among funds for Prisoners-of-War, Soldiers and Sailors Comforts, Victims of Zeppelin Raids and local hospitals. The club also purchased an 'Aston Villa Ambulance Car' and cashed in their pre-War stocks and shares (most of them in railway companies), in order to raise a War loan worth £3,000. The result of all this patriotic activity was that Villa accumulated losses of £7,727 during the War.

But if that ruled out any immediate re-start of Rinder's ground plans when football resumed in September 1919, any anxieties the board might have harboured were soon swept away in a totally unexpected tide of enthusiasm. Desperate for some light relief after four long years of anguish, the nation flocked to football matches as never before. Villa alone broke all their previous records. Despite finishing only in 9th place, in 1919-20 their average gate shot up to 32,155, a 20 per cent improvement on their previous best (in 1912-13). Gate receipts reached a mind-boggling total of nearly £66,500.

One of the reasons for this hugely increased income was that, since 1915, minimum admission prices had been doubled to 1s, largely owing to the introduction of Entertainment Tax in 1917. But Villa also had the added bonus of a record breaking sixth FA Cup triumph, thanks to a 1-0 win over

❖ *Villa blamed bad weather and a trade union work-to-rule for the late completion of the Trinity Road Stand, but as this Albert Wilkes photograph shows, taken in late summer 1922, the progress in such a short time was still fairly remarkable. Note the exposed steelwork of the upper tier balcony. Most Leitch stands left this open to view, but Villa concealed it behind the curved wooden panels. During the construction a workman was badly injured. Although not Villa's responsibility the directors sent him £5 to ease his pain.*

❖ *The familiar face of the Trinity Road Stand, at the time of its completion in 1923, with the less familiar figure of photographer Albert Wilkes on the stairs. None of the details shown here – the stairs, mosaics, stained glass windows or pedimented towers – appeared on the original plans, which helps explain why the stand ended up costing 50 per cent more than the 1922 estimate. Since this photograph was taken, the iron lamp stands have disappeared, and in 1992 the whole frontage was extended and refurbished.*

Huddersfield in the Final at Stamford Bridge. This feat alone had been worth over £13,000, while even the reserve team, who had just switched from the Birmingham League to the more competitive Central League, earned a handsome £4,301 in receipts – four times the total from 1913-14.

Addressing the 1920 AGM, a delighted, and no doubt relieved Fred Rinder told the shareholders that the League president, John McKenna had recently joked that Aston Villa ought not to be called a football club, but 'a gramophone club', because they were always making records.

But for all the renewed confidence at Villa Park, developments in the wider world already suggested that post-War Britain was not so much a 'land fit for heroes' as promised, but a seething cauldron of industrial unrest, strikes and mounting unemployment. It was now quite common to see ex-servicemen begging on the streets, including outside Villa Park on match days.

Crippling inflation would exact a heavy toll on Villa's finances. For a start, the new Entertainment Tax wiped out over 17 per cent of their income straight away, with a further drain being hugely increased insurance and travel costs. Whereas before the War a return rail trip to London had cost only 7s, now the ticket price was over 27s. Limited services and strikes also meant a greater number of overnight stops.

Concerning the ground redevelopment, the economic signs were even more alarming. So high had the costs of materials and labour become that when Rinder and Leitch sought new quotes for building the Trinity Road Stand, the estimated cost had shot up from £27,000 in 1914 to a frightening £66,000 in 1919, too much even for an architectural agitator like Fred Rinder to contemplate.

So the ground works were reluctantly put in abeyance for a couple of years, as Rinder waited for the economy to turn, content at least in the knowledge that Villa's own finances were continuing to show remarkable signs of recovery. There would be no further successes on the pitch, but gates were still rising, reaching a new record peak of 66,094, for a derby match v West Bromwich in November 1920, and a new record average of 35,052 for the 1920-21 season overall.

At the end of that season Rinder obtained a revised estimate for the new stand, but although the price had dropped slightly, to £54,000, it was still far too high. Finally, a third set of figures arrived at in early 1922, was deemed sufficiently low for the board to agree unanimously that the new Trinity Road Stand should be started the following summer.

Three main contractors bid successfully for the work. The builders were to be the Birmingham firm of E. GARFIELD LTD, whose estimate of £25,393 was the lowest of no fewer than 10 tenders. Yet Villa still beat them down to £25,225! There were even more firms – 25 in total – bidding for the steelwork contract, which was eventually given to FRANCIS MORTON & CO, at a price of £9,650. This was not the lowest tender but Leitch had little confidence in some of the rock bottom bidders. Villa might also have saved money by accepting the use of imported steel. But, patriots that they were, the directors insisted on nothing but British materials, even though this may have added over £2,000 to the bill.

Finally, the flooring contract, worth £6,900, went to a firm called KLEINER'S, making a total estimate for the whole project of £41,775.

This was still way above the 1914 price, but Rinder was now clearly intent upon making a start. Gates had continued to be high throughout the 1921-22 season, at an average of 32,690, while just as importantly the demand for seats in the Witton Lane Stand was now far outstripping demand. The longer they delayed, the more potential revenue Villa would miss out on.

Perhaps significantly, however, when the decision to proceed was agreed in March 1922, life was already changing for Fred Rinder.

In 1917 – after nine failed attempts – he had finally achieved his long held ambition of being elected to the FOOTBALL LEAGUE's all-important Management Committee, thus marking his transition from a 'stormy petrel' on the outside to an upright member of the inner circle. This gave Rinder more status than any other Villa representative since William McGregor, and clearly he revelled in it.

Yet small signs of discontent with Rinder's chairmanship were already starting to emerge at Villa Park. Superficially the causes seem to have been fairly petty; for example, complaints that shareholders were not being guaranteed enough seats in the centre section of the Witton Lane Stand, and that too many civic dignitaries had been invited to the 1920 Cup Final at Villa's expense. But the fact that certain shareholders openly defied the chairman at the 1920 AGM, and that he in return clearly lost

his temper with them, did not bode well for future relations. Thus Rinder may well have considered the Trinity Road Stand as a chance to re-establish his supremacy, as well, of course, as providing a lasting legacy of his office.

There may have been one further factor in the timing of the decision to proceed with the stand.

By 1922 Rinder was aged 64, and after forty years as a surveyor with the CITY OF BIRMINGHAM CORPORATION he finally decided to retire. Thus he found himself with more time than ever to devote to Villa Park. By all accounts FWR, as he was often known, was not an easy man. In common with many

❖ Wyndham Malins, an Aston Villa shareholder and critic of Rinder, said sarcastically 'the directors must have their temple.' If so, this was their inner sanctum – the Board Room in the new Trinity Road Stand – where Malins himself would turn up after the 1925 coup. Were the two vases on the mantlepiece the ones which raised so many hackles among shareholders?

❖ The Trinity Road Stand's Oak Room restaurant may well have been the first such facility at a British football ground. Years later the area is still in use, as the McGregor Suite.

❖ *In the days before fast-food, betting booths and decent toilet facilities (for women in particular), a football stand concourse was a simple affair. Yet 75 years later most Trinity Road regulars will still recognise the style. No other ground would have such stained-glass screens.*

single-minded chairmen of successful clubs he was respected more for his achievements than for his personal charms. Some said he was of 'a naturally retiring disposition' while others thought him aloof. He was described as 'coldly logical, a trifle didactic' and an inveterate workaholic. He could also be a strict authoritarian, as shown on a railway journey returning from an away match when he threw three bottles of whiskey out of the window in order to clear Villa's carriage of hangers-on. 'There were plenty of black looks,' he later recalled. But no one dared argue.

Yet he was no prude or abstainer. Indeed, in the earlier part of his professional career Rinder was busily involved in Arthur Chamberlain's campaign for 'fewer and better' public houses in Birmingham, a drive which had seen many a back-street drinking den and shebeen closed down in favour of custom-built licensed houses, many of them tied to the likes of ANSELLS and MITCHELL AND BUTLERS. Between 1909 and 1922, Rinder later estimated, he was responsible for the licensing of no fewer than 2,000 pubs, billiard halls, music halls and clubs across the city. He also became an important figure in the city's burgeoning cinema industry, as an adviser on their design in particular. (Birmingham, it should be noted, gave to the film world Sam Goldwyn – born Sam Goldfisch – and Oscar Deutsch, founder of the ODEON chain.) Two early cinema owners whom Rinder helped were former Villa players, John Devey and Harry Hampton, who formed the WINSON GREEN PICTURE HOUSE COMPANY in 1915.

Since his retirement from the game in 1902 Devey had served as a fellow Villa board member with Rinder. In 1909 he was joined by another former stalwart, Howard Spencer. The pair were still on the board in 1922, along with Captain P. W. M. Bate (a former League referee, elected to the board in 1906) and J. E. 'Jack' Jones (elected 1907), of whom more later.

None of these men could remotely be described as weak. But nor could any of them match Rinder's experience as a football administrator, or his inside knowledge of the building industry.

Besides which, Rinder had ridden successfully through enough challenges in the past, from the Barwick Street showdown in 1893, through the battle with the FA over a maximum wage, the formation of Villa as a limited company, the move to Villa Park, the purchase of the freehold and most recently, the difficulties encountered during the First World War. Under his chairmanship the club had won more honours than any other club, and consistently made larger profits than most. Surely he could be trusted to oversee the construction of one football grand stand? After all, it was his third, if one counted the original Perry Barr stand in 1887 and the Witton Lane stand a decade later.

Two and a half weeks after the decision to proceed, on April 8, 1922, Villa Park staged its third England international v Scotland, a crowd of 33,000 watching the visitors gain a one goal victory, their first win on English soil since 1903. Three Villa players were in the England line-up: Dickie York and Frank Moss, who were making their international debuts, and striker Billy Walker.

GARFIELD'S moved onto the Trinity Road site a month later and continued work throughout the rain-sodden summer. As the steelwork went up, the BIRMINGHAM MAIL reported excitedly in mid-June, 'Even the regular supporter will hardly recognise Villa Park when he goes to the ground for the Villa's opening match next season.'

Although there had been some delays because of the weather, 'already quite a large stretch of the framework has been put up, and the work proceeds so rapidly that the scene suggests to the mind a group of earnest and enthusiastic boys jointly erecting a constructional toy model.'

The MAIL added that the steel members had all been prefabricated in a factory and brought to the site by rail, carefully numbered in readiness to be bolted together. It also commented that 'the public will be glad to know that the whole of the work is British.'

Rather optimistically, Villa had hoped to finish the Trinity Road Stand in time for their first home match of the new season, on August 26, 1922, appropriately enough when Blackburn were to be the visitors (Rovers having been Villa's first opponents at Villa Park in 1897).

However, as the VILLA NEWS AND RECORD for that match explained, not all had gone according to plan.

'There is one important matter to which we should like to draw special attention, and that is with regard to the new grand stand which we had hoped to see completed today, and which, no doubt, would have been quite ready if it had not been for certain ill-considered and irritating obstacles raised by the trades unions concerned. But, if the stand is not actually completed, sufficient progress has been made for its occupation in part, and visitors to Villa Park this afternoon will find a great transformation has taken place since last season; and, not only in the appearance of the ground, but in the general arrangements for the accommodation of the public, prices of admission, etc. We should like our friends and supporters, however, to particularly bear in mind that these arrangements and prices are tentative only, and may be revised and varied as experience of their working may dictate and show to be advisable. In these circumstances the directors ask the indulgence of members of the club and the public generally for any inconvenience which may arise until the new stand and the alterations its erection have necessitated have been completed and are in full working order. We can assure our readers that not an effort will be spared nor a moment lost in hurrying on the good work.

'The inability to get the new stand completely finished in time for the opening match is a source of keen disappointment, not only to the directors of the club, but also to the contractors and all concerned in its erection. The whole of the work could easily have been done in time but for two things. First of all the very wet weather of the last six weeks has caused the workmen to lose quite a considerable number of days' work, but by far the greater portion of the delay has been due to the absurd restrictions imposed by the trades unions with regard to working overtime. An instance or two will be quite sufficient to show the ill-considered attitude taken up by the union officials. In one week alone the workmen engaged on the job lost two and a half days' work owing to the rain in consequence of the union refusing to allow them to work overtime on the fine evenings to make up that lost time. Further, we are led to understand there is not a single plasterer – not merely in Birmingham but in the whole of the country – out of work, there being more plastering work to do than there are men to do it. The contractor who is erecting the new stand asked the plasterers' trades union for permission for the plasterers to work overtime, undertaking at the same time to find work for every man they sent him who was physically fit and competent to do plastering. But no, not a single hour's overtime would the Union permit to be worked!

'And here's another point with regard to the bricklayers. The contractor put on as many men as the job would carry – that is to say as many men as could move on the scaffolding at the same time, 33 bricklayers with their attendant 33 labourers, 66 men in all – and this complement of workmen could just raise the brickwork one scaffold height in a day's work. The contractors asked the joint trades unions for six labourers (scaffolders) to work over after the other workmen had knocked off at 5 o'clock in order to get the scaffold ready for the other 66 workmen to be able to start again first thing in the morning. But again, no! They would rather some of the men should lose time whilst the scaffold was being raised than permit six labourers to work overtime to get all in readiness. These illustrations will give our readers some idea of the difficulties which have had to be faced – difficulties which, in our opinion, and apart

altogether from the question of the wet weather, might very well have been obviated by a little sensible consideration and a spirit of good will and conciliation on the part of the trades unions concerned.

'Notwithstanding all these little "troubles and trials", however, practically two-thirds of the new stand will be ready for the public to get a seat to view the Blackburn Rovers match, though the painting and decorative work and the many conveniences which the directors are introducing for the comfort of the public are still in an embryonic state. We need hardly add that the work will be pushed on as fast as possible, and due announcement will be made of the date of the formal opening – an event which we rather fancy will prove a "red-letter day" in the annals of Aston Villa. The arrangements for the supply of refreshments are merely temporary; the full scheme will not be decided upon until the stand is completed and the directors know exactly where things are.'

Having vented its spleen on the trades unions, the programme went on to describe the new stand; a description which will not be repeated here since so many readers will already be familiar with the building.

A few facts may be of interest, however. The upper tier was to accommodate 6,500 people in tip-up seats – a novelty for Villa fans, since the Witton Lane Stand had, until then, had only bench seats. (By comparison, in 1996 the Trinity Road's upper tier held 5,230, as a result of new seats and gangways being installed, plus stricter regulations on emergency escape.)

The newly terraced lower tier was able to hold 11,000 standing (compared with 3,931 seats in 1996).

❖ *Fred Rinder did not forget the players' comforts in the new stand. X-ray machines and a wealth of medical equipment was installed, together with this large washing area, which contained what were described as plunge, slipper and needle baths (that is, showers). Note the single exposed light-bulb.*

❖ The Duke of York takes off
his hat to the Villa crowd, as
Fred Rinder leads him and the
Lord Mayor out onto the pitch
to meet the players, before
the game v Bolton. Villa's
players and directors had
already met the Duke of York
before the 1920 Cup Final at
Stamford Bridge, and would
meet him again at Wembley
three months after the Bolton
game.

Prices ranged from 1s for standing on the lower
terrace, up to 5s to sit in the central section of the
upper tier.

One innovation the club was particularly proud of,
although it had yet to open, was the Oak Room
restaurant, which would allow supporters,
particularly those who travelled a long distance for
games, to dine before matches. In 1922 this was quite
unheard of at football grounds.

But then there were several aspects of the Trinity
Road Stand which were quite unique. The frontage
we all know about. Juxtaposed with the already
distinctive former Lower Grounds buildings, no other
ground in the world ever boasted such a grand facade,
with its classical central stairway, two pedimented
pavilion towers, mosaic embellishments and Dutch
gables (to echo those of Aston Hall and of public
buildings all around Aston). The central roof gable
facing the pitch was also far more elaborate and larger
than any Leitch had designed for his other stands –
such as at Hillsborough, Stamford Bridge or Craven
Cottage – and was topped by ornamental iron
railings, to match those on the tower of the former
aquarium.

Another unique feature was the curved wooden
panelling on the stand's upper tier balcony. Painted
initially in light blue with claret bands (the reverse of
today), this panelling concealed the steelwork frame
which was always left exposed at other Leitch stands.
Indeed, as can still be seen at Ibrox Park and
Goodison Park, the criss-cross steelwork pattern was
very much a Leitch trademark. But Fred Rinder was
not interested in a stand which looked like all the
others, hence the unique detailing with which we
have all become so familiar.

And so it was that Villa Park now took on the
dignified air which would set it quite apart from the
mainstream of British football. All it needed was for
the internal areas to be completed and for 'the red-
letter day' of its official opening to be arranged.
(Behind the scenes Fred Rinder was negotiating for
the Prince of Wales to do the honours.)

As the 1922-23 season wore on, work continued
at the ground. Rinder's fellow directors occasionally
expressed their frustration at the delays. There were
also frequent questions about the mounting costs.
Each time Rinder seemed to deflect any discussion,
although it was admitted in February 1923 that the
bill now stood at £38,661, despite there clearly being
much extra fitting out to complete.

Nor was work confined to the new stand. The
arched promenade which made up the former
aquarium was converted into a basic ball-court, while
the former mineral water manufactory became a cosy
one bedroom house for the groundsman and his wife,
complete with bathroom, toilet, sitting room and
combined kitchen and scullery. This cost a mere
£250, petty cash compared with the ongoing work
elsewhere. More costly was the provision of new
mains supplies for gas, water and electricity, all of
which fell outside the original budget.

The problem was, how to pay for it all?

Rinder's answer came in June 1923, when he
somehow persuaded the shareholders to agree to two
crucial changes in the company's Articles of
Association. As they stood, ASTON VILLA FC LTD was
not allowed to borrow more than £10,000 in total,
while any individual borrowings by the directors of
over £500 had to be ratified by the shareholders.
Rinder now argued, however, that the scale of the
current ground developments required greater
flexibility than that. It is, no doubt, a measure of the
trust in which he was then held by the shareholders
that Rinder won the debate, for thereafter all
restrictions were lifted, giving the directors a
completely free hand to borrow whatever amounts
they saw fit.

On the other hand, how large could these sums possibly be, especially as the Trinity Road Stand – or the New Pavilion as it was also called – was all but complete. And though Rinder had been called many things in the past, profligate was never one of them.

As the VILLA NEWS AND RECORD of August 1923 declared, all members and supporters will look upon the finished stand 'with pride and satisfaction, because its lay-out, its wealth of accommodation, and the organised detail of its complete equipment, go to make Villa Park the most perfect football ground in the country.'

Its capacity, gushed the programme, was 80,000 – not a guess, it insisted but a genuine calculation – which, once both end terraces were extended, as proposed in the Rinder-Leitch masterplan, would rise to 120,000. (In fact these figures were erroneous. Only when the Holte End was extended in 1939 would the ground be capable of holding near 80,000. But one has to accept that all clubs like to engage in such hyperbole, and the date of Villa's claims is also significant. It was just a few months after Wembley Stadium had opened.)

Another claim to fame was the new restaurant, which was now being run by the PATTISON-HUGHES CATERING COMPANY, and the press room, which, with its writing room, telephones and other appointments was 'better than that at any other football ground in England or out of it.'

What the article did not admit was that Villa were already massively in hock to the banks in order to pay for all this, and that, after the immediate post-War boom, Villa's average gates had now slipped to under the 30,000 mark.

But if Fred Rinder was worried, he certainly did not let it show when the promised 'red-letter day' arrived on January 26 1924, just two months short of the club's Jubilee. Villa had not managed to book the Prince of Wales, but they were able to welcome the next best royal in the Windsor's pecking order, the equally grand but not-so-old Duke of York (a.k.a. 'Bertie', the future King George VI and father of the current Queen Elizabeth).

Never before had Villa Park played host to such an important personage, and although Birmingham City had drawn a larger crowd earlier in the season, there were still 56,000 at the ground to welcome the Duke. Also there was Archibald Leitch, Mr Garfield the builder, the Right Hon. Austen Chamberlain and his wife, and the Lord Mayor of Birmingham, Alderman T. O. Williams, who had arrived earlier in the day quite unnoticed until George Ramsay bumped into him in the stand.

But was there a prouder man in Birmingham that afternoon than Fred Rinder? As he led the Duke out onto the pitch to be introduced to the two teams – Bolton being the visitors – he must surely have felt fully vindicated in his determination to carry forward his masterplan. The ground which he had done so much to create had never looked so good. The crowd

❖ *Villa welcome the Duke of York for the Bolton game on January 26, 1924. From left to right: Howard Spencer (director), Capt. P. W. M. Bate (director), Archibald Leitch (architect/engineer), Fred Rinder (chairman), Howard Vaughton (director), E. Garfield (contractor), The Duke of York, George Ramsay (secretary), Lieut. Buist (Duke's equerry), Alderman T. O. Williams (Lord Mayor of Birmingham), Mrs Austen Chamberlain and the Rt. Hon. Austen Chamberlain.*

was in raptures (since many had never seen a member of the royal family in the flesh before). Best of all, the normally shy Duke seemed genuinely impressed, telling Rinder that he had no idea that 'a ground so finely equipped in every way – and devoted to football – existed.' And though more of a tennis man himself, throughout the game he swapped opinions with a beaming Rinder, even going so far as to disagree with a few of the referee's decisions.

Villa sneaked a 1-0 win that memorable afternoon, little realising then that they would be seeing the Duke only three months later at Wembley. On that second occasion they would not emerge as victors, however. Newcastle beat them 2-0 in only the stadium's second FA Cup Final, thus depriving Villa of a record breaking seventh Cup win.

Nevertheless, how could any shareholder complain? To have undoubtedly the best grand stand in Britain – which it genuinely was at the time – to have been visited by a Duke, to have finished sixth in the League and reached an eighth Cup Final, was hardly a record to dismiss lightly.

Accordingly, there was surprisingly little debate at the 1924 AGM – the first, incidentally, since the death of Joseph Ansell, who had been club's president for 30 years. Moreover, at a time when the country was now in the grip of a worsening recession, Villa had at least managed to make a small operating profit of £3,353.

It might have been more, but as Fred Rinder explained, over the past few summers, as well as finishing the new stand, every inch of terracing at the ground – or some 16 miles in total – had been concreted over (whereas before they had consisted of shale with timber footings). That work, combined with the rest of the ground improvements and the building of the new stand, had amounted to a staggering £70,000.

And yet far from being staggered, or even perturbed, the chairman seemed amazingly relaxed about the total, despite the fact that Villa's debt to the bank had reached nearly £30,000 and there was 'still a considerable sum owing to the contractors.'

Now, either the recent visit to Wembley had numbed the shareholders' usual powers of criticism, or perhaps they were genuinely lulled by Rinder's air of confidence. But in any event these worrying figures were barely discussed, and one shareholder's suggestion that perhaps a new share issue might be raised in order to pay off the debts was considered politely by Rinder, but not taken further. 'Up to the present,' he reassured everyone, 'we have managed to get along, and I don't think we shall have any great difficulty in continuing to do so.'

In fact, about the most animated anyone became was when Rinder announced that Frank Moss, who had just received a benefit worth £650, had had the audacity to refuse to re-sign unless the club guaranteed him another benefit in three years' time. In those days players simply did not make such demands, even if they were War heroes and had England caps to their name.

That unpleasantness aside, Rinder and his fellow directors were all duly re-elected, and the meeting ended with Howard Vaughton, the former player and son of Tom, being unanimously voted in as the club's new president.

But if the AGM passed off without a hitch, eleven days later the board sat down at Villa Park to face the awful truth of their situation. Villa were now in deep financial trouble, as Rinder well knew, judging by his preparedness for the meeting.

Firstly, to pacify the club's bank, the chairman had negotiated the issue of 30 debentures, each worth £1,000 and payable at a rate of 5 per cent interest per annum. (These debentures were, in effect, loans secured from two finance brokers, one in Lozells, the other in Threadneedle Street).

Secondly, to keep Mr Garfield sweet for a while longer the War loan, worth nearly £3,000, was to be cashed, and thirdly, it was agreed that further debentures would also be issued once it was agreed how much was still owed on the building work.

Nothing of this nature had been discussed at the AGM.

In January 1925 the board learned from Archibald Leitch just how much had been spent since 1922. The total had reached no less than £87,335, of which £64,711 was for the Trinity Road Stand. It was, in other words, more than double the original estimated expenditure, including more than a 50 per cent hike in the price of the stand on its own.

The next few months were desperate for all concerned. In March Fred Rinder was taken ill. In June, his fellow director, the former player Howard Spencer begged to resign, also on health grounds. But if Spencer was in dread of being dragged down by a sinking ship, he was instead persuaded to go on a cruise.

Meanwhile, as if in anticipation of the chairman's impending removal, Jack Jones, the vice-chairman, proposed that an oil painting of Rinder be commissioned, to hang in one of the club rooms.

For his part, Rinder soon returned to the fray, drew up various contingency plans with the bank, and at one stage even met with Garfield to discuss him accepting a directorship of the club, presumably in lieu of payment. (This was an old trick, commonly used by clubs who found themselves unable to pay their builders.)

The beginning of the end for Fred Rinder came at the club's 50th AGM, on June 19, 1925, at the Temperance Hall, Temple Street. (This was only a few hundred yards away from the rooms in Barwick Street where FWR's Villa career had begun, so famously, 32 year earlier.)

This time there were no great deeds to cover up the cracks. Villa had been knocked out of the Cup in the fourth round, by Albion. Their placing of 15th in the Division was the worst since 1901, and gates were down again, to an average of 25,059.

But worst of all were the accounts. Apart from having to pay off the £30,000 worth of debentures, Villa still owed £21,581, which Rinder now hoped would be paid off by the issue of £20,000 worth of second debentures. In a long and defensive speech he

CODES USED: A B C (5th Edition); A. 1. 1888.

LONDON 7th July, 1925.

OFFICES:
———
LONDON—
18, VICTORIA STREET,
WESTMINSTER. S.W.1.
———
GLASGOW—
30, BUCHANAN STREET.

TELEGRAMS
— AND —
TELEPHONES:
—
VICTORIA
6474.
—
CENTRAL 7526

To:-

The Directors of

Aston Villa F. C. Ltd.

IN ACCOUNT WITH

# ARCHIBALD LEITCH, M.I. MECH. E.

### CONSULTING ENGINEER AND FACTORY ARCHITECT.

GRAND STAND & TERRACING &c &c.

| 1922 - 4. | | | | | | | | |
|---|---|---|---|---|---|---|---|---|
| To Total Cost of Work | | | | | | | | |
| £87231 - 6 - 11 | | | | | | | | |
| Proffessional Fees on above res--tricted to 5%. = | 4361 | 11 | 3 | | | | | |
| To alterations on original plan, making 2nd design, and final 3rd. design. | - | - | - | | | | | |
| To/ making complete survey of Ground. | - | - | - | | | | | |
| To/Model of Terracing (paid in cash) | 113 | 6 | 10 | | | | | |
| To/ Services of Special Assistant at Ground for 3 months including his wages (£8. 0. 0. per week) and expenses. | - | - | - | | | | | |
| | | | | £4474 | 18 | 1 | | |
| By Cash | | | | 2000 | - | - | | |
| Balance. £ | | | | 2474 | 18 | 1. | | |

E. & O.E.

Secondly, how had the board allowed the costs of the stand to escalate so ruinously? Had Rinder kept his fellow directors informed, and if so, why had they not reigned him in?

There were other lesser charges, including disputed expenses, allowances, and a complaint that Villa no longer admitted boys at half price, as did Birmingham and West Bromwich. (Rinder claimed it was not safe to admit boys into such large crowds.) But perhaps the most inflammatory revelation was that a letter from George Ramsay had been discovered in which the Secretary had described the shareholders dismissively as 'mainly composed of small monied and illiterate men.'

As if to prove otherwise, the irate shareholders – now apparently supported by two of the directors, Jack Jones and John Devey – demanded that a Committee of Inspection be set up to go through the entire accounts with a fine toothcomb.

Nothing Rinder could say would sway the meeting now, and by a vote of 80 to 47, the proposal for a five man Committee of Inspection was approved.

For Rinder this was a crushing blow. His personal honesty had been attacked, and now two of his fellow directors were siding with the doubters. By now it was clear that Jack Jones was being lined up to take over the chairmanship, to which Rinder responded that he would leave the board altogether rather than remain, as he put it, 'in a subordinate position.'

A worrying month later, on a hot night in July, the Committee of Inspection reported its detailed findings to the shareholders, again at the Temperance Hall. The 'Aston Villa Crisis', as it was now being billed in the local press, was about to reach its bitter climax.

There turned out to be no good news. Instead of owing £51,000, it now turned out the figure was over £55,000. Archibald Leitch was still owed a large part of his fees, while Garfield were still waiting for over £20,000.

How on earth has this happened? The Committee had questioned both Leitch and Garfield on this, and found that all the expenditure had been genuinely and honestly accounted for. No-one could therefore be accused of feathering their own nest. Instead, it was clear that most, if not all the extra expenditure had come about as a result of Fred Rinder changing or amending the plans.

Some of the extra costs had plainly not been anticipated, for example the need for expensive new water and electricity mains. But we can easily imagine what the other unexpected bills were for: that wonderfully curvacious balcony panelling; the gold-leaf detailing on the mosaics; the central stairway which had not appeared on the original plans; the oak-panelled board room and restaurant; the stained-glass windows. All these features were luxuries. Stylish ones, delightful ones, much loved by all. But luxuries all the same.

But there were other causes for concern, said Wyndham Malins. Why, having spent all this money on a stand – 'for the Directors, you know, must have a temple' – was it still necessary to lay out a further

❖ *This is one of five much admired mosaic panels commissioned by Fred Rinder for the Trinity Road Stand. The work of a terrazzo tile firm called MARBELLO & DURUS, based in Cambridge Street, Birmingham, it is thought that each panel was laid first on a sheet a toughened glass before being mounted on the brickwork. As the name suggests, most of MARBELLO &DURUS' craftsmen hailed from Italy. One of them, Oreste Bortoli, arrived in Birmingham in 1902, like so many, in search of work. Yet having imposed his artful stamp so vividly upon Villa Park, Bortoli was rewarded by being interned as an 'alien' during the Second World War.*

detailed a whole list of mitigating circumstances concerning the players, injuries and the difficulty of finding a decent centre forward. But this time it clearly was not going to wash.

One shareholder immediately retorted that he had not come along to discuss injuries to players but injuries to the shareholders. The speaker was a hitherto unknown man called Wyndham Malins, who would prove to be the chief spokesman for the anti-Rinder lobby.

Malins listed a catalogue of discrepancies in the accounts put forward by the board. Many of them are too arcane to detail here. Should readers wish to follow the dispute in all its gory details they should refer to reports of the AGM and its follow up meeting, both of which were reported in admirable detail in the VILLA NEWS AND RECORD of July 1925.

But the gist of the charges against the board were as follows:

If the ground redevelopment had been completed by the time of the Duke of York's visit in January 1924, how come the extent of the debt had only been brought to their attention in mid 1925? Were there any other debts lurking in the background that they should know about?

£220 on furniture and carpets, and then another £37 18s 6d on vases from Burslem?

Malins insisted that he was not accusing anyone of dishonesty. He had supported Villa since 1887 and was only interested in the future of the club. His seconder, a Mr J. S. Cornwell, went back even further to 1879, and admitted that in calling for the board to resign he had never undertaken a more unpleasant duty. But the good name of Aston Villa was not merely a parochial affair. Its tradition was known the world over. Why, he had even heard some native friends of his in Egypt discuss Villa's chances in the Cup! There was no use crying over split milk, he added. 'Now we are in the soup and we have to get out in the best and quickest way possible.'

Another shareholder demanded that the old Articles of Association be restored. The 'squandermania' of the board, and of any future

board, had to be curbed, once and for all.

And so it went on, before finally Fred Rinder rose to answer his critics. Still frail from his recent illness – or at least claiming to be so – the battle weary chairman denied having acted as a dictator, or of having failed to keep his fellow directors informed. But he was prepared to shoulder the blame.

In a long, but clearly controlled speech, Rinder defended his position on virtually every count. True, the stand had gone over budget. But he had not concealed the extra costs from the shareholders in 1924. They were there on the balance sheet for all to see. It was hardly his fault if no-one sought to question them then. He also reminded shareholders that many of the costs were for facilities they now enjoyed in the new stand, and which earned the club a clear £5,000 a year. Nor could he or anyone have predicted the onset of the depression.

Notwithstanding the personal hurt he felt at his stewardship of the club being questioned, Rinder had assisted the Committee of Inspection as best he could, and believed the facts were these:

'We all set out to obtain the best stand and ground in the kingdom. We have got it. We engaged and acted upon the best advice of the leading and most experienced architect in football matters in the whole world. We engaged a competent clerk of works, who checked everything and was on the job the whole time. We have had the whole job measured up by a competent quantity surveyor and although the expenditure may have exceeded our expectations, I am perfectly satisfied that you have got full value for the money spent.'

Admitting that he was perhaps guilty of 'misguided optimism', Rinder then delivered his stirring conclusion.

'Let me say I have given the best years of my life to the interests of the club. I have always kept in mind what I believed to be the best interests of the club.

'Nevertheless, if this representative gathering of the shareholders of the Aston Villa Football Club think the time has come when I should make room for someone else, my resignation is here, and I am prepared to hand it to your secretary.'

And with that, Fred Rinder sat down.

But he was not to be spared, and nor were his fellow directors. John Devey, for years a close associate of the chairman's, tried to get off the hook by claiming that he and other directors had been kept in the dark. But Charlie Johnstone, another former player, considered that a lame excuse. It was each director's duty to keep himself informed, and if he felt something untoward was happening, to make it his business to find out.

Captain Bate was also brought to task by Wyndham Malins for his expenses. Bate, it transpired, had attended an England match in Paris, and stayed for seven days at the club's expense, attending theatres and other amusements. His other expenses included 48 pots of French mustard, soft herring, roes, pineapple slices and peaches. Even when the depth of the club's woes were known, these purchases continued.

❖ *Fred Rinder (above), chairman from 1896 to 1925, and (left) Jack Jones the man who replaced him. In 1936 the tables were turned and Rinder took Jones' place in the boardroom.*

*❖ Stained glass windows were among the many delights and extravagances of the Trinity Road Stand. Yet without such luxuries, Villa Park would not be the unique ground it is today.*

Next for excoriation came George Ramsay. The letter he was accused of having written, criticising shareholders, had been dug out after all. True it was dated 1896 and Ramsay had subsequently apologised. But that could not make up for the fact that the Secretary had originally denied ever having written such a letter.

But enough blood-letting. It was now obvious what the mood was. Fred Rinder rose one more time, offered his resignation, and thus brought to an ignominious end the most successful period of chairmanship in the club's history.

Three days later he sat down at his home in Lordswood Road, and wrote to his old colleague.

*Dear Mr Ramsay,*

*In confirmation of my resignation given verbally at the adjourned annual meeting of the shareholders of Aston Villa Football Club on Friday last, I beg to hereby formally resign my office as a Director of the club which I have faithfully served during the last 33 years.*

*I enclose my master keys.*
*Please acknowledge receipt.*
*Faithfully Yours*
*Fred W. Rinder*

Was there a tear in his eye as he wrote this painfully formal note, or was he relieved to have put the whole episode behind him? We cannot know. But we do know that Rinder did not, then, realise quite how completely he was about to be ostracised. At the very least he might have expected to be made a Life Member, but even this nominal honour was denied him.

After the meeting which ousted him, his and Captain Bate's positions on the board were taken by

Howard Vaughton, who stepped down from the presidency, and Wyndham Malins. As expected, Jack Jones became the chairman. Thus Villa now had three former players on the board; Vaughton, Devey and Spencer (who was now back after his timely cruise). Vaughton's place as president was taken by the Conservative MP for Moseley, Patrick Hannon.

Of Jack Jones little is known other than that he had been a shareholder since 1897, a director since 1906, and was so fond of the club that he had named his house in Erdington 'Aston Villa.' He was 54 when he took Rinder's place. Even less is known about Wyndham H. Malins, the leader of the rebels. The SPORTS ARGUS called him 'a successful solicitor and a keen sportsman' who was otherwise little known to the fans. THE ARGUS also stressed that the new men would have to have their wits about them, because Villa's coffers were now 'as bare as Old Mother Hubbard's cupboard.'

Despite this, when Rinder made his next public appearance he was given a warm welcome by the shareholders. This was the occasion of an EGM on September 25, 1925, again at the Temperance Hall, intended to amend the company's Articles of Association so that no director might ever again be tempted towards 'squandermania'.

Even then the former chairman could not hold back from one last defence of his actions, or from a chilling riposte to Jones and Devey. 'I leave my old colleagues to their conscience,' he said.

But his most poignant remark came at the end. 'Your directors,' he told the shareholders, to cries of 'shame' from the hall, 'have ignored me since the last meeting. They have not had so much as the common courtesy to offer me a seat in your enclosure, or invite me to the match.

'Notwithstanding that, I say, sink all differences, give them a chance, help them all you possibly can.'

And so dear reader, whether you are a died-in-the-wool Villa supporter, a modern-day shareholder, or simply just one of the thousands of sports lovers who, on their visits to Villa Park, never fail to look up at the Trinity Road Stand and declare their admiration for its distinction and grandeur, think of poor Fred Rinder as he walked away from the Temperance Hall that night in September 1925. Cast out from the club he loved so dearly, and which had defined his entire adult life, what pleasures did retirement hold for him now?

For sure the man had abused his powers. For sure he had landed the club in an almighty pickle. But he did so because he had a vision; a vision which may have turned into an obsession, but a vision which also clearly shaped the image of the club for many years to come.

In that sense one could argue, as did Rinder, that the £89,000 spent on the ground between 1922-24 was money very well spent. For imagine Villa Park today without the Trinity Road Stand. Of course it would still be an excellent stadium. But in truth, would it be any different from all the rest?

Fred Rinder had his faults, but he always instinctively knew that Aston Villa had to be different.

# Down the Match

VILLA PARK AND THE WHOLE experience of supporting Aston Villa in the 1990s has altered so rapidly and so radically from how it was, even as recently as the 1970s or 1980s, that it is sometimes hard to remember the football worlds we have lost. In just the space of four or five years the lessons of Hillsborough and the medicine administered so strictly by the Taylor Report have scarcely allowed any of us to take stock of our new high powered, all-seated Premiership, afloat on the Stock Market and steered by satellite.

In stark contrast, for those older fans who can still recall what it was like to support the club in the 1920s and 30s, the process of change between the wars was so, so gradual as to be almost imperceptible. Indeed a visitor to Villa Park in 1925 would hardly notice much different had he or she returned 30 years later.

That is not to say that those were halcyon days. In many respects the times were tough. Depression in the 1920s, World War, rationing and austerity brought pain, suffering and hardship on a scale unknown in today's Britain. And this before we even mention Villa's seven goal hammering by Arsenal in 1935 and their subsequent humiliating relegation to the Second Division.

Yet they were riveting times too. Between 1928 and 1933 Villa never finished out of the top five, and in 1930-31 their dazzling strike force of Mandley, Beresford, Waring, Walker and Houghton amassed the record breaking total of 128 goals in 42 games. The following season yielded another 104 goals. Even when they went down to Division Two in 1936 Villa did so in rip-roaring style; spending lavishly, scoring

freely (81) and shipping goals with extraordinary abandon (110!), including the aforementioned 7-1 home defeat to Arsenal and another, best forgotten 7-0 collapse against West Bromwich, also at Villa Park. Even more remarkably, that disastrous campaign was followed by a record average home gate of 39,106. If they had to go down, seemed to be the Villa's approach, then at least do it in style!

Nor was the two-year Second Division spell all bad. In 1938 Villa romped to promotion, reached another FA Cup semi-final, and managed to pull in even higher average crowds than ever, of just under 42,000.

No great honours then, but goodness knows, Villa fans of the period could never complain of boredom. And nor did they. Many still speak of this era as the most exciting they can ever recall.

So what was it like to follow Aston Villa between the wars, and how different was Villa Park as an experience in itself?

Talking to older supporters who recall that period, a number of favourite themes emerge.

Perhaps the most fundamental difference between now and then was that the vast majority of fans were based locally, and either walked to the ground or arrived by bicycle, or public transport. The matchday scenes around Villa Park were thus much busier, noisier and more animated. A procession of trams clanked along both Trinity Road and Witton Lane. On Cup days, in particular, fans often brought bells (and later rattles). Queues for the terraces snaked along the pavements as far, and often farther than the Holte Hotel or the Aston Hotel, sometimes even doubling back on themselves or carrying on round into Witton Road.

So long and tedious were these queues that a bevy of hawkers and buskers plied their trade, patrolling up and down, becoming familiar to all the regulars. It was no use telling folk they should have come earlier. Many had rushed away from their Saturday morning shifts as quickly as they could. Some remained in their work overalls. Others were in jackets and ties. A few wore colours, rosettes mainly, while the luckier kids sported claret and blue scarves or mufflers, knitted specially for them by doting mothers or aunts. Cup matches seemed to provide the most inspiration, with fans turning up in all kinds of outfits or top hats specially created in the club colours. But there were no replica shirts or club shops to feed their Villa cravings.

Furthermore, you could be standing on the terraces next to an away supporter and never know it until their accent gave them away. Not that there was ever any serious trouble. Indeed all supporters from this era agree that even swearing was frowned upon, especially if there were women or children in the vicinity. And nor were stewards ever called upon. As Frank Beach, a Witton Ender from 1935 onwards, recalled, 'In those days everyone would chat with the visiting supporters. If there was any sign of trouble people around would soon shout them down. Even for swearing. Now that was seen as a real crime.'

Segregation would thus have seemed an absurd

❖ *Whenever it was too wet to train outside, trainer Harry Cooch would take the players into the former aquarium, under the club offices. As can be seen on page 150, in 1958 the ground floor was later converted into a properly equipped gymnasium.*

notion to the fans of the 1920s and 1930s. As several fans from that generation have remarked, there was more chance of a punch-up between Villa fans than between fans of rival teams!

Besides which, not so many away fans turned up *en masse*. Travelling was so much more restricted then, not only because of the cost but also because Saturday morning shifts did not allow for any long journeys. Hence there was often likely to be more fans of the Blues or Albion on the Villa Park terraces than fans of the visiting team, just as many Villa regulars frequently spent their alternate Saturdays at St Andrew's or the Hawthorns. Birmingham was never a divided city in that sense.

Another feature of the times was that there was no real differentiation between the type of supporters who stood on Witton or the Holte Ends. Whereas from the 1960s onwards the Holte End came to be seen as largely the preserve of the younger, more vocal elements, before then people simply went to whichever end of the ground was nearest their home or their bus stop. And if they wished to swap ends at half-time then, providing the crowd was not too dense, all they had to do was make their way through either the Trinity Road or Witton Lane enclosures.

It has often been claimed that football used to be a family affair in the old days. But this was not quite

true. Villa had their share of female supporters in the seated areas, as we shall discover. The vast majority on the terraces however – at least 95 per cent – was male. If there was a family link, it was between fathers and sons.

Alf Pursall's experience was typical. Alf grew up in the Slade Road area of Erdington, but his father Jim had attended Upper Thomas Street school and had followed the Villa in their Perry Barr days. He was also at Villa Park on the opening day in April 1897. There was never any doubt therefore that young Alf would follow in his father's footsteps. It was merely a question of waiting until he was old enough. Alf's big day finally arrived on September 12, 1921, when he was just eight years old.

'That's a day I shall never forget,' he recalls. 'It was a 3 o'clock kick-off, so we started in good time and walked the whole way. There was no outer circle bus or anything like that. We walked down through Brookvale Park, up over the hill towards Witton – there was no motorway in the way then – through the allotments, over the canal, into Deykin Avenue. It was very quiet up till then, but then into Witton Road, on the left was the tramway depot at the junction with Witton Lane, and of course trams played a big part in the transport of the spectators. During the week the number 3 was the Witton route which went via Perry Barr, and the 3X which went

❖ *Villa's players of the 1920s relax in their recreation room. Very few clubs could provide such spacious and well equipped quarters.*

via Aston Cross to Witton. They all finished up at Witton. But on a match day the numbers were removed and the trams all said *Football Special* on the front, and that was a great excitement to me.

'It took us well over an hour to walk, but you didn't bother about eight-year-old legs. Dad and me were going to the Villa and that was it. I was that thrilled. I was going to see the Villa! I was going to see the great Knocky Walker!

'We walked from Erdington there and back for my first two seasons and then, when I was 10 or 11, we graduated to the tram which ran from the bottom of Kings Road, the old Number 1. I had a penny child's fare and that took us to Aston Station. From there you walked up Lovers Walk and Queens Road and then across Aston Park. There were always those lovely odours emanating from the ATKINSON'S BREWERY on Queens Road and the MIDLAND VINEGAR works down at Aston Cross, where they make HP sauce.

'I remember, as you approached the Holte Hotel, it had two flagstaffs in front of it, and every match day they flew the Villa flag plus the colours of the visiting side.'

Charlie Parker was born in Summer Lane in 1918, and in common with many young boys his first experience of Villa Park was a reserve match. Charlie's father had been badly burned during the First World War and after he was demobbed seven long years passed before he managed to find a proper job. Charlie thus spent the first eight years of his life sharing a dingy, bug-infested attic with his uncle and grannie, sleeping in the same bed as his parents.

'Dad did everything, postman, rag and bone man,' recalls Charlie. 'As you can well imagine, money was very short, conditions were bloody terrible; no lights, three families shared one toilet, though we were lucky because we had a tap in the back of the kitchen and all the other families had to share one tap in the centre of the backyard. I used to love going to school because it was so clean.

'Try to imagine. No TV, no wireless, the only means of finding out anything that happened was the newspaper. The BIRMINGHAM GAZETTE, EVENING DESPATCH, the MAIL and the POST. Try to imagine that situation. What did a lad have to look forward to? Football! That was the one thing everyone could understand. People in Aston didn't follow the Villa. They loved the Villa. It was something to look forward to, to live for. Anyway, I was seven at the time. "Charlie," my dad said, "I'm taking you down to the match." Down the match. He didn't say the Villa or anything. Just down the match. It was assumed it was Aston Villa.

'I was taken to a reserve match, because the first team cost a bob and that was too much. We walked it, automatic. No cars then. Through Aston Park, into the Holte End, and when the game started Dad sat me on one of the wooden barriers and stood behind with his arms around me. I was just a kid. It was against Huddersfield Town Reserves, the Villa won 3-1. Where he got the money from – sixpence for him and threepence for me – I don't know because he was out of work. And he treated me at half time to a cup of Bovril, served in a very heavy porcelain mug. I don't know if it cost a penny or a ha'penny. I put my hands round it... lovely, ahh, Bovril!'

How powerfully the smells and sounds of football in this period waft our way, across the generations.

'Outside Villa Park,' remembers Alf Pursall of the early 1920s, 'there were people selling the colours and even hot potato machines and things you never see these days. We used to buy fruit drops from a corner shop before the game, but in Trinity Road, come hail, rain or shine, standing in the gutter with his back to Aston Park was a very elderly gentleman. He never had a handkerchief as far as I know. He used the back of a mittened hand but he ought to have used a handkerchief, because he was carrying a circular tray, and on this rusty tray were tiny little packets of 'troach'. Now troach isn't on general sale anymore, but it was a sort of aniseed sweet, and you'd hear his rather painful, strained voice calling out, "Troach! Pennybag troach!" He was there for years. In the pouring rain sometimes you could hear this voice, groaning from under the umbrella. "Troach! Pennybag troach!"

'Then there was the man, always shouting the same thing, "Villa News! Names and players! Both teams!"

'Where now there are the big steps going into the stand, well at that time on the Trinity Road there was just the old tin roof. That's where Dad always stood. He saw me through the children's turnstile, sixpence for me, a shilling for him, and then we'd meet up inside. I never felt scared. You see it was quite different in those days. I remember many years later I read 'The Good Companions' by J.B. Priestley and in his first chapter he talks about Bruddersford United and refers to the spectators coming out of the ground as "a tide of cloth caps". That described the Villa perfectly. I think there were a few Trilbys, but they were over in the old stand. Where we were it was all cloth caps and my father was no exception.

❖ *The billiard room next to the offices was a favourite haunt of Villa's younger players. Alan Wakeman, a Walsall schoolboy who joined Villa in 1934 at the raw age of 14, trained in the mornings and worked as an office boy in the afternoons. He remembers many an occasion when secretary Billy Smith would catch him potting a few balls in between errands.*

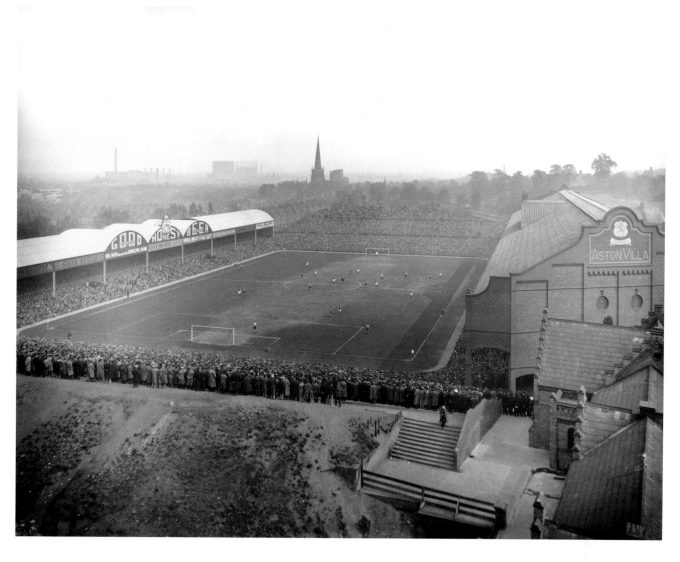

Nobody didn't wear a hat. Even I wore my school cap.'

Another boy in a school cap was Robert Tighe, who grew up to become a doctor and who has supported the Villa for nearly 70 years.

Robert's father, also a doctor (as was his father before him), had been a Villa reserve player before the First World War, much against the wishes of his family, who disapproved of football as a professional career. Villa wanted him to carry on playing after he returned from the trenches, but instead he took over the family surgery in the Duddeston-Nechells area and, together with his new wife, Robert's mother, became a season ticket holder in the Trinity Road Stand in the early 1920s.

Although they would not take their youngest son to a first team match until 1930, Robert remembers being taken to Villa Park with his brother Peter in the late 1920s, at the invitation of the club secretary, Billy Smith.

'We were very excited seeing the stands, terraces and dressing rooms and being able to walk on the hallowed turf. I remember the word "Hookey" scrawled on one of the dressing room walls. This, we learnt, was the nickname of the famous Billy Walker.

'My first League match was the 1930 Boxing Day game against Chelsea, an exciting 3-3 draw. My father usually parked his car in Frederick Road or Albert Road and we'd walk down Bevington Road and into Trinity Road and then through the famous gates and up the steps into the Trinity Road Stand. Just before we actually went up to our seats, I remember my father asking the very imposing steward, who was bowler-hatted with a waxed moustache, if he could tell us who had scored for the Villa in their 2-0 win at Stamford Bridge the day before, that is, on Christmas Day.

'"Waring and Walker, Sir!" he replied in an instant. And that was the only way for us to have found out, because there was no television in those days, the radio coverage was very limited and there were no newspapers at Christmas.

'When we arrived at the top of the steps, what an amazing scene greeted my brother and me! A sea of cloth caps on the terraces and in the stands. There were bowler hats, as well, in the stand. There was a crowd of close on 50,000 there. The sloping embankments were packed, so close that it was almost impossible to see what people were standing on. And there were still new groups of fans threading

❖ *Villa Park in all its late 1930s splendour, photographed by Albert Wilkes Junior, from the very same aquarium tower where his father, who died in 1936, had stood to capture the ground in 1907 (see page 85). The Witton Lane Stand was re-roofed in 1935 at a cost of £2,000, and tip-up seats installed throughout the stand two years later. Also in 1937 the penalty arc, a continental innovation, was introduced to English pitch markings. Notice how precarious was the rear of the Witton End banking, with no barriers to prevent fans from falling backwards down the slope. The Holte End would be almost doubled in height in 1939.*

into the gaps at the top of the terraces, particularly on the Holte End. Most of the men wore white chokers, or scarves, round their necks. Floating fumes of tobacco smoke rose above their cloth caps.

'Before the game a brass band played in a circle in the centre of the pitch. They usually commenced with *Colonel Bogey* to get into their stride and initiated the rhythmic stamping of feet in the stands. They played other light airs, including light classics and popular tunes of the day, such as dance band, theatre and film music.

'While they were playing, just like at the cinema, a youth carried a tray around the ground, shouting "Chocolates and cigarettes!" Villa's centre forward, Tom 'Pongo' Waring, had apparently carried out this same duty at Tranmere Rovers' ground before he signed for them as a player. So after his transfer to the Villa you would sometimes hear terrace fans ribbing with him with the same cry of "Chocolates and cigarettes!"'

Robert and Peter Tighe already had their own chocolate, however. 'Our Aunt Eileen, who lived with the family, worked at CADBURYS,' he remembered with a smile.

Alf Pursall also regarded the brass band with great affection.

'For a while they were called *Ye Olde Aston Silver Prize Band*. Resplendent they were, in dark uniforms with gold braid all down the front. I can remember there was one very tall man who played the big drum at the back and next to him was a man half his size who played the little drum. They used to play what we thought at the time very tuneful melodies, the *Desert Song*, popular marches, that sort of thing. Every tune was listed in the VILLA NEWS.'

As many contemporaries recall, one of the biggest attractions of the band was watching the rather self-important drum major send his baton spinning high up into the air. Thousands of eyes around the ground would then follow its trajectory, young and old alike wondering if this time the bandmaster was going to miss it as it fell. They rarely had the satisfaction!

Other than that there was no pre-match entertainment or even a public address system at Villa Park until the late 1940s. Nor did the players have any shirt numbers to identify them until 1939. Instead, team changes from the programme were chalked up on a board and paraded around the perimeter track, just before kick-off. This was fine for those with good eye-sight, but if it rained the board was often illegible by the time it had done a full circuit.

One of the commonest complaints about all-seated football grounds today is that there is no longer the same vibrant atmosphere which once prevailed. But it has to be said that synchronised chanting and clapping were only popular after the mid-1960s. Before then, football crowds were often quite sedate, if not entirely sedentary.

'There wasn't a lot of community singing, and definitely no chanting,' remembers Alf Pursall of the 1920s. 'But the atmosphere was still so much better. There wasn't a lot of abuse for one thing. You'd hear

things like "Come on Villa!" and that sort of thing. Encouraging shouts. But no abuse, or language or fighting. This was a period just after the First World War when a lot of men had come back and there was terrible unemployment. But everybody was really very orderly, just Priestley's tide of cloth caps. We used to stand near the front for my benefit, so we were quite near our heroes – the likes of York, Kirton, Capewell, Walker and Dorrell – and sometimes Dad would lift me up and I'd sit on the barrier. But you'd never dream of reaching out to touch any of the players, not like they do nowadays. It was quite different like that.'

On the other hand, it was not uncommon for fans to spot their favourite players sitting next to them on the tram on their way to the ground, or turning up at the players' entrance on their bicycles. Until the 1950s very few players had their own cars, and even then it was regarded as a luxury.

❖ Even though the goal posts appear not have to been moved, Villa Park's original pitch is dug up and replaced during the summer of 1931. One of the part-time helpers was a young lad called Bert Bond, who joined the groundstaff four years later and became head groundsman after the war. The much-respected Bond always reckoned the pitch would last for 50 years, and he was almost proved right. It sufficed until 1977 (although the drains installed in 1931 still remain intact, a few inches underneath the modern system). As this photograph shows, the upgrading and concreting of the terraces, begun in 1922, was almost complete, with only a few wooden barriers still remaining at the top of the Witton End. Notice also the decorative ironwork capping the Trinity Road Stand's roof gable. The ironwork, it is thought, was taken down (or damaged) during the Second World War and never replaced.

Another common practice of the pre-modern era was that at half-time or, in later years, some twenty minutes before the final whistle, the huge wooden exit gates on Witton Lane and Trinity Road would be swung wide open. But instead of people leaving, thousands more entered Villa Park: small boys who had not managed to sneak under the turnstiles earlier; unemployed men who couldn't possibly afford the shilling entrance; shift workers who were simply too late for kick-off, and amateur or schoolboy footballers whose games had just finished nearby. It was thus not uncommon for a crowd numbering, say, 20,000 at kick-off, to be over 25,000 by the second half.

There were also usually a hundred or more people who regularly gathered on the slopes of Aston Park, from where they could see half of the pitch, despite the tall advertising boards Villa erected in the corner. After the construction of the Trinity Road Stand in

1922 the free view was limited to just the goal area nearest the Holte End, but the huddle on the slopes was not to be deterred.

Among those in the park were gangs of small boys from the surrounding streets, all of them waiting for the gates to open so that they could duck and dive onto the terraces and start to collect the beer bottles which, in those days, fans could take into the ground without being stopped or searched.

For boys like Charlie Parker this bottle hunt was a vital form of income.

'As soon as they opened those gates the kids would run in. The coppers would be there and we knew they couldn't stop us all, even if they could stop a few. When the game finished and the people were coming out we used to go down to the front of the terraces, down where all the empties ended up being kicked, and started putting them in a special bag. We got a penny apiece, you see.'

❖ *One Villa fan died and several received minor injuries as a result of overcrowding at the Arsenal Cup tie in February 1926. Although the worst trouble was reported in the corner of the ground nearest the players' tunnel, as this photograph shows, much of the wooden fencing on the Witton Lane side of the Holte End appears to have collapsed in the crush.*

One of Charlie's rival bottle collectors was Jack Watts, whom many Villa fans will know today as the man who guides visitors around Villa Park for tours of the ground.

Jack grew up in Pritchett Street, less than 100 yards from William Shillcock's shop in New Town Row, from where the FA Cup was stolen in 1895.

'I was very very young, actually only four, when my brother Ted, who was ten years older than me, first took me down to Villa Park on his shoulders in 1922. We watched the game from Aston Park. In those days it seemed like everybody was out of work. Unfortunately, my father died through injuries he sustained during the First World War, so with just my mother, brother, sisters and myself, there was no fear of getting sixpence a year, never mind sixpence to go and watch a match.

'When I was a bit older, say six or so, there was a gang of about five of us and we resorted to getting into the ground by sneaking under the turnstiles. We'd take in a kind of a bag made of cloth, like a rag bag. After the match we used to go round collecting the old beer bottles, because everybody then could drink in the ground, you know. Oh yes and there were quite a few gangs of us doing it, but the point was there were quite a few empty beer bottles. Nobody ever stopped you.

'Well after we'd collected all the bottles we'd meet up in our back yard to sort the bottles out, MITCHELLS, ANSELLS and all that, to take to the various pubs or outdoors – which is what we called the off-licenses then – for maybe a penny a time. It seemed like a fortune at the time. Remember we were all under ten years of age. Parents were very strict in those days but they had to turn a little bit of a blind eye, because they couldn't give you any money themselves.'

While Charlie Parker, Jack Watts and their pals were collecting up the beer bottles after the match, long queues formed for the trams which lined up in

Park Road, Trinity Road and Witton Lane. But it was such a well-honed operation – and an extremely profitable one for the Corporation – that the streets cleared relatively quickly, and certainly much quicker than is the case nowadays with so many fans choosing to drive.

And whereas now most ears are glued to transistors or car radios, in the 1920s and 30s the only way to get the final results for the whole country was to buy one of Birmingham's rival sports papers.

Villa Park did have its own half-time scoreboards. Between 1906 and the First World War these were fairly rudimentary boards mounted on the roofs of refreshment huts at the back of each end terrace. Then in the late 1920s the more familiar self-contained A-Z scoreboards were put up in two opposite corners, each with their own manual operators mysteriously hidden inside. (Jack Watts would eventually be one of them.) After the final whistle, however, Villa were bound by a gentleman's agreement not to put up all the final scores, since this would have adversely affected Saturday night newspaper sales. Instead, only the results of games involving the Blues, Albion and Wolves were allowed. Then, as much as now, those scores were always greeted by the usual groans, cheers or snorts of derision.

In the city centre, shoppers could find out the latest scores by hanging around outside the newspaper offices, but there also appears to have been a fairly effective jungle telegraph. Robert Tighe remembers that in April 1931 Villa had conceded three goals to Newcastle in the first 20 minutes, before launching a thrilling comeback to win 4-3. His grandmother told him later that she had been out shopping in Duddeston that afternoon and long before 4 o'clock had seen small boys running around shouting 'Villa are three down!' How word had spread so swiftly remains a mystery.

'As we came out after the match,' remembers Alf Pursall, 'there were the newspaper sellers outside, and you could hear the shouts, "Get your Despatch and Mail, Despatch and Mail!" I can hear them now. There was the EVENING DESPATCH, or you could get an early edition of the GREEN MAIL just as you came out of the ground, and then later on, as we got nearer home, you'd get the latest edition of the GREEN MAIL or the ARGUS from our local shop.'

Charlie Parker was another avid reader. 'Now if Villa were playing away you wouldn't know how they had gone on until the final MAIL came, or the ARGUS. Some bloke would call down "Final Argus, City final Argus!" and I used to read from the front page all the way through to the back. And I'd cut out the photograph of the Villa fella – old Billy Walker or somebody like that – scoring the goal and get some flour and water and stick it in an exercise book.'

But it was not all men and boys. In 1905 a visitor to the ground noted that while there were 'no ladies on the reserved side, there are almost as many ladies in the reserved side as men.'

Among them in later years was Mildred Britton, a regular at Villa Park for over 70 years. Mildred was the daughter of one of Aston Villa's original shareholders in 1896, a manufacturing jeweller in Hockley. As a shareholder he was able to buy one season ticket plus one lady's season ticket for just six shillings. Mildred first started attending matches in 1919, as a wide-eyed eight-year-old prep-school girl, and was only 13 when her father took her to the 1924 Cup Final at Wembley. In those days very few young girls would ever be taken to football, but young Mildred was never daunted.

Speaking in 1997 she recalled, 'My brother, funnily enough, was not interested at all, so my two sisters, Katy, Nora and I used to have an early lunch and go on the one o'clock train from where we lived in Four Oaks, have a leisurely walk to the ground and meet Daddy there. He came straight from Hockley. We used to watch the players going in wearing their flat caps and get their autographs. There were quite a few girls doing that. And then we sat in the stand. There was only the one stand then and it hardly seemed more than a Dutch barn. The seats were endless forms with no backs, though the most expensive seats had a bit of carpet tacked onto the actual bench. You had somebody's knees in your back and your knees in somebody else's back. We used to sit in the middle. There were very few other ladies, though where we sat there were never any, what you would call swearing types. I remember there was one old lady who used to stand at Villa Park in a white overall and white cap, selling homemade throat drops. There was also a tuck shop in a cabin opposite Aston Church where we used to go and get liquorice allsorts.

'We sat in that Witton Lane Stand until the new stand was built on Trinity Road and there we had the same seats for years and years and years. I remember the lovely oak staircase, in the old directors' room, more or less like Aston Hall. And of course the old Oak Room. If I was in there without my father or sisters on a match day I used to go up to the bar and get myself a sherry and because everybody knew everybody there I'd say to people, 'Would you like a drink?' They looked at me as if I'd suggested something horribly immoral. It just wasn't the done thing for a woman to offer a man a drink in those days.'

Not all in the Villa garden was rosy during this period, however, particularly when the ground was packed to capacity.

Recalling the afternoon of a Cup tie v Walsall in January 1930, which drew the ground's then record gate of 74,626, Alf Pursall had less than happy memories.

'After they built the new stand – yes, in our own minds we always used to call it the "New Stand" – we moved over to the Witton End. I'd gone to work as an insurance clerk in Steelhouse Lane by the time of the Walsall game, so I had to work on the Saturday morning, nip home for some home cooking, and then get to the Witton End and stand there for ages before kick-off. It got so pressing hard on me I thought, I have to get out or I'll stifle. So I sort of fought my way to the back, towards the top part which was just rough earth. I stood right at the back, where at least I could breathe, but I kept getting pushed down the back of the bank. I'd fall down and had to stagger back up, so I didn't see a lot of the play! It was quite a frightening experience.'

It could also be dangerous. Compared with most grounds Villa Park had, and always would have, an

❖ *Although the period would only witness one major triumph – the FA Cup win in 1920 – many older Villa fans reserve their greatest affection for the players and characters of the inter-war years. Several in the squad shown here, in August 1921, including York, Moss, Dorrell and trainer Freddy Miles (himself once a popular player) were real Brummies who had grown up and still lived among the ordinary supporters. One local hero, Tommy Smart, from the Black Country, was particularly remembered for cycling to the ground wearing the fashionable flat cap of the day, while the name of Tommy Ball would forever be tainted by tragedy after he was shot dead by a neighbour, in November 1923. Back row: Freddie Miles (trainer), Llewellyn Price, Tom Jackson, George Blackburn, Ernie Blackburn, Ian Dickson, Tommy Ball. Centre row: Dickie York, Frank Moss, Andrew Young, Billy Walker, Frank Barson, Tommy Smart. Front row: Arthur Dorrell, Billy Kirton, Tom Weston.*

excellent safety record. But on one occasion the wheel did come off.

This occurred on Saturday, February 20, 1926, when Arsenal were the visitors in the FA Cup. Although the great days of Herbert Chapman's Arsenal were yet to come, Villa's Cup tradition was still sufficient to attract over 71,000 fans, with an estimated 20,000 more locked out. So great was the pressure, particularly in the corner nearest the players' tunnel, that hundreds of fans at the front of the terracing clambered over the railings and sat on the perimeter track.

But that was not all. As the SUNDAY MERCURY reported the day after the 1-1 draw, 'At Villa Park, where the record for the ground was eclipsed, it was necessary to close the gates half an hour before the kick-off, and the huge crowd broke over the barriers and onto the pitch. There were several minor casualties, and one man had to be treated in hospital. Villa officials said that if the early comers had "packed" with a view to giving late comers a chance, there would have been room for another 10,000.'

That was hardly any consolation for the man being treated in the General Hospital. Alexander Bartholomew, of Whitehead Road, Aston, was later reported to be in a critical condition, with serious back injuries. On the following Friday he died.

Villa maintained that it was not their fault. In the VILLA NEWS AND RECORD, published on the day after Bartholomew's death, they made an official statement that 'although the crowds broke over the barriers at one part of the ground, it was not because the ground was full. There was room for a good few thousands more, could the spectators only realise that there is a necessity for them to properly distribute themselves over the area available.'

At the inquest, Villa director Wyndham Malins – the scourge of Fred Rinder the year before – stated that there had been 130 stewards and 163 police officers on duty for the Arsenal game. The club could hardly do more. And the coroner agreed, passing a verdict of accidental death. Bartholomew was buried on March 3 at Witton Cemetery.

As the years went by there would be gradual improvements to the ground. Steel barriers gradually replaced the remaining wooden ones, and the concreting of terraces, begun under Rinder's regime, was eventually completed.

Nor were there any further accidents – at least not reported ones – despite a steady rise in gates, particularly for Cup games. After the Arsenal match the record would rise to 74,626 for the 1930 Walsall game, then to 75,540 for the visit of Manchester City, on March 5 1938.

Among the packed crowd that day was Robert Tighe. 'City had won the FA Cup in 1934, after being losers in the 1933 final. But this season they were not doing well, being in the lower reaches of Division One, while Villa, on the other hand, were riding high in Division Two. They were said to have the fastest forward line in the country and played some thrilling football that season.

'Hours before the gates were opened, eager

rosetted fans waited patiently, vanguard of the biggest crowd ever to besiege Villa Park. That day more so than ever before, Birmingham was in the throes of a severe attack of Cup-tie fever. Villa officials said they had never known a week like it. The Villa manager Jimmy Hogan said that he hadn't realised how many friends he had. Every day, people – many of whom he swears he'd never heard of before – were ringing him up, calling him by his Christian name, and then popping the question, "Can you get me a ticket?"

'Outside Villa Park profiteers mingled in the crowds. Tickets were changing hands for as much as £2 – a lot of money in those days. A full hour before the kick off there were at least 55,000 in the ground. They kept up an ever-swelling volume of cheers, which worked up now and then to a deafening crescendo. One by one, gates had to be shut as the terracing developed into a surging, swaying mass of humanity, bathed in spring-like sunshine. It was such a glorious day. There was a heat haze right across the ground.

'We were seated in the old stand because my father couldn't get us tickets in the Trinity Road Stand. Over a hundred policemen were stationed on the grass fringe of the playing-pitch, and for the first time since the Walsall Cup-tie in 1930, people were allowed to sit in front of the railings. In places they were ten deep around the cinder track!'

It turned into an epic encounter. Villa hit the woodwork twice, took a 3-1 second half lead through Frank Broome, who had injured his knee shortly beforehand, Fred Haycock and Frank Shell, who played much of the game with a large plaster over one eye after a collision. The referee had to change places with a linesman after receiving a blow to his head. Villa's captain Jimmy Allen then put through his own goal in the final minute for a tight, nerve racking climax.

'The final whistle was the signal for a remarkable scene,' remembered Robert Tighe. 'The crowd surged on to the pitch until it was absolutely covered. They lifted Jimmy Allen and other members of the team shoulder high and carried them triumphantly from the field. It took some time before police could scramble the players to the dressing rooms. But it was truly a great victory and a game I'll never forget, because at that moment in time, we were only 18 months from the Second World War and actually less than 20 years from the end of World War I. But on that particular afternoon, all Villa fans were on a high – full of optimism and very, very happy.

'After the game, we eventually made our way through the crowds to Albert Road, where my father's new car, a Wolseley 8, was parked.

'The small lad who always looked after the parking received his shilling gratefully and said "The Villa didn't 'arf do well, sir. We knew they were doing well by the roars!"'

Stirring times indeed. But alas, they were not to last.

# ROUND VILLA PARK
# WITH BILLY WALKER

## *ASTON VILLA'S FAMOUS INTERNATIONAL FORWARD SHOWS YOU ROUND HIS CLUB'S ENCLOSURE*

S AY, can I help you? You're evidently looking for something or someone. For Villa Park? That's easy! Come with me–I'm going there.

I suppose you're not by any chance some chappies I'm expecting to see, some readers of SPORTS BUDGET? My name's Billy Walker! Well, now, it certainly is strange that I should meet you like this. Come along, we'll soon be there. Just down Trinity Road here.

Not much of a morning for your look round, is it? Never mind, you must make the most of it.

Here we are, lads. Go right through the gates! No one will stop you if I'm with you. There you are! You are now in Villa Park.

Isn't it an imposing entrance? See the name painted up over there in great letters? No one can mistake the place, can they? You're right, this large expanse is used as the car-park, and on match-days the vehicles out here run into several hundreds.

Up the stairs here is the inquiry office. That's where I suppose you would have found yourselves if you had not met me.

Well, where would you like to go first? On to the pitch or into the stand to see the rooms? Come out on to the pitch first, eh? Righto, then! We can get down this way.

## WHAT A STAND!

I 'M proud to show you round our ground, for it is one of the finest grounds in the country; in fact, in some quarters it is looked upon as THE finest in many respects. First of all, what do you think of that grand-stand? Isn't it simply stupendous? It's just about the best stand I know, second to perhaps one other, and that's at Wembley. Of course, we've been there, so we know.

You're right: our stand hasn't been built so very long. The other one–oh, that's been up a jolly long time, and it was our best stand until this one grew up. Now, of course, it's properly put in the shade. Come out on to the pitch, you'll get a better view! Over here!

There's room for 8,000 people in the new stand. All of them are provided with tip-up seats. Yes, you know, like you find in cinemas and theatres. Well, that's 8,000. Then in front of the seats is the enclosure, which holds another 18,000, and all of 'em under cover, too.

The rooms? Ah, you've heard of them! They're all under the stand. See that lot of windows just under the rows of seats? Well, they're the windows of the various rooms. We'll go in there in a moment or two.

Cost of the stand? Oh, I don't know exactly: somewhere about £40,000 I think.

Stupendous, wasn't it? Nevertheless, it's been worth the money.

## THE PITCH TOO!

W HAT do you think of our pitch? Like it? So do we! A bit different from some of the pitches you've seen, I guess. Round the edges, I mean. The track's about six yards wide. If you want to get your fat down take a run round our track a few times.

I say, here come some of the lads for training. We'd better get inside, I think. Come on, this way. We take the field for our matches through this gate. You'll find the passage leads right into the heart of the stand and to the various rooms. There you are. Twig what I mean?

Come along up to the dressing-rooms first, before there are too many of the chaps about. This way!

Whacking big room, isn't it? Plenty of space to move about. See the pegs around the walls. There's accommodation for about thirty chaps in here, and then tons of room to spare. Over there is the trainer's room, all up-to-date, like the rest of the Villa's property. Take a look in if you like. No, I think Harry Cooch, the trainer, is with the lads somewhere or other.

See his massage table, his cupboards with

kit, etc., in them? The trainer's an important person, so naturally his room has to be of the best.

## DICKY TAKES A BATH

SEEN enough? Right! Come out here again and take a peep at the bath-room. In here.

Come on, there's no one to bite you. What? You're right, isn't it a grand room? One of the finest. I guess it cost a small fortune for white tiles for the lining of this room. And baths, too. Look at 'em; there's practically every sort that were ever invented in this room. Swimming tanks, see! Then there are the ordinary kind over yonder; and also showers, slipper, needle baths–all the whole lot. If we're not clean we ought to be, don't you think?

What's the matter? Feeling the heat? Well, that's not to be wondered at. The place is artificially warmed. Put your hand on these pipes. There you are: that's why it's so warm in here. Besides, the boilers are going ready for the lads to take their baths later on. Hallo! Here comes someone already. 'Morning, Dick! How's things? Enjoy your spin yesterday? Pity it rained, though. Bathing? Righto, see you later. Come on lads, let's clear!

That was Dicky York, our flying outside-right. In what? Yes, that's right, his car. He and I often go out together for a drive. Oh, no, we've each got our own car. Mine's a Morris–Oxford saloon. It's all right, too, I can assure you. But come on, let's keep on the move. Better come along here and see the doctors' rooms. I guess you've never encountered such places on footer fields before.

That's the room. You see we possess our own club medico, Dr. Jessop. Dr Milne? Well, of course, he helps at times, but he has his footer to think about, too.

## X-RAY ROOM

IN there–no, I don't think you can get in–is our X-ray room. When a player hurts himself at all badly, he is shot into there like lightning and put under the light. There's something new to you, isn't it? Thought so!

Along here is the entrance to our restaurant. Don't look so surprised–I mean it. All slap-up it is, too; just like the best class London shows, with chefs, waitresses, etc. You see, the Villa management realises that the working man must have his meal; so if he cannot get home on a Saturday to his lunch in time to get back to the match, he can come here. It's useful for us players, too, at times. No, don't go in there, it would be a waste of time and we haven't many more minutes to spare.

The directors' and ladies' rooms are also along there. But better come upstairs now; there's more to be seen up there. Come on, this is the second storey. Over there are the offices and board-room. This side are our own rooms. This way!

First of all, in here–come on!–is the billiards room. See the two fine, full-sized tables. Keen? Not exactly. Arthur Dorrell and Alf Yates are our two best cueists. They'll be up here after work, you bet. Now then, this way!

## HEAR OUR JAZZ-BAND!

HERE you are–the cards and reading room, where a restful hour or so can be spent, either with the cards or with a book. At least, that's all O.K. providing "Jock" Johnstone and some of the others are not present. See that piano over there? Well, get Jock on to that and there's no holding him.

But that's nothing to the noise made when our jazz-band get going. There's Jock on the "johanna", Tommy Smart with his mouth-organ, "Toby" Corbett on the triangle, Harry Cooch, our trainer, with a tin-whistle, Jimmy Gibson, using his ribs as a banjo, and Joe Bache, our coach, to conduct.

Some of the lads can dance, too. We have four real Charleston Kings in George Jakeman, Joe Beresford, George Stephenson and Billy Armfield.

## IN THE GYM!

OH, before you go, one other room –through here–the gymnasium. Have a peep in. That's where the chaps put in spells with the Indian clubs, etc. All right for wet weather. But come on, time's simply flying. Mind you don't fall!

I can hear some of the chaps out on the pitch, can't you? I shouldn't like you to go without seeing some of the wearers of the claret and blue. Come along out!

Hallo, Harry! No, I shan't do much to-day. I should like to see you later–before you go!

That was Harry Cooch, our trainer. He was the assistant for several years until poor Freddy Miles died. Harry used to wear the Villa's colours, too. He lives on the premises. No, not in the stand here, but in that house over in that corner of the ground.

## MEET THE BOYS

IT'S still dull, isn't it? Have some rain later, I reckon. Everyone's not training, I see, for there's Frank Moss standing over the other side talking.

You'll remember fair-haired Frank, I guess. Been our skipper for several years. But this season has been out of the side at times to allow Billy Kingdon to play.

Frank's one of our keenest bowls experts. Oh, but then I was forgetting, Frank's also more than a trifle keen on his back garden.

By the way, our goalie, Tom Jackson, is another of the bowls fraternity. Can't see much in it myself. Motoring's my hobby. Of course, in the summer it's cricket. But, then, that's the case with a number of the lads–Arthur Dorrell, Dicky York, George Jakeman–that's him dribbling up there by the far corner-flag–Billy Kirton and George Cook.

## THE FAMOUS STEPHENSONS

SEE the chap running round the track fit to break his neck? George Stephenson –that's right! Clem's brother; Jim, another brother, plays for Queen's Park Rangers, doesn't he? Thought so! George, by the way, is another of our "bowlers".

Hallo! Arthur Dorrell's gone over to have a chat to Frank Moss now. Arthur amuses me; he's keen on fishing. One of his rod-and-line confederates is Harry Cooch. Arthur also keeps chickens.

There's Len Capewell with the skipping rope. See the two looking on? The one on the right is Billy Kingdon; the other Toby Corbett, one of our jazz merchants, and one of the funniest lads ever. I'd like you to see Toby, Jock Johnstone and Tommy Smart when they get together; they're the three "lads of the village", and no mistake.

Well, I don't want to sling you off, but I really must get busy now. You must go, too? Enjoyed yourselves? That's the ticket! Well, lads, all the best! Good-bye!

*"VILLANS" OF THE BATH. Some of the famous claret and blues enjoy a soak after training. Left to right are Tom Jackson and Tom Mort (front bath), George Blackburn and Billy Walker (rear bath), with Tom Smart (left), Dickie York (centre) and Joe 'Toby' Corbett (right) already changed.*

# Chapter 10

# From Bombs to Boomtime

THE OUTBREAK OF WAR IN SEPTEMBER 1939 would find Aston Villa a quite different club from the one which Fred Rinder left behind in 1925. Relegation in 1936 had brought the club down to earth with an horrendous bump, and though Villa Park itself changed very little between then and 1939, behind the scenes there were a number of significant developments.

The first of these was the retirement of 71-year-old George Ramsay in June 1926, thus severing the last remaining links with Villa's once-powerful Scottish elite. Ramsay had been secretary for a remarkable 42 years, and would be elected a vice-president in 1927 (a position he retained until his death in October 1935).

Assistant secretary Wallie Strange had been next in line, but tragically, in December 1925, on his return from a match in Cardiff, he fell down some steps at Snow Hill Station and fractured his skull. Strange died a week later, aged 50. Ramsay's post was therefore handed to the 33-year-old William J. Smith, who had only just been promoted to assistant.

Billy Smith was a genuine one-off. He joined Villa in 1910, as a 17-year-old office junior, and although diminutive in stature, rapidly became a huge power. Tales abound of how he managed to sign this or that player, often sneaking in front of rival clubs at the last minute. According to former player Amos Moss, 'Billy loved the players, and loved being among them.' But he also watched them like a hawk. He thought nothing of reading the players' mail before handing it over with 'Sorry, opened in error' scrawled on the envelope. Moss also remembers how he and other players would be waiting for their bus home from Villa Park, and would see Smith across the road, fag in his mouth as always, spying on their antics from behind a newspaper while he waited for his own bus home to Handsworth.

Both Moss and goalkeeper Alan Wakeman were teenagers on the groundstaff in the years immediately preceding the Second World War. Wakeman recalls that Smith had a prodigious memory, for the rules of the game, for the minutiae of League and FA regulations, and particularly for players.

'What d'you want?' he would snap when anyone approached. Larry Canning, a young Scot who joined Villa in 1942, remembers that after he took a two year course in chiropody, he went up to the offices to show Smith his diploma. 'What d'you want?' came the usual greeting, followed by 'I don't want to see your bloody diploma. How much did that cost you?' Canning told him, only for Smith to write out a cheque there and then to cover the entire course fees. But that was his way. 'He was a darling,' said Canning. 'Everyone loved him.'

That was not quite true. Some thought Smith a little tyrant, and remember him for his legendary drinking, which usually meant that he stopped work at mid-day, once the pubs were open. Jack Watts, who turned out regularly to sweep the terraces after the war, remembers seeing Smith at the ground one Sunday morning. 'What's he coming in for on a Sunday morning?' someone asked, only to be told, 'He ain't come in, he's just going home!'

In Ramsay's day most club secretaries were in charge of both administration and the players (although team selection was largely handled by the board). But in June 1934 Villa's directors decided on a change of policy, and for the first time in the club's history appointed a team manager.

But if the time was right – especially given the success of men like Herbert Chapman at Arsenal, Leslie Knighton at St Andrew's and Major Frank Buckley at Molineux – the man Villa chose was not. When he arrived at Villa Park, Jimmy McMullan, a former Scottish international with Manchester City and Partick Thistle, had spent only one year in full-time management, at Oldham. As every club history recounts, McMullan spent the then astronomical sum of £35,500 on players, only to find himself sacked after two years and Villa humiliatingly dumped into Division Two.

McMullan did help initiate one important development, however. In 1935 Villa agreed to rent the Alexander Ground, home to Birchfield Harriers, for training and as a base for the third team. Named after a founder of Birchfield Harriers, W. W. Alexander, the ground was on the site of the current

❖ One of Fred Rinder's first acts on returning to the boardroom in 1936 was to invite one of the most respected British coaches working on the Continent, Jimmy Hogan, to become Villa's manager. Two and a half years later Hogan would lead the procession at Rinder's funeral. War then intervened, but Hogan returned to the club in 1953 to help coach the youth team. He finally retired in July 1959 at the age of 77.

Perry Barr greyhound track and had a small stand seating 1,000. (The current Alexander Stadium, on a different site, was not opened until 1978.)

Apart from allowing a much needed rest for Villa Park's pitch, which had been completely relaid in 1931, the Alexander Ground at last gave Villa a real chance to develop young talent. To oversee this new outpost of the Villa empire, former centre-half Frank Barson was appointed as youth coach.

Now Barson was the most suspended player in football; constantly in trouble with referees, opposing crowds, directors and the football authorities alike. But the Villa Park faithful always loved him, and if some purists thought his appointment akin to putting the devil in charge of choirboys, those who were coached by him remember Barson as like a hen with his chicks; a natural teacher and always protective.

While Barson started to lay down the foundations for the future, in the boardroom a number of new appointments took place.

Wyndham Malins died suddenly in 1932, and was replaced by the Honorary Secretary of the Shareholders' Association, Joe Broughton. Howard Vaughton stood down through illness a year later and was replaced by a prominent fishmonger and councillor, Fred Normansell. John Devey also fell ill and in 1934 his place was taken by another former player, the photographer Albert Wilkes. Then two years later Wilkes died, and a leading shareholder, Joe Riley, stepped in. Riley owned a pianoforte showroom in Paradise Street from where 5s. seat tickets for all Villa matches could be purchased throughout the 1930s.

But the greatest upheaval occurred in the aftermath of Villa's relegation in 1936. Apart from the shock of going down, there was also an unprecedented operating loss of nearly £11,000, due mainly to the expenditure on players and to the £2,000 re-roofing of the Witton Lane Stand.

Not surprisingly the 1936 AGM at the Grand Hotel turned into a showdown, almost as vitriolic as those that had occurred in 1925 and 1893 (the latter, coincidentally, just around the corner, in Barwick Street). Not only that, but one of the central figures in the debate proved once again to be that old warhorse himself, Fred Rinder.

After he was ousted from Villa's board in 1925 Rinder had flirted with Bristol Rovers (where his brother Sam was chairman). But by the early 1930s he had clearly made it up with his former critics at Villa. They all attended his wife's funeral in 1932, while Rinder himself was a mourner at Malin's burial a few weeks later. Rinder also remained active in the higher echelons of both the FOOTBALL LEAGUE (of which he was made a vice president in 1930) and the FOOTBALL ASSOCIATION (for whom he was elected an international selector). On one occasion, it was reported, he even tried to revive his architectural agitations by visiting Wembley Stadium to draw up plans for its expansion!

Apart from his lofty position within the football hierarchy, one reason why Rinder still commanded

respect amongst his fellow shareholders was that his predictions regarding the Trinity Road Stand had largely come true. As he foretold in 1925, it did take seven years to pay off the outstanding debentures. In addition, the stand had continued to yield an annual income of £5,000.

But relegation in 1936 was a far worse blot upon the club's record than any financial deficit. Echoing the attack made by Rinder himself at Barwick Street in 1893, several shareholders accused the directors of complacency and poor leadership. Some even advocated the return of the 78-year-old Rinder. When the votes were counted, Chris Buckley, another former player (and brother of Wolves manager Frank), proved to be the most popular of the newly elected directors, followed by Fred Normansell, who would become the new chairman, then Albert Wilkes and Joe Broughton. Rinder came next, but only just. His return to the board after an eleven year absence was secured by just four votes ahead of the sixth candidate.

Nevertheless he was back, and more than that, back at the expense of the man who had done so much to unseat him in 1925, Jack Jones. Jones had been a board member for 30 years, and as the votes now confirmed, he too would taste the bitter pill of rejection.

Despite his advanced years, Rinder lost no time at all in orchestrating a revival. One of his first telling contributions was to introduce to the club a coach whom he had met whilst on FA duty at the 1936 Berlin Olympics. This was Jimmy Hogan, a man whose talents were particularly admired in Hungary and Austria, but little known in England. As the records show, Hogan proved to be the ideal man.

After his first transitional season, in 1937-38 he led Villa to the Second Division championship and to their 14th FA Cup semi-final. Despite the lower standard of opposition, average attendances that season hit a new Villa Park record of 41,596, and on aggregate totalled a massive 1.1 million for all first team matches (including that record gate of 75,540 for the Manchester City Cup tie).

With equally impressive profits of £17,172 to crown this revival, not surprisingly Rinder needed

❖ *Wartime football was often a lottery, dependent on the availability of an assortment of veterans and guest players. But by 1944 both Villa and Blackpool (who included Stanley Matthews) were able to field relatively strong sides for the two-legged final of the Football League North Cup. Despite an imposed crowd restriction of 50,000, nearly 55,000 managed to see the second leg at Villa Park. Villa won a thrilling encounter 4-2, to win the cup 5-4 on aggregate, their first major honour since 1944. Six of the team were aged 32 or over, the oldest being 38-year-old Alex Massie. Pictured here are: Back row, Phil Hunt (trainer), Ronnie Starling, Joe Broughton (vice-chairman), Fred Normansell (chairman), Chris Buckley (director), Mush Callaghan, Alan Wakeman. Centre row: Norman Smith (director), Bob Iverson, Alex Massie, George Cummings, Harry Parkes, Edward Smith (director). Front row: George Edwards, Vic Potts, Frank Broome and Eric Houghton.*

❖ *Despite the deaths of 33 fans at Bolton on March 9 1946, the post-war enthusiasm for football continued to yield record crowds all over Britain. Two weeks after the disaster, Bolton came to Villa Park for their semi-final against Charlton and were watched by three Brummies from an unusual vantage point.*

little prompting to dust down his 1914 masterplan. Nearly 25 years after it had been first drawn up, it was now time for phase three, the extension of the Holte End.

Yet the work would not actually start until mid 1939, by which time, sadly, neither Archibald Leitch nor Fred Rinder were around to see their grand designs finally implemented. Leitch died in April 1939, leaving the business to his son, Archibald Junior (who oversaw the Holte End's construction but seems to have gained little further work at football grounds in the post-war period). Rinder passed away on Christmas Day, 1938, at his daughter's home in Harborne, having suffered a seizure a week earlier during a bitterly cold afternoon at the Alexander Ground, where he had attended a mid-week youth game v Leicester.

'Football will not seem the same without Fred Rinder,' reflected the VILLA NEWS AND RECORD, and with good cause. As the list of mourners at St Peter's, Harborne, confirmed, Fred Rinder may not have been an easy man – although he was said to have mellowed in his old age – but he was quite obviously widely respected.

Villa players past and present helped form a guard of honour, as Rinder's coffin was borne by Frank Barson, Billy Walker, Jimmy Allen, Alex Massie, Eric Houghton and Frank Broome. Behind them, Jimmy Hogan led the procession, which included the entire roster of Villa staff, players, directors, the president, vice presidents and leading shareholders, plus the Lord Mayor, prominent Freemasons from all over Birmingham, Stanley Rous from the FA, representatives from at least 12 League clubs and almost every senior figure at the Football League (who had voted him a Life Member only a few months earlier, in recognition of the fact that Rinder was the only man to have attended all 50 League AGMs since 1888).

Since his timely and forceful intervention in 1893 Fred Rinder had dominated the club's affairs. He presided over the club's glory days, masterminded the move to Villa Park, the purchase of the ground and its redevelopment, while his return to the fray in 1936 had coincided with the start of Villa's revival.

It may seem surprising therefore that there is no memorial to Rinder at Villa Park. But then, rather as Sir Christopher Wren was remembered at St Paul's Cathedral – *Si monumentum requiris, circumspice* – if one wanted to seek his monument, one only had to look around. Furthermore, the ground would continue to develop under his influence, even after his death. For if you look at the basic blueprint for the Holte End, as envisaged in 1914, that is almost exactly how it was built in 1939.

Surprisingly, very little detailed information concerning the construction of this, the largest single terrace in British football, has survived.

Photographs of the terrace during the 1930s show that it was already fairly large, being divided into three sections, the uppermost one of which was irregular banking (albeit terraced, whereas the top of the Witton End was rough earth). The Rinder-Leitch plan provided for the whole terrace to be regularised with sunken lateral and radial gangways (to discourage fans from standing in them during games), new crush barriers and concrete steppings, and most important of all, the addition of one further section at the rear, raised on concrete stilts. To improve circulation, two large vomitories (or terrace entrances) were to be dug into either side of the third level and, to finish off the whole job, red-brick flanking walls were to frame both sides and the rear, thereby giving the massive new Holte End that now familiar Villa Park air of distinction (even if what lay behind those outside walls was relatively basic).

Four years earlier Leitch's firm had performed a similar expansion plan for Molineux's South Bank, which held 30,000. The country's other large end terrace was the Anfield Kop, which held 28,000, but was fully covered. The new Holte End, it was estimated, would hold up to 40,000, and, theoretically, raise Villa Park's capacity to 90,000.

Foundation work at the rear appears to have started in early 1939, and was sufficiently advanced by April 15 for the SPORTS ARGUS to announce *Good News for Villa Bobs*. (Note, the admission price had not gone up since 1919!). Fans, it said, 'shall hardly know the Holte Hotel End of the ground when the changes have been made.'

A few days later, mindful of the worsening international situation, the board agreed that they should make every effort to finish the job, but only if it could be guaranteed that the total cost would not exceed £14,000, excluding Leitch's fees and the hiring of a clerk of works, at £8 per week. The board minutes also confirm that Villa were seriously considering extending the Witton End too. Indeed Fred Normansell went so far as to offer the Territorial Army £600 for part of the drill ground behind the banking. That was in August however, by which time the Territorials knew that, barring a miracle, they would need all the space they owned to prepare for war with Hitler.

# Dick Turpin wins on points

❖ Villa Park has many claims to history, but one of its proudest moments came on Monday, June 28 1948. That magical evening, around a floodlit ring in the centre of the pitch, a crowd of 40,000 spectators cheered on the Leamington-born boxer Dick Turpin, elder brother of Randolph, as he squared up to Vince Hawkins for the British middleweight title. Intermittent rain and hail failed to douse the crowd's summer-time frenzy as, an hour before midnight, Turpin finally won the gruelling fight on points.

But there was a deeper significance to his victory. For although this was Turpin's 77th bout, and he had won most of them, until that night the British Board of Boxing Control had shamefully banned all non-whites from challenging for honours.

So now, as he revelled in the acclamation sounding out from the stands, Dick Turpin was able to raise his fists in triumph – the first black boxer ever to win a British title! And it happened at Villa Park.

It was just like 1914 all over again. Villa Park was in mid-construction. Europe was in turmoil.

Sure enough, construction at the Holte End was suspended immediately Britain declared war on September 3, as was all footballing activity after just three matches of the 1939-40 season. In November the WAR OFFICE commandeered Villa Park (among several grounds). But as barrage balloons floated majestically above Aston Park, there then followed several months of so-called phoney war, during which the pretence of normal life on the home front continued. Thus Villa were somehow able to gain a special permit to complete the new terracing.

How they managed this is not recorded. But they did, thus making the new Holte End the only example of any major football ground construction to have been completed during the war. It was certainly finished by April 1940, for by then Archibald Leitch Jnr. was totting up the final bills.

No sooner had the concrete dried than the Holte would be moth-balled. But the rest of Villa Park was already a hive of war-time activity. The home dressing room was for a while taken over by a rifle company of the Ninth Battalion of the Royal Warwickshire Regiment (one of whom was Peter Morris, later to write Villa's Centenary history), while hundreds of boxes of ammunition from KYNOCHS were stored in various parts of the Trinity Road Stand. Space under the Witton Lane Stand was used to store large quantities of ARP equipment.

Before the war Villa's wealthier fans had been able to pay a shilling to park on the Territorial Army's drill ground, behind the Witton End. Now both fans and a few players were to be found square bashing there. Among them was Vic Ray, a supporter since 1928. One day, his sergeant asked for men to guard the ammunition in the Trinity Road Stand. 'It was the only time I ever knew soldiers to volunteer for guard duty,' Ray remembers.

In between kickabouts on the hallowed turf, he thus found himself on watch in the home dressing room, guarding vigilantly the locker of his hero, Villa captain Alex Massie.

Massie and his team-mates, meanwhile, went off to do their bit for King and country. Several younger players joined the forces, many went to work at KYNOCHS, while Alan Wakeman, Eddie Lowe and Jack Maund became *Bevin Boys*, working in the Hednesford coal mine.

Eric Houghton, who later became Villa's manager, then a director and vice president, was 29 when war was declared.

'We were called to Villa Park, given two weeks money, and told our contracts were suspended until further notice,' Houghton recalled, 40 years later. 'The declaration of war hardly came as a surprise, but wiping out our contracts was absolutely devastating. In those days the top money was £8 in winter and £6 in summer. There we were, out of a job, with no money coming in, and the threat of being called up. It was a very disturbing time.

'I went to KYNOCHS for a while, and then found myself in the police force. PC Houghton was

## Evening Despat

077.   *Lighting-up time: 7.30 p.m.*   FRIDAY, 12 APRIL, 1946.   ON

### nnounces big plans for the Post Office

### PHONES A YEAR IS

He was 30ft. up in the air

THE GIRDER

Here is the girder along which the steeplejacks walked during the Cup-tie at Villa Park, thus, in the words of the prosecuting solicitor, "endangering the lives of scores of spectators." Below is a view of the girder from another angle—as it would be seen by the hundreds of football fans beneath.

**CUP-TIE CROWD ENDANGERED BY MAN WHO TOLD POLICE "I WAS DRUNK"—FINED £5**

# Steeplejack walked on girder at Villa Park

ONE of three steeplejacks who climbed a 30-foot girder at Villa Park during the Charlton v. Bolton Wanderers cup-tie, and walked 40 yards along narrow girder work over the heads of the crowds, was fined £5 by the Birmingham Stipendiary (Lord Ilkeston) to-day for committing a disorderly act.

Prosecuting, Mr. M. P. Pugh said three men, two of whom were not before the court, refused to come down in spite of requests from the police and the crowd, and by their action they imperilled the lives of scores of spectators.

He had been asked by the Chief Constable to emphasise that the men not only endangered the lives of the spectators, but by their action might have caused a panic such as had occurred at another football match in which there was a tragic loss of life.

The crowd at Villa Park were greatly angered at the conduct of the three men, he said.

The prosecution, it is under-stood, is the first of its kind in the country.

Mr. Pugh said there were about 72,000 people present at the match, and at about ten minutes past three a police constable who was on special duty in the scoreboard at the Witton-lane side of the ground saw three men, one of whom was the defendant, William Frederick Pratt, aged 25, of 199, Drews-lane, Ward End, Birmingham, begin to climb one of the girders in the old bomb-damaged stand.

The men got to the top—a distance of 30ft.—and walked along another girder to the roof of the grandstand where they rested themselves. It was a very dangerous operation, and right beneath them were the packed thousands of spectators.

The police did everything in their power to persuade the three men to come down from their perilous position.

"They were not so much concerned with their safety as for the safety of the people beneath them," said Mr. Pugh.

One of the men said: "We've come to see the match and we intend to see it. If you try to get us down, we are steeple-jacks, we'll walk along the stands."

### "If you fall. . ."

Spectators shouted, "Come down, you fools, it's we who will suffer if you fall." The three men remained where they were.

P.C. Prest waited until the end of the game, and managed to catch hold of Pratt when he climbed down.

When he was seen at Victoria-road Police Station by Supt. Frankish, said Mr. Pugh, his explanation was a reasonable one, and the great public men's

### Masked men in raid on "pub"

POLICE are to-day searching for three masked and armed men who broke into the Yorkshire Grey public - house, Leytonstone-road, West Ham, London, early to-day.

An occupant was held at revolver point while the premises were searched.

The men escaped with £10 and three bottles of whisky.

Mr. Jim Berry, aged 60, who assists in the public house, said: "I woke up and found the three masked men in my bedroom. Two of them had revolvers and the other a carving knife.

### Phone cut

They all wore black masks, and when they asked me for the keys of the safe, I told them I had not got them. One of the man handed the carving knife to one who had a gun and said, "If he makes a noise hit him on the head with it."

The phone wires had been cut. The licensee, Mrs. May-nard, slept through the raid.

### Smallpox scare in liner

WHILE the Cunard liner Britannic was disembarking passengers at Liver-pool to-day a message was received that a petty officer who had been disembarked

## M.P.s CHANGE THEIR HOURS OF WORK: ALL SIDES AGREE

THE House of Commons, by a vote of 174 to 17 to-day approved a Government motion to alter the times of its sittings from 2.15 to 9.15 to 2.30 to 10 o'clock.

Mr. Herbert Morrison, moving the motion, said the official Opposition and the Liberals were favourable to the change, as also was the Labour Party by a majority, but there was a minority that did not favour it.

Mr. Morrison said that it was not proposed to vary the Friday hours.

Mr. Churchill, Leader of the Opposition, said that he was glad that agreement had been reached between the

is a time of repose. It may be that the human race would consult its health and advan-tage if people lived more in a natural manner instead of working from morning till night—if they broke the day by a short interval for repose, reflection and refreshment.

Mr. Silverman (Lab., Nel-son and Colne) asked Mr. Morrison, amid laughter, what trade union members of the House should join, and if he did not know he

tele-year, aster-s this

cious," ne to y, but

r 100 and tain

ct few ntry—

master-ing the e Post raphs t of the required 6,000,000 e system. of work nd there make up. hy the n the Bill that asked casions.

shortage of . Burke applications e service in s could not iting list of ications had

tion of hos-for the tele-ured in at an Applications a double pre-it had been ep pace with and prevent of outstand-from increas-

00 to be e Bill, the ed to spend 00 a year. few months had been nes at a rate 50,000 per 0 per cent. e-war rate of

nd telephone month was a as planned to in future by ones at the er year. raph traffic ancial year last was 28 er than in

❖ *Wholly Trinity – local schoolchildren admire one of the finest entranceways in football, in April 1952. When young players first arrived at Villa Park during this era, it was said that the Trinity Road frontage was often enough to persuade them to sign.*

something of a cross between Charlie Chaplin and Will Hay. I was assigned to Washwood Heath police station, along with our centre-half and captain, Jimmy Allen. It was all very different from what our lives had been before, and we were getting only about a third of what we had earned as footballers.'

While the unlikely PC Houghton took up traffic duties outside the METRO-CAMMELL works in Washwood Heath Lane (before taking another job at ROVER, with Alex Massie), Villa helped the war effort in two other, rather unlikely areas. Firstly, they rented 34 turnstiles to the AUSTIN MOTOR COMPANY,

presumably in order to tighten security at the works. For this Villa were paid £400. Secondly, in September 1940 it was agreed to loan a large number of tip-up seats, for installation in air raid shelters. The players' two billiard tables and piano were also loaned, to the Corporation.

With a good many seats and turnstiles missing, plus all the ammunition and stores piled high in each stand, it was no surprise that when regional football tentatively restarted in September 1940 Villa Park should remain closed. Instead, Villa's home games in the Birmingham and District League were staged in front of meagre crowds at the ground of Solihull Town (which lay where Gilliver Road is now, by Shirley Park).

While the players were away from Villa Park, the Luftwaffe left a calling card. Villa were lucky, for the ground seems to have escaped unscathed when Aston was badly blitzed in late 1940. (King George, the former Duke of York, paid a morale-boosting visit to nearby Queens Road in December.) But the ground was eventually hit, it is thought around April 1941, when the roof of the Trinity Road Stand was holed by shrapnel and large quantities of glass were shattered. Amongst the debris were found the ruined instruments of *Ye Aston Olde Silver Band*. More seriously, either that night or during another air raid the same month, a bomb left one bay of the Witton Lane Stand, nearest the Witton End scoreboard, a tangled wreck.

Still, compared with the likes of Old Trafford, Bramall Lane or St Andrew's, the damage was relatively light, and in September 1941 Villa Park was able to re-open after two years under the command of the WAR OFFICE.

Initially only small crowds attended. For example, there were just 750 to witness the ground's biggest ever win, a 19-2 romp against a team from RAF Lichfield, in March 1942. On the other hand, the club was hardly geared up for large crowds. The BOARD OF TRADE and MINISTRY OF SUPPLIES had started renting space in the Trinity Road Stand in August 1941. Fire watchers were now camping out in the dressing rooms, while other areas were rented to the MINISTRY OF WORKS. Between January 1942 and June 1943 these rentals were worth around £2,000 to Villa (though the directors still haggled with the army over who would pay the electricity bill for the dressing rooms).

From 1943 onwards Villa gradually regained control of the ground. Parts of it they found damaged. The players never saw their billiard tables or piano again, and many of the seats brought back from the shelters were broken. For all these inconveniences, Villa were paid a total of £3,650 compensation by the WAR OFFICE and BIRMINGHAM CORPORATION.

Even so, Villa still needed a loan from Fred Normansell to keep going, and so there must have been considerable relief when gates started rising again in season 1943-44, culminating in a crowd of 54,824 for the home leg of the League North Cup final on May 6, 1944, which Villa won 5-4 on aggregate against Blackpool.

For many in the crowd that day, Villa's victory was an emotional occasion. Not only was it Villa's first major trophy since 1920, but, amid the ruins of the Witton Lane Stand and with the new Holte End filled for the first time ever, it also provided a precious escape from the grim realities of war. D-Day was still a month away at that time, but for one afternoon at least, the people of Birmingham were able to enjoy a foretaste of the happier times peace might yet offer.

Incidentally, before that game the crowd saw an old man wearing a cloth cap and scruffy overalls come out onto the pitch to make sure all the lines were clearly marked. Little did they realise that after disappearing back down the tunnel the man then headed straight to the dressing room to get changed for the match. This was the veteran Ernest 'Mush' Callaghan, Villa's balding full-back in the promotion team of 1938, who had recently moved into the small groundsman's cottage next to the offices and effectively become Villa Park's caretaker. When not tending the ground Mush served as a police reservist, being awarded a BEM for his display of 'conspicuous bravery' during the blitz of September 1942.

Callaghan was one of several Villa old-timers who carried on playing throughout the war and, in the absence of young players coming through, managed to retain their places when peacetime football finally and joyfully resumed for the transitional season of 1945-46.

In the four seasons before the war, Villa had vied with Arsenal for the title of England's best supported club. In the post-war attendance boom Villa could not quite match their rivals. But their ageing stars still managed to pack them in like never before.

Famously, the peak arrived on the sunny afternoon of March 2, 1946, for the first leg of Villa's 6th round FA Cup tie v Derby County. (That season all cup matches were played on a home and away basis.)

As mentioned earlier, with the Holte End now extended the ground should theoretically have been capable of holding 90,000 (given that the pre-war record was 75,540). But if that was the case, the theory was never proven, at least not officially. Unofficially, there were almost certainly thousands more in the ground.

It has often been alleged that in the days before computerised counting systems, clubs would frequently under-declare their attendances, particularly during this period, to avoid paying the dreaded Entertainment Tax. (To illustrate how much this ate away at profits, in 1945-46, Villa paid £41,701 in tax, from total receipts of £101,692.) We also know from fans' reminiscences that turnstile operators often allowed workmates, family or friends to slip through without payment, or to jump over the barriers. Many more children opted for a low dive under the barrier.

Among them was a chirpy little ten-year-old from Lozells, who, on the day of the Derby game, slipped in under the Holte End turnstiles at 12.55. Even that early he remembers the terrace being fairly full. 'I

# Fastest try on record

❖ Villa Park has often played host to sports other than football. There was of course regular cycling and athletics before 1914, and on March 31, 1923 an hour-long exhibition game of lacrosse was played before Villa's reserve game v Stoke.

Two rugby league internationals have also been staged. The first was a Test Match, Great Britain v Australia, which despite being played on a Monday afternoon (on February 14, 1909) managed to attract a surprisingly large crowd of 9,000. Great Britain won narrowly by 6-5, but the Birmingham public was clearly not that impressed because when the same two teams returned for a further Test Match on New Year's Day, 1912, only 4,000 turned up. They missed a then record Australian victory of 33-8.

The oval ball game returned to Villa Park on October 8, 1924, this time for a Union match between a North Midlands XV and the formidable All Blacks. The home team fielded seven players from Moseley, but despite managing to become the first English team to score a try against the tourists that year, it was the New Zealanders who looked most at home, winning comfortably 40-3 in front a crowd of around 17,000. Another North Midlands XV played at Villa Park on April 12, 1951, in a charity match against Colonel R. L. Scorer's International XV.

But perhaps the most historic rugby event to be staged at Villa Park took place on Wednesday, September 17, 1947. Immediately after the touring Australians kicked-off, this time against a Midland Counties XV, the visiting captain, W. M. McLean, picked up the loose ball and sprinted straight through to the byeline. Incredibly, his touchdown was timed at just thirteen seconds, the fastest try ever to be recorded in Britain. A crowd of 16,000 saw the Australians go on to win 22-14.

found myself in the lower corner, under the scoreboard, and we were getting pushed and prodded so much they levered all the young lads out and sat us on the side of the pitch.'

Twenty five years later Terry Weir would return to that same spot, albeit this time as Villa's official photographer!

Nowadays the idea of manhandling small children over the heads of thousands of adults would be greeted with horror. But as Weir recalls, in the late 1940s it was a regarded as a natural form of crowd control.

'You weren't necessarily expecting it. It just sort of suddenly happened. Up you went and you thought "here we go!" There was no chance of squealing out. I always used to think everything was going to fall out of my pocket, but I hadn't got a fat lot in them anyway. The Holte End was split into three, with gangways in between. I never knew quite how they passed you over the gaps but they did. They never dropped you, but you couldn't see the floor anyway. It was just, "oh oh, another one coming" and the next thing you'd know you'd find yourself down at the front. Looking back now I might have died of fright, but at the time it didn't bother me. When you're 10 years old, who cares? But I never told my mother. She'd have had a heart attack if she'd have known!'

Outside the ground around 10,000 fans had

# Villa Park's handy man

❖ Talk to any Villa fan from the late 1940s or early 50s and they all remember that funny geezer who walked on his hands.

What would happen was this. The mystery man, of medium height and build, and usually somewhat dishevelled in appearance, would emerge from the Witton End about 15 minutes before kick-off, and to a huge round of applause would run to the centre circle, where he would toss his cap onto the pitch.

'At that point,' recalls Peter Aldridge, 'the man flipped over and stood on his hands, remaining motionless for a few seconds. Then he set off, still on his hands, dribbling his cap towards the Holte End. Arriving there, having left several phantom defenders trailing in his wake, he would then get back on his feet and kick his cap into the goal.'

Arthur Smith adds that 'never once did he take a rest, and he always raised a great roar from the crowd when he scored with the cap. On occasions he'd even make it a cheeky back-heeler! All great fun!'

Few Villa Park regulars ever knew the identity of this extraordinary entertainer. But supporters from the Hockley area knew him well, for amazingly, his real name was Lenny Hands!

Lenny Hands, or 'Andy' to his mates, was a drifter of the old school. Born in Summer Lane just before the First World War, when his wife died he abandoned his seven children and more or less took to living on the streets. Shoppers in the old Bull Ring knew him as a hawker, while in addition to Villa Park he would be regularly seen in pubs, performing his tricks, trying to earn beer money.

'Everybody around Hockley knew our Lenny, who I believe lived in Mott Street for a while,' remembers Villa fan Ted Deakin. 'Sometimes he sold newspapers, and other times Old Moore's Almanacs, at fourpence a time. He'd fling open the pub door, throw the almanacs on the floor, then walk around the pub on his hands. Then the punters would buy him a half of ale, or have a book off him.'

Most of the time the police seemed happy to tolerate Lenny's one-man pitch invasion. 'Usually,' says Peter Aldridge, 'shortly after his performance began, a solitary policeman who'd been patrolling the cinder track, would walk slowly towards him, but not so quickly as to be in danger of ever catching him up. As the performance reached its end the policeman would approach his quarry, who would flip up onto his feet, make a great play of eluding the policeman, and promptly disappear into the crowd.'

Lenny then worked his way around the terraces, cap in hand collecting pennies, until by half-time he reached the Witton End, where he had started.

As the 1950s wore on, inevitably the pickings grew smaller as the novelty of his act wore off. Occasionally Lenny became abusive towards people who spurned him, and then the police started to haul him away. Nowadays of course his antics would have been featured on Sky TV, or he would have been snapped up by a sponsor. But Lenny Hands was a wastrel and a wanderer, and would die in obscurity, it is thought, some time during the mid-1980s.

Not a single photograph of him has survived, upright or otherwise. But talk to any Villa fan over the age of 60 and you can be sure, Lenny Hands provided some of the best pre-match entertainment ever seen at Villa Park.

arrived from Derby, and the queues were now enormous, which meant rich pickings for buskers. Many of them were ex-servicemen who worked the many queues to be found in Birmingham at this time, at shops and cinemas as well as at football grounds. Fans remembers a piano accordion player, a saxophonist, and a man with a hooked arm, singing Ivor Novello ditties and favourites like *It's a Long Way to Tipperary*.

Meanwhile, fans were already clambering up to gain a better view from the exposed steelwork of the bombed-out section of the Witton Lane Stand. Looking up at them from the Witton End was another ten-year-old, Brian Evans, from Smethwick.

'It was a beautiful March day. My father worked as a cricket club groundsman in the morning, so my mother took me into Birmingham to meet up with him and together we got the 3X tram from Martineau Street, to be at the ground for one o'clock. I felt so infinitely privileged to be there that it didn't bother me to wait so long in such a crush. Big games always had massive crowds and were always uncomfortable. People were also very kind. They would look out for us. That generation did not regard themselves as part of the entertainment. They didn't think that it was important to shout louder or out-sing the other end. Nor was winning so important. It wasn't a matter of life and death, not like the war had been. And besides, football was cheap entertainment.'

Barrie Bailey, then aged 16, was also on the Witton End. 'As it was in any large crowd in those days you stood with your arms to the side. It was so tight that if your hands were in your pockets you'd be fortunate to get them out again.'

At the back of the terrace, on the earth banking which crowned the Witton End, stood another 16-year-old, Peter Aldridge.

'Long before the game started the sunken gangway in front of me was packed full with people who had no view of the pitch at all. Somebody standing close to me looked down at this lot and said, "You lot aren't going to see much are you?" And some fellow replied, "You wait till the teams come out, mate!"

So came the moment when George Cummings led Villa out to the sound of the brass band playing their usual fanfare, 'Entrance of the Gladiators.'

'As the roar of the crowd announced the team's arrival,' remembered Peter Aldridge, 'the people on the gangway in front of me, as one man, all shoved forward onto the top terrace step, forcing the packed crowd further forward. From where I was standing at the top I could see young boys literally popping out of the crowd like champagne corks and being rolled like logs over the heads of the crowd. We were fortunate because some thoughtful adults behind us put their arms forward onto the barrier we were standing against to hold back the crowd behind us. It was one of those occasions where if you were actually in the crowd, in the ground, you literally could not get out.'

Those who were in, and could see, watched Villa take a 3-2 lead. But the veteran Rams had the last

laugh, however, because with five minutes left on the clock, 36-year-old Dally Duncan set up Peter Doherty, 33, for the equaliser, and with seconds remaining, 38-year-old Sammy Crooks made it 4-3.

Barrie Bailey and his pals wept unashamedly at the injustice of it all, while in the Trinity Road enclosure stood a bitterly disappointed Eric Woodward, then a grammar schoolboy but later to become a reporter on the EVENING MAIL, and eventually Villa's Commercial Manager. Sensing that the game was going to be a special occasion he had forsaken his normal spot on the Holte End and paid a few pennies extra to stand near the players' tunnel. 'I remember it was the first and last time I ever bought a rosette. I was so disgruntled, the result clouded everything.'

Only when the ARGUS and SPORTING MAIL came out that evening did it become apparent that the gate had set a new record. Officially the attendance was put at 76,588 (with receipts of £8,651), but as we have already noted, there may well have been many more. Also, because parts of the ground had not felt absolutely chock-a-block, and because there were 1,000 seats still missing from the bomb-damaged Witton Lane Stand, it was assumed that this new record would soon be surpassed.

But it was not. A week later 33 fans died in a crush on the terraces at Bolton, and while there was hardly the same official response as occurred after Hillsborough in 1989, tighter controls on numbers were quickly adopted.

Moreover, Villa's star was now well and truly on the wane, so that although the period would bring a number of thrillers at the Villa – most notably an epic 6-4 home defeat by Manchester United in January 1948 – there would only ever be two more official gates of over 70,000 at Villa Park; 70,687 for the FA Cup semi-final, Blackpool v Tottenham, in March 1948, and 70,718 for Villa's 4th round tie v Cardiff in January 1949. That same season Villa also recorded their highest ever average, of 47,168.

If only the profits from these boom times had been wisely spent; if only the leadership of the club had been tougher and wiser, perhaps Villa would have gone from strength to strength.

But as is well recorded in other club histories, Villa were like a rudderless ship during this era, and no matter how many managers and expensive new players they took on board, most fans, and it would seem most of the players, sensed that it was only a matter of time before the once mighty club would run aground again.

And yet in other respects, the late 1940s and early 1950s seem to have been immensely enjoyable years

❖ *Villa Park in 1951, showing the extended Holte End, the patched-up Trinity Road roof, and the still unrepaired Witton Lane Stand, with its unique trio of barrel roofs in the centre. Behind the Witton End banking the old Lower Grounds' aquarium block remains largely intact (although the tower would be removed in 1958), as does the Territorial Army's parade ground, now the club car park and Villa Village. The bowling green behind the Holte End would eventually be built over in the early 1960s.*

at Villa Park. As Eric Woodward recalled, 'There was definitely a feeling of bonhomie on the terraces that I'm afraid has long since gone.' Reinforced perhaps by the spirit of togetherness engendered by the war, this camaraderie extended to visiting supporters also. Many Villa fans from the post-war period recall how they would meet up on the Witton or Holte Ends with fans they had met in previous years from the likes of Sunderland, Sheffield or wherever, to swap sandwiches, scarves and stories. Nowadays such tales seem almost hackneyed, as if the passage of time has wiped out all memories of conflict in favour of a romanticised idyll. Yet the folk memory is too vivid, and too commonly expressed to be dismissed merely as a distortion.

The fact is – to the eternal shame of we segregated fans of the 1990s – that in those days, supporters of rival clubs really were quite able to watch matches together in easy harmony, saw the social mix as very much part and parcel of the game, and actually preferred it that way.

Other fond memories from that era concern the traditional Christmas and Boxing Day matches. For the first decade after the war it was common for Villa to play the same team home and away on both days, or at least within two or three days of Christmas. During six of those seasons Villa's Yuletide opponents were Wolves.

Despite the lack of public transport over the holiday period huge crowds managed to attend. In fact two such games broke the record for League matches at Villa Park. The 1947 game on Boxing Day drew 68,099, and on December 27 two years later, Villa Park's all-time League record was established, when 69,492 saw a bleary-eyed Villa go down 4-1 to their Black Country neighbours.

Many of the fans were pretty worse for wear too,

sharing the last few drops of their Christmas spirit around the terraces, or puffing proudly on a specially purchased cigar, while new scarves were compared and ill-fitting jumpers ridiculed.

'If the home game was on Christmas Day when there were no trams or buses,' recalled Peter Aldridge, 'we'd get up early, cycle to Witton for an 11 o'clock kick-off, see the game, then ride back home in time for our Christmas lunch. There were always a fair number of people who, for a penny a time would park their bikes in front gardens or back yards around Villa Park, but on Christmas day the number of bikes stacked in those gardens had to be seen to be believed. Hundreds of them there were, and after the game you had to somehow find your own and then extricate it from the pile. But you always found your bike. It was never missing.'

Villa continued to enjoy Christmas or Boxing Day games against the Wolves until the mid-1960s. But by then Villa's whole world had changed, as had the world around Villa Park.

The trams stopped running down Lichfield Road in July 1953. More and more supporters started arriving by car. Villa's new public address system, first used in 1944, was used to broadcast team news, and it would not be long before the odd 'pop' record would also be heard before kick-off, as the brass band proved out of step with modern tastes.

In time the last vestiges of the war would also be eradicated. The Trinity Road roof was patched up in 1948. But as for the Witton Lane Stand, only in 1954 – after eight frustrating years of continuous requests for a building permit from the MINISTRY OF WORKS – would the bomb damaged section be finally rebuilt, at a cost of around £20,000. Supervising the work was the club's new adviser, John Jones, of the Birmingham architectural firm, Hing and Jones. Even in 1954, however, materials were in such short supply that the club had been forced to hunt around for second-hand steel.

Villa were still awaiting the final bill for the reconstruction work and their compensation from the WAR DAMAGES COMMISSION when, in March 1955, Fred Normansell died after 19 years as club chairman. His 38-year-old son, Bruce, replaced him on the board, while Chris Buckley was elected the new chairman.

We started this chapter by recalling the retirement of George Ramsay. And so we conclude with his successor, Billy Smith also standing down, in April 1955, to make way for his long-serving assistant, Fred Archer.

Smith's 29 years of high pressure work as secretary, and no doubt his smoking and drinking habits, had ruined his health, and so at the age of 62 he opted for early retirement.

And if, on leaving, he had stopped to ask any Villa fan on Carriage Drive, 'Well, what d'you want?' their immediate answer would have been simple. Survival in the First Division and a trip to Wembley.

Billy Smith lived to see both, then died three months after Johnny Dixon lifted the Cup, in August 1957.

# Chapter 11

# Work, Rest and Play

*in which we see Villa Park from the players' perspective* ❖

*Amos Moss fetches the laundry* ❖

*a snooker professional meets his match* ❖

*a Supporters Association is founded* ❖

*floodlights and a new training ground make for a bright future* ❖

*tea, toast and a few tips at Ernie's greasy spoon* ❖

*the Holte End and Witton Lane Stand gain new roofs* ❖

*1966 and all that* ❖

*'I remember walking for the first time down the Villa Park Carriage Drive and feeling the aura of greatness completely surround me.'*

GOALKEEPER JOE RUTHERFORD, ON SIGNING FOR VILLA FROM SOUTHPORT, IN 1939.

❖ *Until converted into Jack Milner's treatment room in 1958, this was the pavilion of the Holte Bowling Club. The bowling green itself was a remnant of the old Lower Grounds, and remained fenced off from Villa Park for many years. The green was finally dug up in 1966 to make way for the Lions Club. Apparently one of the favourite competitions held among senior players was to see who could chip a golf ball from the bowling green, over the Trinity Road Stand and onto the Villa Park pitch. As Charlie Aitken recalled, 'The balls used to break windows and ricochet off the walls all over the place. No-one cared a damn, and you can imagine how good a shot you needed to be to clear the stand.' The keenest participants, Aitken seemed to recall, were Peter McParland, Nigel Sims, Bobby Thompson, and the best shot of them all, as one might expect, Gerry Hitchens.*

THERE ARE FOOTBALL GROUNDS AND football grounds. And then there is Villa Park. But for the Aston Villa players of the 1990s, Villa Park plays a very different part in their professional lives than it did for their predecessors.

Before the modern era, Villa Park was the hub of all activity. Now it is primarily the place where the first team perform. It is their stage, but no longer their rehearsal room. The pitch is not used for training, and even the reserves do not play there on a regular basis. Apart from match days Villa Park is a place to which players drive, once in a while, perhaps to collect post or to fulfil a specific obligation. Certainly none of the players would choose to live within a mile or so's radius of the ground, while few would know their way around the surrounding back streets, at least, not on foot.

This is no disrespect either to the players or to the residents of Aston, Lozells or Birchfield. It is just the way of the world, the same being equally true for Old Trafford, White Hart Lane, Molineux or St Andrew's. Players have moved up in the world. Most football grounds have stayed put.

Besides which, other than matches, more or less everything else associated with being a Villa player – training, treatment, meetings, interviews – nowadays takes place at the club's training ground at Bodymoor Heath, which opened in 1971.

Before then, Villa Park played that everyday role.

Players would know all the ground's nooks and crannies; where to skive training, where to have a quick fag, where to keep warm in winter and where to enjoy a good old chinwag with one of the backroom staff. Groundsman Bert Bond – of whom more later – had a particularly cosy hideaway under the Witton Lane Stand where he would regale young players with stories of his war-time exploits as a navigator with Bomber Command.

Many of the players, if not locals themselves, also grew familiar with the surrounding area; its residents, shops, cafes and factories. A number took on part-time summer jobs to boost their earnings. Alan Deakin, for example, learned welding during the close season. 'We all realised that no matter how well you did, in the end we'd all have to go out and get a job. No players earned enough not to work.'

Leslie Smith built up a successful electrical shop on Bevington Road. Stan Lynn had a newsagents nearby. Even former manager Dick Taylor ended up running his own sportswear shop a stone's throw from the ground, on Witton Road.

For younger players on the groundstaff, Villa Park was an education in itself, if only in hard work, patience and learning to know one's place. Hours were spent cleaning and polishing the boots of senior players. In his early years Amos Moss scrubbed down the dressing rooms, cleaned all the taps and showerheads with Brasso, rolled bandages and fetched washing. Amazingly, until the 1950s Villa had no washing facilities of their own. Instead, Moss had to carry a huge basket of dirty kit across to a woman who lived in Witton Lane, just opposite the stand's main entrance.

'Of course I didn't want to walk all the way around the track so I'd cut across the pitch, with Bert Bond shouting at me, "Get off the bloody pitch!" I'd keep on walking, then when I got round to the Witton Lane side he and his assistant, who funnily enough was called Bill Clinton, would tip the washing out of the basket all over the track. When I came back with all the clean washing I knew they wouldn't dare do the same so I could walk across the pitch without a care!'

To dry the kit there were huge, wheeled racks which rolled in and out of a boiler room next to the dressing rooms. These had been installed as part of the Trinity Road Stand's original heating system.

Charlie Aitken has never forgotten the racks. 'It was about the only place where you could get warm. But the smell was disgusting... all those soaking wet sweaters and training gear which was only ever washed maybe once a week.'

Until Bodymoor Heath, training itself was conducted at a number of different locations. The Alexander Ground, where Frank Barson had ruled the roost during the late 1930s, became a popular speedway venue after the war. In 1949, therefore, Villa's president, Sir Patrick Hannon, helped negotiate a deal to rent the HP Sauce sports ground on Grange Road, Erdington, for £100 a season, for mid-week training and junior matches on alternate Saturdays. Otherwise, much of the training took

place at Villa Park. Not that it involved much ball-work on the actual pitch.

Writing in his autobiography, *Going for Goal* in 1960, Villa's dashing Irish international winger, Peter McParland, described the situation in the early Fifties, just before trainer Hubert Bourne retired.

'Villa treated their players like kings – and still do – but from a football viewpoint those years of struggling were frustrating ones for the players. There was no live scouting system, no organised coaching, no long-term policy and no reserve build-up.

'Training was terribly slack. Players strolled up at any old time, and the way they trained was a farce. Some would just walk round the track, while one player used to go on the far side for a smoke!

'Friday was known as *Two-lap Day*. Many didn't even bother to do two laps. Some would not even bother to change. They would just pull a sweater over their shirts, often leaving their ties on. Then, they would probably sit in the tunnel until some keen type had finished his training and then calmly walk back up the steps with him as though they too, had been training.'

But if the regime was slack – and the results showed it – it is difficult to find a former player who did not feel at home.

Johnny Dixon came down from Newcastle in 1946 with his brother Ernie as a companion, booked into the Holte Hotel (as did most new arrivals at this time), and has never wanted to leave Birmingham since. As a player, he remembered, 'We had the best of everything. Even though the club was always supposed to be short of cash we always travelled by train, stayed in the best hotels. The club really looked after us.'

That meant decent kit and training gear, even when non-essential clothing items were rationed after the war. It also meant annual, end-of-season tours, with generous spending money thrown in (until that is, one of the team bragged about this to a player from another club, who promptly asked his own chairman for a similar deal. Unfortunately this chairman just happened to be a bigwig at the Football League, which banned such payments. Villa thus had to stop the practice, or at least, like most other clubs, find another way around the rules.)

But if there was one feature of Villa Park during the 1950s remembered by most players it was the sound of laughter, cascading around the dressing room.

'For football it was like a pantomime. It was a disgrace really. But we had the greatest set of lads possible when it came to having a laugh,' was Larry Canning's view. To illustrate this he recalls the time when two new billiard tables were installed in the players' recreation room (the previous ones having been requisitioned during the war).

'A snooker professional called Albert Brown turned up when the new tables were installed, and he didn't win a single match against any of the Villa players. So then he decided he'd take us on at billiards, and George Edwards murdered him at that

too. That's how misspent our youth was!'

Of course it was not all fun and games. After former Villa winger Eric Houghton arrived as manager in 1953, with Bill Moore as trainer, the regime toughened up a little. Jimmy Hogan, now in his seventies, was brought out of retirement to coach the younger players.

As every student of football history should know, Houghton's five years in charge was crowned in May 1957 with Villa's record breaking seventh FA Cup win, against Manchester United. But as every true supporter also knew at the time, deep in their hearts, the Wembley win was not the start of something big. Instead, in the finest traditions of the competition, it was merely a glorious aberration. The following season the team slid back into their losing ways in the League, Houghton was sacked in November 1958, and by the end of the season Villa were back in Division Two.

With hindsight we may view Villa's subsequent fightback under new boss Joe Mercer as a false dawn, at least as far as the team was concerned. But in terms of the ground, there were a number of noteworthy developments.

❖ *Villa's backroom staff pose outside the former bowling club pavilion in 1962. Seated in front are the club secretary, Fred Archer (left) and his assistant Len Latham (right). Latham was a former Stoke schoolboy international who was said to have been so strong in his own position that he forced his rival Stanley Matthews out onto the wing, where he remained ever after! Yet having joined Villa's groundstaff in 1931 Latham never made it to the first team. In the back row, from left to right, are Bert Bond, Mush Callaghan, Jack Milner, Phil Hunt and Ron Liney.*

*'I can still remember getting the train to New Street, being met by Peter Doherty, who was then the chief scout, and driving down the old road from the city centre, past the brewery, past the HP factory, straight down what was then the main approach down Park Road, and just seeing the Trinity Road side and thinking, wow! And then there was the size of the Holte End. I'd been to other clubs but this did impress me. There was something about it all that made an instant impression. It just hit me. They took me up into the old offices, and I remember watching a game. The club were in the Second Division at that time. I just liked the crowd, liked the atmosphere and went home thinking, I hope I get an opportunity to join that football club.'*

BRIAN LITTLE, ON HIS FIRST VISIT AS A 15-YEAR-OLD HOPEFUL, IN 1968.

*'When you saw the front of the ground, on Trinity Road, that was the striking part of it. You were in awe of it.'*

ALAN DEAKIN FROM BALSALL HEATH, ON THE DAY HE SIGNED IN 1956.

Apart from the extra revenue earned from the Cup run, these developments were considerably helped by two important changes in legislation.

A month before Villa's trip to Wembley came the long awaited abolition of the Entertainment Tax (first imposed in 1916). Britain could afford it, or at least that was what the Tory Prime Minister Harold MacMillan told his party followers in his famous 'we've never had it so good' speech of July 1957.

Just as importantly, a year later legislation was passed which allowed football clubs to run their own pools competitions. Villa fans responded immediately.

At a terse 1958 AGM, the SHAREHOLDERS ASSOCIATION had tried to get two of their members elected onto the board. Neither succeeded, but chairman Chris Buckley's appeal for unity and calm rang hollow with many of the frustrated supporters. However, the most vocal among them did not give up. In order both to raise funds for the club, and to make the board realise the power which supporters could wield, when organised, a new Supporters' Association was set up.

One of the founders, and its first chairman, was a builder called Reg Hodgkinson. In 1958 there were eight members, but thanks to its hugely successful pools competition, run by Joan Morley, this had grown to a massive 26,000 by 1968. In those first ten years, Hodgkinson calculated, the Supporters' Association raised no less than £100,000 for Aston Villa.

Before this money could be spent, in 1958-59 the club itself undertook four projects.

The first was to convert the bowling pavilion on

Trinity Road into a fully-equipped treatment room for the players, under the supervision of the club physiotherapist, Jack Milner.

At the same time the basement area where the Lower Grounds aquarium had been built in 1878 was completely refurbished and converted into a modern gym. The area had always been used for wet weather training. But now it was completely sealed in, a couple of the original arches were removed, and various bays were adapted for shooting practice. (Sadly, one of the consequences of this renovation was that the original tower, long since disused, had to be lopped – the first of several truncations which would eventually lead to the entire building's demolition in 1981.)

The third innovation, also completed during the summer of 1958 was floodlighting. As explained on page 154, Villa's board had been embarrassingly slow to take this vital step.

But the fourth, and by far the most significant outlay in the period 1958-59, concerned the purchase, at long last, of Villa's own training ground.

In truth the directors had been looking for a suitable site for some time, but the fact that they struck the deal only four months after Joe Mercer's arrival in December 1958, suggested that Mercer was just the fillip Villa needed. True, 'Uncle' Joe was unable to prevent the team being relegated that season. But a narrow 1-0 defeat for the Cup holders in a semi-final against Forest and average gates of nearly 33,000, combined with the smart new treatment room, the gymnasium, the floodlights and the new training ground, seemed proof positive that Villa's future looked extremely bright. Stan Cullis had brought unprecedented success and attention to the floodlit Molineux of the 1950s. Matt Busby had nurtured his Babes at Old Trafford. Was it now time for Mercer's Minors to step into the limelight?

The training ground itself was perfectly located. Barely 500 yards from Villa Park, it lay on Trinity Road, immediately adjacent to the playing fields of King Edward VI Grammar School, Aston (where Aston Unity had played until 1908).

Villa purchased the five acre site from the bicycle manufacturers, Hercules, and needed to do very little to it before staging Third and Fourth team games there from April 1959 onwards. (One of the earliest matches there featured a young hopeful called Ron Atkinson, shortly before his transfer to Headington United.) Before then the Third team had spent several seasons in exile at the ground of Walter Somers Ltd. in Halesowen, while the Fourths had not played a home match for years. The Hercules Ground therefore not only provided a single point of focus for Villa's 50 strong professional playing squad, but also saved the club both pitch rental and travel costs.

Compared with Bodymoor Heath it was a compact training ground. But in 1959 it seemed perfect. There were two full-size pitches, running lengthways between Trinity Road and Normandy Road, a bowling green, tennis courts and changing rooms, although the first teamers continued to change at Villa Park and simply jogged to and from

❖ *Always looking the part in his white coat, club physio Jack Milner tries out the equipment in his new treatment room, in the former bowling club pavilion on Trinity Road.*

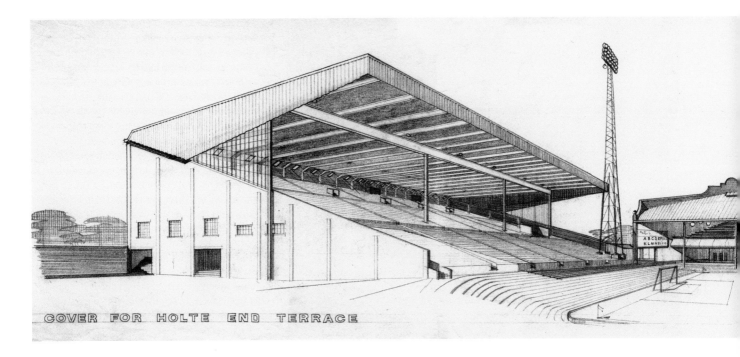

COVER FOR HOLTE END TERRACE

the ground along Trinity Road each day. On occasions they would be joined in training by the local boxer, Johnny Prescott, and by a lifelong Villa devotee, Denis Howell, who was then both MP for Small Heath (which oddly enough included Villa Park) and a serving Football League referee. Howell would occasionally referee Villa's practice matches, taking it so seriously that he once sent off Ron Wylie.

As the VILLA NEWS AND RECORD announced proudly in 1959, supporters visiting the Hercules Ground would 'not only be delighted with all they see, but will also commend the Directors of Aston Villa FC for their perspicacity in acquiring such a wonderful enclosure and a truly great asset to the club.'

But if they applauded the new training ground, the shareholders were far from happy with the financial state of affairs. Those rumblings of discontent at the 1958 AGM grew stronger throughout the season, reaching boiling point in May 1959, as Villa not only plummeted back into the Second Division but at the same time also stacked up debts of £87,000, largely owing to the total of £67,238 spent on the four projects detailed above, plus the purchase of various club houses for the players. To ease the situation an EGM was called, at which the directors sought, and won approval, to extend the club's borrowing requirement from £60,000 to £100,000.

As in 1925, the shareholders tried to set up a committee to investigate the club's accounts. They failed. The board held firm, and would continue to do so as crisis followed crisis throughout the 1960s.

As for the players, now back in the First Division, there were noticeable changes in their conditions. In 1961 the maximum wage was abolished after a strike threat by the leader of the Players' Union, Jimmy Hill. But while certain clubs took to paying their stars £100 a week, Villa's maximum merely crept up from

£20 in 1961 to between £30-50 by the mid-1960s. With larger bonuses, however, it was still sufficient to ensure that more senior players were now turning up to Villa Park in cars, whereas ten years earlier Harry Parkes had been one of the few to drive (though apparently that rarely stopped him from being late for training!).

For those still dependent on public transport, professional football could hardly be described as a glamorous lifestyle. Johnny Dixon took the bus from his digs on the Tyburn Road. When Tony Hateley did not have his car, he and Ron Wylie would catch buses to the station in Nottingham just before 7.00am, board the 7.30 train to New Street, and then nip onto a 5A bus to Aston. Herbie Smith and Larry Canning

❖ The Holte End was roofed in 1962, at a time when behavioural patterns were just starting to change among the game's younger terrace fans. As a result, 'the Holte' – as it now became known – and particularly its newly covered rear, would soon become the noisiest, most raucous, and often the most exclusive part of the ground, leaving the Witton End to Villa's less vocal supporters and any visiting fans.

❖ *Villa players try out their new gym in 1958. Recalling the building's origins, the* EVENING DESPATCH *commented, 'Where monarchs of the jungle used to air their graces, men of Aston Villa will flex their muscles. No leisure in the old aquarium now.' As can be seen, the central arches (shown on page 124) have been removed to create more space. However, this required the demolition of the building's imposing tower.*

would take trams from their homes in Washwood Heath to Saltley. From there they hopped onto an Inner Circle bus to Aston Cross, where Billy Goffin would wait to join them on the 3X tram to Witton. Out near Castle Bromwich, near neighbours Joe Rutherford, Derek Ashton, Roy Gutteridge and Amos Moss were slightly luckier. The drivers of their regular Midland Red bus knew them all so well that he would stop outside each of their homes.

Right up to the 1960s, players continued to arrive at Villa Park on the bus, even on match days. When he broke into the first team in 1961, Charlie Aitken would take the Outer Circle bus from his digs in Yardley at around 1.20, chat with any fans who might recognise him along the way, walk up Trinity Road, stop to buy a Mars Bar, and then play in front of anything up to 50,000 people, before heading home on the same bus.

But from whichever direction they came, and by whatever mode of transport, there was always one place to which all Villa players headed during the week, before and after training. The local café.

In the late 1940s and early 1950s this meant Rose's café, on the corner of Trinity Road and Witton Road. In the late 1950s and 1960s Rose gave way to Ernie, until Ernie set up on the corner of Trinity Road and Nelson Road, within yards of the Carriage Drive, leaving a woman called Pearl to take over the old place. Brian Little remembers distinctly that in the late 1960s only first teamers were allowed to go to Ernie's, while apprentices were given lunch money and told to go only to Pearl's, where there was less likelihood of their impressionable minds being corrupted.

Talking to some of the older players one can understand the club's concern. Most football grounds in those days had greasy spoons nearby where the players would hang out. But by all accounts there was only one Ernie.

Ernie was an Albion fan; a big hearted man and a prankster. Ron Wylie remembers him with special affection. 'I'd get there at maybe 9.30 in the morning for some tea and toast before training. Ernie knew I was a Sinatra fan, so as he saw me come off the bus, he'd put threepence in the jukebox and he'd be dancing to a Sinatra song behind the counter as I walked in. Characters like that just don't seem to be around the game any more.'

But Ernie was also a rogue, albeit more Sergeant Bilko than Reggie Kray. If you needed something, Ernie would fix you up. A tip for the 3.30 at Kempton. Second-hand TVs. You name it, Ernie could get his hands on it. He also acted as a middleman for selling the players' tickets.

This was not always easy money. Charlie Aitken remembers he and his fellow Scottish apprentice, Wilson Briggs, walking from Yardley to Villa Park at 5.00am, simply so that they could queue up to buy semi-final tickets, which they would then sell on. Each was then earning £8 14s a week from Villa, half of which was paid in rent. No wonder Ernie was so popular.

In the end his back door trade in televisions required Ernie to spend a year or so at Her Majesty's Pleasure, and after he died, the café was eventually demolished. By then, however, Villa had already opened up their own canteen at the ground, before all training was switched to Bodymoor Heath.

In one respect the move to Bodymoor was a blessed relief. For the old Holte End may have formed a much-loved and mammoth platform for Villa's most vocal supporters, but for the players it was a mountain they would be forced to climb on a regular basis during training. As if that were not punishing enough, under Dick Taylor they would also have to race to the top with weights strapped to their shoulders. It was a long, long way up, so those players in the know would make sure they grabbed a thick sweater to avoid the weights cutting into their skin.

One of the advantages of using the Holte End for training was that the undercroft areas were sheltered from the rain. So too would be the upper half of the terrace when, at long last, it gained a roof during the summer of 1962.

Apart from the £20,000 spent on rebuilding the bombed section of the Witton Lane Stand eight years earlier, the Holte's new roof was the first major piece of construction at Villa Park since the terrace had been extended in 1939-40. Remarkably, it was also the first time since the old Trinity Road tin roof was taken down in 1922 that ordinary terrace fans had been provided with any cover. Indeed in season 1961-62, Villa Park was the only First Division ground other than Craven Cottage still to have both its end terraces uncovered.

The roof itself, though functional and tidy, was no great beauty, and nor was it ever likely to be, considering the awkward shape and great depth of the terrace, as determined by the Rinder-Leitch masterplan (which significantly never bothered to specify how the terrace might be covered).

Designed by the local architects Peter Hing and

Jones, it did nevertheless provide shelter for roughly two-thirds of the Holte's then (very approximate) capacity of 30,000, with only two slender columns obstructing views. It was also relatively cheap, at only £40,000, all of which was met, not by the £60,000 transfer of Gerry Hitchens to Inter Milan the year before – as was sometimes – but by the still thriving Supporters' Association.

With the new roof finished in August 1962, Villa fans could face the new season with more confidence than perhaps at any time since the war. In Joe Mercer they had one of the finest managers of the day. The likes of Alan Deakin, John Sleeuwenhoek, Harry Burrows and Charlie Aitken were starting to attract rave reviews. Villa had become winners of the first ever League Cup competition, and even the financial outlook seemed rosier than ever. Season ticket sales were well up, and record profits of £106,202 were announced.

On a wider note, Birmingham was booming too. Its factories had full order books, unemployment was low, wages were high and the rebuilding of the city, first planned in the 1930s, was now well in hand after the destruction of the war. The effects of this could already be seen close to Villa Park, where the city's first urban underpass, and one of the first in Britain, was opened to traffic on Birchfield Road, three weeks after the Holte End roof was completed. The new road sliced through the heart of Six Ways, splitting Aston from Lozells and thus changing forever the identity of the area.

The effects of this car-orientated planning policy would intensify throughout the 1960s, culminating in the destruction of Aston village itself in the 1970s.

*'I remember arriving by train from Swindon. I took a taxi down to Villa Park. I had one look at the massive stand and impressive entrance and almost turned home. I thought, this place is too big for me.'*

JOHN NEAL AFTER HIS £6,000 TRANSFER FROM SWINDON IN JULY 1959.

*'Life at Villa Park was a dream. They're the greatest club in the world as far as I am concerned.'*

JOHN NEAL LOOKING BACK ON HIS THREE YEARS AS A VILLA MAN.

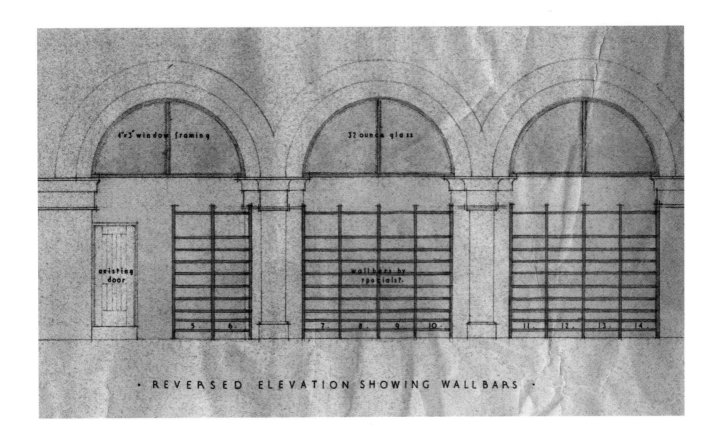

· REVERSED ELEVATION SHOWING WALL BARS ·

this to happen, and that there could be financial aid available from the FA and possibly the government too.

During the summer of 1963 the old barrel roof of the Witton Lane Stand came down, to be replaced by a plain, sloping roof not dissimilar in style to the Holte End roof. Designed again by Peter Hing and Jones, and also largely funded by the Supporters' Association, it was in truth a huge letdown after the quirkiness of the original roof, which though basic, did at least have the benefit of three arch-fronted gables in the centre. The mundane lines and low-slung roof line of the new Witton Lane cover were also in stark contrast to the dignity and detail of the Trinity Road Stand.

But while the rest of the city was being remodelled according to the dictates of modern architects – with their underpasses, functional high-rise blocks, characterless shopping arcades and slavish adherence to concrete and steel – why should a humble football ground have been immune? Besides, the Witton Lane side was far too narrow and too close to the houses opposite to be built upwards, so a new roof and a few improvements under the seating deck were about all that could be reasonably expected. Or at least, reasonably expected from an ageing set of directors who now seemed totally out of touch with the rapidly changing world of football.

A year later, as the board sacked Joe Mercer – who then suffered a nervous breakdown – it was decided to double Villa's overdraft facility to £200,000, so that the club could purchase the Serpentine car park. That led to an end of season debt of £53,806.

Thus Villa veered from a record profit to a record loss within two years.

Something had to give, and in 1965 it did, when astonishingly, the board sold the Trinity Road training ground for £63,000. (Housing on Townley Gardens soon took its place.)

A number of close observers of the scene have since described this decision as the biggest single mistake that Villa's beleaguered set of directors would ever make. For sure the training ground was small, and the Serpentine – the site of the annual

❖ *Wembley winners one and all! Villa Park's groundstaff in 1957 make sure that this time no-one dares nick the FA Cup. Former full-back Mush Callaghan (back row, far left) and his first wife Wyn lived in the cottage attached to the offices and were in overall charge of cleaning and maintaining Villa Park. To help them there was Mush's brother Arthur , Jim Snape, Jim Callaghan, Bert Bond, Arthur Callaghan, Gilbert Darke and Jack Watts . On the front row there are more of the Callaghan family, Harry, Graham and Roy, joined by Fred Hook.*

But then as Villa's club historian Peter Morris would point out, Villa's summer of hope in 1962 would also prove to be a 'great illusion'.

True, Villa were unlucky. Their form was badly hit by the big freeze of 1962, and Joe Mercer eventually fell ill with the strain of Villa's worsening form. Gates dropped dramatically as a result, from an average of 32,074 in 1962-63 to only 22,322 the following year, a fall of some 30 per cent. This was Villa's lowest peacetime average since 1911-12.

Moreover, instead of spending the 1962 profits on players, as would many of the more financially astute clubs at this time, Villa allowed nearly half their surplus to be swallowed up by tax. Who now can fathom the Villa board's spending policy during this miserable period?

Briefly, or at least as far as the development of the ground is concerned, the spiral of events was as follows. In 1962 it was known that Villa Park was likely to be chosen as one of the venues for the 1966 World Cup, that more seats would be necessary for

Onion Fair – might just have been bought by developers, thereby depriving Villa fans of a much needed car-park. But what football club in its right mind would buy a car park and sell a training ground? Or did they hope to convert the Serpentine into a better training ground?

Over 30 years after the event, who can say whether the directors were foolhardy, poorly advised, or whether they simply took a gamble which failed? Whichever, Villa players were now jolted out of their routine and forced back onto the road, using various training grounds around Witton, Erdington and Kingstanding, rented from companies such as DUNLOP, DELTA and LUCAS. After the optimism of 1962 it all added up to a crushing reversal of fortune.

Meanwhile, that same group of tired old directors – four of the six were over 70 – now had to prepare for the biggest event in Villa Park's history, the World Cup (see pages 155-156).

For those men that magical summer of 66 proved to be their swansong. Two and half years later they were swept aside, and the new regime which took their place took a long, hard and penetrating look at Villa Park – its nooks and crannies, its dusty corridors, its locked cupboards and outdated facilities – and discovered what many a shareholder had long suspected. That behind its majestic exterior, Villa Park was not a pretty sight.

*'My cousin played for Rangers and was always on about Ibrox. Well, the first time I came to Villa Park I couldn't believe it. The thing which always gave me a thrill was the Carriage Drive, with the offices at the end, the bowling green on the side, and up on the facade of the stand, the lion. There was never a ground that came up to it, not even the marble halls of Arsenal. It looked old fashioned, but there was a real pride about the place.'*

LARRY CANNING, A SCOTTISH WING-HALF WHO ARRIVED IN 1943 AND LATER REPORTED FROM VILLA PARK FOR BBC RADIO.

❖ The last surviving feature of the Villa Park of 1897 – the distinctive barrel-shaped roof on the Witton Lane Stand – finally succumbed to the ravages of time during the summer of 1963 (shown left). The stand's front paddock, however, survived a further two years before being converted to seating in time for the World Cup (above). As can be seen, the Witton End (in the foreground) was also converted to seating for the World Cup, albeit temporarily, with wooden benches on the terracing.

❖ The changing face of Villa Park, as depicted on these programme covers ranging from 1957 to 1963. Notice that before the floodlights arrived, Saturday afternoon matches in winter kicked-off at 2.15pm.

# Lighting up time

❖ For football fans of the Fifties they evoked modernity and glamour; the promise of magical evenings and exotic opposition from faraway places. For the residents living nearby they were an unwelcome intrusion, and for anxious cinema owners they represented yet one more counter-attraction. If nothing else, they provided invaluable navigational aids for visiting fans trying to find the ground through a maze of unfamiliar backstreets.

But forty years on floodlight pylons are already becoming icons of the past. The modern lighting systems of today, as at Villa Park, are largely to be found mounted along stand roofs, not on spindly great towers which dare only the brave to provide maintenance.

As recounted in CHAPTER 3, the old Lower Grounds Meadow had staged a floodlit game as early as 1878. But as was indicative of the club's torpor during the 1950s, once the modern floodlit era began around 1951, Villa were painfully slow to switch on. In fact they were one of only three First Division clubs still without lights by the end of season 1957-58, and were the last of the West Midland clubs to light up, Wolves having been the first in September 1953.

Installed during the summer of 1958 at a cost of £31,283, Villa's system consisted of four pylons, each 180 foot high and each carrying forty eight 1500 Watt lamps, linked by some ten miles of cables.

Their debut came during the second home match of the new season, against Portsmouth, on Monday, August 25, 1958. Villa were level at 1-1 when, as reported in the VILLA NEWS AND RECORD, 'the lights we had all been waiting for' flickered into life during the half-time break at around 8.00pm, growing in intensity until the ground seemed brighter even than in daylight. 'And how we were pleased with them!' crowed the programme.

The second half was just nine minutes old when Villa Park cheered its first floodlit goal, appropriately enough scored by Villa's longest serving and arguably most popular player, Johnny Dixon. (Just for the record, Villa went on to win 3-2 in front of a 34,797 crowd.)

But no club in the 1950s could possibly install floodlights without inviting top opposition from Europe, at least not after Wolves had so captured the imagination of the nation with their luminous shirts and night-time epics against Honved, Moscow Spartak and others in 1954.

Thus arrived at Villa Park on October 29, 1958 the recent Swedish champions from Gothenberg, G.A.I.S., hardly in the same bracket as Honved, it is true, but foreign all the same, which in those days was all that mattered.

Villa beat G.A.I.S. 3-0, one of the goals being scored by debutant Harry Burrows. Further floodlit friendlies followed against Hearts, on November 19, 1958 (on the night Eric Houghton's contract was terminated), Rapid Vienna, on October 19, 1959, and Dynamo Kiev, on November 13, 1961.

❖ *Lights and action – this was the scene on the night of August 25, 1958, when Villa Park's lights were first switched on.*

❖ *Not many clubs get to see their name splashed in lights across the night sky, but for 20 years the letters AV were familiar to thousands of motorists driving past along the M6 or Aston Expressway. Villa's new, ultra-powerful lights were first installed at the behest of ATV, when they wanted to relay in colour the Leeds v. Manchester United semi-final replay in March 1970. With only days to go before the game, the new lamps were ordered from Cologne. Switch gear which normally took six weeks to obtain was hastily assembled in three days, and with just 24 hours left before kick-off, ATV had to charter a plane to Germany to bring over the final pieces of the jigsaw. Miraculously all was in place by kick-off, thus allowing Villa Park to be the first ground to host a match televised in colour by independent television. Villa liked the new lamps so much they ordered 40 of their own. Each one emitted the same light as 12 old ones, but used the power of only two. The familiar AV formation was unveiled for the FA Cup semi-final replay, Arsenal v Stoke, in March 1971.*

❖ *The beginning of the end for Villa Park's four floodlight pylons came in 1989, when the one in the Witton Lane – North Stand corner was removed in order to make room for a superbox. Its partner on the Trinity Road side (left) took the same route to the scrapyard in March 1990, to make way for a proposed hotel and office development.*

# 1966 and all that

❖ It took four years to plan, two and half months of hectic building work and preparations as soon as Villa's season ended in April, and then, after just eight fleeting days, it was all over.

But for those who were there, the 1966 World Cup was a never-to-be-forgotten event which would bring a novel cosmopolitan clamour to the city of Birmingham, and thrust Villa Park onto the greatest of all international football stages. For this was in the days before saturation TV coverage of world football, before every leading club had its own array of foreign stars, and when Birmingham, for all its futuristic Bull Ring shopping centre and Rotunda, still retained a measured introversion. Thus the arrival of the moody Argentinians at the Albany Hotel brought out hundreds of wide-eyed autograph hunters and staring office girls. Few knew any of the names. But in their sharp suits and slick hair-dos they seemed, quite literally, a race apart. One of their strikers, Luis Artime, was known as 'El Hermoso', the handsome one.

The West Germans were better known. This was Uwe Seeler's third World Cup, and the tall, elegant Franz Beckenbauer's first. When a few of the squad turned up in Cannon Hill Park one sunny afternoon and had a kickabout – in bare feet – they appeared like Olympian gods.

Around Villa Park the scene had never appeared so festive. Although it could not match the vibrancy of *Euro 96*, the Trinity Road Stand was modestly done up with flags, while FIFA shields were mounted on the balcony. On the Holte End visiting fans waved banners and filled the ground with the trumpeting of a thousand klaxons. After years of tedium for Villa fans, here was a rare glimpse of what a future in European competition might yield.

It was also a memorable social occasion; for international journalists who were feted on the roof of the Post and Mail building; in the pubs around Villa Park,

where Brummies who had been on package tours to the Costa Brava – no doubt some of them with the ELLIS TRAVEL AGENCY – tried out their phrasebook Spanish, to loud groans all round. Even the police enjoyed themselves, particularly Jim Chalmers, a recently converted Villa fan from Cowdenbeath. He was then a 26-year-old sergeant, who managed to wangle the plum spot in the ground – guarding the players' tunnel – and thus ended up on TV screens across the globe. Chalmers even posed in all the team photos, simply because every foreign visitor just *had* to have their pictures taken with a traditional British bobby.

On the field, the 1966 World Cup reserved most of its epic moments for other venues. North Korea's shock victory over Italy was at Ayresome Park (in front of a mere 18,727), followed by their memorable 5-3 defeat against Portugal at Goodison Park. England, as always, never set foot outside London.

But three near-capacity crowds at Villa Park still had plenty to remember. There was the appearance of Spain's Luis Suarez, the World's first £200,000 player, in a rain-sodden game won 2-1 by Argentina, El Hermoso scoring twice. The South Americans then conspired with West Germany to hammer out a bruising goalless draw, a match mainly remembered for the juvenile play-acting of both sets of players and the dismissal of the brutal Argentinian defender, Albrecht. Argentina were subsequently reprimanded by FIFA for their violent approach, and left Birmingham unbeaten but unloved. The final and most entertaining of the three World Cup games saw West Germany beat Spain 2-1, a result which meant that coach José Villalonga left Villa no longer in charge of the Spanish team.

'Villa Park was the right setting, even in those days,' said the BIRMINGHAM MAIL's Eric Woodward.

'Bert Bond had done a fantastic job on the pitch. It looked and played well, and the club's staff and all the local organisers coped very well. But when it was over everyone felt very flat. Exhausted, but very flat, as if now it was back to the usual bread and butter struggle with the Villa.'

And so it was.

## 1966 facts and figures

❖ Villa Park staged three games:

July 13  Argentina 2, Spain 1 (47,982)
July 16  Argentina 0, West Germany 0 (51,419)
July 20  Spain 1, West Germany 2 (51,875)

❖ Staging the World Cup required the expenditure of approximately £105,000 on Villa Park, of which Villa received interest free loans of £25,000 each from the FA and FIFA, while the Labour government gave a grant of £45,000, plus a further loan of £10,000. Villa also received £18,000 as their share of the gate receipts.

The main outlay was £90,000, spent on refurbishing the Witton Lane Stand and converting its enclosure to take 2,290 seats. A further 6,000 temporary bench seats were added to the Witton End banking – the crush barriers having been removed – while the gymnasium was converted into a press centre. Another change, required by the FA, was the erection of an ugly wire-mesh cage over the entrance to the tunnel, in order to protect players and officials from missiles. 'We are just obeying instructions,' explained Fred Archer, even though he did not expect any trouble, and in the event was proved quite correct. There was not a serious crowd incident in any of the three games.

# A New Broom

*H*ALL OF MEMORY! CONDUCTORS USED to call out, as their buses pulled up outside Villa Park on match days. Hell, it hurt. But they were spot on.

'It was more like *The Munsters*, actually,' recalled Eric Woodward.

Woodward had been a reporter on the BIRMINGHAM EVENING MAIL for 19 years, before spending two years out in the United States, helping Phil Woosnam to convert the Americans to soccer. On his return he was asked to ring a businessman called Doug Ellis, who had just left the board of Birmingham City to spearhead a £40,000 buy-out of the old Villa regime under Norman Smith. This was just before Christmas 1968.

The next morning Woodward climbed up the creaking stairs of Villa's offices, tapped on the window and was greeted by Villa's long serving secretary, Fred Archer.

'Hello son,' said Archer, in his usual cheery way. 'What are you doing here?'

'I've come to be the new commercial manager,' Woodward replied.

'Oh!' said Fred. 'Well I suppose we'd better find you somewhere to work then, hadn't we.'

Of course there was nowhere, but then Woodward interjected, 'I think there's something else you should know.'

'Oh? What's that?' asked Fred.

'There's going to be about 150 people descending on these offices any minute now,' said Woodward.

Half an hour later Doug Ellis, the new chairman, introduced the assembled press to Villa's new manager, Tommy Docherty, 'the Doc'. Never was a manager more aptly named.

Only those who lived through those stirring weeks spanning the Ellis takeover on December 18, 1968 can possibly know just how timely was the surgery carried out on the ailing form of Aston Villa.

This is not a history of the club, and therefore readers wishing to know more of how the takeover occurred should seek other sources. Peter Morris's excellent centenary history of the club certainly provides as compelling an account as any.

Suffice it to say here that in late 1968 Villa were bottom of the Second Division – their lowest ever placing in 80 years of League football. On November 9 an embittered crowd of 13,374 watched Villa go down 1-0 to fellow strugglers Preston. Standing on the Holte End that miserable afternoon I well remember the growing chants of 'Resign, Resign!' being directed at the directors' box, even from among the more staid supporters in the Trinity Road Stand. Not only that but shortly after Preston scored, I swear a flash of lightning was seen in the skies above.

'That's right God,' shouted an angry old man standing near to me on the terraces. 'You tell 'em!'

Earlier that year there had been riots in America after the assassination of Martin Luther King; street battles in Paris; a spring uprising in Prague; student protests in Mexico City on the eve of the Olympic Games, and, in October, a mass demonstration against the Vietnam war in London's Grosvenor Square.

❖ *The Lions Club puts out the flags to celebrate its opening in 1967. It was built on the former bowling green as a joint venture between the Supporters' Association and both* ANSELLS *(who used to own the land) and* MITCHELL & BUTLER. *Former Villa centre half Jimmy Dugdale was the club's first steward, followed by Charlie Tabberner. In its hey-day the Lion's Club used to boogy on down to resident band Vicky and the Venoms, with occasional turns from the likes of Jasper Carrott, Jake Thackeray and Gerry Munroe. Villa took it over in late 1970, but declining revenues led to its eventual closure in 1977. For many years thereafter the front of the building served as the club's main souvenir shop, until the Villa Village opened in 1996. The upper storey block at the rear is where stadium manager Ted Small is now based.*

And now, incredibly, the spirit of revolution had spread to Villa Park!

As the Doc's newly-signed captain Brian Tiler rose up in front of the Holte End to thump an orange ball into the Cardiff net, on the snowy afternoon of Boxing Day, 1968, it was as if thousands of Aston Villa supporters felt an enormous weight lift from their shoulders. In the words of the song, they were not such ugly ducklings after all, but proud, beautiful swans. No longer would they have to bow their heads in the office or on the factory floor on Monday mornings. Forget the Hall of Memory. They were living on Paradise Street.

'It's great to be a Villa man these days. Everywhere around us at Villa Park there is an atmosphere that inspires confidence... an air of something being done to fulfil all those promises of restoring the Villa glory.' So said the VILLA NEWS AND RECORD for the third round match against QPR on January 4,1969. In the fourth round replay v Southampton just over three weeks later, the crowd of 59,084 was the largest to see Villa at Villa Park since August 1962. (It also turned out to be Villa's last crowd of over 59,000 before reductions in the ground's capacity started to take effect.)

But as the team clawed its way to Second Division safety, behind the brave words lay a great deal of blood, sweat and tears. Working every hour that God gave, and a few more besides, the new board – Doug Ellis, Bob Mackay, Harry Kartz and Harry Parkes (later to be joined by Jim Hartley) – was only just beginning to realise the immensity of the challenge.

Worst of all, an examination of the books revealed the club to be £182,000 in debt, or, roughly the equivalent £1.7 million in today's values. This may not seem a huge amount, but it needs to be put into context. Until the takeover Villa had virtually no commercial income, other than that raised by the Supporters' Association, which had donated £46,100 since 1964, and the Lion's Club, which had added a further £1,000 since its opening on the site of the former bowling green in 1966. At the same time, the club had no training ground and certain parts of Villa Park, despite having just staged the World Cup, were crying out for modernisation.

Perhaps the most extreme example of this was the telephone system. The entire club was run with just two telephone numbers, one of which, incredibly, still operated from an old fashioned, wind-up system! The boardroom next to the offices, recalled Eric Woodward, was equally old-fashioned. As a devoted fan since 1942, he crossed its threshold in the winter of 1968 experiencing a mixture of awe and reverence. Here was the table where the likes of Rinder, McGregor and Ramsay had sat. But then the reality hit home. The windows rattled ferociously. The coal fire fought a losing battle with the draughts, and the only real source of warmth came from electric heaters suspended from the ceiling, so that after hours of meetings – and many of them ran on into the small hours – the directors would emerge with freezing feet and blistering heads.

In time many of the old fittings would be torn out

and replaced. 'It was crash, bang, wallop right from day one,' recalls Woodward. Despite his other business commitments Doug Ellis was there every day and most nights, making sure lights were turned off and not a penny was wasted. The players' billiard room was converted into offices for Woodward and Tommy Docherty, courtesy of local builders and a carpet company. Another contractor repaired the floor in the press room in exchange for two Cup Final tickets.

After an appeal in the programme, 200 volunteers also turned up on a Sunday morning in 1969 to do their bit to spruce up the ground. A few local businesses provided paint, the volunteers brought their own paint brushes, and Ansells threw in free beer and sandwiches.

Among the early volunteers was a building contractor called Ted Small.

Born in Walsall in 1932, as a youth Small had watched his football at Fellows Park, before two years of army service in Malaya and the demands of business kept him otherwise occupied. Then one day he happened to meet former Villa goalkeeper Joe Rutherford, who handed him two complimentary match tickets.

'It just seemed so completely different to how I had remembered football,' Small would later recall of his first visit to Villa Park, in around 1965. 'The grass looked so green. The white lines were so brilliant. My son David and I were both hooked.'

Small then bought season tickets in the old Witton Lane Stand, a year or so before the December revolution.

'One day, I went to pick up some tickets in the offices above the old aquarium. They'd been asking for volunteers, so I offered. I was told to go through to the boardroom to see Mr Ellis. I told him I'd give any help I could and and never thought any more about it. Then a few days later I got a phone call asking me if I'd go and repair a window in the

*❖ Tommy Docherty and Doug Ellis in December 1968. The Doc's arrival alone brought thousands of disillusioned fans flocking back to Villa Park. For his part, Ellis, then aged 44, was about to discover just how critical were the club's finances, and how antiquated its infrastructure.*

❖ *After a telephone call from Doug Ellis, Eric Woodward became one of the first commercial managers in football. After two years working in the USA he was horrified by what he found, particularly the way loyal members of staff had been treated by the old board. During his twelve years at Villa Woodward helped transform both staff and public relations, initiated a whole range of successful marketing strategies, and was largely responsible for the award-winning revamp of the* VILLA NEWS AND RECORD. *Woodward had first watched Villa as a schoolboy in 1942.*

dressing room. I went there on the Monday and while I was repairing the window, this player came walking through. I actually didn't know who he was but we got talking and I asked him how was the player who'd got injured on Saturday. He said "That was me!" and from that day to this Charlie Aitken and I have been great friends.'

From windows Small moved on to plumbing at Villa Park – always without payment – until Fred Archer offered him a car park pass and four free tickets for every match, so that the club would always know where they could reach him if anything went wrong. Which it did, and often. At its worst, Small had to repair no fewer than 36 burst pipes on one Saturday morning alone.

'At that time all the tea bars were outside. The piping was going anywhere and everywhere. You could never drain it, so there would sometimes be icicles hanging off, or I'd have to lie down in a pool of freezing cold water to get the pipes done. But I was enthusiastic. I'd get there early in the morning, do the burst pipes and then chase all the way back home, get changed, pick up the family and then go back for the match and hope there'd be no more bursts to fix. Then, because I had these free tickets, I'd go around before the game and offer my four season tickets to men with children or to any passing couples and just give them the tickets. I used to get some very strange looks.'

Before long Ted Small became part of the Villa Park scene, along with caretaker Mush Callaghan, groundsman (and now stadium manager) Bert Bond, chief steward Bill Poutney, and regulars like Fred Hooke, Sam Messenger, Jack Watts and Reg Parton (the former programme editor and now press steward).

'One example of the goodwill shown towards the Villa in those days,' remembered Small, 'was when I had to sort out new drainage in the Trinity Road Stand. It was just at a time when the building regulations were changing, and it was in our interests to get the work started before the new regulations came in. The trouble was everyone else was doing the same, and every JCB in the country was booked up for weeks in advance.

'I'd been ringing round everywhere, until eventually I found a place up in Coleshill which had the particular type of small digger we needed. But the man there said, "Oh no, we sent our last one up to Manchester yesterday." He asked, "Where did you want it for?" I said "The Villa" and he said "Aston Villa, as in Brian Little?" So I said "Yes" and he said "*The* Aston Villa?" And again I said "Yes." That was on Friday afternoon.

'I turned up at the ground on the Saturday morning and there were *two* JCBs there. He'd sent the second one round just in case the first one hadn't turned up!'

Not everyone was benevolent towards the club, however. Small remembers putting new copper piping throughout the Holte End, in the early 1970s, only for thieves to steal the lot. That left him just days to replace the whole system – this time in less

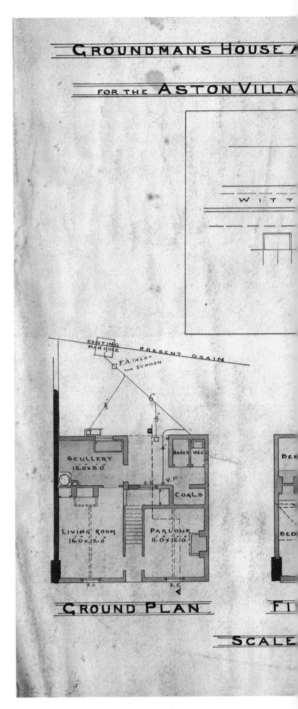

desirable stainless steel – so that the terrace would be ready for a semi-final.

While Ted Small got to grips with the plumbing, elsewhere at Villa Park the revolution continued, for if some of the buildings and equipment were antiquated, so too was the organisation. When Eric Woodward took Tommy Docherty around the ground to meet and greet all the various members of staff, for example, he was amazed at their amazement. No-one had ever taken any notice of them before. It was almost the same at the top, where not one of the three longest serving members of staff – secretary Fred Archer, a club employee since 1920, his assistant Len Latham (1931) or groundsman Bert Bond (1935) – had pensions.

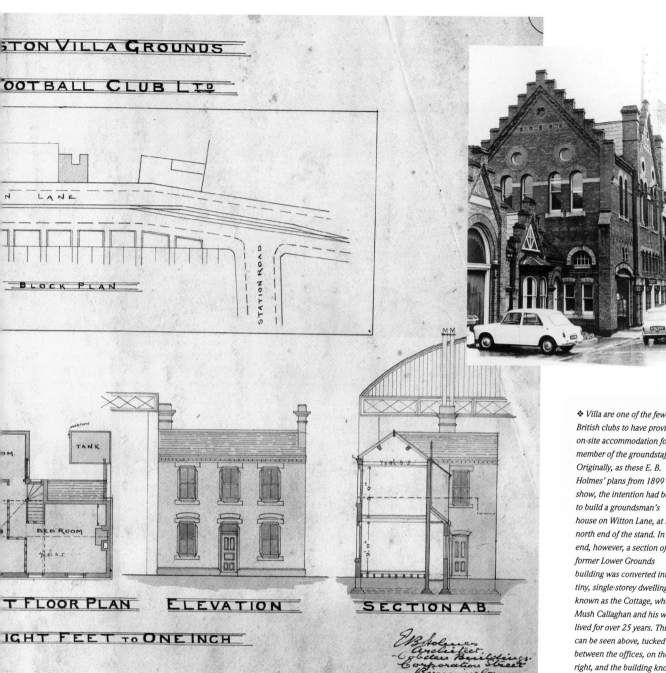

STON VILLA GROUNDS

OOTBALL CLUB LTD

N LANE

BLOCK PLAN

STATION ROAD

TANK

BED ROOM

T FLOOR PLAN    ELEVATION    SECTION A.B.

IGHT FEET TO ONE INCH

MM

*❖ Villa are one of the few British clubs to have provided on-site accommodation for a member of the groundstaff. Originally, as these E. B. Holmes' plans from 1899 show, the intention had been to build a groundsman's house on Witton Lane, at the north end of the stand. In the end, however, a section of the former Lower Grounds building was converted into a tiny, single-storey dwelling, known as the Cottage, where Mush Callaghan and his wife lived for over 25 years. This can be seen above, tucked between the offices, on the right, and the building known as the Barn, on the extreme left. The Barn, which was part of the original mineral water manufactory, was used for storage and laundry, and formed the end wall of the player's five-a-side pitch in the car park. Its archway was the only entrance available to the car park. Demolition of the Barn and Cottage began in May 1972 (left), the rubble being used as hardcore for the new boxes in the Trinity Road Stand.*

Another extraordinary aspect of the club's administration concerned the rights of shareholders – shades of 1887 and 1896 in this respect. As guaranteed by the old Articles of Association, 51 of the original shareholders were still buying pairs of season tickets for only 15s 6d (77.5p), for seats which would normally have cost £8 8s each. And they were not the only set of beneficiaries.

In their early days at the club, Messrs Ellis and Woodward would walk around the ground an hour before kick-off, checking on facilities, services, cleanliness and so on (just as the chairman and his mother had done in his days as a pioneering charter flight operator during the 1950s).

'On our first trip (around Villa Park),' Doug Ellis

❖ *Many fans remain baffled as to why anyone would pay extra to watch a match from behind a sheet of glass. But Villa have never failed to sell a single executive box since these first ones were installed in the Trinity Road Stand in 1972. The boxes cost £36,000 to construct, but paid for themselves within the first three years. In order to provide a clear view for box holders, the Trinity Road enclosure (right) had to be converted to seats, during the summer of 1971.*

told the 1969 AGM, 'we walked to an area known as the No. 1 tea room. I pulled open the door and the door knob came away in my hand. Inside, about 120 places had been laid for guests of the club, who had free passes to that room. Indeed, most of them also had a free car park ticket for Trinity Road.'

At the opposite end of the spectrum was the man who wrote to Eric Woodward to complain that he had tried to buy a pie at half-time, only to be told dismissively that the half-dozen or so in the oven were all reserved for regulars!

Back in the boardroom, meanwhile, a London merchant banker called Pat Matthews (who had masterminded the Ellis takeover, but who was himself a season ticket holder at Chelsea), helped to organise a new share issue through the Birmingham Industrial Trust.

The response was overwhelming. With new shares issued at £5 each, £205,835 was raised, an astonishing demonstration of loyalty which not only wiped out the debt but gave the club a far more solid financial footing.

Doug Ellis later recalled in the VILLA NEWS AND RECORD how he and the staff spent hours in the boardroom opening up all the applications and letters of support.

'I shall never forget one letter. It was written in broken English, enclosing 20 Deutschmarks from a German who had seen my appeal on Eurovision for all Villa supporters to come to the aid of the club. He wrote that he had been a prisoner of war at Cannock Chase and his only pleasure had been crawling under the wire and walking to Villa Park.'

After another appeal in the BIRMINGHAM MAIL a further 2,000 individuals who were unable to afford a share sent in £1 donations. Another 2,500 well-wishers attended an *'I support the Villa'* dance at the Locarno Ballroom. Villa even managed to raise £10,000 by selling off to a road-builder the top layer of clinker which coated the surface of the Serpentine Car Park (much to the relief of those fans whose shoes would get caked in the stuff on wet days).

Doug Ellis particularly remembers one other money raising scheme from that period. Talking to Dennis Shaw in the VILLA NEWS AND RECORD in 1994 he explained that a businessman had agreed to pay Villa £3,000 at the end of the season if his perimeter

track advertisement was seen on television for a total of three minutes.

'We dutifully logged every second that we saw the advert on TV but, as the end of the season approached, we weren't going to make it. We had only logged about two of the three minutes, so when we were next on TV I asked one of our star players to go down 'injured' in front of the sign and stay there as long as possible.' This he did, and so Villa earned their £3,000!

As far as ground developments were concerned, the transformation of Villa Park under Doug Ellis began in earnest during the summer of 1969, and with very few exceptions has continued every year since.

Each of those major developments will be covered in the following chapters. But it is worth outlining some of the wider trends and changes affecting football grounds during the past 30 years to put these developments into their proper context.

By far the most important concerns safety. For the first 78 of its 100 years history, the only two outside sources of advice Villa needed to call upon were its professional advisers, such as Archibald Leitch, and the police. The arrangement worked remarkably well – admittedly more by luck than judgement on occasions – so that Villa Park always enjoyed a reputation for being a safe environment.

Since 1975, however, three pieces of safety legislation have made British football grounds among the most highly regulated in the world, and with good reason. The disasters at Bolton (1946), Ibrox (1971), Bradford (1985) and Hillsborough (1989), plus dozens more smaller but still serious incidents at over 20 other football grounds, combined to give British football the worst safety record in international sport.

The first government move to reverse this appalling record was the Safety of Sports Grounds Act 1975, which followed the Ibrox disaster of 1971. As a First Division ground, Villa Park became 'designated' under the Act in 1976. This meant that in order to open its doors to the public it now had to be issued with an annual safety certificate by the local authority. In that certificate was stated the maximum safe capacity of each section of the ground, calculated either on the size of the terrace or the number of seats, in relation to the number of turnstiles and exits. For example, in 1978, after the new North Stand was opened, the certified capacity stood at 48,000, compared with 63,000 in 1970, before the Act was introduced. Furthermore, in order to maintain the certified figure, all work at the ground now had to be regularly assessed by the local authority and emergency services.

Fortunately, Villa have mostly enjoyed excellent relations with all the various parties to the 1975 Act, as a result of which Villa Park's certified capacity has never been far short of the maximum each stand or terrace could hold at any one stage (whereas other clubs found their capacities slashed as a result of poor standards). But the cost of keeping up high standards has often been enormous. New barriers, fencing and

re-surfacing of the Holte End in 1978, for example, cost Villa £180,000.

The second safety related piece of legislation concerned fire safety, in the wake of the 1985 Bradford fire. This required extensive checks and fire-proofing work to be carried out to the upper deck of the Trinity Road Stand.

Finally came the Taylor Report in 1990, as a result of the Hillsborough disaster in April 1989. The Report made 76 recommendations overall, of which four concerned the elimination of all standing accommodation at First and Second Division grounds (now Premier and First), by August 1994. Villa met that deadline at a cost of £18.5 million, with the results we all see today – a completely revamped Villa Park with two brand new stands. But just as importantly, the club also met the other Taylor recommendations relatively comfortably, having already overhauled its safety management thoroughly during the 1980s.

Running parallel with the enormous changes required by safety legislation since the 1970s has been a radical move towards the commercialisation of football grounds.

Manchester United were the first club to install executive boxes in 1965, closely followed by Chelsea. Aston Villa's new administration wasted little time in following suit. During the summer of 1969 the old director's room, two tea rooms and the former manager's cubby-hole in the Trinity Road Stand were ripped out and turned into a new Director's Guest Lounge and a Vice President's Club, with windows overlooking the pitch (just next to the players' tunnel). Joining fees for the 100 Vice Presidents were 100 guineas.

Overall, while Tommy Docherty splashed out £110,000 on the Rioch brothers, £37,000 was spent on Villa Park that summer. Apart from the lounges,

*❖ Many of the 54,437 crowd who attended Villa Park on the night of February 21, 1972, consider it to have been one of the craziest, most fraught and most wonderful occasions in the history of the club. Villa were in the Third Division. Pele was the greatest footballer of his generation. So naturally Eric Woodward invited him and his club side, Santos, to Villa Park. Unfortunately, by the time the Brazilians arrived, Britain was in the midst of a power crisis. Doug Ellis managed to buy a generator (shown above by the club offices) for just over £5,000. A capacity crowd flocked to the ground, with thousands more locked out. But when the generator started up, only three of the four floodlight pylons worked. Santos agreed to play in the reduced light, until Pele emerged for the second half to find that a different one of the four pylons was now out of action. This time he refused to play on. Tense consultations followed before the lights were returned to their first half setting, and Villa ran out 2-1 winners.*

there were new toilets, new telephones (which did not need winding up), a new public address system, and at long last, a proper ticket office with a modern frontage. This was built on the ground floor of the old offices, thus saving fans from having to queue up those creaky stairs.

The expenditure continued over the following years, despite Villa's unscheduled two year stint in the Third Division.

In 1971 £12,000 was spent on new lamps for the floodlights and £21,000 on the installation of 3,800 seats on the Trinity Road enclosure. These seats reduced the ground's overall capacity to approximately 58,000, but made it possible for the construction of the ground's first purpose-built executive boxes, just behind the seats under the stand's balcony, the following summer.

Accommodating six people each, these 17 boxes cost £36,000 to complete, an outlay which was covered by their first lease period of three years, so that from 1975 onwards they would yield a straight profit of £12,000 and more every year.

The completion of the boxes meant that the space usually cleared for a scaffold platform for television cameras, on the Trinity Road enclosure, was no longer available. Instead, a permanent gantry was now slung underneath the Witton Lane roof.

Beyond the stands there were yet more changes during the early years of the Ellis revolution.

Two personnel changes were particularly noteworthy. In May 1969 secretary Fred Archer retired. Fred had started with Villa immediately after leaving school in 1920, at the age of 14, originally on a month's trial. One of his first jobs, he remembered, was to polish the FA Cup before its return to the FA in London. Whether he passed the trial or not no-one ever told him, so he stayed on at Villa Park without a contract – ever cheery, ever reliable – becoming Billy Smith's assistant in 1926, and finally secretary in 1955. He eventually died in March 1975. (Fred's brother Sid also worked in Villa's offices for over 50 years until the early 1980s, in a part-time capacity, and for a while was joined by his own son, Keith.)

Another long-serving Villa stalwart was Ernest 'Mush' Callaghan, the much-loved, hard-tackling full back with his distinctive polished pate. Born in New John Street, Mush signed for the Villa in 1930, and after serving gallantly as a policeman during the war had moved, with his first wife, Wyn, into the small cottage next to the offices, becoming the ground's caretaker and odd-job man.

Poor health eventually forced his retirement in early 1972, at the age of 62, after which Mush and his second wife Lillian, moved a few hundred yards away to Jardine Road. Then on May 1, 1972 a

testimonial match was played in his honour at Villa
Park. This raised £679 for the now ailing Callaghan,
a figure which the directors made up to £1,000, only
to learn that the day after, Mush had been found
dead at home, the victim of a faulty gas-fire.

It was a tragic end for a popular man. And yet
Mush was at least spared one painful sight – that of
his old cottage and the barn next door (the old
mineral water factory) being demolished in May
1972, to make way for a wider entrance to the car
park alongside the offices. The hard-core from the
demolition work was carried over to help lay the
foundations for the new Trinity Road boxes, leaving
only the offices and gymnasium still standing as a last
reminder of Thomas Naden's 1878 Lower Grounds
complex.

Mush Callaghan was not the only familiar face to
be missing from Villa Park. For perhaps the most
important change of all effected during the new
administration's early years was the acquisition of a
new training ground, six years after the sale of the
Hercules Ground in Trinity Road. This meant that
during the week the players would be seen at Villa
Park even less than before.

Opened in November 1971 by the man who had
done so much to lay out its new pitches, Bert Bond,
Bodymoor Heath truly represented a new beginning
for Aston Villa. No longer would players have to train
on works pitches. No more would they have to flit
back and forwards to Villa Park for treatment. With
all mod cons in the club house and three pitches laid
out by Bert Bond on 20 acres of farmland near Sutton
Coldfield, Bodymoor Heath was possibly the best
£65,000 the club had ever spent. The dedication of
its main approach road, fittingly named Bond Street,
was also a well deserved tribute to a tireless worker
for the club's cause.

Bodymoor Heath opened at a significant point in
Villa's history. Relegation to the Third Division in
1970 and the sacking of Tommy Docherty might
easily have proved to be the beginning of the end of
the 1968 revolution, rather as Joe Mercer's short-
lived revival had failed to bear fruit earlier in the
decade.

And yet quite the opposite was true. Almost as if
Villa had been sent to a health farm in order to
emerge leaner, fitter and more determined than ever,
the club's two year spell in Division Three turned out
to be a memorable roller-coaster for everyone
concerned. While the likes of Doncaster, Halifax and
Gillingham delighted in the record receipts Villa
attracted to many of their away games, Villa Park
itself maintained the extraordinary buzz which
Tommy Docherty had infused so powerfully in 1968.

The Doc had joked that Villa fans were so devoted
that they would turn up just to see the shirts drying
on the line. But Third Division football at the Hall of
Memory? It could have been a disaster. Instead, to
adapt a phrase from Dickens, the worst of times also
turned out to provide some of the best of times in the
history of the club.

Many of the 58,667 fans who saw Villa's
pulsating 2-1 semi-final win against Manchester

United in the League Cup, just before Christmas
1970, still regard that evening as their best ever at
Villa Park – this writer included. The following
season, Villa's average gate of 31,952 was the highest
recorded in the Third Division since the days of
Tommy Lawton at Notts County in the late 1940s.
Among four Third Division games which drew over
40,000 to Villa Park that season was Villa's
scintillating 2-1 win against top-of-the-table rivals
Bournemouth, seen by 48,110 at Villa Park and
millions more on television a few hours later.

Stirring days indeed, and so full of hope too.

Apart from promotion back to the Second
Division, there remained the feeling that whatever
the club's travails, and whatever the causes of
dissension which seemed to plague the boardroom
during the early 1970s, Villa always maintained First
Division standards.

Big name signings. Floodlit friendlies against
Pele's Santos and Beckenbauer's Bayern Munich.
The expenditure of over £178,000 on the ground in
under four years. The purchase of Bodymoor Heath
and a hostel for young players, and last but not least,

❖ Both dressing rooms were
modernised in 1972, although
not all the old charms seem to
have been discarded.

*165*

the emergence of young starlets such as John Gidman and Brian Little.

Brian Little, who made his full, first team debut in April 1972 – scoring one goal in Villa's 5-1 romp against Torquay – was among the last of the club apprentices to spend much of his working life at Villa Park before all attention turned to Bodymoor Heath in 1971.

So before we plough on into the 1970s, a last word from Brian about the Villa Park of old.

Speaking in 1997, he recalled, 'Whereas nowadays all YTS lads go to college one afternoon a week, generally speaking we apprentices in the late 1960s would be expected to do at least one afternoon a week working around the ground. I remember things like the old boot room, the old drying room with its great big hot water pipes on castors. Just the old fashionedness of it all compared to how it is now. There were hard wooden floors in the dressing rooms which we used to have to scrub with industrial cleaners.

'One thing I remember about that floor was in my first reserve game, at half-time, two or three of the older players sat there with a cup of tea and a cigarette. One even managed to smoke two. You wouldn't see that today. And then after the game someone had to make sure that none of the cigarette ends had got stuck between the grooves in the flooring.

'In the afternoons we used to do circuit training and play head tennis in the old gymnasium. Next to this was the laundry area in what we called the Barn, then next to that was the cottage where Mush Callaghan lived.

'In my early days with Tommy Docherty, every Friday morning the whole club trained at Villa Park. Not on the pitch, though. We used to do something like twelve circuits on the track. Then the whole playing staff went into the car park with one ball, and it was like a bit of a free for all. It was a regular occurrence for people to end up with bust noses and cuts here and there.

'In my second year as an apprentice we helped Bert Bond dig up and resurface the whole pitch. I had one week's holiday that year when I was allowed to go and see my parents.

'To be honest with you, we really enjoyed those days. Even sweeping up the Holte End, which I did loads of times. It was always hard work, but we would often find a few bob lying around on the terrace, or even the odd ten-bob note or pound note which had fallen out the fans' pockets in their excitement, jumping up and down. What we used to do was pool all the money, then at lunchtime go over to the fish and chip shop on Witton Lane, just opposite the Holte pub, then take it back to the ground and just sit on the terrace eating our fish and chips or scallop and chips.

'After the terraces had been swept one of our last jobs was to burn all the rubbish at the back of the Witton End. Every now and again, as a treat, say if we had been sweeping up a lot, the club would open up the storage rooms and give us each a bar of chocolate or a packet of crisps. We'd often get home at 7 or 8pm at night, really tired, have something to eat than fall asleep, ready for training in the morning.

'It was hard, but as lads together we had some great laughs and a great deal came out of it; camaraderie, teaching us to be respectful to older players. All that cleaning the boots, folding the kit, it brought you into the club and gave you a sense of pride. In fact I have to say that my early years here have probably formulated the way I think about this place. Even now when I'm coming into Villa Park and I drive onto the flyover from Spaghetti Junction, I still look over the ground and think "Look at that!"

'I like it that much.'

# Villans and Villains

N EVER LET IT BE SAID THAT LIFE AT VILLA
Park is predictable. Cup winners in 57,
relegated in 59. West Germany in 66,
Gillingham in 70. Rochdale in 72,
Rotterdam in 82.

In the Third Division Villa Park's average gates for
season 1971-72 were just under 32,000. The visit of
Chesterfield on May 5 drew 45,586. Each and every
one of the Villa fans in the crowd that glorious Friday
evening – this writer included – wanted one thing,
and one thing only. A return to the First Division,
where Villa belonged. Yet thirteen years later gates in
the First Division barely averaged 15,000, and one
game against Southampton drew a mere 8,456.

In Villa Park's centenary season, 1996-97, Villa
won no honours. Ticket prices were at their highest
levels ever. But average gates topped 36,000 and
seven games were sell-outs.

Whoever it was who first said that football is a
funny game must surely have been a Villa supporter.

From fathers to sons, and yes, from mothers to
daughters, Villa fans have been born and bred never
to take *anything* for granted.

There was a time when the vast majority of them
came from Birmingham, South Staffordshire or the
Black Country, with a few commuters from the likes
of Coventry, Kidderminster and Worcester. But in
1933 the VILLA NEWS AND RECORD reported that their
VILLA ANNUAL, despite being sold only in Birmingham,
had elicited responses from Southern India,
Switzerland, Dublin and all over the British Isles.
'Wherever people live,' rejoiced the programme,
'there lives a Villa supporter.' (The same is true today,
as shown by the list of subscribers to this book in
CHAPTER 17.)

Nowadays of course Villa fans in far off places do
not just follow the club in a casual sense. They travel
to Villa Park on a regular basis; from London, the East
Midlands, the South Coast, the South West, Wales,
even Ireland. According to a survey in 1995-96, just
over 72 per cent of all Villa fans attended every single
home game. Yet only three per cent live within a mile
of Villa Park. Some 58 per cent live within ten miles,
but nearly eight per cent travel 50 miles or more for
each home game. It is not just Manchester United and
Liverpool who set hearts racing in Surrey.

Another survey in 1996 found that 14 out of every
100 Villa fans are female, that three out of four have
jobs, that nearly 15 per cent are students, eight per
cent are retired, and overall, nearly 99 per cent
describe themselves as white. As to how many think
Brian Little walks on water, no data is available.

And as to their memories of Villa Park, good or
bad, hazy or precise, another, rather less scientific
survey carried out for the purposes of this book,
found that no less than 100 per cent of them were
wonderfully evocative, as this, regrettably, brief
selection will now demonstrate.

### ❖ BARRIE BAILEY

Four generations of the Bailey family from Aston have
been regulars at Villa Park. I started on the Witton
End. The back of the terracing then was a mixture of

grass and ashes. Towards the end of the game I used
to walk up towards the back, and as soon as the
whistle went we could scramble down the slope and
get out of the gates before the mad crush started.
Often going down that bank meant a few roly-polys
and the rest of it, so by the time you got to the
bottom you could be quite a scruffy little boy. Mum
would say, "Litttle wretch has been to Villa Park and
got himself all filthy dirty."

Of course I grew up, married and then before I
know it I'm taking my two little boys, Roger and
Brian. One of them was five. I used to carry him
through the turnstiles, with the other holding my
hand. The man on the gate used to look at the little
one and say, "Alright, he's only a baby," and let him
in with a nod and a wink. And then as they grew
older they wanted to stand behind the goal.

We always used to see the same people around us
on the Holte End. It was a kind of ritual. People did

stand in the same place. You discussed the merits of what was going on in the football world and how the Villa were getting on, what the opposition were like, and you'd talk to them like old friends. You never knew their names but you'd talk to them for years.

❖ SYLVIA CHINN
I was born in Whitehouse Street, near Aston Cross. Mum came from a Villa family, she was the eldest of 12. Dad was a Bluenose, so we'd go to Villa one week and the Blues the next. There'd be six or seven of us kids. Mum knew the fellow on one of the turnstiles at Villa Park. She used to work with him at Shelley's, a subsidiary of Norton motorbikes on Miller Street. And she used to send us through, saying to us, "Tell him I'm coming, tell him I'm coming!" We used to say, "She's coming!' And he'd let one through. "She's coming!" Let another one through. "She's coming!" Let another through, and then when Mum

finally got there she'd pay him about 1s 6d or whatever. I used to be so embarrassed.

We used to stand in the same place behind the Holte End goal, about a quarter of the way up in the middle, because I loved the goalie's legs. People used to part to let us all through. Mum used to take a big bag of tea and biscuits and they'd say "Get the tea out, Lil!" And they'd all gather round, the same crowd every time. They all knew us. No one knew names, just faces. There was great camaraderie.

We've moved all around the ground over the years. Holte End. Trinity Road lower, just behind the dug-outs. Witton Lane. Now we have a block of eleven seats on the Doug Ellis lower. Malcolm Stent calls us the Von Trapp Chinns. We meet in the Aston Tavern pub down the end of Witton Lane, with another crowd from Cheltenham who have a room at the back of the pub just for them. We all go in there for a drink before the match.

❖ *Parklife, Aston. In 1888 they gathered in their thousands to watch Professor Baldwin make a parachute jump. From 1897 onwards the focus became a patch of green. Before the Trinity Road Stand was built in 1922 half the pitch was visible. Thereafter, the patch became a sliver. But it was not what could or could not be seen which counted. You had got so far, only to be turned away at the turnstiles. It was cruel, and yet you knew that going home would not ease the pain. Being there was still better than nothing.*

Sometimes you stop in your tracks, you look at us all and you feel proud. Not because it's football, or its the Villa. You're proud because it's your family and you're all together, me, Buck, the kids Carl and Darryl, and their kids, enjoying this one thing together. Obviously we've been born into it but no-one has ever forced anyone. I'm sure plenty of other mums and dads must feel proud like that, knowing that it's been handed down through the generations.

❖ MALCOLM EVERALL

When I was a young lad of maybe ten or eleven, I went from Kingstanding to Villa Park to queue for a ticket. My mom had packed me a flask, which I opened while the queue was moving, spilling the hot soup over my hand and making it go very red. Then to add to my misery all the tickets were sold and we were all asked to go home. This just about did it for me so I started crying. A nice man then asked a passing policeman to look at my hand, as a result of which I was taken into the ground. The St John's ambulance people treated me and I was given a tour of the ground and introduced to two of my favourite players, Nigel Sims and Stan Lynn. That really made my day, as did the two complimentary tickets they gave me, especially as my hand never really hurt at all. The aged one back home still couldn't understand how I'd managed to get two tickets when he'd only given me the money for one.

❖ ROY FIFIELD

After the Supporters Association was set up in the late 1950s it was decided to convert an old coffee shop on the corner of Holte Road and Witton Lane into a souvenir shop. We'd stock ties, badges, scarves, programmes and have black and white team photos from Albert Wilkes Junior. It was about the time Peter McParland brought out his book, 'Going for Goal,' and he would turn up an hour or so before kick-off to sign copies.

The committee would meet every Wednesday night at the Holte Hotel, in what was known as the coffee room upstairs. M&B eventually did the Holte up and called this the Florida Room. We each paid sixpence a week membership, and on match days we'd invite supporters from the visiting team, either to the Holte or to a room at the Aston Tavern.

Opposite the Florida room was a billiards room where some of the players used to go*. One old player we used to see regularly having a half pint on Sunday lunchtimes was Frank Barson.

There was amateur boxing in the back room, jazz on Saturday night. Behind the Holte, where they built a bowling alley in the 1960s, there were two bowling greens where they used to have dog shows.

* In 1956 the Holte Hotel actually staged a World Snooker Championship match between the two greats, Fred Davis and Rex Williams. During the five day match Williams achieved a then world record break of 141, a record which lasted for ten years until he himself beat it. But at the Holte, Davis emerged as the overall winner, by 35-26 frames.

❖ JOHN GREENFIELD

I was born in Erdington just before the end of the War, and was first brought to Villa Park by my parents to see the FA Cup paraded around the ground the day after Villa had won it against Manchester United in 1957. I honestly can't remember much about that day but I've been hooked on the club ever since.

One of my favourite memories was of Villa's famous Cup-tie against Peterborough in the Mercer Minor days, in January 1961. We'd drawn at Peterborough, who were then in their first season in the Football League and already had a real reputation in the Cup, so the replay was a floodlit mid-week game.

There was congestion everywhere, with thousands arriving late from Peterborough, and long queues still waiting after the kick-off, and over 60,000 already inside the ground.

A pal of mine and myself were struggling to get in until, amazingly, a policeman helped us both to leg up over the wall and get into the ground, free of charge! Can you imagine a policeman helping two teenagers break into the ground now?

❖ STEVE STRIDE

I was brought up in Castle Bromwich. My father had become a Villa supporter after he came to Birmingham in the 1940's from Wales, and to start off with he used to bring me down to reserve

matches. I would have been nine or ten, in around 1959. Then I had my first season ticket for the Trinity Road Stand in 1962, as a reward for passing my 11 plus.

I used to really enjoy reserve matches. There just seemed to be a unique atmosphere, and after a while I started coming down on my own, on the number 11 bus. You were always likely to see some star players from the other team, perhaps just over the hill or coming back from injury. I used to wait afterwards to get their autographs, and then occasionally I'd travel home on the bus and some of the Villa players would be on it as well. The one who sticks in my mind, although he wasn't a famous player as such, was Stan Horne, who eventually went to Manchester City in 1965, then Fulham. I remember actually sitting next to him, right next to him on the bus on the way home, and I was so thrilled.

Not that I dared say anything to him. I was far too scared for that.

### ❖ KIERAN McMAHON

Dad first took me to see Villa when I was six, against Leyton Orient. The match was pretty awful but I remember it because I was sitting high up (or so it seemed) on a crush barrier and, being frightened of landing on the concrete below, kept reminding Dad not to let go of me. Fearful of the battering he'd get off my mom if I was returned home damaged in any way, he managed to do this, at least until Harry Burrows struck Villa's only goal of the game. What my Dad did then, like most other people in the ground, was to thrust both arms high and wide into the air in celebration. While his left fist saluted the boy Burrows, the right connected with my nose, which followed the rest of my body in a backward dive towards the dreaded concrete.

Somehow, my hands managed to grasp the bar as my head swung back and forth above the concrete, leaving me swinging upside down, facing the kneecaps of the person behind. This good-natured chappie, believing he was witnessing a deliberate and well choreographed celebration, proclaimed "Cor, that's clever. I wish I could do that!" I was still too stunned to say anything, but I remember thinking at the time "It'd be easy for you if you had a dad like mine."

Anyway, I had to save face and pretend it had all been done on purpose. Needless to say, Dad never even noticed my unscheduled acrobatic display and helped me climb back up level with his shoulder again, wondering why I'd got off at all and how come the sight of Villa scoring had given me a nosebleed.

### ❖ CARL CHINN

Our Nan told us that "We never had none of this (hooliganism) when we used to come to the match. We'd all stand together and have a chat and shake hands after." But later in the season she showed us that as an Aston wench she could mix it with the best of them. We were playing Sheffield United. It was almost the end of the match and we were losing 2-0. This Sheffield fan was leaving the ground and as he passed us he pulled the claret and blue bobble hat off Our Kid's head, threw it on the floor and stamped on it. "Why, y'barstud!" she cried and hit him with a right hook which we called a 'Nanny Punch'. She belted him again, all 4 foot 11 of her, and he covered his face up, this hard man. And all the blokes around were laughing and shouting in a sarcy way, "Leave him alone, y'big bully!" and "Pack it up, he's had enough!" And he had 'had enough'. With the marks of Our Nan's fist on his face and the taunts of the crowd in his ears, he legged it.

❖ *Mutual admiration – Villa's youth and apprentice players express the club's gratitude, a week after the replayed League Cup Final at Old Trafford, in April 1977. To the left, Brian Little can be seen warming up in front of the Holte End.*

❖ *Tough, uncompromising Ron Saunders loved the Birmingham area so much that between 1974 and 1987 he became the only man in history to manage all three major clubs, the Villa, Blues and Albion.*

In those first couple of seasons I didn't realise how big the Holte End was, until we played the Blues in April 1969. We'd just moved into seats in the Witton Lane and so had a marvellous view of the great terrace to our left. There was a huge crowd, over 50,000, with a massive contingent from St Andrews. Many of them were on the Holte End, which was split diagonally between claret and blue and blue and white. In the singing before the match the Blues had the best of it. But just before kick-off something happened that when I think of it still sends the shivers tingling over my body and makes the blood rush to my head.

Our manager, Tommy Docherty, walked onto the pitch and came to the Holte End. He stood to the right of the goal and faced the Villa supporters. Every eye in that enormous crowd was on him. I don't know if it really did go silent, but it seemed to become quiet all over Villa Park. In the seats we all stood, straining our heads this way and that way to make sure we could see what was going on.

The Doc raised his arms above him and then bowed to all the Villa on the Holte End. The roar that went up was unbelievable. It was that roar from within, which wells up inside you and over which your mind has no control. That roar from the guts which overwhelms reason and thought and which makes you shake your hands and arms with fervour and forces you to become part of the crowd, no longer an individual. That roar which shouts out who you are and who you belong to.

We roared for the Doc and we roared for the Villa. We'd had it for years, the knocks and the jibes. The jokes about Aston Vanilla – the team anybody could lick. We'd had it and that roar said we'd had it. No more. We were back. This was us, this was the roar that shouted to the world, 'We're on our way!' This was the roar that spat out the bile of all the years of decline and decay. This was the roar that screamed

our pride in our club. Whatever else he may have done, the Doc let us have that roar.

❖ **SOUVENIR SNIPPETS**

After the Supporters' Association's shop on Witton Lane closed down in around 1967, for a while there was a tiny counter directly underneath the steps leading up to the main Trinity Road Stand entrance. But its stocks were painfully limited and the service was dire. Everything was wrapped in brown paper and hidden away in boxes. If you wanted a replica shirt it was either Dick Taylor's sports shop on Witton Road or Harry Parkes on Corporation Street. Even then the shirts had no club badges on them and other than to play football in, few fans would dream of wearing one in public.

In 1969 Dennis McHugh took over as organiser of the club's Development Association, with a new and larger shop opened next to the Lion's Club in 1972. Keith Dale and Keith Smith (a former Albion, Peterborough, Palace and Notts County striker) then took over in 1974, as the range of goods expanded to mugs, lampshades, bikinis, teddy bears and even underwear. But still no replica shirts. Profits from the A.V.D.A. (consisting of the shop, Travellers' Club and around 1,000 sale agents) rose from £15,000 a year in 1969 to over £150,000 by 1980, all of which went towards the purchase of Bodymoor Heath, the seating of the Trinity Road enclosure, new floodlights, the North Stand, and various other developments.

The shop then expanded to take over the whole front section of the former Lions Club, in 1990, before being transferred to the new Villa Village in 1996. In its first year the Villa Village superstore was expecting a turnover of a mind-boggling £4 million. And as for replica shirts...

❖ **RON SAUNDERS (1975)**

I should be a stranger here. I have only worked in the city for ten months and my family have lived here for a lot less than that. Yet I felt at home right from the day of my appointment. I felt it was right for me.

❖ **ABDUL RASHID**

I was born in Rocky Lane, Aston, the second oldest of seven. Mum's English, Dad was from Bangladesh, but I was the only Villa fan. I took after my aunt, she was a supporter. I was about six or seven when I first came, with a friend whose father was taking him.

I found out subsequently that the place where I stood was called the Witton End. I never saw much of the game because I was so small, but I remember Willy Anderson coming out before the game, juggling the ball and then taking the time and trouble to sign autographs.

Then we moved house to Lozells, and me and my friends from school, the Holte Comprehensive – where Mark Walters went – started coming down to games, first team, reserves, youth team. Villa Park was just a magnet for me. If the gates were open that was it, I was there, and it was not long before I became an avid autograph hunter. We'd come down early, get autographs before the game, and then also stay on after. There were one or two players who didn't like signing, but persistence paid off and I got them all in the end.

At the reserve games they used to have two ball boys, one behind each goal. I got to know one of the lads. He told me that for one particular game he wasn't going to be there so on the day I just followed the person in charge round until about five to three, when he realised the other lad wasn't going to turn up, he spotted the first snotty nosed little kid who was nearby, which happened to me, and said "Do you want to do it?" And I said, "Thank you very much, yeah!" I got a pie for doing it and 50p, I think it was.

The first few times I did it I was very eager and followed the ball up the terrace, but by the time I'd got to the top the ball had worked its way back down, so after being ridiculed I quickly found out that it was better to wait rather than chase it.

I got to know some of the players fairly well from getting autographs, being a ball boy, and then I started helping out washing some of the cars. I was about 14 by then.

The very first time Villa Park ever had ball boys for a first team game was an FA Cup semi final, Ipswich against West Ham in 1975. My big memory of that game was that they gave us nice new tracksuits to run out in. They were sky blue, and when we ran out of the tunnel – there was about ten of us – the West Ham fans on the Witton End thought for a second that we were the players, so a great big cheer went up, before they realised. The atmosphere was tremendous, so good that I didn't realise till afterwards that I'd never touched the ball once throughout the game.

As well as being a ball-boy, by that stage I'd got to know the people in the souvenir shop. They had a kiosk in the Holte End, a wooden hut down in the corner by the Witton Lane Stand. I helped them carry boxes of souvenirs over there before the game, helped put the things on display. But then once the turnstiles had opened I'd say, "Fine, I'm off now!" and went off to stand on the Holte End, free of charge.

Looking back I must have been the pain of Ted Small's life at that time. There I was, a conniving little kid, trying to get into the stadium in whichever way I could, for whatever games. And I think Ted at the time used to make it his responsibilty to make sure that I didn't get in. Now we're colleagues we can look back at those times, but it's amazing they didn't ban me really.

When I left school I was helping out in the main shop, part-time on a match day, and when they offered me a position as an assistant, full-time, I jumped at it. That was in 1977, and I've been here ever since.

So all of a sudden instead of me being an outsider I'm part and parcel of the team. Even so, one of my duties was to take the post over to the old offices. But I would always leave it at reception, because I could never bring myself to go up the stairs. There was always that one door, that big brown door which

really led to another world for me. And it took me ages and ages, even as a full time member of staff, to get the courage to go up those stairs. Because to me, that was the inner sanctum.

❖ EARLY HOOLIGANS

Villa fans are not all angels. As we saw in CHAPTER 2 a number of them frightened the life out of Preston in 1885. In 1938, according to the SPORTS ARGUS it required four policemen to drag away 'a pugilistic spectator' who tried to strike a Brentford player. When Manchester United visited Villa Park in the late 1950s certain members of the crowd hurled abuse at the survivors of the Munich air crash. Even worse, in January 1967 Villa fans were blamed for wrecking a train on their return from a Cup tie at Preston. In 1977 a police inspector was so badly injured at Villa Park when fans kicked his head that he was forced to retire.

For Villa's opening match in the Second Division, on 26 August 1967, the VILLA NEWS AND RECORD warned readers:

'If we are to win back our place in the Premier Division then obviously the encouragement of our supporters is a 'must'. And, at Villa Park, we are proud of this support, both to the club and the many ancillary efforts being run for the benefit of the club in particular. However, there is a small irresponsible element who are bringing discredit upon Aston Villa and *themselves*. If it is the modern idiom to chant the praise or shortcomings of a team, then fair enough.

*'But surely today's educational standard is sufficient to warrant that we can express ourselves without obscenity.*

'The Board of Directors have given consideration to the conduct of a group of teenage spectators and reputed supporters of Aston Villa on the occasion of the friendly match with Blackburn Rovers. Many of these youths were armed with walking sticks or long

*❖ It started with a discussion among fans at the Cross Keys pub in Erdington, and ended up as one of the most colourful crazes ever to be seen on the Holte End. The idea was to celebrate Villa's long awaited return to the First Division with a carnival atmosphere. So just as the Villa and Leeds teams ran out in August 1975, the Cross Keys contingent released dozens of claret and light blue balloons. Within a few months the idea had spread, to young and old alike, right across the terrace. Before games, long queues formed outside one of the main suppliers, a small sweetshop in Aston Lane, but the buyers made sure that balloons were handed out to as many people as possible, so that by Christmas thousands were being released before every game. Never had the power of the ordinary terrace fan been so inflated. And as the photograph below, taken at Southampton, indicates, wherever Villa went, so did the balloons.*

❖ *Any policeman who has ever served at Villa Park will agree – manning the tunnel is the plum posting. George Brannigan (below) did the job for seven years. 'My brief was to make sure that the referee and linesmen had no problems entering or leaving the field of play. And if any player was sent off, I had to make sure he'd come to the tunnel. In those days they weren't allowed to go back to the dug out.' When Jim Chalmers did the job for the World Cup in 1966 he ended up being asked to pose in all the team photos. But who was 'Darkie' – Villa's politically incorrect mascot shown here in the earl 1950s? Alas, no-one can remember him at all.*

staffs painted in Villa colours, occasioning incidents during and after the match. It was necessary for the Police to take action in and around the ground.

'After due consideration with the Police Authorities the board have decided that no-one will be admitted into the ground carrying this type of object.

'Instructions have been issued to all officials and gatekeepers accordingly and it is hoped that everyone who has the well-being of the club at heart will co-operate to prevent hooliganism of this nature.'

❖ GEORGE BRANNIGAN

I started standing at the Witton End in September 1967, joined the police four years later and for nine years was police liaison officer for Aston Villa. When I was first up for a posting in the police they said to me, "Well, you're over six foot, you should go to the city centre. That's where all the tall officers go." But I wanted to go to the station on Victoria Road. "What do you want to go there for?" they said. So I told them

it was because I wanted to work at Villa Park. But when I got to Victoria Road and they found out that I was a Villa supporter, of course for the first six months I never got posted to a single game!

Eventually my first posting in the ground was for a televised night match. In those days they used to have a camera platform on the halfway line, in front of the balustrade on the Trinity Road side. I had to stop people going up the ladder onto the television gantry. So I had a wonderful view of the game. And subsequently I was on talking terms with the producer and with the commentators, like Hugh Johns, or "Huge Honds" (meaning hands) as they called him in the Black Country.

One night, it had been an appalling match, I was on the bottom of the gantry as usual and when we scored the winner, Brian Little I think it was, I jumped up with both hands in the air, and it went out on television that night. There I was with my arms up in the air, in uniform!

Well, the following morning I was fetched in by the superintendent and told, "We do not behave like that! We don't show any partisan feelings." And as a punishment I was moved to the Holte End for a couple of months.

Later on, as police liaison officer, I met a lot of the Villa hooligans on our European travels. One of them in those days was a solicitor's clerk, about 20 years of age, well spoken. I used to see him during the week in his three piece suit, smart red tie, legal documents tucked under his arm, and we used to chat. In town, in and out of the courts. And then on a Saturday this same man was out of his suit. Levi jeans, the bottoms folded up with a leather trim on them. A Villa scarf on each wrist. His glasses were gone. He'd wear contact lenses instead, and he used to have stick-on tattooes on each arm. One said *The Villa Villain* and on the other arm was *We hate all supporters*, or something like that. An incredible difference. On a Saturday he'd be out looking for a fight. On Monday morning he'd be back working in the courts.

I believe he's now a solicitor, an upright member of the community, somewhere down south.

As regards away fans, the incident I most remember involved, shall we say, a well known northern club. They were the least violent supporters I'd ever met. But if you didn't nail it down... Well on this occasion, the Villa had provided a little fibreglass kiosk in Witton Lane so the away supporters could buy tickets directly outside the turnstiles, to save them walking round the ground to the main ticket office.

So the first few hundred came up and purchased their tickets, but then all of a sudden a group turns up, hadn't got any money or couldn't afford the tickets, so what do they do? They took the kiosk away. It was on wheels, so they rolled it away, with the ticket operator still inside, all his tickets and all his cash! They took it down the road to Witton Circle. Nobody stopped them. They were so brazen about it that all the stewards and police just assumed they were taking it away because all the tickets had been sold. Unbeknown to everybody the ticket operator was still inside, frightened to death. Only when he returned with an empty satchel, no tickets and no cash did they realise what had happened. Eventually they recovered what was left of the kiosk from the men's urinals at Witton Circle.

### ❖ GARY SHAW

My dad, Maurice, was a carpenter, and like my grandad before him he was a Villa fan. I was born and brought up in Kingshurst, and although I can't pick out my first game I know it was around 1965 or 1966, when I was four or five. We were always on the Holte. Dad used to sit me on the barriers, which

was rather uncomfortable. Then when I got a bit older, maybe seven or eight, I'd go down the front with my mates from Kingshurst Junior. There were times when we changed allegiance and stood on the Witton, but I didn't like getting wet there. Or every January, the nearest game to my birthday, as a special treat Dad would take me to sit in the Witton Lane.

The best was Boxing Day games. All my aunts and uncles were in the Nechells area, so we'd spend Christmas Day at my nan's place in Nechells, stay overnight, then the whole family would walk over to Villa Park, over Cuckoo Bridge. I remember all the balloons on the Holte End when Dennis Mortimer made his debut. I was 14 and we won 4-1 against West Ham. All those balloons. They were good days. And then after the game we'd all walk back to Nan's for tea and have a big party.

Another night I'll not forget was the semi-final against Manchester United. I was ten, and it was that packed on the Holte that even though I saw all the game, sitting on a barrier, at the end I just couldn't move. Nobody could, it was so intense. So I ended up being passed above people's heads by all these strangers, until finally I was put down in the gangway and went down by the old toilets in the corner by Witton Lane and waited for Dad.

Santos in 1972 was another amazing night. We had to go into the Witton End for that one, because the Holte was too full. But the worst time was the Rangers match in 1976. I was on the Witton again, and just remember getting out of the place as quickly as possible, running to Witton Island and getting a bus out of there. It was pretty shocking, frightening in fact.

I was playing for my school on Saturday mornings by this time, then dashing back home in time for the Villa. We never had a car so we always used to get lifts with other dads. Also, for a while they used to run coaches to Villa Park from the Mountford pub, or when I was maybe 12 I'd get on the bus with my

❖ *October 9, 1976. It should have been a friendly. It turned into a drunken orgy of hooliganism. Seventy people were injured, 92 were arrested. Windows were smashed all over the city, buses and shops were wrecked, shoppers were terrorised, and at Villa Park, with Villa 2-0 up, the game had to be abandoned after Rangers' fans invaded the pitch in a hail of bottles. But by then many locals among the 18,000 crowd had already fled in fear and disgust. According to some policemen on the day, even the usually hardened Holte Enders were frightened. But not all Villa fans were innocent. Some goaded the visitors with Irish Tricolours, and many of the Scottish fans behaved impeccably. Nevertheless, at one point, watched by thousands in the Trinity Road Stand, a gang of Tartan-clad fans kicked a young boy unconscious on the pitch. Three days after the game there were still young Scots wandering around Birmingham trying to get home, while Villa fans arriving for the next home match found hundreds of whisky bottle tops trampled onto the terraces. With friendlies like that, who needed enemies?*

❖ *Former Holte Ender Gary Shaw heads home against Watford in an FA Cup tie in February 1983. Andy Gray told Gary to celebrate his goals more openly. But Brummies, said Gary, seldom 'go over the top.'*

or had seen or had watched myself from the Holte, and that the supporters were calling for me. I think the fact that I was the only Birmingham-born kid in the Championship winning team and the European Cup winners meant that I maybe got more criticism, or rather their expectancy level was higher for me. But the Birmingham public always just treat you like one of their own. They don't go over the top.

I've been on the Holte a few times since. The last time was for the European Championships. That was weird. A few of the stewards recognised me, and I went into a toilet that actually had a covering on it. I couldn't quite work that one out. Indoor toilets, on the Holte!

❖ JOHN HARRIS

My first time was against Rotherham in 67, when I was about nine, with my friends the Atwoods. And the only reason we went was because my mate had no-one to go with and his Dad had a spare seat in the car. And that was that. Initially we were at the front of the Holte. That was about being able to see and being a bit safer down there. And being able to run around a bit. The crowds weren't quite as big as now. Then it was halfway back, on the Trinity Road side of the Holte, where there was this big white wall. We leant on the wall itself, over the vomitory. A fantastic view. Then we moved a little bit further back, near one of the stanchions that used to hold the old roof up. And that was the spot for our crowd, for years and years and years.

By this time we were in Marsh Hill secondary school, in the early 70s, and if you looked up from the Holte End over towards Erdington you could see the school, on a hill. One Saturday a whole lot of us had been signed up for an Autumn Fair or something like that, which meant we all had to be in school. In the afternoon between 3 o'clock and twenty to five, maybe 13 or 14 of us went out onto the school roof where you could hear the crowd across from Villa Park, and we were trying to assess the score from the cheers. We weren't quite sure if we could tell until we heard a goal, and then we knew for sure. We got the score right, as well. One-nil it was.

I remember a group called the Villa Steamers. They were from Erdington and they would have been a lot older than us, early twenties. They liked a bit of a rough house, although they weren't out and out thugs.

One of the things they used to do was they'd pick themes for particular games. So one game, for instance, they decided the theme was old women's hats, and they'd all turn up with old women's hats on. This was the days before dressing up was fashionable at football matches.

I shall never forget the *V for Villa* phase on the Holte End. It started off with certain brave individuals being turned upside down with their legs in a V shape, pointing into the air – quite an achievement given the tight crowds there, to actually get the space to get somebody upside down like that. But then people would tie scarves between their legs. On one occasion it was just tremendous. It

friends to the Fox and Goose and then pick up the number 11. I still see some of that crowd if I go over Kingshurst way. They're still around. We used to stand about level with the crossbar on the Holte.

By then I was watching certain players very closely, like Brian Little, Ray Graydon, Chico Hamilton, that era, taking things on board, trying to pick up tips on how they played, how they moved, their balance, the skills they used to beat players. Not just the Villa team either, but players from both teams.

Then I made it into the Villa Youth team, playing at Bodymoor Heath in the Midland Intermediate League, and the club gave me a Schoolboy Pass which gave me free entrance, so I could just walk into the Holte End. That was really rather a pleasant experience, although I never used to flaunt it. It was the same when I made my home debut for the first team in 1979. My dad was there. All my old pals on the Holte. I knew where they were standing, but I didn't wave or make any gestures. It was a pretty weird experience actually. I mean I'd been on the pitch before for reserve games but to actually play in front of a fairly large crowd was quite different.

I can't tremember my first goal at the Holte End – I've never been one for statistics – but I remember it was a good feeling, a great feeling in fact. But even then I was never a player who sought adulation from the crowd when scoring. I remember Andy Gray commenting how I never used to celebrate goals. He would. He'd celebrate in a big way, but I was never like that. I don't know whether it was shyness or arrogance. I just used to treat applause and criticism the same way, always trying to keep level headed.

But I was very emotional on the last day of standing on the Holte, for the Liverpool match in 1994. That was unbelievable, being on the pitch, the fact that there were all the players I used to play with,

# Memories are made of these...

❖ The slow moving queues which stretched down Witton Lane, round by the Aston Hotel and past the billiard hall, and becoming maddeningly familiar with one stretch of brick wall or the pattern on the coat of the person in front of you, always wondering if this would be the day you'd be turned away...

❖ The shiny, steaming tea urns, the obscure confectionery that you never seemed to see on sale anywhere else but Villa Park, and those meat pies that always felt so soggy compared with other grounds...

❖ Down at the front of the terracing digging your hands into the shale, biting the paintwork off the railings, seeing the players come up right close to you to retrieve the ball and getting showered by the dirt – their dirt! – so it didn't matter...

❖ But, if it had been raining heavily, the drains would empty down onto the front steps of the terraces, pouring out in a muddy fountain around people's feet...

❖ Night matches. Scanning the dark masses around the ground, the Witton End almost invisible, except for flickering lights, here, there, everywhere, almost every second, as fans around the ground lit their cigarettes...

❖ Little Terry Weir, the photographer, running around the pitch before kick-off, chasing players, getting the mascot to pose, with all his gear flapping around, then joshing with the fans and throwing his famous wine gums to them...

❖ That Friday night against Chesterfield, when Villa players kicked plastic balls into the crowd, so light that only people in the front were grabbing them, until Jim Cumbes stepped up and managed to blast a few right up to the back of the Holte...

❖ Defensive clearances looping over the top of the Witton Lane roof, as someone would be sent scurrying out of the stand to retrieve the ball, with only the Holte Enders up top able to see if it had bounced down into the street – perhaps to be nicked by a passer-by – or had got stuck on the roof...

❖ Before the Expressway was built and all the underpasses and overpasses, hundreds upon hundreds of Villa fans trooping up Park Road, along Lichfield Road, and into Corporation Street, just in time to get the first edition of the ARGUS...

❖ *Star Soccer* on ATV, Sunday afternoons, Billy Wright, Hugh Johns and, oh no, not Wolves again!

*❖ Starting at the bottom, 1973 style – many a terrace fan gained his or her first glimpse of Villa through the familiar pitch-side iron railings. Some reckoned you hadn't been fully initiated until you'd bitten off some of the paintwork. Others recalled overflowing drains, pools of urine, and being sprayed by shale from the players' boots.*

might have been a Birmingham game, when there were just so many people doing this and we were all singing *Walk On* with these guys upside down for ages, swaying from side to side. This was to the sound of coins falling out of their pockets, so there was all this money spilling down the terraces and everybody diving for it!

I remember the Sunderland game, April 1975, when we won the Second Division Championship. By the time I'd plucked up the courage to go on the pitch at the end there were about 7,000 other people already there.

But I found it all very strange. Villa Park looked very different from the pitch. The pitch itself looked different. For a start it had a hump in it. And I can always remember just walking back and looking up at the Holte End, and it just looked so squat. When you were on it you felt that you were towering over the ground, but actually it was wider than it was higher. That struck me. Walking back with one of my mates and just standing by the penalty area looking up, and thinking, it's not as big as we think it is. Now that was strange.

# Jack in the box

❖ In the days before video screens, TV monitors and transistor radios, the main link between Villa Park and the outside world was provided by the ground's two splendid manual scoreboards.

With their crisp white letters on shiny black backgrounds, the information they imparted at half-time, always randomly, often painstakingly, number by number, took on a fascination far outweighing the significance of the actual scores. Some kids grew up wanting to stand on the footplate of the *Mallard*. Some wanted to fly in the cockpit of a *Comet*. But didn't we all want to climb up into that secret world of the Villa Park scoreboards and discover its hidden mysteries?

Jack Watts − who now conducts an average of 6,000 people a year on tours around Villa Park − started working in the Holte End scoreboard after he came out of the army in 1946, at the invitation of his old friend and neighbour Mush Callaghan. He was paid 10s. for that and 15s. for helping Mush and others to sweep up the ground on Sunday mornings. In a lifetime of service to the club he has also manned the turnstiles, cleared snow, tended the pitch and acted as a host in the North Stand.

But for 34 years the main scoreboard was Jack's Saturday afternoon roost. Working mostly with Mush's brother, Arthur, and Sam Messenger, and later with his two sons, Peter and Steven, Jack would take down all the scores as they were read to him over the telephone by a woman from the Exchange Telegraph office in town.

'I talked to that woman every week for all those years,' Jack laughs, 'but I never met her once.' He also recalls that the telephone line from the telegraph office was an open one, shared between the scoreboard operators at Villa, Blues, Albion

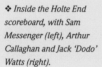

❖ *Inside the Holte End scoreboard, with Sam Messenger (left), Arthur Callaghan and Jack 'Dodo' Watts (right).*

❖ *The final score for a much loved part of the Villa Park furniture. The new electronic scoreboard is already in action, as Jack Watts and Sam Messenger (seen to the right of the old board) sign off on January 10, 1981. The manual system did have one minor drawback, however, as the operators discovered in October 1946, when Newcastle beat Newport 13-0. In the end one of the crew stuck his arms through the gap, holding up a 1 and a 3 as steadily as he could while the crowd below cheered him on.*

and Wolves. 'There was always someone at Birmingham rattling on and on in the background, but one time they weren't playing at St Andrew's, or so I thought, so I said to the woman at the telegraph, "Good news, it'll be a bit quieter today, that Birmingham mob aren't around." And then I hear this other voice down the line saying "Oh yes we are!"'

'Course I was only joking!' adds Jack, mischievously.

As the half-time scores came in, Jack would write them on his sheet, then Arthur and Sam would make sure the metal plates were slotted into the appropriate spaces. The men in the Witton End scoreboard would then simply follow suit (although that didn't stop kids faithfully watching both boards to see which would get the scores up first).

Once all the half-times were up − which usually took about eight minutes − the scoreboard operators could still follow the game through small slits between the boards.

Then after ten minutes or so of the second half they would take out a couple of number plates from the centre, pull up their chairs (or one of the old war-time ammunition boxes) and enjoy one of the

finest views in the ground until it was time for the final scores.

But if the scoreboards provided a useful service at first team matches, at reserve games they were absolutely essential. With no local radio stations to keep fans informed of how the Villa were doing away from home, letter A on the Holte End scoreboard was like a magnet, drawing people's attention away from the reserve game as the first team score was updated every 15 minutes.

Oh the agony of waiting! And the sheer joy of seeing a Villa goal being posted. Not even watching modern day Ceefax can match it for nerve-racking tension.

It was not much easier for Jack. 'At the reserve games you could guarantee nearly all the scores would come up for all the other teams bar Aston Villa. And the people below on the Trinity Road terrace would be shouting up at me. I knew most of them. "Oy, Dodo!" they used to shout, because that's what Arthur Callaghan called me, after the film actress. "Oy, Dodo! Wattie! We'll come up there and we'll bounce you one!" Thinking we were doing it on purpose, leaving the Villa first team till last!'

Only twice did Jack not dare show himself.

When Villa played their infamous 'friendly' against Glasgow Rangers in October 1976 he shut the scoreboard up after a bottle came hurtling through one of the gaps, missing his head by an inch.

On another occasion, for the one and only time in all his years on the job, Jack dropped one of the metal number plates onto the crowd below, where it struck a man in the face.

"Can you imagine! Oh dear, I'm thinking, what's going to happen here? If the fellow sues the club it's going to be for thousands of pounds, so that's the sack for me, straight away. But the biggest coincidence of all was that out of maybe 64,000 in the ground, the fellow it hit happened to be a relation of Mush Callaghan's and one of my old footballing partners, a chap called Martin Moore. If it had been anyone else I wouldn't have been working for Aston Villa now, I'd have got the sack. Afterwards I saw Martin, and said, "Blimey Martin, I aren't half glad it was you!"'

❖ Villa's electronic scoreboards in action. The old scoreboard are (above) was converted into the ground's first police control room.

❖ *Andy proposed to Alison via the scoreboard during a game v. Spurs in 1991. Mark asked Rachel when Forest were the visitors. And when their replies of 'Yes!' were flashed up for all to see, thousands of Villa fans went 'Aah!' But, we never did find out Samantha's reaction in 1990. Nowadays a special licence means that couples are able to go one stage further, and actually get married at Villa Park, in the McGregor suite. And if chairman Doug Ellis's plans for a hotel at the ground had also gone ahead, in 1989, they might also have been able to stay on for their honeymoon! What next? A Villa nursery?*

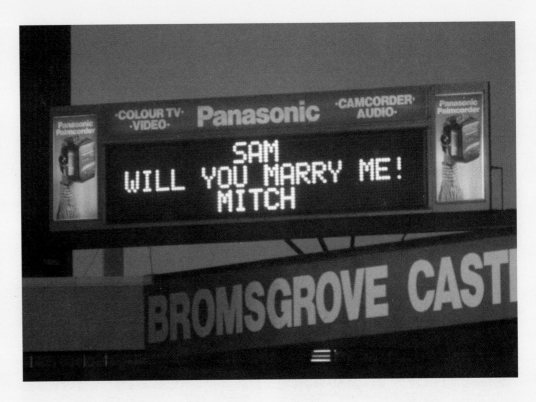

# Lionhearts

❖ Brian and Heather Little, Steve and Carolyn Stride, Abdul and Jane Rashid. What do they all have in common? They all met while working for Aston Villa. Then there was former secretary Alan Bennett, who found love across the counter at the club's bank in Six Ways, and the late Charles Tabberner, former Lions Club secretary, who fell for Pam in the ticket office.

On the terraces, too, passions have not always been reserved for the football. Peter Ray met his match near the end of the 1970-71 season.

'I was on the Holte End in my usual spot. Home for the weekend from college in Reading. After the euphoria at Wembley the season was petering out to a tame ending, yet here I was again, on the Holte, to watch Rochdale.

'And then I noticed her. A duffel coat. Had to be a student too...

'Her friend in the clique was more talkative, but the smiling eyes in a duffel coat were drawing my attention. It seemed that her favourite player was Charlie Aitken, so I found myself making sarcastic comments about him, hoping for some reaction from the duffel coat.

'It worked too. In fact I was severely admonished, albeit amid an air of good nature. I began to admire the fire in the duffel coat's eyes, and thought, roll on the next home game.

'Two weeks later, Villa v Wrexham. A silly game, we lost 3-4. But the match was of secondary importance. After searching for her on the Holte near the usual spot, I talked again to those eyes in a duffel coat. She was so pleasant. A trainee teacher

too, at Crewe. We parted friends, and the next home game could hardly come soon enough.

'Three days passed, then it was Villa v Reading. A sad game for me, the only time I hoped Villa would not win, so that my college town team, Reading, might stay up. They had the draw they needed until Terry Bell headed into his own net and Reading were down. But this was the second and less important blow of the evening. Duffel coat was not at the game.

'Back in my student lodgings in Bracknell, I couldn't rest. Not knowing duffel coat's name was irritating. My own fault. Such a silly thing – not to have asked her name! I couldn't rest. Wouldn't settle. Landlady sewing, landlord laughing a Fulham obscenity at me. What should I do? Write that's it! A general letter. Crewe College of Education. There couldn't be another Villa fan in an all-female college, surely?

'Wrong! Another student collected the letter addressed to *The Aston Villa Supporter*, opened it, then realising it was not for her, posted it on a noticeboard And the girl in the duffel coat found it! She wrote back. We corresponded and met during the summer vacation. Her name was Jenny, the youngest sister of Roly Morris.

'We were married in 1976. Terry Weir took photographs at our wedding reception and we became season ticket holders in the Trinity Road Stand. Pregnant, she saw Chris Nicholl score twice at both ends at Leicester, and we finally came back to where it all started, in 1995. Holte End seats, Villa v Spurs. Both daughters in attendance, young son at home. Saunders, Dean the unstoic, scored a winner and nearly a quarter century was complete.

'No duffel coat this time, but the eyes were flames still.'

# Chapter 14

# The Sensational Seventies

*in which an old Etonian draws up in a Morris Traveller* ❖

*Villa return to the top flight* ❖

*Doug Ellis brings ASDA to the Serpentine* ❖

*the North Stand is delivered* ❖

*the Holte is divided* ❖

*£10,000 is required* ❖

*new offices prompt a police investigation* ❖

*Ron Bendall sells up to Doug Ellis* ❖

*farewell to the old offices* ❖

G OING UP, GOING UP, GOING UP!' THAT'S what they sang on the Holte End in the 1970s, and that, more or less, was the theme of the decade at Villa Park.

The team went up twice, from the Third to the First Division; after years of remaining virtually static, ticket prices went up virtually every year; the balloons went up from the Holte End in 1976, as did the dreaded perimeter fences shortly after; the North Stand went up in 1977, and in 1980, in conjunction with the ASDA supermarket group and the Sports Council, the curtain went up at the Aston Villa Sports and Leisure Centre on the site of the Serpentine Car Park. And then finally the balloon went up in another sense, when both the police and the press called on Villa Park to check out the club's new offices.

Just about the only thing which did not go up during the decade was the ground's capacity, which fell steadily from 60,000 in 1972 to 48,000 by 1977. Thus the attendance of 50,084, for Birmingham City's visit on September 18 1976, turned out to be the last gate of over 50,000 at Villa Park (until the ground is expanded again, that is, hopefully in the late 1990s).

Otherwise, the 1970s and early 80s were characterised by more ins and outs at boardroom level than at any other time in the club's history. Doug Ellis began the decade in the hot-seat (although Jim Hartley was briefly chairman in 1972). Sir William Dugdale was elected in his place in 1975, followed by Harry Kartz (1978) and finally, as the 1980s began, Ron Bendall, who had joined the board in 1975 and bought Doug Ellis's shareholding in late 1979.

Sir William, whose three years in office were dominated, groundwise, by the opening of the North Stand, was perhaps the most intriguing character ever to have occupied the chairman's seat at Villa Park. A combination of country tweeds, old school tie and City nous, he was an old Etonian, Oxford graduate and a Grenadier Guard during the war, and had supported Villa since the age of ten, in 1932.

The list of his clubs included Aston Villa and Warwickshire CCC, and in London, the MCC. But he was also a member of White's, Brook's and the Jockey Club. In short, not your typical football club director.

But Dugdale was no rarefied toff. Apart from the Villa board, he served as chairman for both the Severn Trent Water Authority and Wolverhampton Racecourse. He was also a man of the soil, his family having farmed the estate at Blythe Hall, Coleshill, since the days of Sir Thomas Holte at Aston Hall. Yet for all his wealth, Dugdale would happily turn up for board meetings in a battered old Morris Traveller, in which he used to transport livestock around the farm. And whereas he was plucky enough to have ridden in the Grand National and flown in air races from England to Australia and Vancouver, the 1957 Cup Final got him so worked up that he ruptured his appendix. Truly, the boardroom at Villa Park had not seen his like before.

Other directors who came and went during this period of musical chairs included Dick Greenhalgh

(1971-72); Bob Mackay (1968-72), the last survivor of the old regime, who was credited with being the man behind the Bodymoor Heath purchase; Eric Houghton (1972-79), the former player and 1957 Cup winning manager; Harry Cressman (1973-78), possibly the first American-born director at a British club; Alan Smith (1972-78), Secretary of Warwickshire CCC, and Ron Bendall's son, Don (1978-82).

Two Villa Park stalwarts died during the 1970s; Bert Bond, the stadium manager and head groundsman, in 1972, and four years later, assistant secretary Len Latham. Both men had served the club since the 1930s.

Alan Bennett filled the role of club secretary throughout most of the period. Appointed as successor to Fred Archer in 1969, Bennett was that rare creature in the Villa set-up – a southerner! – having been Chelsea's assistant secretary beforehand (where he had worked with Tommy Docherty). He stayed almost exactly ten years at Villa Park before leaving in May 1979 to join Leicester City.

The decade also saw the club look back, when celebrating the centenary in 1974, and look forward, by taking the first giant leaps into the age of modern technology.

For example, in 1972 one of the most advanced turnstile counting systems in the country was installed at a cost of £3,500. In March 1976 Villa also became one of the first four or five clubs in the League to install a computerised ticketing system. Supplied by GEC, this early system cost £32,000, but was a huge boon, particularly as Villa's return to the First Division had pushed season ticket sales up to a record breaking 9,000. Another innovation was the opening of a ticket kiosk in the Bull Ring Centre.

On the communications front Villa launched their own newspaper, The VILLA TIMES, which surfaced twice during the 1970s, and completely revamped the VILLA NEWS AND RECORD in 1969, so successfully that it won more *Programme of the Year* awards during the decade than any other club publication. In 1975 Villa also launched its first ever telephone information line.

In economic terms, the 1970s were years of rampant inflation, not helped by the imposition of VAT on all football ground admissions. These two factors, combined with Villa's success under managers Vic Crowe and Ron Saunders – and consequently the growth in the club's wages and bonus bill – forced ticket prices to rise as never before. For example, the price of match day entry for adults to the Holte End increased between 1969 and 1981, from 5s (25p) to £2.00, and for the most expensive season tickets in the Trinity Road Stand they increased even more, from £8 8s to £101 within the same period.

Even taking into account inflation these rises still represented a doubling of terrace prices and a tripling of seat prices. Yet Villa's price hikes were hardly greater than those of any other clubs during the 1970s. Every club's costs were rocketing, particularly in relation to safety work.

❖ *Sir William Dugdale – the Villa boardroom had not seen his like before*

At the same time, this inflationary spiral meant that virtually every club which did dare to carry out substantial stand developments during the 1970s suffered the consequences. Fulham's current ground problems can all be traced back to the crippling debts incurred after building a stand in 1972. Tottenham's new stand went massively over budget, while Sheffield United and Wolves suffered so severely from the debts incurred from stand construction that both once proud clubs ended up plummeting down to the Fourth Division.

Understandably therefore, so soon after the club's rescue in 1968, Villa's directors were extremely cautious about embarking upon the long awaited redevelopment of the Witton End, even if the need for a new stand was now quite pressing.

Apart from the fact that the Witton End had remained the most basic part of the ground since the early 1920s, in common with most successful clubs, Villa were now finding that demand for seats was on the increase. Villa also needed extra seats in order to maintain Villa Park's ranking as a favoured venue for Cup semi-finals.

Tentative planning for a new stand began in October 1973, shortly after the Home Office issued the first edition of its Guide to Safety at Sports Grounds (which was based upon the 1972 Wheatley Report, following the Ibrox disaster the year before). This publication represented a watershed in football history, for it was the first time the government had made any specific recommendations on ground safety since an official report on the chaotic opening of Wembley Stadium in 1923.

Villa Park, fortunately, was not in need of major surgery. As Doug Ellis told the 1973 AGM, therefore, the club had to concentrate resources on the playing side rather than on the Witton End. 'We cannot afford a stand before we reach the First Division,' he explained – particularly since gates had dropped, despite promotion to the Second Division – but equally, he added, 'we cannot afford to be without one when we get there.'

Note that Ellis used the term 'when' and not 'if'. For such was the iron resolution which then pervaded Villa Park. As Ron Saunders regularly reminded one and all after his appointment at the start of the centenary season in 1974, no less than 110 per cent effort would do. And no fewer than 57,266 – Villa Park's highest League gate since August 1962 – turned up to see the giddy climax of that extra effort, a tense 2-0 victory over promotion rivals Sunderland, on April 26 1975.

*Going up, going up, going up!* sang a packed Holte End, in disbelief almost as much as in joy.

For it was not only eight years of exile in the lower divisions which ended that year. Two months earlier, Villa's 1-0 triumph over Norwich in the League Cup Final had earned the club its first ever entry to a European competition.

But not everything went Villa's way in 1975.

After several years of negotiation between Doug Ellis and the Leeds-based ASDA supermarket chain, Villa's chairman had hammered out a deal for the

❖ *Read all about it! Eric Woodward's revamped* VILLA NEWS AND RECORD *won awards throughout the 1970s, and in August 1972 was joined by the* VILLA TIMES. *Sales of season tickets, reported the* TIMES' *inaugural issue, had reached 7,200, despite higher costs of between £13 - 17. In 1997 season ticket sales topped 20,000 for the first time.*

complete redevelopment of the now almost permanently waterlogged and rutted Serpentine Car Park.

Essentially the plan was for ASDA to build a £3 million superstore and petrol station on a corner of the nine acre car park, on three conditions. Firstly, Villa would retain the freehold of the site, but would receive an annual rent from ASDA. Secondly, ASDA would part fund a community sports hall on the site, and thirdly, they would resurface the car park, which on match days would be reserved exclusively for Villa supporters. (Villa had already estimated that if the club had gone it alone, resurfacing the car park would have cost at least £165,000.)

For Villa, therefore, the ASDA deal worked out by Ellis could hardly have been more advantageous, and would have considerably helped towards the cost of redeveloping the Witton End. For their part, Birmingham City Council were also in favour, since they were effectively gaining new sports facilities free of charge and, in the process, helping towards the creation of some 300 jobs.

But after lobbying by local residents and shopkeepers, West Midlands County Council decided to reject the plans, and so, not for the last time in the modern era, Villa's directors were left scratching their heads in disbelief and frustration.

Not that they were beaten. ASDA immediately decided to appeal against the County Council's decision, while the Villa's board felt confident enough to proceed at least with Stage One of the Witton End redevelopment.

This was completed during the summer of 1976 and essentially consisted of lopping off the uneven earth banking at the top, refurbishing the front half of the terrace with new concrete and barriers (in preparation for the new stand being built behind),

❖ *Beat 'em or join 'em? Doug Ellis, Pat Matthews and Jim Hartley prepare to meet the shareholders in 1972. AGMs and EGMs during the 1970s were seldom places for the mild.*

and tidying up the rear with new stairways and fencing. Once completed in August 1976, at a cost of £70,000, and with the terrace capacity reduced from 16,500 to 13,000, the Witton End had never looked so neat and trim.

But it was only a transitional state, for in May, before Stage One had even been finished, the board resolved to start planning for Stage Two, the building of the North Stand itself.

And so we come to the first major piece of new construction at Villa Park since the Trinity Road Stand was started in 1922. Readers will recall the hugely disruptive aftermath of that particular development; the massive debt incurred and the subsequent resignation of chairman Fred Rinder. In the inflationary 1970s, would Villa be able to avoid the same pitfalls? Who could be sure, for even if Rinder's ghost did not haunt the boardroom, the news coming in from Alan Bennett's old colleagues at Stamford Bridge was enough to dissuade any club from so much as putting up a tea bar. Chelsea's new East Stand had taken two years to complete, left the club over £3 million in debt, and the team had just been relegated to Division Two.

On the other hand, Chelsea had chosen a firm of architects known more for their prestige than their experience of stand design, whereas Villa's chosen design team, led by Harry Marsden of the Stockport-based CHESHIRE DESIGN GROUP, had recently completed a striking new cantilevered stand at Manchester City's Maine Road (coincidentally also called the North Stand).

CDG also brought on board two companies with whom they had worked at Maine Road; the structural engineers OVE ARUP & PARTNERS, who had an excellent record in stadium work, and the firm of CAMERON, MIDDLETON & LEES as quantity surveyors.

Villa set the team a tough challenge. In order to minimise the loss of revenue the stand would have to be ready for use by August 1977. Furthermore, on no account were its costs to exceed £1 million. Yet it was now August 1976, leaving just three short months to

draw up detailed plans and put them out to competitive tender.

By working through the night the design team just made it, but only after the first set of detailed drawings had to be scrapped and the whole process started afresh. Even then some of the building contractors invited to tender expressed doubts that the job could be finished in the timescale allowed.

One company did convince the Villa that they could do it on time and at cost however – FAIRCLOUGH – and so work on site began, on schedule, on January 19 1977.

The first step was to clear the rear half of the Witton End banking, leaving room for 6,000 standing in front, while the foundations for the new stand were prepared in the space behind. Alas, the price of this progress was that the old scoreboard in the Witton Lane corner had to be sacrificed.

As the various sub-contractors prepared to move in, each one programmed to dovetail into the overall timetable, as in 1922, torrential rain in February caused the first set-back, just as the foundations were about to be laid. There then arose a dispute between the architects and the local authorities concerning the design of the seating treads, gangways and handrails. This required CDG to completely redesign the upper seating deck in mid-construction.

There would be further problems and delays with materials and labour, so that as August approached, Fairclough's men were having to work in shifts, sometimes until one o'clock in the morning. But even if, as the architects admitted later, 'the language did become a bit raw and tempers flared,' the team all pulled together remarkably well, to complete the stand in what was then considered to be a record time.

Only two weeks later than scheduled, the North Stand opened its doors to the public for Villa v Everton on August 27, 1977, and was fully operational by late October. (Stage Three, the fitting out of the offices and various suites, would not take place for another three years.)

Spectators at Villa Park today will be quite familiar with the North Stand, so it needs little description on these pages. But a few points concerning its design may still be of interest.

Firstly, the North Stand was really quite advanced for its time. Or as the VILLA NEWS AND RECORD described it, somewhat equivocally, 'Without doubt, the North Stand is probably the best in Britain.'

Nowadays it may not seem so futuristic, for like many buildings of that period it has dated rapidly, particularly its textured concrete rendering. But in 1977 its entrance and internal executive areas were likened to the Dorchester Hotel, not because they were anything like the Dorchester but because even wealthy guests were simply not used to such luxury at a football ground.

The stand was also innovative.

Its most obvious novelty was the picking out of the letters AV in light blue seats, among the predominantly claret coloured seats on the upper deck. On the North Stand the effect was relatively subtle, whereas in more recent years whole names and logos have become *de rigueur* at almost every ground. (Regrettably so, in this writer's opinion.)

More significantly, the North Stand was the first major stand in Britain to use what is now broadly termed the 'goalpost' form of roof construction, whereby two columns are placed outside the spectators' field of view, supporting a horizontal girder from which the roof is suspended. Deemed to be cheaper than a conventional cantilevered system, the 'goalpost' has since become common at British grounds, including Ibrox Park, Ewood Park, Anfield, the Hawthorns and Molineux. The new Holte End at Villa Park is another clear example.

Another pioneering aspect of the North Stand, later copied at Tottenham, was its double layer of executive boxes. Apparently when the design was originally drawn up with a single line of boxes, even with a handsome input from the Development Association, there was still a sufficient funding gap to make the directors think twice. Which is exactly what Sir William Dugdale did. The first reaction to his suggestion for twice the number of boxes was 'You can't do that! No stand has two layers.' But when he asked, 'Why not?' no-one could think of a good reason.

So instead of 20 boxes on one level, the North Stand expanded to 39 on two levels (one of them being double-sized for the club to hire out on a match-to-match basis). Priced at between £6,000 or £7,500 each, these boxes would yield £250,000 in their first three years, or 25 per cent of the stand's total costs. By 1980 this contribution would increase to half the costs. Put another way, the income from just one spectator in one the 39 boxes would fund the provision of nearly eight seats on the deck above. Such were, and are, the economics of modern stand construction.

As Eric Woodward had predicted, the new boxes were an instant hit, attracting a waiting list before the stand even opened. The seats proved extremely popular too, offering as they did the best, unrestricted views in the ground, and some pretty breathtaking ones of the M6 too (for when the action began to pall). Thus the club sold nearly 2,000 season tickets for the stand in its first few months, double the number originally anticipated. One local businessman, who had just opened a new factory in Queen's Road, went so far as to buy 300 tickets in the new stand for one game, for his entire workforce and their guests.

On the other hand, as the upper deck's early occupants discovered, there was a price to pay for such an excellent view. Fortunately, however, this was solved when extra deflector panels were added at each side to stave off the chilling effects of fearsome cross winds.

Another design problem, albeit one which would only later become an issue, concerns the North Stand's 'goalpost' roof structure. As is the nature of all such stands, the upper deck cannot be extended into or around the corners, at least not without creating restricted views (as has happened at

Norwich). In 1977 this was hardly an issue, since Villa Park's capacity of 48,000 was then deemed to be quite sufficient, particularly since average gates were then around 35,000. But of course the advent of all-seated grounds since then has meant that the North Stand is now smaller than would be ideal, and will thus have to be fitted with an entirely new roof if it is to be enlarged (as Doug Ellis proposed in 1997). But 20 years ago, the board could hardly have foreseen the demands of the Taylor Report.

Nor could they have been held entirely responsible for the increase of violence on the terraces, which required the lower section of the North Stand to be segregated, a sad indictment of changing social standards after so many years of trouble-free mingling between home and away fans on the old Witton End. Even then a simple dividing fence did not prove sufficient, and after hundreds of youths wearing Villa and Everton colours exchanged missiles, abuse and copious amounts of spit during a game in September 1978, the club and police were forced to create a 'no-man's land' between the home and away sections.

But if it was sad enough that supporters of rival teams could no longer congregate together in the same area, even more galling for law-abiding Villa supporters was that not only were perimeter fences erected along the front of the Holte End – in response to that infamous invasion of the pitch by Rangers fans in 1976 – but the year after, a radial fence was placed right down the centre of the Holte End, thus dividing it for the first time ever into two blocks, known thereafter as K and L.

The main reason for this was that Villa Park was now fully designated under the 1975 Safety of Sports Grounds Act, and therefore had to comply with various requirements concerning the management of

❖ *A sign of the times – segregation, and perimeter fences, came to Villa Park in the late 1970s.*

❖ *The North Stand rises up in place of the Witton End in 1977, almost one hundred years after the aquarium block, from which this photograph was taken, was built at the Lower Grounds. This was the view from the verandah outside the club offices.*

large terraces. As the largest single standing area in British football – even with its total capacity now reduced from 28,000 to 22,600 – it was felt necessary to split the entry and exit of fans into two distinct zones, to help control distribution and avoid potential congestion. The radial fence also allowed the Holte to be divided, if necessary, between rival sets of fans attending FA Cup semi-finals.

However, such cold practicalities found little favour with Holte Enders, for whom this ugly, steel intrusion slicing through their favourite playground like a Berlin Wall, cut off friends from each other, created divisions where none had existed before, and implied somehow that Villa fans could not be trusted to manage themselves. Indeed for many a Holte Ender, the installation of that one simple fence was the beginning of the end of the traditional Holte experience.

But on a wider level the fencing actually did symbolise the end of an era. For now that the 1975 Safety Act was in force and the government was showing itself to be more concerned with the issue of hooliganism, no ground would ever be the same again. From the mid-1970s until the Hillsborough disaster in 1989 there would be no doubt as to who called the shots. It was the local authorities, and above all the police. And instead of standing up to the police and saying, 'Wait a minute, these are our customers and they're not all rowdies,' the majority of clubs took a back seat and allowed their grounds to be turned into fortresses.

With hindsight we can now see how wrong that approach was. But in the thick of the fighting it was much harder to see the wood for the trees.

On the whole Villa fans, fortunately, remained a fairly innocent bunch compared with those of certain clubs. But policing the Holte End, once a relative pleasure, was nevertheless becoming an increasingly unpleasant duty, particularly at the rear. Officers would emerge from their duties with their uniforms drenched in saliva. On occasions individual policemen found themselves cornered, punched and beaten in the darker corners of the Holte.

That was a law and order issue. Yet at the same time there were no areas of Villa Park which might

ever have been described as a safety risk. The North Stand was entirely new and non-combustible. The Witton Lane Stand had been recently, if modestly modernised in 1966, and the Trinity Road Stand, though now faded, would only need fire-proofing after more stringent checks were made after the 1985 Bradford fire.

As to the Holte End, apart from the new fencing, every single step was resurfaced during the late 1970s, at a cost of over £150,000, with new crush barriers added throughout which complied exactly with the government's recommendations. This meant that by the time of the Hillsborough disaster in 1989, the Holte End could even merit being described as a model terrace.

But that is to jump ahead of ourselves. For back in the 1970s, there were issues of another sort still to resolve at Villa Park.

The first concerned ASDA's appeal. This was finally successful after a six day hearing, enabling work to begin on the Serpentine in 1978.

The ASDA Superstore itself, with its now neatly surfaced car park, opened a year later. The adjacent £1.25 million Aston Villa Sports and Leisure Centre was then officially opened in September 1980, by the Minister for Sport, Hector Munro. In addition to ASDA's contribution, the SPORTS COUNCIL had provided a grant of £250,000, to which £300,000 was added by the government's Inner City Partnership fund.

Ironically, the store would not prove a commercial success, so that ASDA eventually withdrew from the site to concentrate on a new store at Perry Barr. Yet the Sports and Leisure Centre – which would never have existed without ASDA – has thrived, attracting up to 250,000 users a year for a whole range of sports and events, including the championship winning TEAM FIAT basketball team, boxing, rock concerts, and even the occasional Villa away match, beamed live into the centre by satellite.

Another irony was that the man who worked so hard to broker the deal with ASDA, Doug Ellis, was no longer even on the Villa's board when the Sports and Leisure Centre opened.

Continuing dissension amongst the various board members had led to both Ellis and Eric Houghton leaving the club in late 1979. Harry Kartz, who had succeeded Sir William Dugdale as chairman in 1978, thus found himself leading the smallest board in the club's history; himself, plus Ron Bendall, Don Bendall, and a new appointee, Trevor Gill, who also served as the club's president. In October 1980 Ron Bendall then took over as chairman.

As one of the club's largest shareholders, Bendall had been invited to join the board in 1975. A Birmingham-based accountant who specialised in liquidations, he had stood on the Holte End in the post-war era, but had increased his involvement when his son Donald became infatuated with the Villa during the 1960s. By 1978 he was living as a tax exile on the Isle of Man and was something of a mystery man, certainly to the fans.

On the other hand, what did they care so long as

❖ The North Stand – a complete stylistic contrast to the rest of Villa Park and a trendsetter in its own right. The goalpost roof structure has become commonplace at British grounds, while Tottenham Hotspur copied the double layer of boxes. Since the photograph below was taken the upper storey has been infilled with lounges and offices.

the team were doing well. And of course under Ron Saunders they were now doing extremely well, so that by the end of Ron Bendall's first season as chairman Villa won their first League championship since 1910. As no Villa fan will need reminding, despite the shock resignation of Ron Saunders the following February, under his successor Tony Barton, Villa then won the European Cup in May 1982, their greatest ever achievement since the Double winning season of 1896-97.

Bendall's legacy should therefore have been an entirely positive one.

But it was anything but. For by the time he sold his shareholding back to Doug Ellis in November 1982 – by which time Bendall was in declining health – Villa were £1.6 million debt, an extraordinary turnaround of financial fortunes in such a short period. When Ellis had left the board in 1979 there had been no debt and a surplus in the bank.

Ask any fan which they would rather have – the honours or the bank balance – and it would be no contest. But all the same, someone had to sort out the debt. Moreover, regardless who now sat in the chair, there was another extremely thorny leftover from Ron Bendall's two years at the helm.

To explain what occurred in detail would take a book of its own, for it was an immensely complex affair. But so far it affected Villa Park, the gist of it was as follows.

When Stage Two of the North Stand's construction had taken place in 1977 the Clerk of Works responsible for the building programme had performed such a good job that in January 1978 he was employed by the Villa as a full-time stadium manager. His name was Terry Rutter, and for the first year or so of his contract, on the surface at least, everything ran relatively smoothly.

The summer of 1978 saw Rutter oversee £250,000 worth of improvements. A new pitch was laid – Villa Park's second since 1897 – to replace the one originally laid in 1931. Refurbishment of the Holte terracing (as mentioned earlier) and catering bars began, and in the Trinity Road Stand a large underground area was excavated to provide a new lounge for box-holders.

During the course of this delicate and dirty operation old Bovril bottles dating back to 1885 were found amid the excavations.

Elsewhere, those much needed extra screens were added to the upper tier of the North Stand, while, some 2,000 gallons of paint gave the rest of the ground a shiny new look for the start of the 1978-79 season. A year later a new ticket office, costing £43,000, was opened on the ground floor of the North Stand.

The real problems seemed to start in 1980, when work began on Stage Three of the North Stand development; the fitting out of new offices, a contract undertaken by the Birmingham building firm of CURRALL, LEWIS & MARTIN. (This work had become a matter of priority after the council

pronounced Villa's old offices as unsafe in March 1980, and the board decided that the building was beyond economic repair.)

After work on the new offices began, Rutter and the North Stand architect Harry Marsden formed their own company called SPORTS GROUNDS CONSULTANTS, through which Rutter continued to work for Villa on an annual contract. The company also worked for Aberdeen and Shrewsbury.

Once completed in 1982 the bill for building and fitting out Villa's swish new North Stand offices, amounted to a surprisingly high total of £838,000. Further costs amounting to £460,000 were also incurred for improvements to the Villa Park floodlights, for rewiring work, the installation of CCTV and the creation of a tunnel in the lower section of the North Stand. This latter work was required because the old access to the pitch (from the groundman's area in the Witton Stand) had been blocked in January 1980 by the installation of an advanced rain protection cover, which ran the full length of the pitch and rolled in and out of a special housing on electric motors. Warwickshire CCC were supplied with a similar cover.

So it was that Villa's staff moved happily into their plush new offices. But then no sooner had the celebrations from Villa's European Cup triumph in Rotterdam died down, in mid 1982, than news emerged that an internal report had been carried out into the £1.3 million worth of work carried out during the previous year or so. Conducted by Alfred Harvey, the chairman of a Midlands building consultancy, this report alleged that £700,000 worth of orders and invoices had been unaccounted for. In August the West Midlands Police launched their own probe, and suddenly the European Cup winners were in the centre of a highly damaging and widely publicised corruption scandal, reported in the national press and on network television.

Villa's auditors, DELOITTE, HASKINS & SELLS, meanwhile started to conduct a more detailed investigation into the figures included in the Harvey Report. Their rather different verdict, delivered in

October 1982, was that the final bill of £838,000 for the offices was in fact only 10 per cent above what it should have been, but that nevertheless there had been a serious lack of documentation, breaches of recommended codes of practice and poor site supervision.

As the police continued their own investigations, in November, from his Isle of Man retreat, the now-ailing Ron Bendall decided to sell his 42 per cent shareholding in Villa to Doug Ellis, and thus the wheel came full circle. In 1968 Ellis had taken over a club £182,000 in debt. In 1982 he returned after almost a three year absence, to find it £1.6 million in the red.

Terry Rutter's contract with Villa was terminated the following January, allowing Ted Small to return as the new stadium manager, and as far as the club were concerned, that was the end of the affair. Although they could have taken further action, it was agreed that any money they did have would be better spent on remedying the club's now critical financial position rather than on expensive lawyers.

The police did not ease up, however, until finally the affair reached its denouement at Birmingham Crown Court in February 1985. Harry Marsden admitted to having conspired with Ron Bendall to obtain money by deception from the Football Trust, by inflating a claim for CCTV equipment at Villa Park. He also admitted to a similar offence involving Wigan. Meanwhile, Terry Rutter pleaded guilty to related charges for floodlighting at Port Vale, and for false accounting in relation to rewiring work at Villa Park.

But in sentencing both men to 12 months imprisonment, suspended for 18 months, and while describing the whole affair as 'a seabed of corruption', the judge also said that he did not want to make the two men scapegoats. 'I am quite sure there have been others who have not been through this dock at all.' One of them was Ron Bendall, who had died in April 1983.

On its own this tawdry episode of greed and mismanagement might not have been of much significance, other than to be a warning to all clubs that they should be very careful as to who they let loose on major building projects and who they employ as their professional advisers.

But for a number of individuals caught up in the affair and its repercussions, particularly those who had served the club with loyalty, life would never be the same again. Reputations were ruined. False accusations were made – though the worst were later retracted – and worst of all, as far as the club was concerned, the momentum which it should have built upon after Rotterdam was soon dissipated. The affair also overshadowed the fact that whether one admired its aesthetics or not, the North Stand and its new facilities were, for the time, well worthy of the champions Villa had briefly become.

So far as this book is concerned, however, one of the saddest aspects of this unfortunate interlude was the demolition of the last significant remnants of the Lower Grounds – the old offices and gymnasium – during the summer of 1981.

For sure they were in a much diminished state, having had the original tower removed, the Cottage and Barn demolished, and the ground floor stripped out to house the ticket office (before that too moved to the North Stand).

No doubt also that they were no longer suitable as offices, as the club's current secretary and director, Steve Stride, would later recall. Stride, who joined the club as an office junior in June 1972, remembered the buildings as dilapidated, dusty, poorly heated and very draughty, although he did rather enjoy nipping down to the gymnasium to play squash with Alan Bennett at lunchtimes.

'You could smell the history in those buildings. You could close your eyes and think back to what they must have been like in the old days, particularly the old boardroom, with its huge oak table, large heavy doors and big open fire.

'My first office had been hastily constructed in the room where the players used to play snooker. In it there was a rather large heater which the players and coaches would come and sit on in the winter. For me as a Villa fanatic and a young lad that was great, because they'd talk a lot and reminisce about the old days. But to be honest it was an awful building to work in otherwise, and to be able to move into a brand new office complex in the North Stand was a real step forward. When I started here in 1972 there was maybe six or seven of us. Now its more like 36, and we don't even have enough room in the North Stand offices.'

But if the old offices and gymnasium were no longer suitable as offices, might they have had other uses?

In an age more attuned to the need for conservation, we can easily imagine the old buildings being converted into a restaurant (which is how the upper floor began in 1878), or even better, a club museum, in which the rich heritage of the Lower Grounds could also have been celebrated.

And although pronounced unsafe by the council in 1980, there were many who felt that the structure was not beyond redemption. Ted Small, whorelinquished his position at Villa Park after Terry Rutter became stadium manager, knew the building intimately. 'It was beautiful. I tried to get it preserved but I'd gone by the time it was pulled down and there was no one there at that time who was interested. I agree there were parts of it that would have had to come down, but the brickwork and the arches were not dangerous and it could have been made into something really special.

'Instead,' says Small with regret, 'they sacrificed a beautiful building.'

It was raised to the ground without ceremony, in August 1981, and all that was gained in return was an extra few parking spaces – a poor exchange, for sure, but a lost opportunity too.

For without this quirky building in its midst, Villa Park took one further step away from its rich and unique heritage, and in the process, became just that little bit more ordinary.

# Seven years of lean, seven of plenty

*in which we span the contrasting years from 1982-89, and 1989-96* ❖

*seven years of recession, low gates, no honours* ❖

*but Villa open up to the community* ❖

*Hillsborough, the Taylor Report and seven years of frenzy* ❖

*the Trinity Road Stand refurbished, a new Witton Lane Stand built* ❖

*and Doug Ellis honoured* ❖

*the end of terracing* ❖

*the new Holte End Stand* ❖

*Euro 96* ❖

P ART TWO OF DOUG ELLIS'S REIGN AS
Villa chairman began on November 30
1982. Although now aged 58, far from
seeking a quiet life he not only threw
himself straight back into the football business from
day one – having been a mere spectator during the
interim years – but also became Villa's first full-time,
salaried director (a situation made possible by a
change in FA regulations in 1980).

There was certainly plenty for club chairmen to do
at that time, for the 1980s were to develop into
perhaps the most troublesome decade in the entire
history of the professional football.

The recession of the early 1980s sent crowds
tumbling to their lowest ever levels since before the
First World War, down by a startling 8.1 million
spectators between 1980 and 1986, while Villa's own
gates in the First Division more than halved, from an
average of 33,641 in the title-winning season to just
15,270 five seasons later. At one particularly low
point, in November 1985, there were even reports
that Villa had agreed to help out their crisis-torn
neighbours by sharing Villa Park with the Blues.

But it was not only rising admission prices which
deterred paying customers, nor simply, in Villa's case,
a miserable run of results under managers Graham
Turner and Billy McNeill, which culminated in
relegation in 1987.

Fuelled by such negative images as a televised riot
at Luton in 1985, the perception of football as a
hostile environment drove away casual fans in their
thousands. Then came the agony of the Bradford fire
in May 1985, on the same day a youth died at St
Andrew's in the aftermath of a pitched battle
involving Leeds United and City fans. A few weeks
later, 39 Italian supporters at the European Cup Final
between Juventus and Liverpool were crushed to
death at Heysel. Banned from Europe as a result, the
English game had never been at such a low ebb, or
held in such low esteem.

The Popplewell Report which followed the
Bradford fire hardly affected Villa Park – apart from
fire-proofing work carried out in the Trinity Road
Stand – since the ground had already been
modernised in line with the 1975 Safety of Sports
Grounds Act. But there were other measures which
threatened the pleasures of ordinary law-abiding
fans, particularly those on the terraces. High profile
and often uncompromising policing, particularly for
away fans, not to mention the ban on alcohol sales at
grounds, perimeter fences and degrading body
searches, created a climate of fear and loathing in
which only the most dedicated maintained their
support.

The situation threatened to deteriorate further
when the Prime Minister of the day, Margaret
Thatcher, pressed for all fans to carry identity cards, a
patently unworkable scheme which even some of her
most ardent sympathisers among football's higher
echelons opposed. Villa fans made their own protest
against the proposal when thousands attending the
televised visit of Manchester United, in March 1989,
held up red cards in a co-ordinated action. Even the

referee joined in. Millions of viewers saw the protest,
as did the Home Secretary, Douglas Hurd, who was
sitting in the Trinity Road Stand as a guest of the
chairman.

Not surprisingly, in view of all the uncertainty
and pressure, very little major construction took
place at British football grounds during these dark
days. Nevertheless, there was always plenty to do for
the newly re-appointed stadium manager, Ted Small
and his growing team of workers. Under the ever
watchful eyes of the local authorities, the running of
a modern ground, plus Bodymoor Heath, was now a
highly demanding, seven day a week operation – a
world apart from the unregulated days of old when
the likes of Bert Bond, Mush Callaghan and a few
willing helpers and club apprentices laboured to
keep the ground in order.

Few fans would have noticed many of the costly
improvements effected at Villa Park during this
period; the new lighting, sound and emergency back-
up systems; the new-style, flat-rail crush barriers;
the installation of a police control room where the
old Holte End scoreboard had been, or the
appearance of closed circuit television cameras
around the ground. Yet in several of these areas Villa
were genuine pioneers. (And that is not just club
propaganda. Many an independent expert visited
Villa Park during the 1980s to learn from the club's
experience.)

Costly though these safety measures were, none
of them helped to bring in a single extra spectator
through the turnstiles. As gates declined, therefore,
the profitability of Villa's commercial activities
became ever more crucial. After Eric Woodward's
sterling efforts as Villa's first commercial manager,
his former assistant Sue Walker took over the
operation in December 1980, thus becoming the

first women ever to occupy such a role in British football. Tony Stephens took over the position in 1983, and when he moved on to work for Wembley Stadium, Chris Rodman, formerly at Lincoln City, was appointed in 1986. Finally, the local kid who had once made such a nuisance of himself around the ground, Abdul Rashid, achieved his long-held ambition by becoming commercial manager in 1988, a position he has held ever since.

Together with his newly recruited assistant, Denise Rowe (formerly at Tottenham), one of Rashid's first tasks – albeit a relatively easy one, as it transpired – was to sell the leases for 15 new executive boxes installed at the rear of the Witton Lane Stand in the autumn of 1988. These brought Villa Park's total number of boxes up to 73, a figure topped only by Manchester United.

Another commercial venture was the acquisition in 1986 of the large Colmore Depot on Witton Lane, just behind the North Stand. Built in the 1950s on the site of a coal yard, the depot had latterly been used as a distribution centre by Ansell's brewery. Villa's original intention had been to convert the building into an indoor 'Soccerama' centre, a plan rejected by the council after local residents expressed fears about increased traffic during the week. Ironically, however, when 'soccer' was changed to 'cricket' the idea did win approval, and together with grants from the SPORTS COUNCIL and, again ironically, the FOOTBALL TRUST (who donated £60,000), the new centre, named Stumps, opened in October 1987.

More on Stumps follows in the next chapter. But for now, one aspect of its development is worthy of note. Until the Colmore depot was purchased, Villa's boundaries had remained more or less the same since 1911. From 1987 onwards, however, they were

to increase, bit by bit, until by August 1995 they extended all the way from the Holte Hotel right up to the back of the houses on Witton Road, thus covering almost the same extent as the Lower Grounds had done between 1888 (when the Meadow was built over) and 1897. Again, here was a shrewdly orchestrated development which, although barely noticed by the fans, would contribute crucially to the club's current position of strength.

Moreover, with Stumps soon attracting up to 4,000 users a week, plus another 250,000 visitors flocking annually to the Aston Villa Sports and Leisure Centre, Villa Park and its related facilities were now fulfiling much the same role as had the Lower Grounds – that of a vibrant focus of sporting and leisure activity for both the local community and the city of Birmingham as a whole. Henry Quilter

❖ Back to school – Villa launched their pioneering classroom scheme for local schoolchildren in April 1989, one of several innovations at Villa Park during the 1980s which would later become common at British football grounds.

ground, the children were provided with their own classroom at the ground (in the family clubroom) where everyday aspects of their routine curriculum, for example in maths and English, could be adapted to some of the activities they had seen at Villa Park. In its first two years over 5,000 children from schools all over Birmingham took advantage of the scheme.

In short, whatever else Villa might have lacked throughout these seven lean years without any footballing honours, Villa Park steadily and impressively evolved during the 1980s from a football ground which merely opened its doors only on match days into a major, seven-day-a-week centre of activities for all ages.

Indeed as the end of the decade approached, life at Villa Park was already on the turn. Graham Taylor had led the team back into Division One at the first attempt – just as Joe Mercer managed nearly 30 years earlier – while after the all-time post war low of 1985-86, average attendances were now on a slow but steady rise again. Just as importantly, under Graham Taylor's influence Aston Villa began to feel like a united club again, with a proper youth policy and a positive sense of direction.

But there could be no room for complacency yet. As the 1988-89 season reached its climax, during the month of March Villa failed to score a single goal in five consecutive First Division matches. Even relegation seemed a possibility.

While Villa fans chewed their fingernails in anticipation of a tense end to the season, off the field, Doug Ellis unveiled plans to build a £5 million hotel, conference and exhibition centre at Villa Park, integrated into the rear of the North Stand and its corner with the Trinity Road Stand (where the old offices had stood). A few eyebrows were raised at the very idea – a radical one by any standards – and it would have required Villa to construct new offices. But no-one could accuse the chairman of lacking imagination, especially as 18 of the proposed 93 hotel rooms were to look out over the pitch, at a time when the only other stadium in the world able to offer such a facility – the Toronto Skydome, the world's most advance multi-purpose sporting venue – was still several weeks away from even opening.

As the council sat down to consider Ellis's futuristic hotel plans, elsewhere the football world was in its usual state of late season flux; going through that curious, but compelling interim period between Easter and the Cup Final, when so many fates and fortunes are decided.

Over at the half derelict Molineux, Wolves were preparing to celebrate promotion from the Third Division as champions, under former Villa boss Graham Turner. Taking their place, for the first time in their history, were the now up-for-sale Blues, whose gates in Division Two had slumped to below 5,000. Walsall were destined to be relegated with them, but at least the Saddlers had the prospect of a new stadium at Bescot to instil hope.

Elsewhere, UEFA had agreed to lift the ban on English clubs in European competitions. Forest had just beaten Luton in the final of the Littlewoods Cup,

would no doubt have despaired at all the tarmac which covered his precious gardens. But he would have applauded the spirit. In his day Australian cricketers had performed on the Magnificent Meadow. Now they came to Stumps instead.

Quilter's successors, George Reeves-Smith and Henry Crawford, would also have been impressed with the other events which Villa Park was now attracting, as the list on page 195 illustrates.

Meanwhile, Villa themselves launched a whole series of initiatives designed to bring the community to Villa Park and, at the same time, try to redress some of the negative imagery from which football suffered at this time. A family section for supporters was opened in August 1985 in the Trinity Road enclosure, run by a life-long Villa fan and policeman, Dave Wallis. This proved such a success that a purpose-built club room for families was established a year later in the North Stand, where it has thrived ever since under the sponsorship of PANINI and now, McDONALDS.

Other family-oriented events initiated after the arrival of manager Graham Taylor from Watford, in 1987, included an Open Day at Villa Park, during which some 8,000 fans were given a tour of the ground, a chance to meet the players and take part in a range of competitions and charity events. Taylor also brought with him from Vicarage Road the idea of staging firework displays at Villa Park on Guy Fawkes night – another echo of the once popular extravaganzas staged at the Lower Grounds a hundred years earlier.

But an entirely new idea followed in April 1989, when Aston Villa became the first club in the country to host a Schools Liaison Scheme, whereby local schoolchildren were able to visit the ground as part of their regular studies. Sponsored by BRITISH GAS and the FOOTBALL TRUST, the idea was the brainchild of Rod Evans of the Birmingham Education Department, and was run by primary school teachers Joan Evans (no relation) and Jayne James. Apart from touring the aided by Steve Hodge and Garry Parker. Arsenal and Kevin Richardson were top of the League. At the opposite end of footballing spectrum, Darlington were heading for relegation to the GM Vauxhall Conference, despite the appointment in February of a new young manager, Brian Little.

Such was the state of the football world in April 1989. And then it happened.

Saturday, April 15 was a sunny-in-patches day across Britain. Villa's first team had the day off, while Villa Park itself geared up for yet another FA Cup semi-final. Everton and Norwich, including one Andy Townsend, were the participants, for a game which would yield record receipts of £385,678 from a near capacity crowd of 46,553.

The other semi-final, between Liverpool and Nottingham Forest, was at Hillsborough.

Can you remember where you were that afternoon? Most football fans can, rather as members of the older generation can recall exactly where they were when news of President Kennedy's assassination was announced.

The first reports of an incident came through shortly after 3.06pm. All most people knew then, from radio or television reports, was that the game at Hillsborough had been stopped because of overcrowding behind the Leppings Lane End. As half-time approached at Villa Park, rumours began to spread from those who had radios. There had been some serious injuries. Peter Jones of the BBC, his voice cracking, talked of 'awful scenes,' of ambulances, makeshift stretchers and oxygen cylinders. And then it was known that there were one or two deaths and that angry supporters were claiming that a gate on Leppings Lane had been opened by a policeman, and not broken down by fans as the police were alleging. This was not an outbreak of hooliganism. This was a total breakdown in crowd management.

The reports continued towards five o'clock. But the vast majority of supporters at Villa Park were still oblivious, and when the final whistle went, the Evertonians in the ground celebrated their 1-0 win wildly, most of them only vaguely aware that there had been some 'trouble' at the other semi-final.

By now half the nation was tuned in to radio or TV, disbelieving, horror struck. Pat Nevin, who had scored Everton's winning goal at Villa Park, bounded into the dressing room and instead of champagne, was greeted only by a deadly hush.

By six o'clock the streets around Villa Park were all but deserted, while at Hillsborough the confirmed death toll was rising. It rose and rose until the awful truth was known. Ninety five Liverpool supporters were dead. Another, Tony Bland, would be kept alive on a life-support machine until he too was allowed to die, in 1992.

It was a sunny afternoon. A perfect afternoon for football. And it was the end of football as we knew it.

In common with many other clubs, Aston Villa reacted immediately to the tragedy. On behalf of the club, Doug Ellis donated £25,000 to the disaster fund. 'Watching the scenes on television last Saturday

I cried, and I am not ashamed to say that,' the Villa chairman told the SPORTS ARGUS. On the Tuesday, he, Steve Stride and Ted Small met with representatives of the police and local authorities, to review Villa Park's own safety arrangements. No significant problems were found.

That is not to say that Villa Park was perfect or 100 per cent safe. No ground can ever be that, unless it is empty. Nor were the authorities being complacent. But it was true that the geography, layout and existing safety systems at Villa Park would not permit the kind of overcrowding which had occurred at Hillsborough. For example, clear gangways, or wells, were already in place between the front line of crush barriers and the perimeter fences at each end.

Even so, Villa Park was destined to change almost beyond recognition over the next seven years. Seven years of frenzy they were to be, but happily, seven years of plenty too, including two more Wembley triumphs, twice runners-up in the League, an FA Cup semi-final and a run or two in Europe.

Most readers will be familiar with the main developments at the ground; the construction of the new Doug Ellis and Holte End Stands; the conversion of the ground to seating-only, and the expansion of the club's boundaries to take in the Holte Hotel at one end of the site and the creation of the Villa Village at the other.

But it was not just Villa Park which altered. During those hectic few years the whole business of football would change beyond recognition. The introduction of satellite television coverage and the launch of the Premier League would be the most significant developments, followed by the flotation of the club on the stock market in 1997. But there were many other changes between the Hillsborough disaster in April 1989 and Villa Park's centenary, almost exactly eight years later.

So many, in fact, that as the story of that historic period now shows, life at Villa Park transformed so rapidly in front of our very eyes that, looking back, it seems harder and harder to recall what the football world was really like before that terrible afternoon at Hillsborough.

Some will say that many aspects of the old world were much better. Others will say good riddance to the old attitudes. But one thing we can all agree upon is this. Villa Park has undergone a quite astonishing revolution since 1989.

Here, blow by blow, is how it happened.

### ❖ JULY 1989

While Villa fans look forward to a new defensive partnership of Neilsen and McGrath, FIFA announce that no standing will be allowed at future World Cup matches. Few people believe that the all-seater rule will spread to domestic football, however.

### ❖ AUGUST 1989

Lord Justice Taylor's Interim Report into the Hillsborough disaster is published on August 4, with the promise of a Final Report containing various

HOME OFFICE

**THE HILLSBOROUGH STADIUM DISASTER**

15 APRIL 1989

INQUIRY BY
THE RT HON LORD JUSTICE TAYLOR

FINAL REPORT

Presented to Parliament
by the Secretary of State for the Home Department
by Command of Her Majesty
January 1990

❖ *The Taylor Report changed the face of British football and, many would argue, saved the game from its inherent inertia and complacency.*

❖ *Less than four weeks after the publication of Lord Justice Taylor's Final Report in early 1990, Holte Enders were able to enjoy their first fence-free match since 1977.*

❖ **JANUARY 1990**

The end of an era. To make way for the new hotel, the last remaining section of brick wall which once linked the old offices with the Trinity Road Stand is finally demolished, thus ending all links between the ground of today and the Lower Grounds of old.

On January 29 the publication of Lord Justice Taylor's Final Report contains good and bad news among its 76 recommendations. Firstly, he rejects the government's proposals for an identity card scheme. But he also recommends that First and Second Division grounds become all-seater by August 1994. The shock waves reverberate around the football industry as the implications sink in. Initial estimates suggest that the conversion costs could add up to £350 million, far beyond the means of the game as a whole. A quick calculation establishes that if no new stands were to be built and the existing terraces converted, Villa Park's capacity would fall from approximately 43,000 to 33,650.

recommendations for the following season. Among his interim recommendations is a reduction of crowd densities on all terraces by 15 per cent, with each self-contained section to have a maximum limit, strictly applied. This results in a reduction of the Holte End's capacity from 22,600 to 19,210, while much to the displeasure of Holte Enders, Blocks K and L are cut off from each other completely by the closing of gates in the central dividing fence. Also, gates in the pitch perimeter fences are removed and the openings painted in bright yellow for easy identification. The monitoring of Villa Park's arrangements now becomes formalised under a new Safety Advisory Group chaired by Councillor Frank McLoughlin. He joins five other councillors, two council officials, three club representatives, plus other officials from the police, ambulance and St John's, and a member of the Supporters Club. Although its membership changes over the years, this important watchdog continues to monitor Villa Park until the present day.

❖ **OCTOBER 1989**

Figures released by the Home Office show Villa Park to be top of the arrests league, with 344 arrests in season 1988-89. But Villa Park's ground commander, Chief Superintendent Jim Chalmers – the bobby who manned the tunnel in 1966 – makes no apologies. Explaining that most of the arrests were not for violence, he says, 'If other clubs are prepared to put up with obscene chants, abusive language, drunkenness and aggressive behaviour, well we are not.' For too long respectable fans have had their match-day experience ruined by thugs. Now it is time to redress the balance.

❖ **DECEMBER 1989**

As Villa go joint top with Liverpool, work is nearly complete on a new 42 seat superbox between the Witton Lane and North Stands. This requires the floodlight pylon in that corner to be removed. The Aston skyline will never be the same.

❖ **FEBRUARY 1990**

The hated perimeter fences come down at the Holte End, accompanied by a warning that fans must not abuse the trust placed in them by going onto the pitch. At Villa Park's first fence-less match for 13 years, on February 24, top of the table Villa look defenceless as they go down 3-0 to Wimbledon.

❖ **MARCH 1990**

Another floodlight tower comes down, from the corner between the Trinity Road and North Stands (and is sold for scrap). This is to make room for the new hotel development. Villa also start planning their response to the all-seater ruling. They receive a boost on March 20 when the Chancellor of the Exchequer, Chelsea supporter John Major, announces a reduction in the duty paid on football pools, from 42.5 per cent to 40 per cent. The 2.5 per cent balance, worth perhaps £20 million a year, is to be transferred to the FOOTBALL TRUST, which in turn will use it to grant aid Taylor-related ground improvements. For Villa this could mean grants of up to £2 million.

❖ **SUMMER 1990**

After Villa finish runners-up, and the World Cup gets under way in Italy, Villa Park becomes a hive of activity as the club begins its Taylor implementation plans. The hotel plans are now put on ice. Overall, around £2 million is spent, of which the FOOTBALL TRUST pays £474,000. The main developments are:

**North Stand** – the ground's last perimeter fences are removed and the lower tier is fitted with 2,900 sky-blue seats. This reduces the ground's overall capacity to just over 40,000. Nine new turnstiles, refreshment bars and wider entrances are also constructed in the North Stand's Witton Lane corner, at a total cost of £241,000. Villa Park becomes one of the first grounds to provide a briefing room for police and stewards before games. Grateful for at last having somewhere to go for the odd cuppa during a long stint on duty, the police put up a plaque in the room in gratitude to Ted Small.

# Villa Park – the Venue

❖ In recent years Villa Park has rediscovered its roots as a multi-purpose venue for sport and entertainment.

Boxing returned on June 21, 1972, when Danny McAlinden took two rounds to defeat Jack Bodell in a British and Empire Lightweight title fight *(right)*.

A century after Iraquois Indians put on a dazzling display of lacrosse at the Lower Grounds, the modern American sport of gridiron made its Villa Park debut, when the ground played host to the first ever British Superbowl, London Ravens v Streatham Olympians, on August 26, 1985. Accompanied by all the usual cheerleaders, marching bands and high octane razzmatazz, the Ravens won 45-7. But with less than 8,000 onlookers in the ground the experiment proved to be a one-off novelty rather than the start of something big.

Following in the transatlantic footsteps of Buffalo Bill and Professor Baldwin was the American evangelist Billy Graham, whose prayer meetings in June and July 1984 attracted a total of 257,181 people to Villa Park over the course of a week. Three years later, in July 1987, over 16,000 Jehovah's Witnesses arrived for a two day convention. (While they met inside the ground, over 40,000 more gathered in Aston Park for a three day tent crusade led by another American preacher, Dick Saunders.) The black South African Archbishop Desmond Tutu also chose Villa Park for a religious gathering, in April 1989.

In a somewhat amplified echo of the days when the Lower Grounds staged orchestral and operatic performances in the Great Hall, Barry White and his, ahem, *Love Unlimited Orchestra* provided Villa Park's first summer concert in modern times, in May 1975 *(inset)*. Local band Duran Duran – so good they had to name them twice – followed in July 1982, watched by 18,000 *(right)*, while 'The Boss' – not Graham Taylor but Bruce Springsteen – drew crowds of over 40,000 to each of his two, four-hour concerts at Villa Park in June 1988. Springsteen's high decibel offerings also managed to attract a torrent of complaints from residents all around the ground and even from some living up to ten miles away.

Finally, 35,000 adoring fans enjoyed a memorable evening with Rod Stewart *(centre right)* and Belinda Carlisle in July 1995, which, unusually, was staged in the round, just like a boxing match.

improvements to the car park behind the North Stand and various other minor works. Not since 1922 has Villa Park witnessed such a hectic summer. Moreover, rather than employ large contractors, most of the work has been carried out by sub-contractors hired directly by Villa. Ted Small believes that this offers the club more savings, and more flexibility, given the tight deadlines.

❖ AUGUST 1990

While Czech coach Dr Jo Venglos adjusts to life as Villa's new boss, Doug Ellis announces record profits of £895,000 for the previous season. The club's turnover has reached a record £5.5 million (compared with £4.3 million the year before), of which £2.3 million derives from commercial sources. Villa Park's implementation of the Taylor Report is to be monitored by a newly formed government body, the Football Licensing Authority. Lobbying continues to save at least some terracing at grounds, with Doug Ellis one of the many voices urging the government to compromise.

❖ SEPTEMBER 1990

As part of the nationwide drive to reduce the numbers of police on duty at football grounds, Villa complete the first series of pioneering training courses for club stewards. Run by ground commander Jim Chalmers and assistant secretary Arthur Moseley, the evening courses instruct 167 stewards on safety issues and on the need for a more customer-oriented approach, as recommended by the Taylor Report. Villa fulfil another aspect of the Report by appointing the club's first ever safety officer, John Hood. A recently retired police superintendent who had regularly controlled operations at Villa Park, Hood first attended Villa games as a child in the late 1940s. In common with newly appointed safety officers at other clubs, Hood has to work hard to begin implementing the new policy of high profile stewarding and low profile policing. Among his early responsibilities is the awkward task of phasing out the club's older stewards, as required by the Taylor Report. His three-day-a-week job is soon taking up six days.

On September 25 Villa fans are offered a new facility, the chance to enjoy a flutter at one of of LADBROKES' betting booths around the ground.

❖ MAY 1991

The Football Licensing Authority appoints nine inspectors, each to have the responsibility for overseeing around ten League grounds. Villa are pleased to learn that the FLA inspector for the West Midlands is to be their former ground commander, Jim Chalmers, whose daughter is a Holte Ender.

❖ SUMMER 1991

As Aston Villa sign up to controversial proposals to form a breakaway Premier League at some stage in the future, and welcome back former apprentice Ron Atkinson as their new manager, work begins on the phased refurbishment of the Trinity Road Stand.

*❖ At a time when gates were plummeting, the revenue from adverts fixed onto the Trinity Road Stand balcony – directly opposite the TV cameras – proved too tempting to refuse. The ads appeared when Villa Park staged its first live televised game, on Friday, January 20, 1984. Only 19,566 attended, and Villa lost 3-1 to Liverpool. But the hoardings stayed in place and earned £25,000 a year or more until, much to the relief of purists, they were taken down in 1990 (or rather taken up, to be fitted along the front of the new roof instead).*

**Holte End** – in readiness for the terrace being converted to seats, the 1962 roof is extended to the front, but with two extra columns restricting views. In order to finish the work in time, but much to the consternation of traditionalists, off-the-shelf brown and red cladding is used. Designed by local structural engineers STEWART & HARRIS, with FRANCIS C. GRAVES as quantity surveyors, the development costs £441,000 and requires the removal of the final two floodlight towers. It is estimated that adding roughly 13,000 seats to the Holte End will cost a further £450,000.

**Trinity Road Stand** – the original 1920s asbestos roof is replaced by grey-coloured steel cladding, complete with an access walkway and advertising hoardings along the front. This costs £115,000 and allows the adverts, which had obscured the ornate balcony since 1984, to be removed.

**Witton Lane Stand** – five new boxes are added to the 15 at the rear of the stand. But to make room the number of seats falls to 4,113. (Before the earlier boxes were installed in 1988 the stand held 6,265.)

**Floodlights** – now that all four pylons have gone, 61 extra powerful lights are mounted along the front of the new Holte End roof and on gantries added to the Trinity Road and Witton Lane roofs. The installation costs £75,000, and increases the strength of the lighting system from 400 to 800 lux.

**Pitch** – groundsman Tony Eden oversees the replacement of the uppermost twelve inches of topsoil and the re-seeding of the pitch, by a Stirling firm called SOUTERS, at cost of £110,000.

**Other safety-related works** include the provision of extra CCTV cameras, a new key telephone system and new radios, at a total cost of £35,000. Spending on the refurbishment of the ground's toilets now reaches £127,000. Also, the former Lions Club, which has served as an Executive Club throughout the 1980s, is converted into a large new souvenir shop, with a players' lounge behind. These works total £150,000. There are also

Nearly £693,000 is spent on a variety of works, the most noticeable of which is the extension of the new roof to cover the enclosure, which itself is upgraded with 3,900 new sky blue seats. Villa Park's capacity is now 40,312.

❖ **AUGUST 1991**
Plans for a new 10,500 seat Witton Lane Stand are submitted to the council. Designed by the HUSBAND DESIGN GROUP of Sheffield (architects also of the new Twickenham) and the Birmingham-based structural engineers, STEWART & HARRIS, the plan is to keep the existing tier of the Witton Lane Stand, and add behind it a new mid-level of executive boxes, and an upper tier and goalpost-supported roof. The space to permit this extension has come about as a result of a council plan to realign and widen Witton Lane, which will allow Villa an extra strip of land measuring eight metres wide (although the club would have preferred ten). In preparation for the road change, the Victorian houses facing Villa Park on Witton Lane are demolished, including the house where Villa's laundry used to be done in the post war years.

❖ **SEPTEMBER 1991**
Objections to Villa's stand plans come from three local residents' associations. As with other similar protests at such places as Highbury, Ewood Park, Maine Road and Anfield – where new stands are also planned in response to the Taylor Report – the main concern is the sheer bulk of the proposed structure. The objectors complain that the new roof's height of 26 metres – compared with 11 metres for the existing one – will overshadow homes in Holte Road (behind Witton Lane) and reduce their daylight hours. They are also worried about property values.

Villa promise to screen the stand with trees and landscape the area between, and stress that once the stand is finished the ground's capacity will not increase, so that there would be no more traffic than is usual. It is also emphasised that if Villa Park, and the City of Birmingham as a whole, is to host Euro 96, the ground's all-seated capacity will have to meet the 40,000 minimum. With the Holte End likely to accommodate 12,000, this means that the new Witton Lane Stand cannot be reduced below the 10,500 mark.

Meanwhile, Villa fans are informed that the newly introduced Football Offences Act could lead to fines of up to £1,000, or even a total ban from the ground, for anyone found guilty of racist or obscene chanting or abuse, throwing missiles, or going onto the pitch without good reason. As part of the ongoing implementation of the Taylor Report recommendations, a full scale test of the club's contingency plans is conducted during Villa's reserve game v Coventry.

Fans are allowed in free, provided they agree to evacuate the Trinity Road Stand at half-time. Similar exercises are held in 1993 and 1994, complete with simulated casualties, in order to test the response of the emergency services and the reactions of club stewards.

❖ **NOVEMBER 1991**
Having been pioneers of the computer age in the early 1970s, Villa take another step towards meeting the Taylor Report by completing the installation of a state-of-the-art computerised Crowd Monitoring System. Each spectator passing through a turnstile is counted, as before, but now the numbers in each section can be monitored and analysed in an instant, so that John Hood's team and the police know exactly how many are in the ground, what the flow rate is, and how long it will take for any queues to clear. The system also warns when any turnstiles should be closed, so that stewards can redirect fans to other entrances, and provides vital extra information for accounting purposes. Already Villa's crowd management expertise is attracting visits from other clubs, from Wembley Stadium, and even from stadium operators abroad.

❖ **JANUARY 1992**
Villa open their new Holte Suite social club in the former Granada Bingo Hall, which the club has recently purchased (thus expanding the club's boundaries even further towards the extent of the old Lower Grounds site). The bingo hall was originally built as a ten-pin bowling alley in the mid 1960s, on the site of the Holte Hotel's two bowling greens. Villa now hope that the building will become a regular social club for all supporters, a facility which has been lacking since the closure of the Lions Club in 1977.

There are red faces at the lack of green on Villa Park's pitch. Having been relaid only 18 months earlier, the surface is now looking embarrassingly threadbare. The extension of the Holte End and Trinity Road roofs has not helped, since they increase the amount of shading on the pitch. But the fundamental problems go back further, to when the pitch was completely relaid in 1977. The firm who replaced the surface in 1990, SOUTERS, are now anxiously returfing the North Stand goalmouth and trying a new top dressing in the centre, while groundsman Tony Eden tries another solution for the Holte End goalmouth. This involves putting down seven tons of a new type of fibre sand, in which tiny filaments of synthetic fibre are mixed with the sand, in order stabilise the root growth. But to cover up the bare patches for when Villa's match with Everton is televised in early February, 20 tons of green coloured sand are spread across the pitch, much to the

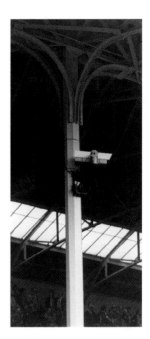

❖ *Big brother is watching you. But violence inside grounds has dropped dramatically since CCTV became a standard tool of crowd management. Once again, Villa were pioneers of its use during the early 1980s.*

❖ *No fences, but a reminder to fans of the cost of a new offence, introduced as part of the Football Offences Act in 1991.*

*continued on page 200*

# The Holte's last stand

❖ The old Holte End was so much less impressive, smaller and dowdier than its successor that future generations might well wonder why anyone could possibly have mourned its loss.

But then if you had never stood on the Holte End how could you ever know?

Everyone had their own reasons for loving the old terrace. For many, this writer included, it was the place where small boys grew up to be big boys; where they learnt to swear, enjoyed their first illicit fags, drank warm beer and mixed more freely among adults than was remotely possible in any other environment. We all had our favourite characters standing around us; the moaners, the wits, the statistical bores, the shouters, the amateur commentators, the old pipe-smokers who reckoned Villa should never have sold Trevor Ford. My personal favourites were some middle-aged inebriates who usually gathered just in front of the first sunken lateral gangway, slightly to the left of the goal. Among them were two brothers, their noses swollen and red like misshapen tomatoes. The worse Villa played, the funnier they became. Then there was a little bloke who used to light up a big cigar at the start of each half. Once I asked him how long there was to go, and instead of looking at his watch he just looked at his glowing stub, and said, 'Bout eight minutes!'

Holte Enders were far more inventive than they were given credit for. Apart from adapting *Bachelor Boy* and *Ghost Riders in the Sky* they sang the Monty Python anthem *Always look on the bright side of life* long before any other set of fans. They could also keep up a rhythmic chant of *Big Fat Ron's Claret and Blue Army* – interspersed with *A.V.F.C.* – for so long that those in the rest of the ground went through the full gamut of reactions; from amusement (to begin with), to boredom (several minutes later), to impatience (alright, you've made your point), to

admiration (such stamina!), to eventual amazement (had the record stuck?).

Yet the Holte could also be divided, sometimes between rival gangs from Castle Vale, Kingstanding or Perry Barr, or more often simply by those on the left and right sides. When matches became especially tedious one side would sing their support for the TV programme 'Tiswas' or Celtic, the other for their respective rivals 'Swapshop' and Rangers. Equally, Holte Enders could be moody and withdrawn, so much so that it only needed a chirpy DJ to try to gee them up over the public address system for the entire terrace to clam up, on principle.

Some feel that the Holte had lost much of its spark by the late 1980s (as would also be said of several other great terraces). But there was also a sense, rightly or wrongly, that the Taylor Report was depriving Villa fans of their right to stand, purely because of the inadequacies of another terrace, far away. Such a view was quite understandable, if only because the Holte End had rarely felt unsafe. In fact, in its latter years the barrier and gangway layouts followed the rule book to the letter.

There was resentment, too, that whenever the demise of terracing was discussed in the media it was always to the likes of Liverpool or Arsenal that attention seemed to focus.

Which brings us to the final afternoon, on May 7, 1994, when 19,210 Holte Enders stood there for the last time. At the other end of the ground were the Liverpool fans, who had paid their own last respects to the Anfield Kop the week before.

Every person entering the Holte was handed a certificate printed by the EVENING MAIL saying 'I

was there'. A phalanx of former Villa stars walked onto the pitch, towards the Holte End, bringing many a lump to older throats, both on and off the pitch. Many fans just stood silently that afternoon, contemplating not only great games from the past but their own lives too; the fathers who had first taken them to the Holte, old schoolfriends, exams, first jobs, preposterous fashions, wild nights, wet nights, dull days and afternoons of escape from the worries of life  While all around the world changed, for rich or poorer, for better or worse, the Holte was always there.

The Holte's Last Stand will be remembered for many reasons. Dwight Yorke's two goals, in particular. But there was also an acute embarrassment on the day. Villa's compere, a local cabaret singer and devoted Villa fan called Dave Chance, was asked to go onto the pitch and lead the singing. Very fetching he looked too in a light pink suit.

Someone at the club had thought it might be a nice idea to get fans from both teams to sing together the favourite Anfield anthem, *You'll Never Walk Alone,* particularly as the Holte had been known to sing it on occasions, and after all, both sets of fans were mourning the loss of their terraces.

Alas, the idea rebounded. The Holte turned on poor Dave with catcalls and jeers. What should have been one of the proudest moments in his life turned into a nightmare. As he later told the VILLA NEWS AND RECORD, 'If you died a death in front of 300 people at club you could just about handle it. But 45,000 at Villa Park...'

When the final whistle went, most people did not know quite what to do. As Martin Jones recalled, 'Nobody moved. Nearly 20,000 people were just standing there, not prepared to go home. The atmosphere was superb, you could feel it in the air. Many supporters decide to take home souvenirs - exit signs and toilet seats being amongst the favourites - but as I started to make my way out and glanced over my shoulder for one last look at the famous terrace, I heard a voice over the public address system pipe up with "I know you want to take souvenirs home, but could you please bring the iron gates back." I could just imagine two blokes charging down Witton Lane with a 20 foot gate!'

❖ *Villa Park's changing face during the 1990s, as seen from Trinity Road. The old Lions Club became the Club Shop, while the stand's frontage gained two extra bays. Despite the changes the ground's entrance remains one of the most dignified and stately in British football.*

amusement of a critical press. For Tony Eden the pitch problems are a nightmare, especially as they could cost Villa Park the chance of staging one of the FA Cup semi-finals in April (which would lose the club up to £100,000 in revenue).

❖ FEBRUARY 1992
Council planners reject Villa's plans to demolish the Holte Hotel. The pub, which has lain unused since 1990 and has since been bought by the club, is now in an advanced state of disrepair. But although not a listed building, the former Lower Grounds headquarters – which was redeveloped in 1897 when Villa took over the site – does lie within the Aston Hall and Church Conservation Area, and therefore the council feel that it should be saved.

❖ MARCH 1992
Villa prepare for another crunch meeting with the council over their plans for the new Witton Lane Stand. The designs have already been modified to meet some of the residents' objections; for example, by reducing the overall height by three metres, at a cost of around 500 seats. But despite general approval by council leaders, one Aston councillor remains vehemently opposed. This does not bode well since the same man is also deputy chairman of the planning committee.

❖ APRIL 1992
On April 2, Villa breath a huge sigh of relief as the council grant planning permission for the Witton Lane Stand. Work is now expected to start in the summer of 1993, a year later than Villa had hoped but still in time for the August 1994 deadline.
    The huge task of restoring the pitch has been sufficiently successful to ensure that the Portsmouth v Liverpool semi-final does come to Villa Park.

❖ MAY 1992
On May 5 England is confirmed as the host nation for Euro 96, with Villa Park as one of the venues. Two weeks later, after a year of legal disputes with the FOOTBALL LEAGUE and the Players' Union, the Premier League prepares for its launch by announcing a £304 million, five year television deal with BSKYB. The potential revenue from this gives Villa new hope of funding the many ground improvements still to be carried out.
    Villa are voted the First Division's Family Club of the Year, by the building supplies firm JEWSON, which sponsors family-oriented schemes across the League. Among the facilities and events cited in the award are the PANINI family lounge in the North Stand, run by Glyn Walters; the ground's provision for disabled and blind spectators; Villa's highly respected Schools Liaison Scheme, run by Jayne James; Ron Wylie's community programme and the regular involvement of Villa players and staff in community affairs. The £15,000 prize will go towards further improvements. 'Aston Villa treats its community relations not merely as a PR exercise but as a built-in element of everyday life,' commented JEWSON, whose panel of six judges includes former England captain, Bobby Moore.

❖ SUMMER 1992
While Messrs Daley and Platt are on England duty at the European Championships in Sweden, and Mark Bosnich plays for Australia in the Barcelona Olympics, the Trinity Road Stand undergoes a major refurbishment on its 70th anniversary. Overseen by Villa director Peter Ellis (son of the chairman), and designed by the architects HOSSACK BROOME (from Rugby), the main features of the development are as follows:
– To create much needed space, but being careful to retain the style of the facade, two bays are added on either side of the original twin towers. These are finished in red brick, with retro-style gables, windows and metalwork on the balconies.
– A revamped entrance is created, with the central stairway being rebuilt, a new reception area replacing the old turnstile area, and above, a glazed-in walkway beneath the famous Villa mosaic crest.
– Inside the stand, the McGregor Suite is enlarged and revamped, together with a new Museum Club and a Press Lounge on the first floor. The Museum Club, which will be open to fans touring the ground during the week, is to be the new home for a collection of historical photographs and mementoes. On the stand's second floor (which had remained unused and neglected for many years) a restaurant and club lounge are created. The general spectator concourses serving both tiers are also refurbished and brightened up, with new toilets, fast-food outlets and TV monitors.
– On the upper seating tier, the gangways are widened to meet new safety standards, the wooden floors are re-covered, and the original wooden tip-up seats from 1922 are replaced by claret-coloured plastic seats in the general areas. In the centre, upholstered seats with arms are also provided for

members of the Museum Club (168 seats) and Premier Club (237 seats). Unfortunately this requires a number of season-tickets holders in these areas to move to other parts of the stand. The refurbishment and safety measures result in the upper tier's capacity dropping from 5,740 to 5,222. This includes the new club areas, the directors box (143 seats) and an enlarged press box (72 seats).

Originally, the costs of this major redevelopment had been estimated at £1.5 million, but as the builders – from SIR ROBERT MCALPINE– delved deeper into some of the stand's forgotten corners, it soon becomes apparent that the structural problems were much greater than originally anticipated. As a result, the final costs reach £2.4 million. Nevertheless, the finished result is excellent, and ensures that the famous old stand should be good for another 70 years of service.

❖ AUGUST 1992
As Trinity Road regulars survey their upgraded surrounds, on August 19 Villa Park hosts its first ever match in the Premier League, a 1-1 draw against Leeds, watched by 29,151. As well as a new retro-style kit, Villa sport a redesigned club badge, while the new League's men in black are now kitted out in green.

Another break with tradition sees Villa stage all their 1992-93 reserve home fixtures at the Bescot Stadium, Walsall. Villa insist that the move is for one season only, and is to allow the newly restored Villa Park pitch as much recovery time as possible. (In fact the improved atmosphere at the more compact Bescot helps spur Villa on to their first Central League title for 29 years.)

❖ OCTOBER 1992
In recognition of the economic hardships now being faced by many fans, Villa cut admission prices from £9 to £8 for advanced sales of tickets for the Holte End. Admission for the Coca-Cola Cup match v Oxford is also cut to £5 for the Holte End and £8 for seats. A reasonably encouraging crowd of 19,808 takes the bait.

The long tradition of regular Saturday afternoon fixtures is no more. On Monday, October 19 Villa Park hosts its first televised match live on BSkyB. Attractions on the night are giant inflated Sumo wrestlers, dancing girls, fireworks and the Red Devils parachutists. But although the satellite broadcasters are delighted with the crowd response, the deafeningly loud music makes for an uncomfortable night for traditionalists and local residents. The attendance seems unaffected, however, with 30,398 watching a tight 0-0 draw against Blackburn Rovers.

❖ FEBRUARY 1993
Despite Villa's challenge for the Premiership title, a series of disappointing gates prompts the club to offer another price concession for Villa's game v Wimbledon. Tickets bought in advance for the Holte End are reduced to £5, while season ticket holders can bring a friend for just £1. The offer is well

received, resulting in a gate of 34,496 – nearly 13,500 more than attended Wimbledon's previous visit, in the FA Cup a month earlier.

Work begins on the realignment of Witton Lane.

❖ APRIL 1993
Chairman Doug Ellis announces that instead of hiring a single major contractor to build the new Witton Lane Stand, as would be normal practice, Villa are going to manage the entire project in-house and use sub-contractors. This is the first time any club has ever undertaken such a major task, as the trade press notes with particular interest. The construction will be carried out under the supervision of stadium manager Ted Small, Villa's own design consultant Keith Smith, and the quantity surveyors, POOLE STOKES WOODS. By taking this unprecedented step Villa not only hope to save up at least £500,000, but they also hope to retain full control and gain extra flexibility with the project. Saving money on the stand will also mean that Villa can devote more of their £2 million FOOTBALL TRUST allocation to the Holte End. Ted Small comments, 'This is something that I've always fancied doing and reckon I can do as well as anyone. Knowing the ground like I do, after being stadium manager for 13 years, I can get things done the way I know is best for the club, not what someone else thinks.'

It is also revealed that changes have been made to the design. Instead of the goalpost roof structure originally planned, a simpler cantilevered design has been chosen. This is on the recommendation of Rollo Reid, the technical director of a company of steel fabricators called JOHN REID & SONS, of Christchurch, who were recently involved in the remarkably rapid and cost-effective transformation of Notts County's

# The Football Trust

❖ Villa Park would not be the ground it is today without the help of the FOOTBALL TRUST. Since 1990 Villa have received nearly £3.7 million in grants and loans from the Trust, including £64,000 towards the Trinity Road Stand improvements, £135,000 for the North Stand, £774,000 for the Holte End and £1 million for the Doug Ellis Stand. These grants have all been paid from funds channelled through the Trust from the government's reduction in the betting duty on pools.

In addition to this source, the Trust receives funds from the three main pools companies, Littlewoods, Vernons and Zetters, and from Littlewoods' Spot the Ball competition (although these funds have been badly affected by the introduction of the National Lottery). From this source Villa have received £678,000 for various safety and improvement works, £51,000 for CCTV installations and £92,000 for improvements to the club's transport infra-structure (such as the away fans' coach park on Witton Lane).

Finally, the FA and Premier League also contribute to the Trust. From these funds Villa have received an FA contribution of £250,000 for the Doug Ellis Stand and a Premier League grant of £600,000 for the Holte End.

weeks without a break, only grabbing a quick break in late September. 'Sometimes my wife has had to ring and order me home,' he jokes. 'But I can honestly say that it's because I'm enjoying the work so much. I can't wait to get here in the mornings.'

But it is not all plain sailing. As happened when both the Trinity Road and North Stands were built, a spell of rain delays the construction sufficiently for extra labour to be called in for overtime shifts, much to the anger of local residents.

Ted and his team are not the only ones working extra. Normally a hired contractor would deal with all the bills. Doing it in-house means that Doug Ellis has been getting through more chequebooks than Joan Collins on a spending spree!

Meanwhile, season ticket sales have increased by more than 25 per cent, to an unprecedented total of around 10,000, while the club announces a record turnover of £10.1 million. The Annual Report also shows that in order to cover the club's mounting running costs and wages bill, for every £7.37 earned per supporter, another £5.54 has to be raised from commercial and other sources.

❖ AUGUST 1993

As Villa kick-off the new season against QPR on August 14, the imposing new Witton Lane Stand is nearing completion. Already Villa Park looks so much larger and lighter, although no-one anticipated just how small the Holte End would look in relation to its new neighbour.

Work continues on the stand's upper tier, but the 36 mid-level executive boxes are ready, as are the 5,500 new light blue seats on the lower tier. However, because these new seats have been installed on the existing treads, which are much narrower than the modern norm, there are soon complaints from fans that they have less knee-room than before. Villa promise that this will be corrected when the whole lower tier and concourse areas are to be rebuilt, adding that there was no time to achieve this and build the upper levels at the same time. But the complaints linger on all season.

Otherwise, traditionalists suffer a double-whammy on the opening day of the season. Not only do Villa kick-off the new season in a new candy-striped strip, but in line with new Premiership rules, they also sport squad numbers and players' names on the back.

After their title winning season at Bescot, Villa Reserves are ordered back to Villa Park by the Central League, much to the disappointment of groundsman Tony Eden, and also the coaching staff, who rather liked the improved atmosphere at the small ground.

❖ Raising the roof – the new Witton Lane Stand's roof in mid-construction, showing the slender cantilevered trusses. The existing lower tier was re-seated at the same time, but underwent a complete refurbishment a year later.

Meadow Lane (a development which astonished the football world and led to REID's involvement at Watford, Charlton, Spurs, Tranmere and Barnsley).

Rollo Reid explains that the use of the more slender 'nutcracker' cantilevered trusses will reduce the visual impact of the stand roof when viewed from both inside and outside the ground, thus allowing the upper tier to regain a few of the lost seats. It will also allow the roof to be constructed from Witton Lane, whereas the use of a large horizontal goalpost truss would have required one tower to go through the centre of the superbox, and space to be cleared for two huge lifting cranes to be positioned in the corners. In short, the new roof design will be simpler and quicker to execute in the 14 weeks available.

The stand's Witton Lane frontage has also been redesigned in a more sympathetic and attractive manner, using predominantly red brick facings and glazed stairwells and bays.

There is one drawback to the plans, however. Villa have already agreed to pay £50,000 for the 135m x 8m strip needed to extend the stand. But the council now demand that Villa pay the extra costs of moving all the services (wires, pipes and so on) laid under Witton Lane. In addition, not only is the road being realigned but it is also being upgraded from a Category B road to an A road, so that it can withstand usage by heavy vehicles. These road works alone will cost Villa an extra £600,000.

❖ SUMMER 1993

Only hours after Villa's defeat at home to Oldham in May, rules out their chances of catching Manchester United at the top of the Premiership, work begins on removing the 1963 roof of the Witton Lane Stand. Also going ahead is the road realignment and the re-seating of the existing lower tier. Ted Small rises with the lark and goes home in the dark. He works 16

❖ JANUARY 1994

Ted Small and his proud (though exhausted) team celebrate the opening of the Witton Lane's upper tier on New Year's day, for the match against Blackburn Rovers (who rather spoil the occasion by winning 1-0). The game is watched by 40,903 – Villa Park's best gate for four years – and yields record gate receipts for a Villa home game, of £345,359.

The new tier has 4,686 claret-coloured seats, bringing Villa Park's overall capacity up to 46,005. Above the seats is a gantry suspended from the cantilevered roof. This is to accommodate TV cameras and the expected rush of media representatives attending Euro 96. Also incorporated into the gantry is a state-of-the-art stadium control room packed with some £100,000 worth of hi-tech equipment, from where John Hood can now supervise match day operations in ideal conditions.

Spectators note two slight disappointments. Firstly, because the club were only able to extend the new stand by eight metres, rather than the ten they requested, the upper concourse is narrower than would have been preferred. Secondly, the type of cantilevered roof structure employed requires a series of narrow columns along the rear, resulting in restricted views for a handful of seats in the back rows. Otherwise, the views are superb, and Villa Park has never looked finer.

The final bill for the new stand is put at nearly £5 million, of which the FOOTBALL TRUST'S overall contribution is £1.7 million.

Now, here's a question. What do Bob Lord, Jimmy Seed, Stan Cullis, Jack Walker, Don Revie, Jackie Milburn, Sir John Hall, Stanley Rous and Bobby Moore have in common.

Answer? All have had individual stands named after them. Three days after the opening of the Witton Lane Stand, to that list is added the name of Doug Ellis. At a gala celebration of his 70th birthday, at the Metropole Hotel, it is announced that fellow directors John Alderson, Dr David Targett and Peter Ellis, have decided to name the new Witton Lane Stand after their long serving chairman. One of Ellis's all time heroes, Tom Finney (who will also have a stand named after himself, at Preston) is there to present a framed painting of the new stand, while the likes of Nigel Kennedy, Jasper Carrott, Jimmy Greaves, Tommy Docherty, Gary Newbon and Dave Ismay are there to entertain the 400 guests. As the VILLA NEWS AND RECORD later describes the scene, 'For once the Villa chairman was lost for words. "I can only say thank you," he said.'

And as to criticism of the naming of the stand, an editorial in Villa's glossy new magazine, CLARET & BLUE, insists that the decision rightly honours 'a man who has led the club's finances through recessionary minefields and multi-million pound rebuilding demands, to establish Villa among the most secure clubs in Europe.'

Referring to Ellis's reputation as *Deadly Doug*, the magazine adds, 'Any Villa fans who want a *nice* chairman, who never sacks anybody, suffers fools gladly, always gives generously and shuns the limelight, they may have to shop around the Kiddywinks Sunday League to find him.'

❖ FEBRUARY 1994

One stand completed, one more to go. With only eight months to go before the all-seater deadline, planning is already advanced for the Holte End. It now transpires that rather than simply install seats

onto the existing terracing, the club now intends to build a completely new stand. There are two main reasons.

Firstly, the existing rake, or angle of the terrace has been found to be too shallow for seating. To re-profile it in order to give everyone a decent view would mean raising the rear sections, which in turn would mean jacking up the roof. Even then the result would not be ideal since seats at the back would still be a long distance from the pitch, and the newly extended roof has four obtrusive columns blocking views.

Secondly, the Holte End was built over fifty years ago, at a time when much less was known about crowd circulation and little effort was put into facilities for standing spectators. To invest heavily in an old and – to be blunt – rather basic structure would therefore not be in the long term interests of either the club or its supporters. All the same, the terrace's demolition means that the roof erected in 1990 becomes the most shortest major structure in the history of British football grounds.

❖ MARCH 1994

Villa end Manchester United's dream of a treble by winning 3-1 at Wembley in the Coca-Cola Cup Final as the council sits down to consider the club's planning application for the new Holte End.

This time there are only two written objections from local residents, and Villa agree to install extra translucent panelling to reduce the potential loss of light. But certain local councillors remain outwardly hostile towards the club. One describes Villa's plans as 'cheap and tatty.'

Nevertheless, the council seem minded to grant approval, on condition that Villa restore the dilapidated Holte Hotel. The go-ahead then follows in April.

❖ MAY 1994

It has been called the Church End, the City End and the Holte Hotel End. But to the modern generation it has always been the Holte End, or even just the Holte, plain and simple.

❖ *Tunnel vision – in line with UEFA directives, a retractable tunnel cover was added for Eur 96.*

Reshaped in 1914, extended 1939-40, covered in 1962 and re-roofed in 1990, the Holte End faces its last stand on May 7, for Villa's final home game of the season v Liverpool.

The week before the Anfield Kop had bowed out. Gone already are Arsenal's North Bank and Manchester United's Stretford End. But the Holte remained the largest of them all, right to the very end, with its final capacity of 19,210.

Because of ground developments across the country, the crowd of 45,347 is a Premier League record. Liverpool take the lead, but two second half goals by Dwight Yorke, appropriately enough in front of the Holte End, seals an emotional victory.

So ends the terrace era at Villa Park. From next season onwards the only people allowed to stand at the ground will be the managers and coaches in their new, open-plan dug-out, complete with crush barrier at the front!

### ❖ SUMMER 1994

While Villa's Irish quartet of Houghton, McGrath, Staunton and Townsend put on a gallant display in the USA World Cup, the Holte End is reduced to rubble. Amongst this rubble are found all kinds of Victorian beer bottles from local breweries. Must be the ones missed by Jack Watts when he was a kid!

In place of the giant earth and concrete mound rises up a new two tier stand, whose lower tier is scheduled for a phased opening starting in August.

One of the contract workers is a Birmingham City supporter. As readers may know, City supporters were always told that when Birmingham took over St Andrew's in 1906 a gypsy placed a curse on the ground. Any excuse! In an attempt to transfer the curse, rumour has it that the Blues fan takes a piece

of rubble from the St Andrew's Kop, which is also being redeveloped, and drops it into a cement mixer at Villa Park. As Sheryl Crow sings, *Well if it makes you happy...*'

### ❖ AUGUST 1994

Lord Justice Taylor's all-seater deadline comes and goes with barely a murmur. (Of the 41 clubs subject to the deadline, only six are granted an extension.) Around 3,000 seats on the new Holte End's lower tier are ready for occupation – giving Villa a temporary capacity of around 28,800 – as Villa Park stages its first ever game without standing spectators on August 24. A 1-1 draw v Southampton is watched by 24,179.

At the club's AGM at the Sports and Leisure Centre, yet another record turnover is announced, this time of £13 million.

### ❖ SEPTEMBER 1994

An extra 2,000 Holte End seats are made available to cater for a 30,533 sell-out crowd for Villa's nail-biting victory on penalties against Inter Milan in the UEFA Cup. But Villa are fined £12,000 by UEFA after fans invade the pitch to celebrate the winning penalty. Doug Ellis warns supporters that their actions could seriously jeopardise the club's European hopes, while John Hood reminds one and all that CCTV cameras can easily identify the culprits.

### ❖ NOVEMBER 1994

Thirty eight fans ignore the warnings and invade the pitch at the end of Villa's UEFA Cup tie against Trabzonspor, as worries mount that the unsavoury behaviour of a small minority of Villa fans in the new all-seated set-up is giving the club an unwanted reputation. Whatever happened to the easy-going, good natured Brummie welcome for which Villa Park was once well known?

There is at least a warm welcome for two familiar

faces who form the new managerial team, Brian Little and John Gregory (later to be joined by former team-mate Allan Evans).

Villa reserves are back at Bescot for the five month winter period.

❖ DECEMBER 1994

Only seven months after the Holte End's last stand, the new Holte End Stand is fully occupied for the first time, with both tiers now in use. Any doubts that former Holte Enders might have harboured after the demolition of their favourite terrace, or even during the awkward transition period since August, are swept away as the full splendour of the stand is now seen. With its roof line now matching that of the Doug Ellis and North Stands, the new Holte End transforms Villa Park from a football ground into a super-stadium.

The upper tier of claret-coloured seats holds 5,751, while the lower level holds 7,750, with claret seats spelling out 'The Holte End' amid a sea of light blue. With 13,501 seats overall this makes the new Holte the largest single end stand in British football, and raises Villa Park's overall capacity to 40,310.

The FOOTBALL TRUST have contributed £600,000 towards the £5.2 million costs, which means that Villa have now used up their £2 million grant allocation. However, the club also take advantage of a new Trust scheme for interest-free loans, borrowing £300,000, repayable over a three year period.

Villa celebrate the stand's first full usage with a 3-0 win against Chelsea on December 28, watched by 32,901.

Best of all, Villa's third goal is a thumping header at the Holte End, scored by new signing Ian Taylor, a Brummie who first stood on the terrace as a 12-year-old, before he went to play for Moor Green, Port Vale and Sheffield Wednesday. Not since Gary Shaw has a former Holte Ender received such a huge, or such a heartfelt cheer.

❖ FEBRUARY 1995

In an attempt to root out or reform the few misbehaving fans still attending, Villa join their fellow West Midland clubs in a new Club Watch scheme. However, the situation is not all bad. John Hood's safety team and stewards are now so much in control that for the game against Wimbledon on February 11 there is not a single uniformed policeman on duty inside Villa Park. Did anyone notice? Maybe Villa should try this more often, as Villa notch up a handsome 7-1 win in front of 23,982 fans and zero bobbies.

❖ APRIL 1995

Villa Park's tunnel loses the mesh added for the 1966 World Cup and gains a continental-style white cover, which folds out when the players enter or leave the pitch, and then retracts during the game in order to avoid restricting views.

❖ SUMMER 1995

Another hectic summer for Ted Small, Keith Smith and the team as work begins on stripping out the entire lower tier of the Doug Ellis Stand in a £971,000 refit.

All the new seats are put to one side, the old concrete raker beams are replaced with ones of more generous dimensions, and the circulation routes and concourses are completely remodelled. One unexpected hitch is the discovery of blue asbestos, a material used for fireproofing steelwork, which is thought to date back to the old stand's redevelopment for the 1966 World Cup.

While this work continues, on June 4 the ground plays host to Brazil v Sweden in the Umbro Cup, a rehearsal for Euro 96. Then on July 23, Rod Stewart performs a concert in the round in front of 35,000 adoring, if noticeably over-age rock and rollers. Speaking of which, young Steve Stride is invited to join the board after 23 years on the staff.

❖ *The demolition of the Holte End exposed Villa Park in a quite dramatic fashion. Amon the onlookers was John Harris.*

*'When they were pulling down the old Holte End I thought I'd have a wander down, see what was happening, only to find there was already a crowd of 20 or 30 people just standing there, in a little knot, whereas I assumed I'd be the only one mad enough to go and look. The demolition crew were just starting to chip off the top layers of bricks. This poor guy, every time he reached the bottom of his ladder somebody would go up to him and ask, "Could I have that brick please?" I went back later in the week and the word must have got around by then because there was a constant flow of people balancing bricks in either hand. Some people were almost screaming for bits to take away. At that time the demolition guys were just giving the bricks away, but later Villa were selling tham at £25 each. I took my brick home, put it on display with a scarf round it. I know other people who mounted theirs on plaques, with brass inscriptions and everything, and one guy whose made display in his back garden.'*

❖ **AUGUST 1995**

The new season starts with a thrilling 3-1 victory over Manchester United, but with the Doug Ellis Stand's lower tier yet to be completed. The capacity is thus temporarily restricted to around 35,100.

The game's other significance is that for the first time in 25 years popular photographer Terry Weir is not on duty. Weir has been injured in a freak road accident and has been forced to retire early, at the age of 59. His familiar presence on the touchline, not to mention his bottomless bag of wine gums, will be sorely missed.

Another break with tradition is that after 71 years of hiring outside caterers, the club follows the growing trend in football by launching its own, in-house Aston Villa Catering service.

But the most significant development of the month is the £600,000 purchase of nearly four acres of land between the North Stand and Witton Road, from BRITISH TELECOM. 'As a farmer's boy,' Doug Ellis tells the VILLA NEWS AND RECORD, 'I always believed that if land became available adjacent to my own farm, I had to buy.' Apparently the chairman had been waiting twelve years to purchase the land, which once formed part of the original Lower Grounds and, as recounted in CHAPTER 7, served as the Territorial Army's drill ground until the 1940s. The GPO took it over after the Second World War. Villa will now convert the office building partly into a new souvenir superstore, and partly into offices for various branches of the club. The plans are being supervised by a new member of staff, the well-known Villa fan and entertainer, Dave Ismay, who is now heading the Special Projects department.

❖ **SEPTEMBER 1995**

Villa Park's first open day since 1988 attracts an unexpectedly massive response when nearly 20,000 fans turn up for a chance to look behind the scenes and meet the players.

❖ **OCTOBER 1995**

The first 1,000 seats on the Doug Ellis Stand's lower tier are brought into use.

Large steel frames go up in two corners of the ground, in readiness for Villa's entry to the new age of video screen technology. Arsenal, Spurs and Wolves are already on air. Villa have chosen to order two 'Superscreen Videowalls' from local company CD Interactive. But although the big switch-on is scheduled for December, owing to circumstances beyond Villa's control the screens never arrive and for almost the next two years Villa Park is without any scoreboards.

❖ **NOVEMBER 1995**

A major milestone in Villa's implementation of the Taylor Report is reached when the new lower tier of the Doug Ellis Stand comes into full use for the near sell-out game against Newcastle on November 18. The capacity of the tier has been reduced from 5,711 to 4,161, but each seat now has more leg room – meeting new minimum standards – and the sightlines have been improved with a slightly steeper rake. The vomitories have also been completely rearranged for smoother circulation, and lead to a whole range of improved concourse facilities. Villa Park's new capacity is 39,339, although 50 seats in the Witton Lane corner of the Holte End's lower tier cannot now be used because the new lower deck on the Doug Ellis Stand creates obstructed views.

The completion of the work comes just in time. Villa's improved form and the increasing popularity of the Premiership mean that sell-out crowds are now becoming regular events. Is it time to get back to the drawing board and start planning some new extensions? Already Ted Small and Rollo Reid are plotting to put a column free roof over the Trinity Road Stand. Tragically, they will not be joined in this work by designer Keith Smith, who suffers a fatal heart attack in September 1996. However, Keith does live to see his last major project finish in time for the Christmas rush, and that is the new souvenir superstore, the Villa Village. So popular is the new store that its turnover is expected to top £3 million in its first year.

❖ **SUMMER 1996**

Villa end the season in 4th place, having reached the FA Cup semi-final and won the Coca-Cola League Cup for the fifth time (after beating Leeds 3-0 in March). Despite the expenditure of some £18.5 million on ground improvements since the Taylor Report, and over £20 million on players in just the last two years, Villa's finances are rosier than ever. Turnover has reached £18.8 million, while the income from commercial, merchandising and travel sources is up to £9.8 million.

Even more remarkably, Villa Park faces one of its quietest summers for years. All the staff need plan for are the European Championships, in June.

Otherwise, Ted Small hardly knows what to do with himself!

*❖ As Villa Park's stands have become larger and taller, regular pitch replacement has become a fact of life. The Doug Ellis Stand, for example, is more than twice the height of its predecessor. The new pitch (below) laid in 1977 was the third since 1977.*

# The new Holte End Stand

❖ After the old Holte was cleared and the barriers removed – some to be re-installed at Wigan's Springfield Park – the new Holte End rose up remarkably quickly. It was built by the construction firm of MOWLEM, in conjunction with Ted Small, Villa's own in-house designer Keith Smith, Rollo Reid (who also worked on the Doug Ellis Stand) and the firm of RT JAMES, Consulting Engineers. The quantity surveyors were POOLE STOKES WOODS.

The roof is a goalpost structure (mirroring the North Stand) but with the steelwork of the towers left exposed, so as to let as much light through as possible. Rather than paint the steelwork (as has been done, for example, at Molineux and the Hawthorns), the surfaces have been galvanised, in order to reduce maintenance costs.

Although it is very difficult to tell, in section both the upper and lower tiers are slightly curved, in a parabola. This is to ensure that good sightlines are achieved from every row. The rearmost row of the upper tier is actually four metres nearer to the goal-line than the back of the old terrace, but is five metres higher.

Internally the stand offers acres of concourse space on three levels, with the added option of a mid-tier lounge (currently hidden behind metal shutters at the back of the lower tier). But the centrepiece is the ground floor Holte Suite, which opened its doors in August 1997 (see next chapter).

As to the design of the stand's frontage, this needs little explanation, since it is so unashamedly based upon the Trinity Road Stand. True, plastic and neon signs have taken the place of mosaic, and the window details are considerably plainer. But the pediments, dutch gables and sweeping stairways are wholly Trinity, as it were, and form as imposing an entrance as any to be found in British football.

But perhaps the stand's greatest facet is that despite being all-seated, its design seems to have lifted the atmosphere at Villa Park, rather than dampened it, as has happened at several other newly converted grounds. The old Holte was always a massive presence. The new one looks positively inspirational, and more importantly, according to its regulars, feels that way too.

❖ Thirty years after Villa Park played host to the World Cup, the European Championships descended upon Birmingham like an international street carnival dedicated to peace, harmony and the combined healing powers of face paint and lager. Some 7,000 Dutch came with their orange wigs and regalia. The Scots sported kilts and a *Braveheart* bravura. Even the staid Swiss managed to amaze with their lederhosen and large cowbells. Then there were times when you could not tell who came from where as orange warriors in kilts cavorted gleefully in Victoria and Centenary Squares.

On the day of the Holland v Scotland game, hundreds of fans from both nations marched together to Villa Park from the official campsite on Moor Lane, behind a lone Scottish piper. At the

ground, two Dutch supporters' bands – called the *Orange Hooters* and *Half-a-Pint-of-Lager* – entertained the crowds both inside and outside. Trumpeter Harry Verdonk said, 'It's simple, if the fans sing they cannot fight.'

But in truth no-one was in the mood for trouble, even those who managed to drink the local off-licenses dry. Such a contrast with the last Tartan Invasion, 20 years earlier, when drunken Rangers fans had rampaged through the city on the day of a friendly with Villa.

Unlike the 1966 World Cup, very little work was needed to prepare Villa Park for the tournament, since so much had already been achieved in meeting the Taylor deadline. Nevertheless, Euro 96 banners and flags lent the ground a wonderfully festive appearance, set off by the exuberant displays of the fans themselves. There were times when, bathed in the warm sun, or looking up at the festooned balcony of the Holte End, one might almost have been in Spain or Italy, so vibrant and celebratory did Villa Park seem. Many a Villa fan asked, 'Why can't it be like this every week?'

Yet for the visitors it was just the same. Both Dutch and Swiss visitors sang the praises of Villa Park; its history, its setting, its intimate atmosphere, its friendly policeman with their funny helmets, its lack of fences. As many a letter of thanks and praise sent to the club in later weeks demonstrated, for continental fans the FA's tournament theme of *Football Comes Home* was no mere slogan.

Apart staging the games, Villa's staff essentially managed them too. Safety Officer John Hood had on duty 132 club Villa stewards, reinforced by 57 others from the Blues, Albion and Wolves. The visiting teams also brought their own stewards, which prompted one wag to observe that the Dutch contingent spoke better English than the natives!

'It was a party,' recalled John Hood. 'A carnival atmosphere. I wish all our supporters could come and enjoy themselves like that. Wouldn't that be wonderful?'

No doubt the Birmingham Chamber of Commerce would heartily concur. Euro 96 was said to have been worth £21 million to the local economy in terms of tourism and extra spending.

❖ *European Championship matches at Villa Park*

| June 11 | Holland 0 | Scotland 0 | (34,363) |
|---------|-----------|------------|----------|
| June 13 | Holland 2 | Switzerland 0 | (36,800) |
| June 18 | Scotland 1 | Switzerland 0 | (34,926) |
| June 23 | Portugal 0 | Czech Republic 1 | (26,832) |

# Major matches at Villa Park

❖ Villa Park has staged matches at almost every major domestic and international level. Here are the most important games:

❖ FULL INTERNATIONALS:

April 8, 1899
**England 2, Scotland 1**
*25,590*
Jimmy Crabtree and Charlie Athersmith both play for England, Athersmith setting up Settle for England's winning goal.

May 3, 1902
**England 2, Scotland 2**
*15,000*
Billy George wins his third cap and Albert Wilkes his fifth, though neither would play for England again. A third Villa player, Robert Templeton, won his first cap for Scotland, and scored after 4 minutes. Wilkes made it 2-2 in the second half.

April 8, 1922
**England 0, Scotland 1**
*33,646*
Three Villa players are in the England line-up: Dickie York (winning his first cap), Frank Moss (his second), and Billy Walker (fourth). Another familiar face was former Villa player Joe Pearson, who was one of the linesmen.

February 3, 1945
**England 3, Scotland 2**
*65,780*
Victory International.

10 November, 1948
**England 1, Wales 0**
*67,770*
Trevor Ford won his sixth cap for Wales.

November 14, 1951
**England 2, Northern Ireland 0**
*57,889*
Danny Blanchflower was an Irish reserve.

November 26, 1958
**England 2, Wales 2**
*41,581*
Villa's Jackie Sewell played for England, along with Peter Broadbent, who scored both goals and later signed for Villa, and Birmingham's Gil Merrick, who was making his international debut. Appearing for Wales for the first time was Villa's Vic Crowe. He lined up with Phil Woosnam, who signed for Villa four years later.

June 4, 1995
**Brazil 1, Sweden 0**
*20,131*
This was part of the four team Umbro Cup, staged partly as a rehearsal for Euro 96.

❖ INTER-LEAGUE:

April 9, 1898
**Football League 1, Scottish League 2**
*22,000*

February 29, 1908
**Football League 2, Scottish League 0**
*11,000*
Villa winger Albert Hall selected for the hosts.

November 7, 1928
**Football League 2, Scottish League 1**
*25,000*
Tom Smart plays for the League.

March 21, 1962
**Football League 3, Scottish League 4**
*18,459*

❖ FA CUP SEMI-FINALS
Villa Park has staged more FA Cup semi-finals than any other English ground. It was also selected as a replay venue for the 1907 and 1938 Finals, but in both cases was not needed. The letters W and L in brackets denotes whether the winners of the Villa Park semi-final went on to win the Final.

April 8, 1901
**Tottenham Hotspur 4, W. B. Albion 0** (W)
*34,979*

March 21, 1903
**Derby County 3, Millwall 0** (L)
*40,500*

March 31, 1906
**Everton 2, Liverpool 0** (W)
*37,000*

March 27, 1915
**Chelsea 2, Everton 0** (L)
*22,000*

March 26, 1930, Replay
**Arsenal 1, Hull City 0** (W)
*46,200*

March 12, 1932
**Arsenal 1, Manchester City 0** (L)
*50,377*

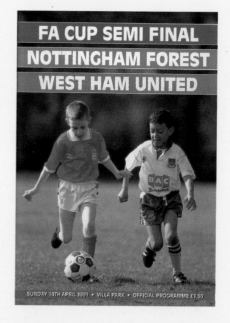

March 16, 1935
**Burnley 0, Sheffield Wednesday 3** (W)
*56,625*

March 23, 1946
**Bolton Wanderers 0, Charlton Ath. 2** (L)
*69,500*
Record receipts for any match at Villa Park, £18,011.

March 13, 1948
**Blackpool 3, Tottenham Hotspur 1** (L)
*70,687*
Record receipts for any match at Villa Park, £18,962

March 21, 1953
**Blackpool 2, Tottenham Hotspur 1** (W)
*68,221*
Record receipts for Villa Park and for any English football match other than Wembley, £20,084.

March 27, 1954
**Port Vale 1, West Bromwich Albion 2** (W)
*68,221*

March 26, 1955
**Manchester City 1, Sunderland 0** (L)
*58,498*

March 17, 1956
**Manchester City 1, Tottenham 0** (W)
*69,788*

March 22, 1958
**Fulham 2, Manchester United 2** (L)
*69,745*

March 18, 1961
**Burnley 0, Tottenham 3** (W)
*69,968*

March 31, 1962
**Burnley 1, Fulham 1** (L)
*59,989*

April 27, 1963
**Manchester United 1, Southampton 0** (W)
*68,312*

March 14, 1964
**Preston 2, Swansea Town 1** (L)
*45,354*

March 27, 1965
**Chelsea 0, Liverpool 2** (W)
*67,686*

April 23, 1966
**Chelsea 0, Sheffield Wednesday 2** (L)
*61,321*

April 29, 1967
**Chelsea 1, Leeds United 0** (L)
*62,378*

April 27, 1968
**Birmingham City 0, W. B. Albion 2** (W)
*60,831*
Record receipts for any Villa Park game other
than World Cup, £37,028.

March 22, 1969
**Everton 0, Manchester City 1** (W)
*63,025*

March 23, 1970, Replay
**Leeds United 0, Manchester United 0** (L)
*62,492*

March 31, 1971, Replay
**Arsenal 2, Stoke City 0** (W)
*62,388*

April 15, 1972
**Arsenal 1, Stoke City 1** (L)
*56,576*

April 3, 1974, Replay
**Leicester City 1, Liverpool 3** (W)
*55,619*

April 5, 1975
**Ipswich Town 0, West Ham United 0**
*57,835* (W after replay)

March 31, 1979
**Arsenal 2, Wolves 0** (W)
*46,244*

April 12, 1980
**West Ham 1, Everton 1** (W after replay)
*47,685*

April 16, 1980, Replay
**Liverpool 1, Arsenal 1**
*40,679*

April 28, 1980, 2nd Replay
**Liverpool 1, Arsenal 1**
*42,975*

April 11, 1981
**Ipswich Town 0, Manchester City 1** (L)
*46,537*

April 3, 1982
**Tottenham 2, Leicester City 0** (W)
*46,606*

April 16, 1983
**Arsenal 1, Manchester United 2** (W)
*46,535*

April 14, 1984
**Plymouth Argyle 0, Watford 1** (L)
*43,858*

April 13, 1985
**Luton Town 1, Everton 2** (L)
*45,289*

April 5, 1986
**Everton 2, Sheffield Wednesday 1** (L)
*47,711*

April 11, 1987
**Tottenham 4, Watford 1** (L)
*46,161*

April 15, 1989
**Everton 1, Norwich City 0** (L)
*46,553*
Day of the Hillsborough disaster.

April 8, 1990
**Crystal Palace 4, Liverpool 3** (L)
*38,389*

April 14, 1991
**Nottingham Forest 4, West Ham Utd 0** (L)
*40,041*

April 13, 1992, Replay
**Portsmouth 0, Liverpool 0** (1-3 pens), (W)
*40,077*
First FA Cup semi-final settled on penalties.

April 9, 1995
**Crystal Palace 2, Manchester United 2**
*38,256*

April 12, 1995, Replay
**Crystal Palace 0, Manchester United 2** (L)
*17,987*

March 31, 1996
**Chelsea 1, Manchester United 2** (W)
*38,421*

❖ By an extraordinary coincidence, every
year between 1983 and 1995 the semi-finals
at Villa Park saw the involvement of at least
one or more players in either of the
competing teams who had either played for
Villa or would sign for them later. The full
list is: 1983, Paul McGrath (Manchester
United); 1984, Geoff Crudgington
(Plymouth), Nigel Callaghan (Watford);
1985, Les Sealey, Steve Foster, Garry Parker
(Luton), Derek Mountfield, Andy Gray
(Everton); 1986, Derek Mountfield, Adrian
Heath, Kevin Richardson (Everton), Gary
Shelton, Garry Thompson (Sheffield
Wednesday); 1987, Steve Hodge
(Tottenham), Kevin Richardson, Steve Sims
(Watford); 1989, Andy Townsend
(Norwich); 1990, Andy Gray (Crystal
Palace), Steve McMahon, Ray Houghton,
Steve Staunton (Liverpool); 1991, Gary
Charles, Garry Parker (Nottm Forest); 1992,
Warren Aspinall, Guy Whittingham
(Portsmouth), Mark Walters, Dean Saunders
(Liverpool); 1995, Ray Houghton, Gareth
Southgate (Crystal Palace), Brian McClair
(Manchester Utd).
So the next time Villa Park hosts a semi-
final, pay close attention to the line-ups. Even
if there are no ex-Villa men playing, the
chances are, one or two of the players might
yet end up on the Villa's books.

FOOTBALL LEAGUE CUP FINAL

April 6, 1981, Replay
**Liverpool v West Ham United** (2-1)
*36,693*

❖ *Alan Hansen and Kenny Dalglish in familiar company
– with silverware that is, after Liverpool's 2-1 victory over
West Ham in the replayed League Cup Final at Villa Park
in April 1981. Twelve months earlier the ground had
staged three FA Cup semi-finals (including two replays
involving Liverpool) within a two week period. No other
ground has staged so many semis.*

# Chapter 16

# Villa Park, today and tomorrow

in which we conclude our tale ❖

Villa Park, the business park, 1897 and 1997 ❖

who's who at the ground ❖

we meet the staff, directors and matchday personnel ❖

the Centenary celebrations ❖

raising the roof on Trinity Road ❖

Villa Park in the 21st century ❖

VILLA PARK IN 1997 IS THE HUB OF A multi-million pound business. But it is also a dream factory. Take away the dream, and the business would collapse within weeks. But take away the business, and the dream would fade pretty rapidly too.

Obvious, perhaps, but no less true in 1997 than it was a century ago. All that has changed are the figures and the scale.

❖ In 1897, playing staff apart, Villa employed a full time staff of no more than four people. There were also five directors, all of whom were unpaid. In 1997, there were 84 full-time staff, and of the club's seven directors, three filled executive posts (including the chairman).

❖ At its launch as a limited company in 1896, Aston Villa FC Ltd was valued at £10,000. When the company was re-organised in 1969 this total rose to £215,000. Shortly before its launch on the Stock Exchange in May 1997, Aston Villa plc was valued at £125 million.

❖ In 1897 Villa were the tenants of a brewery, renting nearly seven acres for £300 a year. In 1997 the club owned the freehold of nearly 47 acres, including the 15.6 acres of the Villa Park site, the coach park on Witton Lane, 10.4 acres at the Serpentine car park and 20 acres at Bodymoor Heath.

❖ In Villa's first season at Villa Park, around 92 per cent of Villa's income derived from gate receipts and season ticket sales. In 1995-96 the proportion was nearer 42 per cent. In 1897 Villa had approximately 250 season ticket holders. In 1997 they had 20,000.

❖ In 1897-98 Villa's turnover was just over £11,000, which, based on the retail price index, would today be worth approximately £575,000. Yet in 1995-96 Villa's turnover was just over £18.8 million. That does not make Villa 32 times richer today than 100 years ago, however.

❖ The cost of ground improvements has not actually increased hugely as a proportion of Villa's income, although in recent years, of course, there has been a significant rush of expenditure. Rather, the growing scale of players' wages has forced the club to seek forms of revenue other than simple gate receipts. To illustrate this point, in 1897-98 a top Villa player would be paid £4 per week. On the basis of one home match per fortnight, therefore, it needed 640 adults to pay for a place on the terraces (at 3d each) in order to cover his wages for that two week period. In 1996-97 the figure was nearer 1,800 adults (that is, with each paying £13 to sit on the Holte End lower tier, after deducting VAT). Put another way, and a fairly blunt way at that, in the modern age the *entire* income from one supporter's season ticket is sufficient to finance only *a few hours* of just one day in the working life of just *one* senior player. A sobering thought, is it not?

❖ Another way of illustrating the gulf between now and then is that in 1897 the top transfer fee Villa had paid was £350 (for Fred Wheldon from Small Heath). This figure represented just over 3 cent of the club's total gate receipts for the season. In 1997 the £4 million paid for Villa's record signing, Sasa Curcic, swallowed up just over 50 per cent.

Small wonder therefore that Villa Park nowadays seldom sleeps, or that its staff can never afford to take things easy, even with all the extra cash pouring in from the likes of BSkyB, and Carling (sponsors of the Premier League). Merely covering the club's running costs is tough enough. But yielding that vital extra cash which aims – though hardly guarantees – to bring success, is a gargantuan task.

Given the constant pressure, it may not be a surprise to learn that a good number of the men and women who work at Villa Park tick are dyed-in-the-wool Villa fans, supporters of the club long before they went on to the payroll. What may be more surprising is how many of them have worked for Villa for periods of over ten, fifteen or even twenty years. For all his reputation as 'Deadly' Doug, the chairman seems to preside over a remarkably loyal and long-serving workforce. It sounds like an awful cliche, but is true nevertheless. Aston Villa really do have two teams, one on the field and one off it.

So who are these men and women who make Villa Park tick while the players are busy training at Bodymoor Heath, and what exactly do they all do?

We start in the club's main reception, in the North Stand, where we are most likely to be greeted by either Marie Priest or Margaret Ward. Their ability to remember names, faces and voices (over the constantly ringing telephones), while remaining cheerful at all times, is quite awesome. Marie started as a 17-year-old office junior in 1980. Margaret joined Villa in 1987. On occasions their place might be taken by another Villa veteran, Pam Bridgewater, who started in the Travel Club but now works mostly in the upstairs offices as part of the overall administration team.

Next door to the reception is the recently extended ticket office. This is the domain of Ray Fairfax, whom some readers may remember as a full back with West Bromwich and Northampton in the 1960s. After hanging up his boots, Smethwick-born Ray returned to the Hawthorns, rose to become assistant to secretary Alan Everiss, then later moved to Port Vale as secretary. When he took over Villa's ticket operation in 1988 there were just two full-timers and a relatively basic computerised system. Nowadays there are eight full-time staff, including Kim Graham, Lee Preece, Keith Brown, Steve McDermott and Pauline Collins, plus a number of assistants who work on match days. There are also two match-day satellite ticket offices, on Trinity Road and at the back of the Holte Hotel.

Even then it is still an uphill task for the staff to meet the demand, particularly for prestige games. For this reason, Villa now make tickets available for sale by telephone and credit cards through the 24-hour

❖ Villa Park in 1996 – more roofs and more space than ever before, but all the familiar landmarks, too; Aston Park in the foreground and the 1837 railway line still cutting through Witton. Notice how the stand roofs feature translucent panels, to increase the flow of light.

TICKETMASTER agency. This accounts for around nine per cent of all sales.

Villa Park's own computerised system, which cost £80,000, was supplied by a company called SYNCHRO SYSTEMS, which serves 48 clubs in Britain (and has also ticketed such events as Euro 96 and the Rugby World Cup).

In the not-so-old days, of course, the majority of fans paid for admission by cash at the turnstiles, whereas all-seater stadiums have meant all-ticket games, requiring both supporters and the club to plan much further ahead than was once necessary. In addition, more and more fans prefer to receive their tickets by post, rather than having to queue in person.

Another departure from the past is that nowadays all tickets are printed on the premises, as and when needed (rather than in pre-printed books). After dealing with some 20,000 season ticket sales during the summer, this means that in a typical year Fairfax and his team have to sell, print and distribute over 300,000 individual tickets. In season 1996-97 they handled no fewer than seven complete sell-outs.

Inevitably, everyone wants to be friends with the

ticket office staff. But beware! Flattery or bribery is futile, and that's official. Fair play is the Fairfax creed, as one would only expect of such an incredibly wise, handsome and terrifically good guy..!

Immediately above the main ticket office is the sumptuously fitted first floor office of the chairman, Doug Ellis, next door to which are the offices of his personal assistant, Marion Stringer. After working for the chairman in his other companies for four years, Marion moved to Villa when her boss resumed the chairmanship of the club in 1982. Not that she needed much persuading, having been a Witton Ender back in the days of Gerry Hitchens. Also working for the chairman is secretary Sharon Barnhurst.

Further along the corridor is Brian Little's secretary, Debbie Ritchie, at Villa since 1978, and Pam Silk, who arrived at Villa Park a year earlier. Her immediate boss is club secretary and now director, Steve Stride.

Steve was the Castle Bromwich schoolboy whose reward for passing the 11-plus was a season ticket for the 1962-63 season. Though he can scarcely believe it himself, he has now worked at Villa Park for a

The Corner Flag restaurant (above) is one of countless building projects undertaken by Villa's indefatigable stadium manager, Ted Small (below). No one has worked harder to make Villa Park the stadium it is today.

quarter of a century, and all being well could come close to the long serving records of his predecessors, George Ramsay (secretary for 42 years) and Fred Archer (at the club for 49 years).

Following in a long line of unsung, assistant secretaries, going back to Wallie Strange and Len Latham, is Arthur Moseley. Originally from Bournville, since joining Villa in 1978 and being appointed as Steve Stride's assistant the following year, Arthur has fulfiled a number of vital administrative roles at the club, not least on match days. In the pre-Taylor 1980s Arthur was in charge of Villa's pioneering match-day control centre in the North Stand. Nowadays he is as busy as ever, being responsible, among many duties, for the match officials and media. He rarely sees more than the final 15 minutes of any home match.

Another department which gains little of the limelight but performs a vital role is that of the accountants, headed by Phil Longmore (from Kidderminster, on the staff for 13 years) and Birmingham-born Mark McGuinness, whose total service to Villa adds up to 21 years. Phil and Mark are assisted by Maxine Taylor, Becky Davis, Mary Lenehan and Samantha Gregory.

Moving further around the first floor are the offices of safety officer John Hood (of whom more later) and·Cyril Smith, the part-time registrar. A retired accountant, Cyril took over from the late Bert Sisk a few years ago, and had the important task of keeping track of and verifying all the club's thousands of shares in the run-up to the May 1997 flotation.

Then comes the offices of the Commercial Department. This consists of Abdul Rashid, Sharon McCullagh, Gary Birch, Sarah Jones, Karen Salsbury, Anne-Marie Newey, Nazia Razaq and Joanne Lane. Since Abdul, the former ball-boy, was appointed as commercial manager in 1988, the department has

brought in over £30 million, including £6.8 million in 1995-96 alone (and that does not include a further £3 million from merchandising and travel income). Second only to match receipts, the Commercial Department is Villa Park's main source of income.

Now we move up to the second floor of the North Stand. This consists of the Centenary Suite, Executive Suite, and in the Trinity Road corner, the Board Room (which is also used for corporate hospitality on match days). Just outside this room, in the corridor, stands an imposing, if rather overbearing mahogany sideboard, capped by a carved lion – the last surviving relic from the old offices and thought to date back to 1897. (It can be seen in the photograph of George Ramsay on page 79.)

Up on the third floor of the North Stand, which was only recently in-filled for use, is the new McDONALDS Family Room. This holds up to 200 and is run by Dave Wallis, who started the original family enclosure in the Trinity Road Stand back in 1985 (on the suggestion of former commercial manager Tony Stephens). On paper Dave seems an unlikely sort of person to spend matchdays in the company of hundreds of excitable junior Villans, given his career as a detective in the Commercial Fraud Squad (for whom he recently spent a few years fighting fraud in Hong Kong). But apart from being a lifelong Villa fan, Wallis is also a qualified youth leader with a real commitment to family schemes in football – a commitment which has led to him sharing his knowledge and ideas with clubs all over the country.

Next to the family room are the offices of Villa's newest department, Aston Villa Catering services. Formed in June 1996 after 72 years of outside catering at the club, the department has two responsibilities. On the executive side, Pam Wincott oversees the provision of up to 2,400 meals on every match day in the ground's 17 different dining and hospitality areas (such as the McGregor Suite, Museum Club, Premier Lounge and Carvery, Corner Flag Restaurant, Banqueting Suite and Holte Suite), while Alma Andrews and Linda Broadhead ensure that all catering outlets in the general spectator concourses are running smoothly.

But the department does not just cater for match days. In common with an increasing number of football grounds, Villa Park is now open seven days a week for a whole range of lunches, dinners, banquets and conferences, which means that the club's catering service has to compete with all the top hotel and restaurant facilities in the Birmingham area. Hence Villa now have their own Sales and Marketing team, consisting of Carol Deakin, Jim Scott and Tina Cole, plus a number of other highly trained specialists, including Simon Murphy (Banqueting Manager), Peter Reed (Executive Chef), Norman Dodd (Head Chef), Tony Lolley (Banqueting Chef) and Sue Wadley (Restaurant Manageress). With such expertise to hand, Holte Enders should now be able to look forward to the best servings of *boeuf en croute* and *consommé* in the Midlands – or meat pies and Bovril as they are better known down Aston way.

Leaving the North Stand offices for now, our next

stop is the former Lions Club building, just in front of the Trinity Road Stand. Now looking rather out of place in the smart new Villa Park set-up, the building has housed many a department over the years, plus dining facilities, a players' lounge and of course the club shop. Upstairs at the rear, opposite the players' official entrance, is where stadium manager Ted Small and his ever-ringing mobile phone can be found, usually under a mountain of plans, samples and all the paraphernalia of a site office. Ted is one of the few current members of staff who was around in the early days of the Doug Ellis revolution of 1968.

In those days Ted turned his hand to most running repairs. But such is the scale and complexity of the modern-day stadium that, apart from a regular stream of sub-contractors, his department now includes nine staff. The maintenance manager is Tony Diffley, aided by Sue Birch, Harry Corrigan, Warren Corser, David Phillips and Jose Crego. Bridget McLoughlin looks after the ground's plumbing, Barry Hitchman is the electrician, and Dave Tipper is Villa Park's carpenter.

Dave's workshop is situated in the corner between the Doug Ellis Stand and North Stand, a few yards away from head groundsman Tony Eden's hidden lair (which lies in the bowels of the North Stand, at the end of the tunnel near the Witton Lane corner). Tony and his two assistants, Steve Harper and Richard Hill not only tend the Villa Park turf (along with 12 match-day part-timers and volunteers). They also have the responsibility of caring for Bodymoor Heath's four grass and one all-weather pitch.

And talking of Bodymoor Heath, although not strictly part of Villa Park, how could we fail to mention the staff at the training ground? Trevor France is the caretaker. On the coaching side there is of course Brian Little, his assistant Allan Evans, plus first team coach Kevin MacDonald, physiotherapist Jim Walker, fitness coach Paul Barron, reserve team manager Malcolm Beard, youth team coach Tony McAndrew, chief scout Peter Withe and youth development officer Bryan Jones.

To make sure they and their many charges are kept clothed and fed there is kit man Jim Paul, and the two cooks, Annette Horsefall and Annette Evans. Jim – who used to run the Villa's hostel for young players with his wife Sylvia – has to look after over 500 home and away kits for the first team squad alone, plus all the training gear, boots, studs, track suits (for work and leisure), balls, shin pads, towels and so on that form part of the every day needs of a modern professional footballer. Still, at least Jim does not have the problems of his dressing room predecessors, the likes of Charlie Wallace (a former player who worked at Villa Park for many years), Walter Cowans (father of Gordon) and John 'Pop' Ward (who saw that epic Villa v Sunderland game in 1913 and was an attendant to the first team from 1968-78). For a start the modern kit is not washed by a washer-woman on Witton Lane, or dried on those steaming pipes in the Trinity Road Stand, and nor does it need ironing. In addition, instead of each player – whether he be tall or short, bony or stout –

# Record attendances

| | |
|---|---|
| November 6, 1920 | **66,694** (new record at Villa Park, also given as 66,094). Villa 0, West Bromwich Albion 0, Division One. |
| February 20, 1926 | **71,446** (new record at Villa Park - also given as 71,297). Villa 1 Arsenal 1, FA Cup 5th round. |
| February 18, 1928 | **23,667** (reserve team record, to see Pongo Waring make his debut for Villa). Villa 6, Birmingham 2, Central Lge. |
| March 2, 1929 | **73,686** (new FA Cup record at Villa Park). Villa 1, Arsenal 0, FA Cup 6th round. |
| January 25, 1930 | **74,626** (new FA Cup record at Villa Park). Villa 3, Walsall 1, FA Cup 4th round. |
| January 14, 1931 | **73,632** (midweek record at Villa Park). Villa 1, Arsenal 3, FA Cup 3rd round replay. |
| October 30, 1937 | **68,029** (all-time record for Second Division match). Villa 1, Coventry 1. |
| March 5, 1938 | **75,540** (new FA Cup record at Villa Park). Villa 3, Manchester City 2. |
| 1945-46 | Seasonal receipts of **£101,692** were a record not only for Villa but also for any League club. |
| March 2, 1946 | **76,588** (all-time Villa Park record). Villa 3, Derby County 4, FA Cup 6th round. Match also yielded then record receipts for any League or Cup match staged outside London, of £8,651 2s 6d. |
| December 26, 1947 | **68,099** (new League record at Villa Park). Villa 1, Wolverhampton Wanderers 2, Division One. |
| December 27, 1949 | **69,492** (all-time League record at Villa Park). Villa 1, Wolverhampton Wanderers 4, Division One. |
| February 21, 1996 | **39,334** (all-time club record receipts at Villa Park **£504,958**). Villa 0, Arsenal 0, Coca-Cola Cup semi-final. |
| 31 March, 1996 | **38,421** (all-time record receipts at Villa Park, **£1,067,620**). Manchester United 2, Chelsea 1, FA Cup semi-final. |

having to fit into the numbered shirt appropriate for the position he was selected for, nowadays each player has his own numbered, personalised and correct-fitting shirt.

Because all the players' equipment is stored, washed and maintained at Bodymoor Heath, Jim has to transport the necessary kit to Villa Park in several large hampers, just as he would to games played away.

So now we and the kit are back at Villa Park, we move from the ground itself to the indoor cricket centre, Stumps, at the rear of the North Stand. This opened in 1987 and is run by Bob Manca. The son of a well known Italian restaurateur – Marcello Manca, of the La Galleria – Bob was a Holte Ender in his youth and in the late 1980s became Villa's promotions manager. He finally concentrated on Stumps in 1990, since when this unassuming building has become something of a mecca in the indoor cricket world. It has staged test matches, the British Open (which is a three-day event involving 30-40 teams) and is home to one of the country's leading National League teams, which over the years

# A dream come true

❖ It was late 1971. Bored rigid with his job in accountancy, 20-year-old Steve Stride wrote to his beloved Villa. Did they have any vacancies? It was a long shot, so he was hardly surprised to receive a standard reply. The club would keep his letter 'on file'. Oh yeh! That old one. Six months later he was called for an interview, and the rest, as they say, is his story.

I started here on June 11, 1972 – a dream come true. On my first day I bumped into Ian Ross. He was very friendly, asked who I was, and then introduced himself, as if I wouldn't know! Villa's secretary, Alan Bennett, went to Leicester in April 1979. I thought they'd appoint someone else. Then the chairman at that time, Harry Kartz, said, "Look we've interviewed four people, they could all do the job, but so could you. Why don't you do it?" So I thought, well, why not? It was the chance of a lifetime. We played West Brom the day I was appointed secretary of Aston Villa, May 11, 1979. I was 28 then, maybe the youngest secretary in the League and younger than many of the players. So Ron Saunders called them together and said, "Right, from now on it's not young Steve, it's Mr Stride, and if I catch any of you calling him anything else you're in trouble."

One concern of mine in my early days as secretary went back to when I came down with my father, as a 10 or 11-year-old. I used to go through one turnstile, he'd to go through another, and that was after queuing separately for perhaps 30-40 minutes. I found that quite frightening, as I'm sure lots of other small boys did, waiting to meet up inside the ground, never knowing how long it might take. That's why we started up a father-and-son turnstile.

What I soon learnt was that if you've got 35,000 people coming to a match you only need a very, very small percentage to complain and you've got one hell of a lot of letters on a Monday morning. And that whatever system you adopt for selling big match tickets, whilst you please some people, you upset others. Mind you, I remember this chap asked for two standing tickets for the League Cup Final at Wembley and then he asked, "Are these two together?"

The one match that really sticks in my mind was before I started work here – the League Cup semi final in 1970. We were the underdogs. Manchester United were the top boys. George Best, you name it. And it was very near Christmas. We've had great matches since then, but for me that night was the greatest I've known at Villa Park, for atmosphere, and emotion. I mean, I was too young to remember 1957. I did watch it on TV but I can't pretend I remember it. So this was the first chance for a whole generation of Villa supporters to go to Wembley to see their team. Kids today have perhaps been two or three times. Perhaps some of the glamour has worn off a little bit. But for us, to see Aston Villa at Wembley was just... oh it was fantastic.

Since working here the biggest thrills have been winning the League, winning the European Cup, and the day Mr Ellis called me in to invite me onto the board. That just knocked me back, to think that from being a supporter on the terraces I was now on the board.

Being here every day you don't notice the changes to the ground so much. I know people who've been abroad, come back and can't believe it's the same Villa Park. I'm very proud of it now, but I'm also conscious that there's still lots to be done; seats that aren't quite right, refreshment areas which need upgrading. We're attracting more and more families, and we all expect a lot more than we did 20 years ago.

Just one example of how things have changed. Carolyn, my wife, worked here for 12 years. This is where we met. Now we've got three children. Matthew, who's seven, is becoming a Villa supporter. He's been down to about a dozen games here so far, but I don't push him. The other night we'd played down at Wimbledon and I got home at 1.30 in the morning, the adrenalin still flowing. Seven o'clock, Matthew wakes me up and he says, "Dad, can I have a Newcastle shirt for Christmas, with long sleeves and Ginola on the back?"

I said, "But son, you're a Villa supporter."

"Not this week, Dad," he said. "I'm a Newcastle supporter."

It's not easy, is it?

has featured the likes of Mike Gatting, Gladstone Small and Tim Munton. (For the uninitiated, indoor cricket matches last for 75 minutes and are contested between teams of eight players, each of whom get to bat and bowl.)

In addition to cricket, Stumps also stages regular netball league matches, plus daily five-a-side or seven-a-side football. It also hosts special match-day packages arranged for kids and corporate clients alike. Overall it is reckoned that 4,000 people use the centre every week.

Leaving Stumps we now cross the car-park to the Villa Village, the newest outpost of Villa Park's burgeoning empire.

On the ground floor is the Villa Village superstore. Opened in November 1995, the store is one of the largest in football, with 3,200 square feet and a turnover which reached £3 million in its first year. During the week it needs 12 staff to cater for the regular business, rising to 30 on match days. All a very, very far cry from its origins in that small corner shop on Witton Lane in the late 1950s, run by the Supporters' Association.

Indeed so successful and large did the subsequent Development Association become that in June 1995 Villa took the merchandising and travel departments under its own wing.

The whole operation is now run from Villa Village by John Greenfield, with Alan Williams concentrating on the merchandise. Erdington-born John's first taste of Villa Park was as a 12-year-old, seeing the FA Cup being paraded around the ground in 1957. He later became a part-time rep for the club lottery, before joining the staff in 1982. In those days the shop was a small outlet next to the Lions Club with 100 different products on sale. Now the Villa Village stocks over 500 different lines.

It will come as no surprise to learn that the best selling lines of all are the replica Reebok shirts. Apparently 28 per cent of all Villa kits sold worldwide are sold from Villa Village.

Many of them are also sold via the club's rapidly expanding mail order department, also run by John Greenfield from offices in the Villa Village. Over 20,000 people have taken advantage of this facility, with Villa fans writing in from all over the world, including, believe it or not, Iran and Iraq. (So at least there's one thing the two nations have in common!)

There are three staff working in this area; Karen Sanders, Julie Cooke and Jane Thomas. They also help with the Travel Club, which runs coaches to all away games and has over 1,000 members.

In past years the third arm of the promotions department was the club pools. This is now a lottery, run by Robert Dobson, also from Villa Village. But the organisation itself remains a separate entity, as it has to be by law, so that all its profits can be donated to the football club. The advent of the National Lottery has hit club lotteries hard – not just in football but across the sporting spectrum – with Villa's own operation down by 25 per cent in the past two years. Nevertheless Villa still have over 2,000 agents selling around one million scratch cards a year and

contributing £100,000 to Villa's coffers.

There are a further three departments on the upper floor of the Villa Village building. In one corner is the Community Liaison Office, run by former Villa player and assistant manager, Ron Wylie, with Warwick Adams, Nigel Macrow and Alan Thomason. This quartet run Soccer Specials for up to 300 children on match days, using facilities at Bodymoor Heath, Stumps and the Holte School, and week-long coaching schools during the summer. The rest of the year Ron's team take their coaching expertise out to schools all over the region, as part of a nationwide 'Football in the Community' scheme, co-ordinated by the PROFESSIONAL FOOTBALLERS' ASSOCIATION. Every club chooses its own way of meeting the scheme's aims. The prime motive behind Villa's is not to track down local talent – although naturally the coaches do not turn a blind eye to likely lads – but to provide genuine soccer-based fun and games for all children; boys, girls, able-bodied or otherwise. Ron reckons that each year his team reaches some 60 schools and 20,000 children overall, making Villa's one of the most active schools programme in the country. Moreover, Villa foot the entire bill, without any cost to any of the participants.

Next door to the Community Office is the Special Projects Department. This is another fairly young, but increasingly active branch of the club, run by Dave Ismay, with assistance from Tamara Williams and Tina Robinson. Dave, who was once a regular on the cabaret circuit and has always been a Villa fan, is effectively Villa's *Minister without Portfolio*. He works on new building projects (such as Villa Village), runs the Villa Villans Supporters Club, handles the club's many contacts with charities, organises the daily ground tours (led by Jack Watts), and also manages one-off events, such as the club's visits to Wembley – may his workload be heavy! – or the recent Centenary celebrations for Villa Park. Dave has also had the task of co-ordinating the club's response to a recent Supporter Satisfaction survey, conducted by the University of Central England.

❖ *Villa Village – the latest addition to the Villa Park scene, and a major contributor to the club's funds. The building and its adjoining offices once belonged to BRITISH TELECOM, and occupy the northern end of the former Lower Grounds.*

One further responsibility of the Special Projects department is the vitally important Villa archive. Most football clubs are extremely careless of their own records, mementoes and relics of the past. Sad to say, until the 1970s Villa were no different, and many a valuable item or bound volume was needlessly lost or destroyed. Fortunately that neglect is now a thing of the past. Linda Fletcher was Villa's first part-time archivist, with a room put aside in the North Stand. She was followed by long-time supporter Derrick Spinks, whom many a Villa fan will know from his numerous historical articles and publications, and later David Goodyear.

Now carefully housed in their own special room, the archives are currently being organised by Reg Thacker. Reg will also be known to Villa Park regulars. He is the dapper chap who has run the Trinity Road programme kiosk for over 20 years, and is a dealer to whom hundreds of desperate collectors turn for such elusive items as the Gillingham v Villa

programme from 1971. (Don't all write at once.)

And that, ladies and gentlemen, concludes our whistlestop tour of the day-to-day departments at Villa Park in 1997. As can be seen, they form quite an enterprise, but a sharply focused one, packed with experienced administrators and Villa fanatics alike. To these dedicated people, Villa Park is plainly more than just a place of work, and more even than simply a football ground. It is a symbol of the success to which their own efforts have contributed.

Yet as has already been stated, by its very nature Villa Park is also an entity founded upon a dream, and for the workforce, therein lies a paradox. An unsuccessful team means a quiet life for the staff, whereas a team which is regularly challenging for honours brings with it a mountain of extra work, long hours, extra pressure and increased public scrutiny. That surely explains why so many of the folk working for Villa are also rooting for them – they have to be fans in order to cope with the workload. It might also explain why once in the job, so many of them appear to get hooked on the adrenalin rush.

And who are we to judge them, for given half the chance would we not be exactly the same?

But whether we go to Villa Park to work, rest or play, as the ground reaches its 100th year – in finer fettle than ever, most would agree – we are all of us as hooked as ever. However much we moan about rising ticket prices, or feign indifference, or try to wriggle from the hook, we can never quite escape. For we are all would-be dwellers in the Villa Village, as we gather around the hallowed green and cheer on our favourite sons. And when they're not around to delight or deny us, there is always plenty else for us to gossip about. Who said what about whom. Who's coming and who's going. Who's mad with whom, and did you see what he did on Saturday? Highlights on TV and low spots at Grimsby, we've seen them all.

We wear the colours. We pay as much as we can afford to follow the circus. We know all the characters but can never quite work out the plot.

There have been thousands and thousands before us. They flocked to Perry Barr in their charabancs. They descended upon the Lower Grounds in trams. They have honed in on Villa Park from the motorways and railways and they have made the rafters of the Holte End reverberate across the ages.

And, no doubt, there are plenty more where they came from. Enough, surely, for Villa Park to enjoy another hundred years of pilgrimage.

We can but hope.

But what of the Villa Park of the 21st century? What changes might our children and their children witness over the next 100 years? Or will there even be a football ground on Trinity Road by the year 2097?

As to the immediate future, as this book went to press a package of ground improvements costing an estimated £20 million had just been unveiled, shortly before the club's flotation on the stock market. The club also announced a £6.5 million, three-year deal with their kit suppliers, Reebok. Three developments were definitely scheduled to take place during the

# Something money can't buy

❖ Abdul Rashid has worked full-time for Villa for 20 years. Before that he was an autograph hunter, ball-boy and part-time assistant in the souvenir shop. He met his wife, Jane, when she worked at Villa Park and they married on the day Villa played Penarol in the World Club Championship in Tokyo, in December 1982. It was the only day they could find when neither of them were working and when the Lions Club was available for the reception, of course.

The biggest thing for me, becoming a full time member of staff in 1977, was having to sit down to watch a game. When I was still part-time I used to go up the Holte End. But then coming onto the staff I found it very frustrating, sat in the the Trinity Road stand. And then I was working for the commercial department and all of a sudden I'm in a box and thinking, I don't want this. But then the comfort factor comes in and it's soon a matter of what you get accustomed to.

Two years after I started full time I was interviewed for the match programme. Mike Beddow asked, 'What's your ambition?' At the time I was 17, selling bingo tickets in the pools office and I'd just become the Travel Club rep at all the away games. So I should really have said that my ambition was to become souvenir shop manager or promotions manager. Instead of that I reached for the stars and said I wanted to become a commercial manager.

When Eric Woodward was leaving he told me he'd been very impressed that I showed such ambition and gave me some great advice. He said, always ask questions. Go and ask Gerald Harris how he knows how many programmes to have printed. Go and ask the caterers how they know how many pies to order? Ask how do you do this, how do you do that. And I've always done that, from being a souvenir shop assistant, to serving on the counter of the lottery and the bingo, to being in charge of the Travel Club, to being a rep out on the road, to being assistant promotions manager, assistant commercial manager and finally commercial manager in 1988. I had a lot to prove to an awful lot of people.

No matter what happens, a commercial manager gets judged on results. The bottom line is what revenue you bring in. When I took over I think the commercial income was about a million a season. And now it's approaching £7-8 million. But it's not really any one person's effort. I look at the senior staff here and we've all been here an awfully long time.

Being a Villa supporter and a local lad, there's no two ways about it, I've got a feeling for this club. I've wanted to do things at this stadium because it's my club. I know I've said that a commercial manager gets judged on results. But for me one of the major achievements has been the schools programmes that we've set up. We were the pioneers, and after us 19 other clubs took it on. I'm very proud that we were voted *Community Club of the Year*.

To me, the thing that's different about this club is the people. Take our sponsors. They can't believe how friendly the part-time staff are, not only the stewards but the gate men, the security people. As a department we have an awful lot of supporters working for us, and yes, they do get paid. But I don't think they do it for the money. They do it for the fact that they can go home on a Saturday night thinking that they've helped their club. That the players may know them on first name terms. I get told so many times about the friendliness at Villa Park. That loyalty to the club, it's something you just can't buy.

❖ *Ron Wylie shows the youngsters a thing or two on one of the Community Scheme's numerous programmes for local schools. Ron reckons the scheme takes 20,000 youngsters a year.*

summer of 1997, in readiness for Villa Park's 100th season of action.

Firstly, the ground is to have an entirely new playing surface, its second in successive summers, and an entirely new type of surface to boot. Readers may recall the advent of plastic pitches in the early 1980s, at QPR, Oldham, Luton and Preston. Their unmourned demise led to the assumption that synthetics were dead and buried. Well, buried anyway. But since then a new generation of pitch has emerged, mixing natural and synthetic materials.

The £250,000 Desso Grassmaster surface which Villa are installing in 1997 is one such innovative turf system, developed first in Holland and used only once before by an English professional club, Huddersfield Town, at their award-winning McAlpine Stadium. Although fans will not spot any difference, the sand-based pitch will have hundreds of synthetic fibres injected at regular intervals among the blades of grass, so that the overall surface will actually be 97 per cent natural turf and 3 per cent artificial. By adding the fibres the surface should be much stronger and capable of withstanding much heavier usage.

The second development to take place during the summer of 1997 is that, after nearly two years of waiting, Villa Park is to have its first video screens in two corners of the ground. Costing in the region of £1 million for the pair, the 35 square foot screens are said to use a form of LED technology not yet seen in Britain.

Thirdly, the new Holte Suite is to open in the centre of the Holte End Stand. This extensive and lavishly fitted new facility, costing £2.7 million, is to be used as a conference and banqueting suite during the week, and on match days will provide three different levels of service (depending on demand); for corporate hospitality, for silver service dining, and for ordinary supporters using it as a members' club. Not so much *Holte Enders in the Sky* then, as *Holte Enders in a Tie*.

Overall it is anticipated that the Holte Suite will

cater for up to 800 people on match days, and 650 on weekdays.

Finally in 1997, Villa Village is to have a smaller offshoot – a Villa Hamlet as it were – in the ground floor of the Holte Hotel. This will be open on match days only, and represents the first phase of what is hoped will lead to the complete overhaul of this landmark building.

Beyond 1997, two further developments are proposed for 1998 and the following years. The first concerns the re-roofing of the Trinity Road Stand and phase two of the stand's overall refurbishment.

Planning for this began several years ago, but because it soon evolved into such a technically complex proposal it was not possible to start any work until Euro 96 was out of the way.

Essentially, the current sloping roof is to be replaced by a goalpost-supported roof, thus eliminating all ten intermediate columns from the stand.

However, there is a price to pay for column-free viewing, for taking away the old roof will render the two screen walls with their familiar circular windows and mosaic emblems, dangerously unstable. Sadly, therefore, they will have to be replaced, albeit in a sympathetic style. The old roof's central gable will also be lost, although again it is hoped that, as has happened at Hillsborough, a modern replica might be added to the new roof.

Once the old roof has been removed, a temporary cover will be erected, to protect the upper tier seats (because knowing Villa Park's past history, whenever the work is done it will rain heavily). Meanwhile, the entire lower tier of the Trinity Road Stand will have to be cleared in order to create a flat space immediately in front of the stand. This space will be used for two purposes; firstly, to assemble the goalpost structure's massive horizontal girder, which will measure 135m long, 10m high, and weigh 370 tons; and secondly, to provide room for two of the country's largest moving cranes to move into position so that the assembled girder can then be lifted into place, resting upon its two end towers.

Once this spectacular operation is completed, work can then begin on re-instating the lower tier, but this time with the seats and treads being designed to modern standards for sightlines and comfort.

When viewed from the rest of the ground, the fascia of the new roof will match up exactly with the other three stands, thus tying together Villa Park as never before, visually if not structurally. When viewed from Trinity Road, the existing frontage will not have altered, but stepped behind the uppermost brick parapet there will be an extra storey and of course the roof girder itself will have a considerable impact on the skyline. However, a similar engineering exercise has been accomplished on another redbrick stand of the 1920s, at Ibrox Park in Glasgow, and the effect there is by no means jarring.

Finally, inside the stand Villa are hoping to make a number of changes. These may include the provision of 36 executive boxes immediately underneath the roof girder, at the rear of the upper tier, the possible removal of the existing boxes from the rear of the lower tier, and the opening out of the lower concourses so that fans have much more room for circulation and enhanced facilities. It is also possible that these new facilities will made be accessible to fans sitting on the upper tier, thereby reducing some of the congestion experienced on the first floor concourses.

Overall, this major work is expected to cost around £3.4 million, and add perhaps only another 250 seats to Villa Park's overall capacity. On the other hand, it will provide those spectators in the Trinity Road with the same viewing standards and catering facilities currently enjoyed on the three other sides, while ensuring that Villa Park is still able to boast one of the most distinctive frontages in world football.

As readers may be aware, Villa had confidently hoped to start the work on the Trinity Road plans in May 1997. But the council's planning committee thought otherwise, and in April sent the plans back to Villa for a re-think. Part of their objection was that at the same time as planning the Trinity Road redevelopment Villa also submitted outline proposals to extend the North Stand (with an enlarged upper tier and new roof), in order to bring the overall capacity nearer to 50,000. Before passing any plans, the planners demanded to see an overall development plan.

Villa Park, said one Erdington councillor, was 'an ugly mess' that stuck out 'like a sore thumb.' Another, the same Aston councillor who had objected so vehemently to plans for the Witton Lane Stand's redevelopment in 1992, dismissed the ground as a 'hotchpotch of four different sheds.' This, from the same council which had happily given approval for such architectural turkeys as the Copthorne Hotel and dozens of crinkly-tin retail warehouses all over the city (but presumably whose members have the most chic garden sheds in Britain).

Doug Ellis was obviously very disappointed with the council's attitude. After all, the club and its designers had worked closely both with council planning officials and the local conservation officer in drawing up and amending the Trinity Road Stand plans, and there had not been a single objection from local residents. The plans were therefore expected to sail through. Ted Small was devastated too. After over 25 years service to the club, he dearly wants to see the ground's redevelopment completed before his retirement.

But in whatever form the designs are eventually approved – as surely they must – there can be no doubt that the basic aims of the redevelopment will not be altered. The Trinity Road Stand roof does need to be replaced by a column-free version, and if Villa are to continue to be successful and meet current levels of demand, they are going to have to raise the capacity above its 1997 limit of 39,339. Furthermore, the only way they can achieve this is by extending the North Stand. Beyond that, who can say?

In October 1972 Doug Ellis told the VILLA TIMES that his long term ambition was to create a stadium

# Keeping count

❖ Some of Villa Park's 86 turnstiles may date back to the days of Pongo Waring and even Perry Barr, but they all count. The only difference is that nowadays a computer does most of the arithmetic. The main terminal is located in a match day control room in the North Stand, where accountant Mark McGuinness and his assistants, Mike Maher and Bob Scott monitor the flow of spectators into each part of ground. Now that Villa Park is all-seated and admission is by ticket only there is less need to guard against overcrowding, or worry about turnstile operators carrying large amounts of cash. Nor can small children squeeze under the turnstiles and slip through as so many did in the past.

Nevertheless, the match day control room staff still have to watch carefully, to cope with a late flurry of arrivals or to guard against long queues building up, or even the small, but still ever present possibility of ticket forgeries.

In charge of the turnstile operators is John Partridge, whose father George preceded him as senior turnstile supervisor for 48 years. John has to ensure that all turnstiles are manned and ready for the 1.15pm opening (for a routine 3.00pm kick-off). On a typical match day some 50 per cent of the crowd will arrive in the last 15 minutes for the game. The majority of turnstiles will then close ten minutes after kick off, leaving just one 'late turnstile' in each stand to remain open until 4.10pm. Meanwhile, the turnstile operators report to the match day control room for a final count and check of their ticket stubs. In the days of terracing the final attendance would be known by around 25 minutes before the final whistle. Nowadays the figure is available in an instant, and earlier of course if the game has been a sell-out. But a 'house full' sign of 39,339 does not necessarily mean that there are 39,339 spectators actually inside the ground. Every ticket may well have been sold, but not everyone makes it to the ground.

As to the more distant future, what does our crystal ball reveal?

From Holland in the late 1990s there comes two developments, from Amsterdam and Arnhem, which may well influence the stadium of the future; that is, retractable roofs and retractable pitches. Realistically, Villa Park (and very few other English football grounds either) is unlikely to need either of these. Although technically a retractable roof could be developed for Villa Park, the cost would be enormous and the economic benefits dubious, particularly as the city already has two major indoor arenas. And if there is no sliding roof, there is hardly a need to slide the pitch in and out, which is just as well since there is no room to do this at Villa Park anyway.

Otherwise, it is reasonably safe to predict that season ticket books will almost certainly be superceded by plastic, laser-read smartcards, within the next 20 years. These same cards might also be used like credit cards to purchase refreshments, souvenirs and tickets within the ground.

There might be interactive consoles attached to certain seats, for spectators to call up information, match facts, or perhaps vote for their man of the match. Spectators might also be able to hire headsets for match commentaries, or even hand-held mini-TVs for replays, statistical data and so on.

Who knows, if the television companies continue to exert ever more influence over the game, we could reach a stage at which clubs like Villa do not need any income through the gate, and instead will invite fans to matches at Villa Park as studio guests; no longer needing to pay but having to dress and behave in a manner likely to please the television directors.

A horrifying scenario perhaps, but then whoever would have imagined, fifty years ago, that one day first team games would be staged on Sundays and Mondays, but never on Christmas Days?

And what of the location of Villa Park itself? Could

❖ *Villa fans anxiously watch the first team fight for their Premier League survival on a video screen relaying live action from Norwich, on the final day of the 1994-95 season. But success has its drawbacks, too (below). These signs went up seven times in 1996-97*

'on the lines of Real Madrid.' By that he meant that instead of leaving his wife and kids at home a family man could take them along to the match and sit in comfort and safety.

Ellis went on to say that this dream stadium of the future would have swimming pools, restaurants, cafes and tennis courts, and would be covered by a huge glass dome.

Well, there are no swimming pools or tennis courts – yet – and a glass dome may have to await until Dan Dare returns to the planet. But essentially the rest of the chairman's vision has come to fruition. Villa Park now offers a safe and comfortable environment for all ages and sexes, and it is in use most days of the week as a sporting and leisure centre.

one ever imagine Villa moving, lock, stock and barrel to a new location, just as they did in 1897?

Of course it cannot be ruled out. But then realistically, Villa Park already conforms with many of the requirements which look likely to shape stadium developments in the early 21st century. It has excellent links with public transport, particularly its two nearby railway stations, Witton and Aston. It is also handy for the major road networks.

But what about all those small streets and local residents around Villa Park, you ask. Surely the stadium of the future will be built on out-of-town sites where no-one will be inconvenienced? Again, not so. That trend ended in the United States in the 1980s and is now largely discredited. Stadiums which stand in the middle of nowhere serve very little purpose other than on match days and only transfer the traffic problems to motorways. Conversely, stadiums in urban settings – if designed and managed appropriately – can offer huge benefits to both their local and wider communities. Indeed, instead of acting as a blight, they can be vibrant forces for urban regeneration, particularly if well served by public transport.

So, in this writer's humble view at least, Villa Park is ideally located to meet the needs of the next century.

Nevertheless, no-one would deny that there is still much work to be done at the ground, and that there are still many lessons to be learnt in this ever changing world. It is no secret that Villa Park in 1997 is not perfect, or that there exist differing views as to how it might be further developed.

But then the same is true of all public buildings, whether they be football grounds, hospitals, schools, libraries or theatres. As times change, so too must ideas and solutions. In fact living proof of that lies within a goalkick or two of Villa Park. Aston Church is an amalgam of several different styles, added and amended by builders separated by hundreds of years, stretching from the early medieval period through to the modern era.

Aston Hall, too, is no longer the same building commissioned by Sir Thomas Holte in 1618. It took 17 years and many design changes to complete the stately home, and it has undergone another 350 years of change since.

Much the same may be said of Villa Park. For as an architectural critic once put it, a building is never finished, it is only started. On that basis, Villa Park on its one hundredth birthday can certainly claim to have made a pretty good start.

So, here's to the next one hundred years! May they be as eventful, as enjoyable, and, as I hope this book has shown, as compelling as the first one hundred.

The VILLA NEWS AND RECORD surmised in 1924 that 'if the history of the big plot of land on which the Villa teams play, and all its many "accessories" are included, ever comes to be written, it will form quite a romantic tale, full of sporting and financial adventure.'

And so it has proved.

# Seat for seat

❖ Coincidentally, Villa Park has almost the same capacity in 1997 as it did in 1897. By 1946, with the completion of the Holte End extension, the maximum figure rose to above 76,000. But not until the safety legislation of the mid 1970s were accurate assessments of the capacity made. Since then, this is how the Villa Park numbers have altered:

| 1970-71 | 62,500 | (11,927 seats) |
|---|---|---|
| 1972-73 | 60,500 | (15,682 seats) |
| 1977-78 | 48,100 | (19,914 seats) |
| 1990-91 | 40,277 | (21,067 seats) |
| 1993-94 | 46,005 | (26,795 seats) |

In 1997 a sell-out crowd at Villa Park means 39,339 all-seated specators, distributed as follows:

| | |
|---|---|
| **Holte End Stand** | **13,501** |
| upper | 5,751 |
| lower | 7,750 |
| **Trinity Road Stand** | **9,254** |
| upper | 5,222 |
| lower | 3,912 |
| executive boxes | 120 |
| **North Stand Stand** | **7,360** |
| upper | 3,980 |
| lower | 3,086 |
| executive boxes | 252 |
| super box | 42 |
| **Doug Ellis Stand** | **9,135** |
| upper | 4,686 |
| lower | 4,161 |
| executive boxes | 288 |
| For blind supporters, wheelchair users and their helpers | 89 |

# The Garden of Eden

join the groundstaff at Bodymoor Heath. He eventually became head groundsman for Villa Park in January 1980.

Even then he was on familiar ground, for not only had he played on the pitch as a youth but he had also popped in regularly to learn all he could from Bert Bond. 'A wonderful man,' says Tony. 'He was very knowledgeable, very amiable, and very chatty. He would help anyone if he could; us at ICI, the groundsman at Walsall, anyone.'

Tony's seventeen years as groundsman have been more challenging than those experienced by any of his predecessors – the likes of Ruben Leeson, Bert Bond, Les Bates and George Murphy. The original Villa Park pitch was replaced in 1931, and that second one lasted until 1977. Since then, however, it has been relaid and upgraded three times, with a complete new drainage system installed in 1990 (leaving the 1931 pipework untouched underneath) and undersoil heating added in 1996. Yet another new pitch was laid in 1997, using the innovative Desso Grassmaster system (as explained elsewhere in this chapter).

Villa are not alone in having to invest heavily on turf technology. The old mud heaps of yesteryear were never so closely scrutinised by a critical television audience as they are today. Indeed Tony recalls how manager Ron Saunders actually preferred the Villa Park pitch to be as muddy as possible.

'I remember in the European Cup when we had to beat Dynamo Kiev to get to the semi-final. The night before, the pitch was completely impervious, so I got about 3-400 hundred people down. All brought their own forks. That was some night, that was. The Russians came out, expecting to train and suddenly they were sinking into the pitch. Ron said, "My team's the fittest in the country so I want it heavy." And he was right. We took them out 2-0. A great night.'

Since then Tony has had more than his share of nightmares. There was the infamous green sand interlude in 1992. On another occasion, in the early 1980s, the pitch was draining so poorly that he reckons that he and his staff had to drill 84,000 holes to pierce through the compacted top surface. In more recent years, as the higher stand roofs have cut out more and more natural light he has also had to contend with poorer growth. Another recent problem, common to grounds all over Britain, has been the dreaded 'black layer,' a slimy, black, algae-like disease which infiltrated the pitch's 80 per cent sand base and stunted the root growth. None of the experts have a solution.

'There have been times when I've hidden myself away during games and just been out at half-time,' admits Tony. 'I just can't stand looking at the players cutting up the pitch, knowing that I can't do anything about it and that I've just got to get it back as best I can and wait until the next game.'

A groundsman's best friends are time, and the healing power of nature. Summer concerts and events like Euro 96 do not help in that respect. But

❖ When it comes to roots, few staff at Villa Park can match groundsman Tony Eden. Brought up in Deakin Avenue, he started watching Villa in the late 1940s and signed on for the club as promising centre-half in April 1958 (twelve months after his namesake had signed off from Downing Street). Unfortunately Tony could not oust Jimmy Dugdale from the first team, so in 1960 he joined Walsall, where he stayed two years before enjoying his best spell at Kidderminster Harriers.

All the while, however, he was learning his trade as a groundsman with ICI (now IMI) at the former KYNOCH works in Witton. In those days the company employed a full-time sports coach, Frank Mitchell (the former Birmingham City, Chelsea and Watford player), and needed a full complement of groundstaff to tend no fewer than three football pitches, two rugby pitches, two hockey pitches, two bowling greens and eight tennis courts. By the mid 1970s these wonderful facilities were being sold off, so Tony was delighted to accept an invitation from his former ICI colleague, George Murphy, to then Tony admits that he is lucky to have a board which is not afraid to shell out for improvements (which in recent years have amounted to over £600,000). In an age when postponement owing to a waterlogged or frostbound pitch is little short of a cardinal sin, the pitch cover installed in 1978 has proved to be a huge bonus in wet weather, as has been a system of eight large quilt-like covers which help to fend of frost. And now there is the new undersoil heating system. This automatically comes into operation whenever the temperature drops below a certain point, pumping hot water through a system of one inch plastic pipes, laid just below the surface. Another boost in recent years has been the reserves' temporary sojourn at Bescot, and the fact that the design of Villa Park still allows for wind to penetrate through the corners.

Even then, Tony and his fellow Premier League groundsmen accept that in the modern age it may be necessary for clubs to replace their pitches every few years, rather than every few decades as before. But then when you pay £8 million for a player, and have Sky TV watching your every divot, nothing but the best will do for this, the 'Garden of Eden' upon which all our dreams unfold.

❖ For the statistically minded, Villa Park's pitch exactly meets the international recommended dimensions of 115 x 75 yards. There are five yards of turf behind each goal-line and four feet beyond each touchline. To help drainage, the surface is cambered, being eight inches higher in the centre than at the touchlines. Underneath the turf, in addition to the irrigation system, there are 26,000 metres of heating pipes.

❖ *Tony Eden (above) needs two assistant groundsmen and 12 matchday helpers to cope with the changing weather conditions and Villa Park's increasingly sophisticated pitch systems.*

# Safety first priority

❖ High up, suspended under the roof of the Doug Ellis Stand, is the Villa Park stadium control room, one of the most sophisticated of its kind in British football. Before the Taylor Report such facilities, if they existed at all, were usually cramped, ill-equipped and were run totally by the police.

Nowadays the hi-tech Villa Park control room is run by the club, with the police working side by side with safety officer John Hood.

Brought up near Tamworth, Hood comes from a long line of Villa fans (which currently extends to his own grandchildren). He started policing at Villa Park in 1974, and was appointed as the club's first ever full-time safety officer in September 1990. (He also serves as a Conservative councillor for the Sutton Vesey ward on Birmingham City Council.)

'When I first arrived it wasn't an easy task,' says John. 'People were saying to me, "You've only just come to the ground. I've been doing this job for 20 years and it's always gone alright." But of course football clubs in those days used to rely totally on the police or the fire service to organise them, and they had no say in how many police officers came to the ground. If the ground commander wanted 200 or 250 police in the ground that was it.

'When I first started the police numbers were down to maybe 100-120. Now the maximum is probably 30, but five times last year we managed matches without any police in the ground at all.

❖ Monitoring the monitors – John Hood (below) keeps a watchful eye on the safety team high up in the Doug Ellis Stand, while Villa Park's new breed of high-profile stewards stay on the alert.

That just shows the difference between how we operated in the 1980s and how we operate now.

'We currently have in the region of 140 general stewards. Then we have 30 safety stewards, who are normally off-duty fire or ambulance officers, or school teachers, people who've got qualifications in first aid and fire fighting. But the general stewards now do everything, too. They can search supporters or eject them. We average probably only about three or four arrests at the ground per game, and they're mainly drink related.'

It is all a far cry from the days when, as for example before Villa's Cup game v Sunderland in February 1903, the 72 stewards were chosen by each director 'submitting half a dozen names of good workmen.' Indeed until 1990 most stewards did the job for free, in return for a pie, a programme and a free view of the game.

For many years after the Second World War Villa's stewarding operation was run by Bill Pountney, a well known character who ran a shop on the corner of Trinity Road and Bevington Road, with his wife Hilda. He acted as a steward in the Trinity Road Stand while groundsman Bert Bond looked after the Witton Lane Stand. As the steward numbers rose from 70 to nearer 200, in 1986 Bill Pearson took over as Chief Steward.

Currently, John Hood's safety team consists of his deputy safety officer, Brian Good (thus making an ideal pairing of Hood and Good). Eaton O'Connor is the club's Chief Steward, with Dave Steel as his deputy. There are then a further ten senior stewards, including a radio controller, based up in the stadium control room.

'In total, if you take in all the 24 hour security staff, plus the turnstile operators, on a match day I'm responsible for about 350-400 people,' says Hood. 'That's why I'm dependent on having good people under me to make sure the operation works.'

Joining him in the control room are the current Chief Superintendent for Villa Park, Colin MacDonald from Queen's Road, and Villa's Football Liaison Officer, WPC Belinda Gill. Keith Richards is the Fire Officer delegated by the West Midlands Fire Service, while there are also regular visits from Birmingham City Council's Errol Stuart, who is a member of the Safety Advisory Group, and from Jim Chalmers, the Football Licensing Authority inspector.

One of John's responsibilities is to link up with Villa Park's public address announcer, Dave Poulton. The most common announcements are for lost children, partners who lock themselves out of their homes and need a key, sudden illnesses, or births, and cars parked in the wrong places. Then there was the time, in the middle of a game, when one of the players' car alarms went off, and the police had to send a message down to the bench, to ask how they could turn it off. And you thought Brian Little was shouting out some tactical instructions!

'There's always something going on,' says John. 'Fraudulent tickets, forged notes, people turning up who are wanted by the police. No match is ever quiet.'

And nor can John's team ever be complacent, even though he is convinced that the all-seater revolution has quite transformed crowd behaviour at Villa Park.

'You only have to look at the families we get along nowadays, and the fact that people keep coming back, whereas before they might easily be put off. Plus the fact that if there are troublemakers – and we do still have a small hooligan element – we can identify them now quite easily. I'm happy that we've got an operation at Villa Park which is the envy of a lot of clubs.'

# Gone to blazers

❖ When Lord Justice Taylor decreed that stewards over the age of 55 should be pensioned off, there were a fair few grumpy souls around Villa Park. But now several of them are happier than ever, acting as commissionaires for hospitality areas all over Villa Park and looking rather dapper too, in their smart claret blazers. Among them can be found, in the Trinity Road Stand the three Kens, Messrs Binks, Davidson and Clarke, and looking after the players' lounge (in the former Lions Club), Peter and Brenda Bosley. Each has cheerfully served the club for over two decades.

The longest serving match-day helper of all, Jack Watts (who is the ground's official tour guide during the week) helps out in the boardroom, while Jack's former scoreboard colleague, Sam Messenger, who started working for Villa in 1950, can also be found as part of the welcoming party. Other members of the commissionaires' brigade include Ken Morgan, a former turnstile operator and supervisor since the 1960s, Jim Hannis and Nick Hoverd.

Three other blazered gentlemen who perform an important role are the Press Stewards, Malcolm Greatrex, Peter Pritchard and Reg Parton.

Reg has worked in the Villa Park press box for longer than any other single individual. Born in 1919, he saw his first Villa game in 1930. He later developed closer ties when working as a typesetter for the printing company which produced the Villa programme, JOHN GOODMAN & SONS (having earlier worked on BLUES NEWS for a rival printer!). There he became friends with a man called, oddly, Shirley Bladon, who would go on to become the longest serving editor of the VILLA NEWS AND RECORD (from 1937-63). Bladon invited Reg to help out in the press box in 1955, and remarkably, he has been there ever since. From 1963-69 he also edited the programme.

In the old days, recalls Reg, Villa's pressbox, near the front of the Trinity Road Stand's upper tier, held 45, and was filled only rarely. Those who did attend could find refuge in a small, dingy room under the stand with a spluttering gas fire. Now, the new box at the rear of the stand accommodates 72, while the press lounge on the first floor is smarter than many clubs can offer their VIPs. There is also a purpose-built interview room for the coaching staff and players, replacing the cubby holes and corridors reporters used to have make do with.

Genial Reg is a fanatical compiler of information about the Villa, and has every copy of the programme dating back to 1919. But he perhaps became best known to visiting pressmen by offering a unique service. Sitting on the front row of the press box, where all behind him could see, every 60 seconds Reg would flip over a card showing the exact number of minutes that had passed. In the days before electronic scoreboards, this one, simple service endeared him to a whole generation of harassed reporters, and was just one more little detail which helped to make Villa Park different from all other grounds.

*While Reg Parton (top) counted the minutes in the press box, Jack Watts (above) manned the Trinity Road scoreboard.*

# The Boardroom

❖ In 1897 Villa had five directors; a surveyor (Fred Rinder), a tobacconist (Josh Margoschis), a publican (James Lees), a doctor (Vincent Jones) and a school-teacher (Charlie Johnstone). The president, Joseph Ansell, was a solicitor. This is the line-up for 1997.

Herbert Douglas Ellis (below) will need little introduction. The man largely credited with masterminding the complete transformation of Villa's finances, he has served on the board for a total of 27 years, and as chairman for 23 years – from 1968-75 and from 1982 to the present day – thus making him Aston Villa's second longest serving chairman, after Fred Rinder (1897-25).

Born in Cheshire in January 1924, Ellis was brought up in a farming family and would earn extra money by milking cows before catching a train to Chester for school. He had ambitions to be a professional footballer, and was taken on by Tranmere while working in his first job as a railway booking clerk. After war broke out he also played a few games for Southport, until called up to the navy in 1941. Ellis served for five years, two years of which he spent in the Far East, taking command of a transport division within the Fleet Air Arm. This invaluable experience led him to Birmingham, where he was appointed as the manager of a FRAMES TRAVEL AGENCY in Sutton, in April 1948. It was then that he started to watch Villa from the Witton End, before devoting his energies to organising affordable foreign travel – previously regarded as a preserve of the rich – in the form of package holidays from Elmdon Airport. During these pioneering years, Ellis would do everything short of piloting the actual planes. He collected the tickets, weighed in all the passengers and their luggage, and, helped by his mother, served them with home-made sandwiches during the flight, too.

So successful were these efforts that by the end of the 1950s the Ellis group of companies included the largest provincial tour operator in the country. A lover of motor sport, Ellis also became involved in Birmingham speedway racing, at the Alexander Stadium in Perry Barr.

As one of the city's leading businessmen it was not long before he was being courted by directors from both Birmingham clubs. But although he wanted most to join Villa, the board in the end preferred to close ranks, and so it was that he became a City director in 1964. Those few years as St Andrew's, he would later say, taught him how not to run a football club. Finally, the call to Villa Park arrived in December 1968, and thus claret and blue fortunes were to change, almost literally, overnight.

Apart from his efforts on Villa's behalf, Ellis would continue to be a successful businessman. After selling his travel interests in 1976 he branched out into farming, property, and among various other leisure-related enterprises, the ASTON MANOR BREWERY. In between pursuing his love of salmon fishing and cruising on his private yacht, he has also worked hard for charitable causes, a long tradition at Villa Park and one which Ellis has formalised under the banner of the ASTON VILLA CHARITABLE TRUST. He is also chairman of the GOOD HOPE HOSPITAL TRUST.

Villa fans will know the rest. For a quarter of a century Doug Ellis has dominated the affairs of the club, earning himself a lasting memorial in the form of the stand which now bears his name.

Everyone has a view on the chairman. He has enemies, but many friends. He has critics, but many admirers. Some call him 'Deadly' in a spirit of animosity. Others use the same term in affection. Yet as we have noted, his staff at Villa Park are amongst the most loyal in football.

And surely all will agree that reticent or weak men do not make successful chairmen of football clubs. Fred Rinder was no shrinking violet, and nor is Doug Ellis. Both chairmen led the club through major constitutional reforms – Rinder when the club became a limited company in 1896, Ellis when the company floated on the stock market in 1997. Both craved success for Aston Villa and worked long hours to achieve it. But above all, in the context of this book, both pushed through considerable ground developments at Villa Park. From 1897 to 1939 Villa Park was effectively the house that Rinder built. The Villa Park of today is no less a symbol of Doug Ellis's leadership.

❖ After the numerous upheavals of the 1970s, Villa's boardroom has been remarkably settled since Doug Ellis returned to the club in 1982.

One of the first new directors, appointed in November 1983, was **Dr David Targett**. 'Doc' Targett had been the club doctor since 1970, having first

attended Villa Park as a small boy with his father (who was also a doctor, in Handsworth). A warm and exceptionally humorous man, the doctor was also actively involved in local speedway and boxing. But Villa was his first love and he gave up many hours to care for the welfare of the players, many of whom became close friends as a result. Tragically, 'Doc' Targett died in May 1997, at the age of 65.

Elected alongside him in 1983 was **Tony Alderson**. Like 'Doc' Targett, Alderson was already a familiar face at Villa Park, having been a partner in the firm of solicitors which acted for the club for many years, HATWELL PRITCHETT. In fact, Sir Theodore Pritchett was Villa's president from 1963-69, so it was fitting that Alderson should have been chosen for that same role on his retirement from the board in 1996.

It was equally appropriate that **David Owen** should become a director in 1997. Owen is a partner with the firm EDGE & ELLISON, which took over HATWELL PRITCHETT in 1971 and has acted for the club ever since. Owen, whose father worked at KYNOCH, first stood on the Witton End in 1949 and has followed Villa religiously ever since, attending games home and away with his wife Pat, and sitting in the Trinity Road Stand with his three children. For many years he served as chairman of the Aston Villa Promotions Association.

Joining him in the 1997 intake was **Tony Hales**, who hales from Blackpool and grew up watching the Tangerines. After moving to the Midlands he eventually became a director of ANSELLS in 1987 and took up a regular seat in the North Stand, with his three sons. More recently he has become the chief executive of ALLIED DOMECQ PLC. Villa have always had connections with the brewing industry, and with ANSELLS in particular, so again Hales fits in well with the club's traditions.

The third director to join in 1997 was **Mark Ansell**, who, despite his surname, has no connections with the brewing family. He does, however, have impeccable credentials. Although brought up in Small Heath, he comes from a family of Villa fans. His brother Barry made one first team appearance in 1967, and Mark himself played for Villa as an amateur. Starting as a Holte Ender in the late 1950s, he has acted as an adviser to the club for 15 years, and was Head of Corporate Finance with DELOITTE & TOUCHE MIDLANDS before becoming Villa's full time finance director in 1997.

Finally, Villa's fifth current director is **Peter Ellis**, who joined his father on the board in 1984, but inherited the family bug long before then. His first visit to Villa Park was in 1958, and he was a keen player himself while attending school in Birmingham and then Repton. Since training as an accountant Ellis Junior has had involvement with fifteen different businesses, his main role now being as finance director of the ASTON MANOR BREWERY, Birmingham's largest independent brewery, in Thimble Mill Lane. At Villa his responsibilities have extended to the refurbishment of the Trinity Road Stand, the development of Villa Village, Stumps, the ASDA site and the club's catering operations.

# St John Ambulance

❖ When Bert Harris met his untimely fate on the cycle track, in April 1897, there was not a single ambulance on duty at the Lower Grounds. Nowadays, the average game at Villa Park sees in attendance three ambulances (one from the West Midlands service and two from St John); a major incident unit and two paramedic crews (under the command of Superintendent Paul Bayliss); a specially trained crowd doctor (currently either Dr Naj Rashid or Dr David Bowden); the club doctor (Dr Barry Smith); nurses in each of the ground's two first-aid rooms (in the North Stand and Holte End); numerous trained first-aiders among the club stewards, and last but by no means least, around 40-45 dedicated members of the St John Ambulance Brigade, all of whom are unpaid volunteers. For example, Paul Cook, their Operational Commander, works at the BBC's Pebble Mill studios when not on first aid duty.

Some would joke that there is no better place to fall ill than a modern football ground, and yet ironically, since the advent of all-seater stadiums, the numbers of fans needing treatment has plummeted. Before the Taylor Report there would be, on average, about 30-40 casualties at each Villa Park game; the commonest complaints being crush injuries, cuts and bruises, twisted ankles, concussion and the occasional broken limb (and Villa Park, it should be noted, was much safer than many other grounds). Since 1994, however, only around 4-6 fans are treated per game, usually for minor ailments such as scalding from hot drinks, asthma attacks or headaches.

Nevertheless, there is no room for complacency. There might be six or seven fans who experience heart attacks during the course of the average season (most of whom, but not all, are saved, thanks to all the modern medical equipment now at hand). There are also the occasional pregnant supporters who do not quite make the final whistle, or the odd case of hyperthermia.

Just about the only crisis Villa Park's superb medical team cannot properly deal with is a mass outbreak of depression. The Taylor Report covered most of the issues, but alas counselling in the event of a home defeat was not among them.

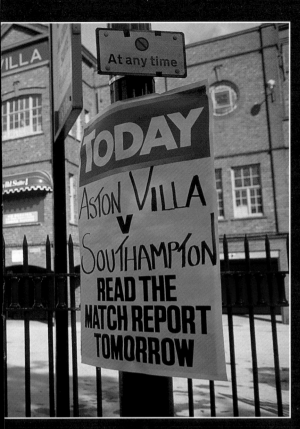

# Supporters
# Roll of Honour

*in which we honour our subscribers* ❖

Philip George Dutfield, Gosport, Hampshire

Martin John Guise, Solihull

Terence Donald Measey, Tamworth

Brian C. Seadon, Shrewsbury

Peter Harrold

K. Brookin, Birmingham

Steve Wall, Holte End

William James Moore, Talaton, Devon

Richard James Moore, Chichester, West Sussex

David Hodges, Southam, Warwickshire

Martin & Emily Kender, Highworth

John L. Balmforth, Halesowen

Ross Griffith, Pelsall

Keith & Josie Richardson, Ludlow

Adam H. Rose, Leicestershire

Michael Rose, Leicestershire

George Bernard Baker, Shareshill

Robert Thomas, Doug Ellis Upper Tier

Philip Gray, Holte End

Cameron Dunbar, Birmingham

Karl Bowater, Gornal, West Midlands

Jeff Winters, Birmingham

Andrew D. Bate, Stourbridge, West Midlands

Mr R. G. Birch, Holte End (L5)

Andrew Fox, Holte End

Keith & Scott Taylor, Holte End

James Alexander Curry, Doug Ellis Lower

Susan Pudge, North Stand

Dave Clarkson, Cheltenham, Gloucestershire

Sandy Walshe, Birmingham

Ian Clark, Doug Ellis Stand, Upper Tier

Ralf Schulz, Hamburg

Daniel Chappell, Prestatyn

Nick Stanton, Lower Holte

John & David Hughes, Cinderford

Paul Ford, Birmingham

Paul & Jenny Bailey, Yeovil

Kevin J. Powell, Coventry

Alan G. Burchell, Solihull

Thomas James Knibb, Knowle

Greg Dollery

John Brealey, Henley-in-Arden

David Goodwin, Holte End

Mark David Goodwin, Holte End

Glen Paul David Goodwin, Holte End

Martin K. James, Tamworth

Robert Griffin, Halesowen

Mr Paul Tullett, Quinton, Birmingham

Stan Chambers, Alum Rock

Ian Paul Sanders, Holte End

Wayne Tandy, The Deers Leap

Bob & Louise Turley, Walmley

Richard M. Wincott, Shirley

Gregory Upton, Stafford

Ken Whittington, Erdington

Lee Day, Grendon

Peter Curry, Holte End

Derek, Kerry, Carly & Jean Day, Baxterley

The Sutton Family, Birmingham

John Westcott, Milton Keynes

Mr G. E. Pritchard, Leicester

Dean Baker, Cannock, Staffordshire

Ian G. Lowe, Birmingham

Stephen Tovey, Birmingham

Chris Flynn, Birmingham

Mark Thornley, Hednesford

George Brannigan, West Midlands Police

Brian Etheridge, Holte Lower

Nicholas Hay, Solihull, Doug Ellis Upper (AA 261)

Mark Stoneman, Stourport

C. W. Plummer, Walsall

Robert Connelly, Solihull

Sid Ravenhill

John William French, Witney, Oxon

Barry & Wendy Geddis, Polesworth

Chris Harris, Trinity Road Upper

Robert Parry, Hodge Hill, Birmingham

Albert Poulton, Aston

Mark Pearce, Holte End

John Goodman, Dudley

Norman R. Heaton, Trinity Road Upper

Pam Bridgewater

Matthew & Daniel Smith, Wolverhampton

Ian Macdonald, Studley, Holte End

Robert Edward Garratt

D. S. Willetts

Stuart T. Swann, Holte End

Tony Lines, Great Barr

R. L., R. J. & R. L. Elwell, Sutton Coldfield

John Hadgkiss, Knowle

Paul, Marc & Luke Thomas, Bearwood

Colin & Wesley Perry, Sutton Coldfield

Craig Vigurs, Holte End

Mr J. M. Richmond, Holte End

Alan S. Johnson, Sheffield

William Edward Batty, Balsall Heath

Mr V. A. P. Kiely

William Pearson (Former Chief Steward), Nechells

Craig Ramsey, Holte End

David Bridgewater

Chris Ashmore, Brownhills

Andy Collins, Hampshire (formerly Erdington)

David Parker, Handsworth, Birmingham

Paul Perry, Lichfield

Michael James Lovesey, Cotteridge, Birmingham

Dr Mark Wilson, Tettenhall Wood

The Day Family of Droitwich, Holte End Lower (L)

Paul Mahoney, Waunarlwydd, Swansea

Geraldine Coffey, Quinton, B68 0PN

Edward McNeill, Holte End (L4)

Campbell Wiseman, Hartford, Huntingdon

Andy & Steve Jackson, Coventry

Adrian Thomas, Malvern Wells

Roy Lilley, Perry Barr Exile

Chapman Family, Hartley Wintney

Michael Caiden, Gloucester

M. V. Tamplin, Billesley, Birmingham

Philip Richard Bennett, Pedmore, Stourbridge

David Woodley, Doug Ellis Lower Tier

Colin & James Daly, Cubbington

Stephen Smith, Rubery, Birmingham

John Andrew Clover, Rubery

Keri Thompson, Doug Ellis Upper, Row UU, 250

C. J. Riordan, Birmingham

Matthew Dale, Holte End

Nicholas Cox, Castle Bromwich

Neil Byrne, Northampton

Big John, West Heath

Patrick Dunlea, Newcestown

Steve Newburn, Redditch

Paul Randle, Stroud

Rob Rodway, Stevenage

Martin J. Watson, Four Oaks

H. 'Hoppy' Holman, Cornwall

Anthony Watts, Poole, Dorset

Mr M. Whitehouse, Cheslyn Hay

J. T. O'Brien, Rubery

Ian & Bridget Tait, Willenhall

Philip Chandler, Clayton West

Linda M. Treadgold, Studley

R. M. Lanning, Stonehaven

Tom Blackwell, Minehead, Somerset

Carol Maguire, Great Barr

Kevin T. Dalley, Holte End Upper Tier

Anita 'Chucky' Harris, Trinity Road Stand Lower

Philip Patterson, Dorridge

Ian Edward Beesley, Perry Barr

Mr Alan L. C. Rainey, Kings Heath

Michael John Leahy, Perry Barr

Michael P. Baylis, Rubery, Birmingham

Robin David Wilkes

Robert Victor Williams, Walsall

Dave Whitehead, Wolverhampton

Kevin David Birch, Hanbury

Paul Nixon, Solihull

The Donnison Family, Tamworth

Peter, Carole & Teresa Bell, Gary Hall, Northfield

Steven Paul Butler, Nant Peris, North Wales

Clive Hicks, Henley-on-Thames

Gareth C. Jones (Bones), Bristol

Colin Brookes, Stroud

David, Susan & Oliver Eagle, Marston Green

Colin Brown, Holte End 1959

Daniel Richard Evans, Kings Norton

Roger Wooldridge, Bournville

Alan Bobbett, Sedgwick

Yves Geens, Booischot, Belgium

L. J. Taylor, East Grinstead

Derek T. Hough

Anthony Sargeant, Cannock Chase

Edgar Sargeant, Brewood

Michael John Richard Page, Billesley

Timothy Jackson, Wolverhampton

Paul Cummins, Birmingham

Darren Paul Hunt, Holte End

David Banner, Abingdon, Oxon

C. & J. Marcantonio, Ward End

Robin Pleaden, Denham

Warren, Karen, Ellie & Harry McDivitt, Solihull

Rich & Andy, Holte Enders

Colin Bishop, Portishead

Malcolm Corfield, Norton Canes

Mr J. A. Powell, Kings Heath

Adrian J. Mullis

Martin Jackson, Lower Holte End

Alan Gee, Brazil

Bill Willcox, Harborne

Noddy & Honey Monster, Solihull

Ray Halford, Kings Norton

D. Wilcox, Birmingham

Dave Nicholson, Worcester

Nicola & Andrew Friel, Sutton Coldfield

Jeff Corfield, Brownhills

Edward Mills, Weoley Castle

John Collins, Tamworth

Matthew Buck

Darren Hudson-Wood

Gido Kirfel, Cologne

Martin Lawlor, Bartley Green

Dale Southall, Cannock

Geoffrey Horton, Wollaston, Stourbridge

David Foster, Hoggrills End

Clive, Philip & Michael Cross, Rothwell

Adrian Batsford, Chelmsford

Frank & Ben Antram
Keith Rickett, Atherstone
John A. Higgins, Handsworth Wood
Rev. Leo Osborn, Cullercoats
John (Villa) Power, Tramore, Waterford, Eire
Donald & James Whyte, Shirley
David Lawlor, Sutton Coldfield
Richard Beckett, Lichfield
Graeme Preston, Frimley, Surrey
Geoff Bryant, Sutton Coldfield
Bob Moore, Frankley
John Green, Erdington
Tony & David Harris, Bulkington
Rod Snelson, Trinity Road, E4
Anson, Luddington
Roy Joyner, Warwick
Jens Martin, Luxembourg
Matthew John Collinge, West Hagley
John Joseph Downey, Holte End
Leni & John Ward, Bournville
Owen Suter, Bicester
Norman Hughes, Halesowen
Jim Stelfox, North Stand
Geoff Baker, Bromsgrove
Kevin Fowler, Great Barr
John Ball, Walsall
Marc Troth, Bromsgrove
Stewart & Gareth Marsh, Nottingham
John A. H. Marriott, Sheldon
Ken & Lorna Marriott, Woodbridge
Daniel Reeves, Gibraltar
Anthony Woolley, Doug Ellis Upper
John S. Brown, Sutton Coldfield
Carl & Sylvia Morris, Blackburn
C. D. Hartshorne, Worcester
Terry Stone, Alcester
G. M. & H. Sutton, Evesham
Adrian Goddard, Lichfield, Holte End
Kevin Stratford, Oxford
James Powell, Sutton Coldfield
Simon Plester, Smethwick
David Hockenhull, Prestatyn
Ken Phipp, Holte End
Michael Weller, Stirchley
K. G. Wilkinson, Cradley Heath
Dave Skinner, London
Philip A. Hughes, Halesowen
Mick Watkins, Redditch
C. L. Highfield, Walsall
G. P. Highfield, Walsall
P. J. Highfield, Walsall
Rev. M. B. Sanders, Walsall
Mark Bradshaw, Neasden, London
John & Mary Gallivan, Great Barr
M. D. Fellows, Halesowen
Marcus Edwards, Rugeley
Johan Sunnerstam, Karlstad, Sweden
Steve Webb, Holte End
Rod Evans, Sutton Coldfield
Andrew Mearman, Kingswinford
Paul Mills, Bewdley
Bob Woodward, Burntwood
Thomas Johansson, Halmstad, Sweden
Robert Henry Doyle, Hartford
Paul John Drew, Streetly
P. E. Roberts, Tamworth, Staffs
B. & S. Minshull, Cowes & Tamworth
Michael Mykola Halaj

Herwig Witthohn, Cuxhaven
Bernard, James & Paul Bemand
Keith Puttick, Horsell, Woking
Garry, Carol & Jordan Moore, Erdington
Ken Noon, Walton-On-The-Hill
Stein Carlsson, Tungelsta, Sweden
Harry Turner & Descendants, Christopher & Daughters
Gerald H. Lodwick, Wem, Shropshire
David R. Ismay, Birmingham
Mr D. C. Hayward, Stourbridge
Bert Perkins, 124 Rectory Park Road
Paul J. Edwards, Great Barr
A. J. Bemand, Weston-Super-Mare
Duncan K. S. Laws, Holte End Lower
Lester N. Corrall, Reading
Ron Close, Holte End
Andrew & Elizabeth Buck, Coleshill
Paul A. Webb, Lichfield, Staffs
Dean Strange, Mildenhall
Dean Shepherd, Wakefield
Andrew John Francis, Rugeley
Jennie Taylor
M. E. C. Wilson, Pailton, Nr Rugby
David & Alan Ostojitsch, Rowley Regis
Colin P. Kinneir, Coventry
Miss Anna Peak, Sutton Coldfield
Reg Thacker, (Archivist) AVFC, Edgbaston
Roger & Louisa Winn, Holte End
Mark Jenkins, Alvaston, Derby
David Poole, West Midlands
Michael Macwillson, Shrewsbury
Michael Halcrow
Peter Hopkins, Southampton
Gerald Leek, Yardley
Robert Taylor, Holte End
Graham Phillip Bird, Hall Green
Lesley Ann O'Donnell, Doug Ellis Stand
Glyn, Lori, Caerwyn & Celyn, Newnham-on-Severn
Stephen R. Shaw, Streetly
Bruce Ball, Worcester
Bruce Ball Jnr & Ross Wood, Kingswinford
Ian David Spray, Warley
Ian R. Wilson, Bearsden, Glasgow
Bob Peach, North Stand
Christine & Ian Rossiter, North Stand
Michael Murphy, Frankley
Stan Jones, Yardley
Ralph & Wendy Willis, Middlesbrough
Mike Jehan, Sark
Maurice Carter, Leighton Buzzard
Dr Robert Tighe, Edgbaston
Russell John Farley, Brixham, Devon
Mr Clive Dickens, Redditch
Terry J. Davis, Halesowen
James Cox, Erdington
Bob Reynolds, Holte End
Carl A. Tate
Ray Pearson
Graham, Marlene, Stephen, Garry & Julie Brown, Albert Village
Frank Andrew Francies, North Stand
Dennis Newport, Great Barr
Anthony, Gordon & Glynn Wood, Tipton
Stuart Palmer, Villa Youth
Denise & Paul, Daventry
J. & A. Ward, Redditch
David James, Tojay Records, Hamburg
Neil Brailsford, Southam
Nigel Groves, Halesowen

Keith Feaver, Sheffield
David O. Cox, Voisins Le Bretonneux
Andrew McAllister, Cheltenham
Michael Wurm Pedersen, Copenhagen
Mark Tamburro, Abingdon
Richard S. Lewis, Bristol
Malcolm Taylor, Wallheath
John Ernest Phillips, Burntwood
George A. Soden
John Knight, Great Barr
Graham D. Cockayne, KK 204, Witton Lane Upper
Michael Hrab, Cannock, Staffordshire
Leo Pinnock, Flitton, Bedford
Jack Pinnock, Flitton, Bedford
Gary Burbidge, Solihull
Carol & Philip Gill, Brownhills
Heather Stroud, Loughborough
Ian Gray, Ward End
David Whittall, Redditch
Peter J. Ross, Belbroughton
Catherine, Derby
Jayne Margetts, Erdington
Gary Corbett, Bromsgrove
Geoff Underhill, East Grinstead
Margaret Edkins, Wychbold, Droitwich
John A. Gould (1934)
Keith, Natalie & Vicki Stubbs, Doncaster
Danny & Martyn Bacchus, St Neots
David Yeomans, Oxfordshire
Gordon Cull, Nuneaton
Dave O'Neill, Birmingham
John Matthew Gardner, Warwick
Jonathan Helm, Maidenhead
Paul Ellis, North Wales
Matt Lydon, Church Broughton, Derbyshire
Jon & Tom Northover, Holte End
Tracey & Roy Hatfield, Sheldon, Birmingham
Michael John Moss, Holte End Upper
Antony Ibbotson, Castle Bromwich
Carl Stephen Portman, MCIPS, England
Tony Mason, Erdington
Matthew O'Brien, Lifford, Co Donegal
Andy Brookes, Cheltenham
Michael John Cooper, Stetchford, Birmingham
Mark & Scott Ginger, Gloucester
Dave Beale, Hither Green Lane, Redditch
Mark Santy, Doug Ellis Stand
E. David Payne, Switzerland
Peter J. Payne, Switzerland
Dean & Michelle Beresford, Holte End
H. John De Saulles, Premier Club
Richard D. Webb, Swansea
Pamela Harris, Holte End
Kevin Bulgin, Kingstanding
Stuart Michael Coates, Kingston-Upon-Hull
R. J. Bailey, Sutton Coldfield
Bill Ford, Evesham
Betty Leonard, Burnham-On-Sea
Jeffrey J. Sheridan, Great Barr, Birmingham
Mr & Mrs S. Pride, Exeter, Devon
Rebekah Jane Hassall, Brownhills
Elliott & Victoria Lee, Seisdon
Tim O'Brien, London
Geoffrey Wright, Ware, Hertfordshire
Alan F. Jasper, Doug Ellis Upper
Keith Lowe, Victoria, Canada
Derek Wisdom, Canada
Benbow Family of Boraston

Bully, Lisa, Leanne & Shannon, Maypole

T. & L. Dowling, Maypole

Simon Barron, Holte End

Thomas Algernon Taylor, Donnington, Gloucester

Andrew Holmes, 22 Warple Road

Nobby (Lisa), Holte End

Philip Clive Wharton, Ashford, Middlesex

Kelvin Davis, Dorton, Buckinghamshire

Jack & Kate Hughes, Great Barr

Dave Ashman, Kinver

Stephen M. Ryan, London

Ralph Williams, Somerset

Ray Holland, Droitwch, Worcestershire

Ashley Dawson, 14 Occupation Road, Walsall

Richard & Maria, Cardiff

Daz Stephens, Plymouth

Carol Smith, Coventry

David Alan Taylor, Rubery, Birmingham

The Cox Family, Alrewas, Nr Burton-on-Trent

John Warren, Solihull, West Midlands

Richard Pedrick, Holte End

David Orme, Glossop

Tom Monks, Birmingham

David McCullough, Ravenhill, Belfast

Robby Watkins, Stafford

Chris Gooda, Tunbridge Wells

Dean Morris, Burford, Shropshire

David Lewis, Holte End

Alan Hunt, Burgess Hill

The Waters Family, Sutton Coldfield

Ken Baker, Poole, Dorset

Carl Binnions, St Albans

Darren Holden, Holte End

Robert Lerner, Elstree

John Adkins, Billericay

Kevin Lowbridge, Wolverhampton

Shane McVey, Drummullan, Northern Ireland

P. R. D. Smith, Peaton

Graham F. J. Hill, Malvern

Laura Caswell, Isle Of Man

Terry Parr, Handsworth

Pybus Family, Market Drayton

Arthur Montgomery, Chesterfield

Noel Lewis, Witton Lane

Michael Abbott, Doug Ellis Stand Upper

Thomas David Pulling, Doug Ellis Stand (Upper)

A. & L. M. Colclough, Tamworth

William Powell, Sutton Coldfield

William Kilmurray, Dublin

Julie Nerney, Trinity Road Stand

Liam Foley, Harpenden

Mr Pete Bishop, Wolverhampton

Paul Biddlestone, Blackpool

Bob Nicholls, Trinity Road

Dawn McCarrick, Gloucester

Jon Broad, Minworth

Mark Fullbrook, Holte End

The Pallots, Wolverhampton

Paul Hughes

Chris Dennis, Solihull

Thomas R. J. Evans, Fradley, Lichfield

Robert C. Taylor, Perry Barr

John Fitzgerald, Edinburgh

Robert Bevan, Baddesley Ensor

Anthony Thomas McNicholas, Erdington

James Thomas, Rowley Regis

Andy Black, Hereford

David Brearley, Bromsgrove

William Rangeley, Holte End

Pountney Family, Holte End

Tom Eadon, Melton Mowbray

Mark Williams, Stourport-On-Severn

Nicholas T. Watts, Chichester, Sussex

Matthew L. Watts, Chichester, Sussex

Trevor Watts, Epsom, Surrey

Rob Aston, Gaunts Common

Malcolm, Gregory & Stewart Everall, North Wales

Michael O'Brien, Tamworth

Andy Perry, Sutton Coldfield

Paul Pilkington, Northfield

Stephen J. Hanks, Birmingham

Darren & Mick Wilkins, Epping, Essex

Adam Paul Patterson, Hemlington, Cleveland

R. C. Brown, Banbury

Mr R. Howkins, Weston-Super-Mare

James Egan, Trinity Road Enclosure

Doug & Eira Shirley, Witton Road End

Caroline Helen, Hall Green

Les Willetts, Dudley, West Midlands

Stuart Day, Redditch

Graham Goodwin, Frittenden, Kent

Iain Chipper, Maidstone, Kent

Geoff Ellis, Rugby, Warwickshire

Michael Dessington, Penyffordd, Nr Chester

David Marshall, Northern Ireland

Tom Corby, London

J. M. Braniff, Lichfield, Staffordshire

A. J. Braniff, Atlanta, Georgia, USA

Bill & Thomas Wiggett, St Albans

Rob Kirby, Holte End

Norman & Sean Hodson, Holte End

Alan Gilder, Holte End

Mark Byrne, Stourbridge

Matthew Kennell, Atherstone

Paige Nevada Harris, Holte End

Gerald Chishick, Madrid

Ian Thomson, Trinity Road Stand

Stephen Thomson, Trinity Road Stand

The Aston Villa Supporters Club of Canada

C. Warren, Smethwick

David Hemming, Birmingham

A. J. Newman, Northfield

Patrick Clarkson, Holte End

Sarah Hemming, Birmingham

Hewlett Family, Ockham, Surrey

Wendy Jordan, Cannock, Staffordshire

Robin Peck, York

Philip Piper, Holte End

Peter Aldridge, Sussex

Peter & Nikki Long, Doug Ellis Lower

Lars Nilsson, Halmstad, Sweden

Steve Knott, Reading

Simon Daykin, Cannock

David R. Beddows, Bromsgrove

Martin Crump, Catterall

Richard McEnarney, Banbridge

Ron Nutt, Salford Priors

Kris Rowell, Leeds

Mac McCarthy, Norfolk

Michael Bradley, Sherborne

Matthew Murphy, Preston

David Tether, Kingswinford

Simon Kerr-Edwards

Stephen Mullins, Wednesbury

G. P. & S. M. Blaszkiw, Warminster, Wiltshire

John Smith, Welford-on-Avon

James M. Deeley, Scarborough

Paul Fogarty, Sheepy Magna

Mike & Matt Freeman, Upper Holte (208+209)

Charles Derrick Dewsbery, Handsworth Wood

Bob Harvey, Lichfield

David & Trish Gilbert, Sutton Coldfield

David Nicholls, South Shore, Blackpool

Jonathan Betts, Holte End

Leigh M. J. J. Bull, Holte End

Michael J. Mullen, Castle Vale

Crooks, Guildford

Andrew & Sally Grant, Sheffield

R.S. Hutchison, Morden

David Bradley, Harborne

James Lockley, Birmingham

Frederick Thomas Barrett, Guardschapel, London

Raymond Haston, Hodge Hill

Peter Walker, Hong Kong

Michael Shorthouse, Nanaimo, Canada

Adams Family, Walsall

B. M. Bartlett, Harborne

Diane Fitton, Birmingham

Alan Beale, Studley

Adrian, Katie, Peter, Sylvia & Alison Smith, Knowle

Robert Gough, Daventry

K. Batson, Stockport

John Cullen, Tomhaggard, Wexford, Eire

A. J. Clarke, Great Barr

Steven Clarke, Great Barr

Martin Clarke, Great Barr

Charles B. Carter, Stirchley

John Morgan, Birmingham

Kim Sykes, Birmingham

Nigel Thompson, Coleraine, Northern Ireland

Kieran McGarr, Birmingham

Richard Burton, Beckenham, Kent

Bernard Day, Painswick

R. A. Jones, Erdington

Valerie Downes, Loughton

Darran Boulter, Hereford

R. A. B. Bottomley, Newick, East Sussex

Al Craig, Canadian Villan Supporters Club

Mr W. E. Catherall, Llandudno

Darren Miles, Rickmansworth

Gareth Powell, London

Giovanni Cantone, Hockley Heath

Dave Smith, Arley

G. Day, Birmingham

Terry Goode, Tamworth

John A. Tooth, Trinity Road Upper (Section E)

Louise Barnsley, West Hagley

B. R. Veal, Pulborough, West Sussex

David & Peter Hitchman, Lichfield

Alan West, Northfield

Peter Brett, Holte End

Roy, Dorinda & Aaron, Stourbridge

Bob Hughes, Sidmouth

Mrs Diane Marvin, Woodgate

Rich, Sue & Dan Ford, Evesham

M. H. Russell, Bromsgrove

James A. V. Lane, Pelsall

Dawn Lesley Taylor, Hednesford

Robert Taylor, Shareshill

Hilary Cole, Doug Ellis Upper

Nigel, Kim, Aaron & Rae-Anne Carr, Rugby

Mark McDonagh, Kings Norton

Colin Draycott, Sutton-in-Ashfield

David Matthew Robinson, Lichfield

Curtis Mynard, St Austell, Cornwall
Pauline A. Holloway, Solihull
Steve Thorne, Croydon, Surrey
Samuel McCoy, Welsh Newton Common
Mark Jenkins & Ralph Edward Hogg
Paul Joseph Naylor, Solihull
Leslie Hobson, Hereford
Keith & Joe Ridout, Newhall
David Llewellyn Tamplin, Holte End
Peter, Martyn, David, Ross Underhill, Co. Cork
Julian & Aston Turner, South Africa
Mark Napier, Stafford
Steve & Matthew Allen, Stone
James A. S. Blackstock, Lydney
Phil & Sean Woodlock, Birmingham
S. & J. Reynolds & Family, Pershore
Fernie, Bournville
David Simon Billingham, Pedmore, Stourbridge
P. J. Hosier, Walmley, Sutton Coldfield
Andy Clark, Birmingham
Darran Cox, Birmingham
John F. Gibbs, Holte End 1950-97
Ian, Andrew & Matthew Mayne, Penkridge
Fred Moland, Gomersal, West Yorkshire
Bruce Woodcock, Cradley Heath
Jamie Stuart Tate, Curdworth
The James Villans, Holte End Lower
Duncan Carney, Stafford
John Salmon, Solihull
Rob Tate, Handsworth & Dunstable
Mark Lawton, Wordsley, Stourbridge
Ken Hobbs, Sutton Coldfield (now Somerset)
John Hartill, Bodmin, Cornwall
Rod Rigby, Holte End
Timothy John Bailey, Stone
Russell Turvey, Olton
Guto Siôn Williams, Penygroes
Ken G. Banks, East Grinstead
Sam Guy, Wrexham
Kathryn & David Knight, Kidderminster
C. J. Hughes, Longbridge
James Price, Malvern
Adrian Price, Malvern
Adam J. Miles, Worcester
Bruce Hulston, Slough
Chris Leedham, Castle Bromwich
Richard A. Hales, Bridgend, Mid Glamorgan
David J. Barron, Doncaster
Holmes, Villa Fans, Chatham, Kent
Ashley Goodwin, Gloucester
David Beament, Poole
Kraut, Tonna
David Kane, Newick, East Sussex
Chei Sam Ip, Redditch
Paul Evans, Wolverhampton
Benjamin Thomas-Egan, Trinity Road Enclosure
Mark Heslington, Lichfield
Gilbert M. Jones, Solihull
Graham & Janet Luckhurst, Stratford-upon-Avon
Mick Kenna, Halesowen
Paul Kenna, Halesowen
Arthur James, James A. & Kenneth Hinton
Steven J. Giles, Los Angeles
Anthony John Beaman, Redditch
J. Black, Chelmsley Wood
Sam Gamble, Chelmsley Wood
David Daniel, Stafford
Matthew & Charlie Lingard, Edinburgh

Richard Fitton, London
Dennis Shaw, Centre Sport
Dudley H. Janes, Trinity Road Stand
Norman D. Crandles, Canada
Richard Johnson, Trinity Road Stand
Mr M. D. McDonald, Chelmsley Wood
C. C. Gough, Holte End
Walter Bull, Rednal
Peter Stokes, Trinity Road
Bill King, Quinton
Chris Smith, Redditch
James Blundell, Redditch
Robert James Evans, Yardley
H. & J. Gilchrist, Erdington
Mr Graham Spilsbury, Yardley Wood
Chris Deakin, Southampton
Terry Butler, Portscatho, Cornwall
Nick Becerra, Barnet
Tony Brandal, Norway
Jon Noden, Sutton Coldfield
Roy Scrivens, Evesham
Teresa Ecija, Wolverhampton
David John Edward Clayton, Tamworth
Reine Bladh, Alstermo, Sweden
Bobby, Anna & Roisin Mendonca
John Simmonds, Spalding
Paul & Richard Hinton. Pamela Wood
Robert Hughes, Trinity Road Stand
Sean Beale, Brownhills
Chris Ballantine, Cannock
Colin Eaton, Derby
Bob Watler, Westgate
Vincent Clark & Debbie Winchester, Kent
Barry, Pat, Carolyn, Rosalyn Etheridge
Ian Richards, Bromsgrove
John Dee, Sheffield
John E. Smith, Weston-Super-Mare
Trevor Victor Collins, Exeter, Devon
L. J. & J. H. Richardson, Weston-Super-Mare & B'ham
Reevo, Holte End
David Warman, Darlington
Jonathan Hill, Yardley, Birmingham
Sewell Family, Handsworth
John Walls
Alastair Rhodes, Tal y Bont
Malcolm, Sharon, Jamie Cooper, Harborne
M. A. Arscott, Taunton
P. M. Arscott, Taunton
Tracy Ashford, Holte End Upper
Nigel Iwanski, Holte End Lower
M. Brown
Jürgen Hohmann, Germany
Van De Sÿpe Ignace, Belgium
Iris Barford nee Nightingale, Trinity Road
Frank McNally, Trinity Road Stand
Stephen (Staga) Higgins, Northfield
Adam Moorby (10) & brother Luke Moorby (2)
Mr Ray Poultney, Milking Bank, Dudley
Roy Winnall, Holte End
Alan Booth, Holte End
Mark Anthony Found, Holte End
Nigel Harris, Great Barr
Mr David James Moon, Warwick
Neil David Porter, Holte End
Vernon Wareing
Simon Foxall
Andrew Foxall
Tony Williams, Tottenham, N17

Andrew & Trevor Clayton, Holte End
Simon Brooker, Gresford
Neil Jones & Jane Benton, Holte End
Simon Towe, Cradley Heath
Barry Flowers, Whitkirk
Alan Tucker, Solihull
William Annison, Holte End
Lasse Sørensen, Nykøbing SJ
Peter J. Baker, Vista, South Australia
Philip Jennings, Hodge Hill
Raymond Hemus, Birmingham
Simon Bonnick
Orjan L. Bratland, Bergen, Norway
Geoff Swann, Western Australia
John Penlington, Belbroughton
Philip Golding, Malvern
Benjamin Hancox, Woodford Green
Andrew Knight, Great Barr
Paul Underdown, Holte End
Martin Roberts, Holte End
Mark Penny, Holte End
Ian Ward, Holte End
John Evans, Rowley Regis
Daniel Kane, Kettering
John Bullock, Norwich, Norfolk
Chris Nason, Hednesford
Chris McCormack, Holte End
Beryl Stanyard, Doug Ellis Stand
Michael, Andrew amd Steven Lucas, Streetly
Jason & Simon Crowe, Stratford-upon-Avon
Kevin Fern, Newhall, Derbyshire
Newey, Birmingham & West Midlands
J. D. Haddon, Northfield
Stan Beaumont, Belgrave, Tamworth
Neil Harvey, Chester
Graham Padget, Solihull
Marie Sandland, Tamworth
Philip J. Thompson, Wetherby
George E. Sherwood & Hannah, Holte End
Brian M. Orchard, Rashwood Hill
Martin Samuel Alexander Orchard, Droitwich Spa
James Drew, Tamworth
Mr & Mrs Adam David John Cooper, Holte End
Mark Farmer, Holte End
Alan Sparks, Trinity Road Stand
Stephen Sparks, Holte End
Graham Jackson, Holte Ender, Coventry
Shirley & Geoff Blizard, Solihull
Ralph Grimes, Stratford Upon Avon
Nicholas Hampson, Pebworth
Dennis Coleman, Thame
Mrs Susan Byrne, Kingstanding
Mr David Byrne, Kingstanding
J. A. Muirhead
Stephen Amery, Northamptonshire
David Webley
Mr Albert Jones, Holte End
Kate Atkinson, Maulden & Holte End Lower
Ken Smart, Co. Durham
Phil Smart, Co. Durham
James Robert Smart, Yardley
Peggy & Michael Knight, Malvern
Brian Harris, Surrey
Andrew Davis, Holte End
Patrick Magennis, Santa Monica, California
Brian Lane, Lea Village, Birmingham
Paul Ellison, Westcliff-on-Sea
Christopher E. Hardy, Tunbridge Wells

Yvonne Davies, Llangeitho
Barry Fellows, Oxford
Peter Reed, Redcar, Cleveland
Si Priestley, West Yorkshire
Mr Andrew Light, Holte End
Mr Phil Sneddon-Coombes, Holte End
Thomas Deeley, Bentley Heath
Brendan Geary, Sutton Coldfield
Andrew Sanders, Pleck, Walsall
Tim Stephens & Family, Wilmcote
Mr Stuart Reading, Fort Lauderdale, Florida
Paul, Karen, Roger & Pauline Reaves, Rugby
Stuart Robb, Smethwick
Paul Tomlinson, Oxford
Alan, Neil & Chris Masters, Burntwood
Kai Gopsill, Future Holte Ender
The Burns Family, Kings Heath
Mark Alexander Smith, North Stand (G48)
Julie A. Evenson, Stirchley
Julie Rowbottom, 64 Valley Road, Lye
Jim Sparrow, Quinton
Frank MacDonald, Trinity Road Stand
B. M. Dain, Birmingham
Eileen McGuckin, Wolverhampton
Martin J. Owens, Trinity Road Stand Upper
Stan Hill, Holborn Hill
Philip John Shakespeare, Erdington
Ernest Henry Pearman, Woodlands Farm
Richard H. Weaver, Bearwood
Ronald Field, Redditch
Andrew Little, Chatley, Worcestershire
Lily Anstey, Hall Green
Andrew C. Beattie, Stone, Staffordshire
Mike D'Abreu, In Memory of Dad & Bert
Keith Potter, Birmingham
John Baker, Little Aston
Barry Silver, Greenford, Middlesex
The Bissett Family, Erdington
Ben Morse, Burford
Andrew Secker, SJAB, Handsworth Wood
Derek & David Fletcher, Witton End
Pat & Eddie Higgs, Sutton Coldfield
Richard Connolly, Rasharkin
John Peter Reidy, Holte End
Steve Sturman, London
Graham Carlin, Great Barr
Carl Thornton
D. J. Silver, Kenilworth
Andy Seal, Telford
S. J. Lavery, Coventry
Mark Ferriday, Sutton Coldfield
Bob Morton, Ex A. P. Rovers, Great Barr
Andrea Warren, Holte End
Martin A. Bird, Sutton Coldfield
Mark Barrow
Keith T. Smith, Sutton Coldfield
Edward Harris, Cradley Heath
John Alan Dunn, Holte End
Vera Ellen Ragsdale, West Midlands
Paul Rostance, Aldridge
Julia Greenfield, Camberley
Roy Farmer, Beer, Devon
Joanne Haddon, Dordon
Paul Bateman, Holte End
Peter & Michael Wells, Holte End
Michael John Carey, Hereford
Mr Ron Boon, Chelmsley Wood
Philip Hunt, Stratford-on-Avon

Philip Wint, Brownhills
G. B. & E. A. Jinks, Birmingham
Christopher Allen, Harborne
Oreste Bortoli Family, Sequals, Friuli, Italy
Barry Hucks, Sutton Coldfield
W. E. Egginton, Birmingham
Keith Anthony Foster
Gary Clarke, Sutton Coldfield
Jean Dryhurst, Trinity Road
Catherine Pritchard, Sutton Coldfield
Harold W. Parker, Birmingham
Nigel Aust, Northampton
Alex Blanchard, Chelmsford
Gary Blanchard, Chelmsford
Richard Whitehead, Basingstoke
Vic Whitehead, Tamworth
Andrew Mason, Sutton Coldfield
Tracey, Kieran, Tamara, Nuneaton
A. Murray, Walmley
Michael Byrne, Walsall
Antony Goudge, Milton Keynes
Brian & Robert Miles (E3 A 43-44)
Si Watson, Oundle
Silvestre A. Tangalan Jr, Seattle, USA
Roger Jones, Erdington
Dominic Harper, Stourbridge
Paul Jarvis, Torpoint, Cornwall
Antonio Durante, Rome, Italy
Albert E. Heath, Droitwich Spa
Albert Heath, Handsworth
Craig Swann, Australia
Eric & Philip Overton, Uttoxeter
Trevor O'Loughlin, Ennis, Co. Clare
Robert Rogers, Lozells, Birmingham 19
Tony Peck
Dean Tye, Holte End, Evesham
Jamie Cash, Streetly
A. Holmes, Tamworth
Michael Hanbury, Aberdare
Terence Anthony Barker, Crewe
John Ernest Barker, Crewe
Molyneux Family, Monkspath, Solihull
Roy Thornton, Sutton Coldfield
Andrew Gledhill, Holte End Upper Tier
Paul Freeman, Uxbridge, Middlesex
Eric Freeman, Lower Quinton, Stratford-on-Avon
A. P. Johnson, Salisbury
Fred Taylor & Family, Sutton Coldfield
Graeme R. Pallant, Tarleton
Nick Bowles, Faringdon, Oxfordshire
Adam Richardson, Cowplain, Portsmouth
Stan Russell, Wiltshire
Anna Wheeler, Quinton
Mr George Allen Stafford, Great Barr
William Hughes, Harpenden
Michael Hughes, Harpenden
Patrick Drummey, Dungarven, Republic of Ireland
Philip Shakespeare, Great Barr
Philip Yardley, Kitts Green
Keith D. Gavin, Shenstone
R. K. Morgan, Cardiff
Nigel Renshaw
Norman Renshaw
Stephen (Rennie) Renshaw
Dan (Villa Man) Renshaw
N. J. Holbrook
Nathan David Stevens, Sutton Coldfield
I. Angus, Great Barr

Stephen John Davies, Hammerwich
Kimberly Frances Angus, Streetly
Mark Ford, Erdington
Steven White, Doug Ellis Stand (Upper)
Gary Harris, Holte End
Teague & Peter Roarty, Holte End
Frank Smith, Aldridge
Rob & Karen Wardle, Castle Bromwich
Nigel Sadler, Walthamstow
K. R. Pursall, Buckinghamshire
S. M. Pursall, Cheltenham
Paul Griffiths, Holte End Upper
John Holder, Cheltenham
John Partridge, Castle Bromwich
Gary Sanders, Worcester
Barry Williams, Lichfield
Luke Atterbury, Northfield
Richard Geary, Knaresborough
Peter Lawrence, Bloxwich
George Barker, Smethwick & Knightwick
Robert W. Jeffries, Evesham
Nigel Lee, Kings Bromley
Adrian Paul Rogers, Holte Ender
Mr Philip Michael Tansey, Harrow
Andrew Elston (HE 1725), Redditch
Harry Gatward, Therfield
James Mitchell, Kenilworth
Luke & Thomas Millard, Kings Heath
Andy Campkin, Wendover, Aylesbury
Thomas William Skinner, Burntwood
C. J. Ball, Walsall
J. K. Stelfox, Hurley, Atherstone
Mr Lewis Gwynne, Streetly, Sutton Coldfield
Tony, Angela & Craig Webb, Erdington
Kenneth F. Denham, Erdington now Sutton Coldfield
Ian & Simon Galbraith, Shelfield, Walsall
Dennis & David Harris, Kingswinford
J. H. H. Rutherford, Goalkeeper, Chester-Le-Street
Raymond J. Lewis, Willenhall
Stuart Caldwell & Family, Stratford-upon-Avon
Kevin O'Neill, Sutton Coldfield
Phil Martin, Geneva, Switzerland
Morton James Price, Holte End
John Hill, Melbourne
Jim Spencer, Walsall
C. N., R. N. & P. K. Newell, Trinity Road Stand
Robert Cooley, Holte End
Kevin Smith, Balsall Common
Benjamin Smith, Balsall Common
Tamburro, Redditch
Sue & Mick Tilt, Trinity Road Stand
Adrian Thorne, Horsham, Sussex
Becky Tompkins, Hollywood, Birmingham
Kevin Whittick
W. Harvey, Nuneaton
W. A. Harvey, Nuneaton
Lally Family, Sutton Coldfield
Melvin Thickett, Trinity (Lower Stand)
The Harris Family, Great Barr
Michelle Diggins, Erdington
Terry Hall, South Africa
Liam Davis, 95 Newbrook Avenue
Steve Ewer, Great Barr
Peter & Paul Vos, Halesowen
Barry Wall, Gloucestershire
Amanda & Karl, Castle Bromwich
Michael Milne, Streetly
Paul Palmer, Sutton In Ashfield

Ian Murphy, Birmingham/Hollyhead
Peter W. Giles, Ellesmere, Shropshire
Maria, Emma & Clare Ganner, Alton, Hampshire
Carl & Luke Davies, Rugeley
C. I. Adams, Kenilworth
R. I. B. Bottomley, Wandsworth, London
R. J. P. Bottomley, Battersea, London
J. J. Lee, Wandsworth, London
J. F. D. Lee, Wandsworth, London
Mr William Fitzpatrick, Walsall
Tim Cookson, Eastbourne
Vaughn & Maria Parker, Kidderminster Branch
Paul Best, Toronto
Roy Billingham, Pedmore, Stourbridge
Paul James Hunt, Lozells
Nicholas John Hunt, Lozells
Brian Thomas Cotton, Holte End
David Bevan
David Watson, David Watson Jnr, Wayne Watson
Jason Magan, Castor, Nr. Peterborough
David Sharred, Castle Vale
John Kreeger & Maxine Thornton, London W3
Craig Jaques, Ringwood, Australia
Len Lawley, Adelaide, Australia
Richard Lawley, Adelaide, Australia
Alan James Kelsey, Walsall
Allan Dunn, Gt Yarmouth
S. E. Ablewhite, Bourne, Lincolnshire
Richard R. Carter, West Sussex
Derek Hollis, Daventry
Roy Pearce, Holte End Upper
Michael, Danny & Declan Sheehan, Doug Ellis Stand
R. Townsend, Birmingham
Marc A. Dawson, Devon
R. J. Castle
Peter Rodgers, Sutton Coldfield
Christopher Harper, Holte End Upper
John F. Ratcliffe, Upper Trinity Road Stand
Jean & Diane Gledhill, Holte End Upper Tier
Philip Weston, Bristol
John Arnold, Dosthill, Tamworth
Chris McEvilly, Smethwick
Raymond John Wilson, Holte End Upper
Damian Tarbuck, Willenhall
Adam J. Small, North Stand
Amanda Primina Pagliari, Sutton Coldfield
Remo Renato Pagliari, Sutton Coldfield
David B. Kelly, R.A.F. Henlow
Gareth Paul Jones, Llanelli
Neil Alcock, Birmingham
Ian Shackleford, Holte End
Daniel McLaughlin, St Albans
Chris Newton, Cambridgeshire
Ashley Harris, Walmley
Robert Head, Shard End
A. Boyns, Gillingham, Kent
Nick & Julie Gossage, Bromsgrove
John Gossage, Bromsgrove
Jamie Gossage, Bromsgrove
Richard Gossage, Bromsgrove
Neil Doble, Bideford, Devon
Douglas O'Brien, Stroud
M. Asson, Handsworth
Evans, Acocks Green
S. J. M. Eccleston, Trinity Road
Robert Cope & Family, Winson Green
Darryl Chinn & Family, Hall Green
Mr S. F. Pittaway, Birmingham

Malcolm Ronald Ellis, Leigh, Lancashire
John Bannister, Walsall
Adam Bannister, Johannesburg
Lee Jarrod Slater, Pelsall, Walsall
Debbie Slatford, Didcot
Mark Wheeler, Shard End
Stephen Cooper, Milton Keynes
James S. Raphael, Holte End
B. F. A. Poole, Great Barr
Vernon Grove O.B.E., Ackleton
Peter Beardshaw, Great Barr
Alexander & Daniel Berwick, Hopton, Stafford
Terry Wright
Roger Spencer, Langley, Oldbury
Dave Cox, Unionville, Canada
Mr Carl A. Lewis, Redditch
Matthew Idoine, Netherton
Russell Briggs, Erdington
M. Roberts & C. Briggs
John Briggs, Erdington
Robin Dean, Holte End
Maurice, Michael & Richard Powers, Holte End
Malcolm John Banks, Portsmouth
Michael J. Reidy, Erdington
Mark Robinson, Holte End
Calvin James Cummins, Churchill
Bridie Mulligan, Ward End
Michael Pearson, Wingerworth, Chesterfield
Leonard Arthur Mellor, Sutton Coldfield
G. J. Daniels, Castle Bromwich
Claus Kotzebue Jørgensen, Denmark
Bjørn Hansen, Ravnkilde
Hans Christian Hansen, Hillerød
Chris Mander, Warwick
Nick Harper, Birmingham
D. T. Barlow, Shirley
Dennis Killeen, Birmingham
Paul Badger, Berlin
Mr Lee David Ellis, Leigh, Lancashire
Ian Harrison, Warwick
Simon Harrison, Warwick
Dave Hodge, Holte End
Ben Hussey, Exeter
Arthur Buxton, Woking
David R. Ward, Netherton
"Jimmy Re" Ward, Hockley
T. J., Terrance & James Partridge, Trinity
Leonard G. Taylor, Plymouth, Devon
Christopher Privett, Dorridge
Mr G. Edwards, Selston, Nottinghamshire
R. K. Jones, Stourport-on-Severn
Arthur Zammit, Holte End, L6J62
Helen Kavanagh, Marchwood, Hampshire
Mark Neal, Yardley Wood
Paul Colborne, Warminster
Meakin-Wager, Holte Lower, Row X 106/7
Ron, Rob & Rick Vincent, Ruskington
Caroline James, Stafford
Simon Wheeler, Tamworth
Paul Hooton
Andrew Williams, Hall Green
Edward & Leonard Reading, Erdington
Mark S. Waldron, Halesowen
Gerald L. Kirwan, Clonsilla, Dublin
Dave Alan Turner, Woodgate
Burton Family, Lancing, West Sussex
Mr Jason Webb, Weoley Castle
Nigel Ainge, Northfield

Craig Millard, Great Alne
Roger Levicki, Marlow
Sylvia Neal, Birmingham
Donna 'Ra Kilt' Chisholm, London
James Dagley, Cheltenham
Philip, Lynsey & William Clover, Trinity Rd Upper
Dennis Clover, Old Witton Lane Stand
Keith Gleadall, Manukau, New Zealand
Peter Colborne, Warminster
Patrick F. J. O'Reilly, Kings Norton
Kevin Gledhill, Leamington Spa
Downes Family, Hall Green & Nottingham
Bladon Family, Hall Green & Perth, W.A.
Steven Buckley, Isle of Wight
Lee & Paul Causer, Holte End
Richard A. McCormack, Reading
Internet Field Family, Weston-Super-Mare
Alexander Moore, Northampton
Kevin, Stephanie & Jack Portley, Northampton
Michael Bishop, Northampton
Les Bumford, Bloxwich
Tony Corfield, Aldridge
Andrew Willetts, Water Orton, Holte Ender
Harry Taylor, Skidbrooke
Sara Tovey, Telford
R. F. Harris, Evesham
S. M. Goodall, Evesham
Stuart Ramsell, Holte End
Simon John Wiggin, Walsall
Alan Goulding, Newport, Shropshire
Peter J. Atherley, Selly Oak
Harry Tether, Stourbridge
David Woolley, Amblecote, Stourbridge
John T. Lock, Nechells
Ian & Daniel Haden, Neil Bradey, Halesowen
A. Whiley Snr & A. Whiley Jnr, Northfield
Antony K. Bullivant, Trinity Road Stand
P. W. Barrell, Sutton Coldfield
Brian Martin, Bristol
D. C. Morgan
Sam D. J. Jones, Solihull
S. D. Pallett, Holte End
Stephen Dent, Lydbrook
Kenneth & Philip Veal, Great Barr
Guy Spreadbury, Warwick
Tony, Jimmy, Lauren & Jenny Taylor, Holte End
Desmond Moore, Cheltenham
Derek Fox-Roberts
Gordon, Paul, David & Harry Reeves
Louise Alasan Morris, Hall Green
Zoë Jayne Morris, Hall Green
J. Hudson, Redditch
Victor Pawlin, Barry
Christopher Pawlin, Barry
Jason Pawlin, Barry
Gough Family, Cannock
John W. Daw
Ian J. Walker, Henley-In-Arden
Des Suckling, Aldridge
G. Walden, Holte End
Zosia Mace, Birmingham
Nicholas Blewer
Hooper, Worcester
Miss L. Bunn, Great Barr
Hayden Wakeling, Hammerwich
Rob & Penny, Solihull
Leighton Bullivant (1/4/77), Birmingham
Barrie Bailey, Plymouth

Brian Bailey, Plymouth
Roger Bailey, Nottingham
A. C. Woodhull, Sandpiper Close, Worcester
K. C. Woodhull, Grey Uplands, Malvern
Bill Gubb of Barnstaple, Devon
David Foster, Rothwell
Andrew Day (7), Erdington
David Willetts, Hackney, London E5
F. J. Bettles-Hill, Newport Pagnell
Peter R. Hill, Dunblane
George Earl, North Stand
Peter Collings, Four Oaks
Terry Leonard, Kidderminster
J. Weaver
Douglas Mayo, 1950
John Wyatt, Upper Trinity (E) Road
G. D. Haviland, Kidderminster
Reg Ash, North Stand
Frank Harvey, The Holte
Chris Newton, Cheltenham
Martin Blogg, Hastings
Butler Family, Cambridge
Malcolm Morley, Lichfield
David Charles Baldock, Halesowen
Samantha Greenfield, Wythall
Rosin & Alex O'Mahony, Dublin, Ireland
Paddy Kelly, Dublin, Ireland
Joe O'Reilly, Dublin, Ireland
FC Villa Football Club, Dublin, Ireland
Irish Aston Villa Supporters Club, Dublin, Ireland
Phil Innamorati, Great Barr
Tony Cowdrill, Great Barr
Mr B. & Mr N. J. Bindoff, Birmingham
Miss K. E. & Master G. A. Bindoff, Birmingham
Ian Hoskison, Doug Ellis Stand
Keith Evans, Holte End Lower
A. A. Bent, Holte End
McWilliams Family, Kings Heath
Christopher C. Fleming, Hamstead/Great Barr
D. E. Hall, Birmingham
J. A. Hall, Bromsgrove
David Wootton, Sutton Coldfield
Robert Mackenzie Smith
John Grey, Evesham
Thomas James McNamee, Rednal, Birmingham
Andrew J. Davis, Sutton Coldfield
Jason Hynes, Holte Ender, Cradley Heath
Liz Ratcliffe, Doug Ellis Lower, Row N, Seat 101
Andrew Richard Maddern, Maesteg
Allen Gumbley, Castle Bromwich
Peter Keady, Redditch
John, Lynsey & Ian Bousfield, Solihull
Martin Davis, Wisbech
Michael Ross, Chelmsford
Sue, Nick & Daniel Kendrick, Worcester
Mr James Malcolm Grove, Trinity Road Stand
Paul Lawrence, Holte End
W. S. Davis, Streetly, Sutton Coldfield
Peter (Pedro) Badlan, Holte End Lower
Darren Lippett, Trinity Road Lower
Jonathan Muir, Bromsgrove
Gary & Jenna Dale, Warley
Matthew R. Brown, Rowley Regis
Murray Jukes, Kidderminster
Terry Griffiths, Castle Bromwich
G. W. Batters, Sutton Coldfield
Mr D. E. Cross, Tamworth
Simon & Frank Croft, Sutton Coldfield

Andrew Brooks, Chase Terrace
Iris Marlow nee Evans, formerly Winson Green
Bernard Sydney Cole, North Stand
Scott Maciver, Newhall
Mr J. F. Gavin, Walsall
Reg & David Tutt, Trinity Road
Michael Brooks, Upper Holte
Kevin Brown, Great Barr
Kevin John Williams, Holte End
John Leydon, Sligo, Roscommon
Keith Morris, Holte End (U)
Michelle & Anthony Thickett, Trinity Rd Enclosure
Matthew C. Thickett, Trinity Road Enclosure
Mike Simmons, Melbourne, Australia
Neil M. James, Birmingham
Adam White, Hook Norton, Banbury
The Nugent Family, Templeogue, Dublin
Paul Tierney, Erdington
D. W. Close, Holte End
J. D. Close, Holte End
George Meacham, North Stand
Claire Hughes, Birmingham
Lee Hermitage, Middlesex
David A. Lancaster, Eccleshill, Bradford
Bob Hickman & Family, Holte End
Keith Terry & Lisa Day, Neath, South Wales
Shirley & Robert Bowker, Telford
Abbie Elizabeth Horton, Rowley Regis
Bill Coleman, Boscombe, Bournemouth
The Beale Family, Witton Lane
John Rouse, Stafford
Neil Edwards, Brackla, Bridgend
Sally Davis, Staines, Middlesex
Neil Edwards, Rochdale
Gary Arthurs
David Harrison, Torquay
Lynn Ruston, Doug Ellis Lower Stand, M1, N102
Matthew Hanney, Llanelli, Wales
Simon Keley, Great Barr
Henry Anthony, Brownhills
Terry Leedam, Ironbridge Gorge
Tony Evans, Witton & Holte End
Kellie Louise Hathaway, Walsall
Richard Henman, 30 Years A Villa Fan
John & Andrew Fairfield, Lancaster
Brian Boot, Borth
Dyfed Lewis, Borth
Stephen Ludlam, Stourbridge
Dr. Julian Stringer, Shrewsbury
J. P. Jennings, Sutton Coldfield
Simon Ash & Thomas Brunskill, Droitwich & Plymouth
Walter Neumayr, Aalborg
Andrew Webb, Oxford
Eddie Nicholls, Adelaide, Australia
Mr M. Lockley
The Fell Family, Birmingham & Bristol
Chris du Bois, Steve & Pete
Roy, Andrew & Nicholas Smart
C. J. Whitaker
D. R. Highfield, Seaton, Devon
R. A. Highfield, Seaton, Devon
Dominic Burnett, Yardley
Matthew Griffiths, Burntwood
Alexander Thomas Berry, Fairington, Lancashire
Andrew Wibberley
John David Drower
Christopher John Austin, Bishampton, Worcester
Christopher Mansfield, Redditch

Ralph Stride, Castle Bromwich
Brian Kelly, Stafford
Peter & Luke Williams, Reading
James Burnett, Lichfield
Terry Rumble, Poole, Dorset
Vic, Nottingham
Martin Phillips, Burntwood
Andrew Willis, Leicester
Kennerson, Leicestershire
Nigel John Richardson, Taunton
Mr G. Collins, Beauvezer, France
Jim McCranor, Coventry
Dave McCranor, London
D. Dekker, Hoorn, Holland
David Keats, Thornton Heath
Mr T. A. Turnbull, Hemel Hempstead
John Harris, Southgate
Stephen Todd, Redditch, Worcestershire
Ray Hodgetts, Alcester, Warwickshire
Mr J. Slim, Kingswinford
Ross Dubberley, Holte End
Gregory W. A. Skitt, Cannock
Vic Pendry, Birmingham
Keith Coburn, Cambridge
Roger Fullbrook, Holte End
Tony Tongue, Holte End
John Byrne, Barrhead
J. Ringrose, Romford
Roger Wash, Newmarket
Ross Leach, Dunstable
Andreas Prodromou, Cyprus
Tony Shaw, London
Tina Rees, Gloucester
Mr K. P. Newton, Adelaide
David M. Prescott, Ontario, Canada
Mrs Eileen A. Griffith, Bangor
Ger Breen, Clare, Ireland
Des Brennan, Moseley, Birmingham
David Yates, Great Barr
Alan G. Davis. Sutton Coldfield
Steven Horne, Halifax
J. T. O'Brien, Rubery
J. C. Ison, Birmingham
Christian Jahnsen, Denmark
Rolan Tunney, age 11, Staffordshire
Neil Gallagher, Bearwood
Mark Gallagher, Bearwood
John Cox & Family
Peter Drake and Family
Phil Lees, Erdington
Vic Millward, Erdington
Nadine Goldingay, Erdington
Frank Beach, Erdington
Terence Francis Weir, Great Barr
Trevor Hartley, Tamworth